Economic Theory of
NATURAL RESOURCES

Orris C. Herfindahl

Allen V. Kneese

Resources for the Future, Inc.

CHARLES E. MERRILL PUBLISHING COMPANY

A Bell & Howell Company

Columbus, Ohio

This book was researched under the auspices of Resources for the Future, Inc., Washington, D.C.

Published by
CHARLES E. MERRILL PUBLISHING COMPANY
A Bell & Howell Company
Columbus, Ohio

Library of Congress Catalog Card Number: 72–95935

International Standard Book Number: 0–675–08895–X

Printed in the United States of America

2 3 4 5 6 7 8—79 78 77 76 75 74

Preface

The writing of this text has involved at least some difficulties not found in the case of texts for well-established and well-defined fields. Some of our decisions on what to exclude and how far to go with topics that are included no doubt will appear debatable to many users. There are many aspects of applied natural resource economics on which we do not touch. Since our main goal is to provide theoretical constructs (in a somewhat narrow sense) that are useful in analyzing problems in the management of natural resources, we include empirical material on particular natural resources only to show how theory can be used. The reader will look in vain for a full-blown discussion of the industrial organization of any one of the natural resource industries, such as forestry, fishing, or mining, although thumbnail sketches of certain basic features are necessary in some cases if only to provide a setting in which theory can be discussed.

There is no pretense at all of an adequate discussion of the regulatory problem. In practically all cases the implicit point of view is that there are no obstacles to the effective operation of whatever regulatory device might be imposed in order to move to a more efficient position. This is an important omission. No student should be misled into thinking that an optimum scheme of regulation based on this assumption is necessarily the optimum scheme for the real situation. An attempt to find an optimum scheme of regulation in a practical context necessarily must include the regulatory machinery itself and responses thereto as a part of the system whose behavior we are trying to optimize. For instance, if taxes are imposed on effluents but they are measured inaccurately or not at all, if inspectors are bribed, or if taxes are not collected, it will be of no avail to have calculated the "optimum" effluent charges even to the last mill. In practice, direct regulation and enforcement schemes are probably even more subject to shortfalls in operation than incentive schemes.

Perhaps rather arbitrarily, we have chosen not to discuss the formal work that has been done on problems of resource management involving massive uncertainties, although they are not ignored entirely. The discussion of uncertainty in the context of benefit–cost analysis has taken on a more definite shape, however; and this aspect of the uncertainty problem is discussed at length.

Because the field covered by the text is extensive, its writing and test runs have by now covered a rather long period. The number of persons who have given us their criticism of part or all of the manuscript is so great as almost to be embarrassing. The principal results of their comments are not to be seen, for these are the errors and confusions that have been eliminated. We must take responsibility for those that remain. We are deeply grateful to our critics for their very careful efforts.

Early versions of the manuscript were inflicted on students in an engineering economic systems course at Stanford University and students in resources economics courses at the University of Michigan, the University of New Mexico, and George Washington University. Geoffrey Berlin, Paul Bugg, and Gene Mumy, then graduate students at Johns Hopkins University, conveniently close to us, were able to give us detailed comments on several occasions. We have benefited greatly from the comments of economists in universities, including Professors M. A. Adelman (Massachusetts Institute of Technology), Ralph d'Arge (University of California, Riverside), Paul Bradley (University of British Columbia), Gardner Brown (University of Washington), Charles Cicchetti (University of Wisconsin), Anthony Fisher (Brown University), John Gray (University of Manitoba), Steve Hanke (Johns Hopkins University), Jack Hirshleifer (University of California at Los Angeles), Karl-Göran Mäler (University of Stockholm), Herbert Mohring (University of Minnesota), Robert Rooney (California State College, Long Beach), Gunter Schramm (University of Michigan), Nathaniel Wollman (University of New Mexico), and anonymous reviewers engaged by our publisher. Our indebtedness to colleagues at Resources for the Future is great and diffuse, but we should like to mention especially John Krutilla, Talbot Page, and V. Kerry Smith.

O. C. H.
A. V. K.
October, 1972

Author's Note

While writing this book Orris Herfindahl and I were helped by many people. First and foremost were our associates at Resources for the Future. Various ones of them read and commented on all or portions of the manuscript and provided numerous opportunities for discussion of the contents. In a few cases we drew heavily on their past writing as well. Next must come our students in several courses we taught using materials from this book. Many economists at other academic institutions also helped us in various ways.

My co-author and excellent friend, Orris Herfindahl, died while on trek in Nepal in December of 1972. He and I had been associated in a number of enterprises at RFF over the past decade. To work with him was always an adventure. He had read and thought deeply about many things and he was my teacher as well as my associate. His love for nature was infectious, and he was a superb outdoorsman. The world is a lonelier place without him.

Allen V. Kneese
May, 1973

Contents

PART I

Introduction and Basic Theory

CHAPTER 1

Introduction

In this day of the literature explosion and rising concern about solid waste, authors owe a word of explanation for adding another tributary to the flooding stream. The incentive to write this book arose from two sources. First, both of us have tried our hand at teaching courses in natural resources economics and found ourselves facing multiple dilemmas in trying to do so efficiently and effectively. Second, we are seeing once more a large scale concern with natural resources although in a broader context than that which characterized earlier "conservationist" concerns.

One product of the new situation is the establishment of many new courses and even degree programs in natural resources economics. Recent concern is a product of a renewed awareness of the finiteness of our natural resources base, in this nation and in the world. This means concern with scarcity of the traditional natural resource commodities in the face of rapidly growing population and industrial production. To many it means, even more urgently, scarcity of resources which had long been regarded as infinitely great in supply—"free goods" in the economist's terminology.

Clean water and pure air are now perceived as being natural resources— scarce ones, and in many areas urgently scarce. Ecologists have made it impossible for anyone who can hear or see to be unaware of the problems we face with respect to the natural environment. It appears that all natural resources issues can best be thought of as part of the general problem of wise use and management of the natural endowment of minerals, fuels, land, air, water, ecosystems, electromagnetic properties of the natural world, and landscape.

We have written this book in an effort to contribute to an understanding of the economic issues, concepts, and methodologies surrounding such management.

To return to our reason for writing this text, we recall the multiple dilemmas we have faced in trying to teach a satisfactory course in natural resources economics. The first dilemma is that while there is a vast amount of literature in the area, it is a rather unhappy experience to guide students through it. On the one hand, if one asks them to read everything of importance, the library load becomes not only intolerably large but they find themselves repeatedly plowing through similar material as the author establishes a theoretical context for what he is doing. Also they find themselves suffering through books and articles where the ratio of words to important ideas is extremely high. On the other hand, if the student does not read extensively, he will miss many wholesome grains buried in the chaff. This book is intended to provide a compact introduction to the main theoretical components of the economics of natural resources use and management.

Another dilemma results from the inherently interdisciplinary nature of natural resource use and management. Disciplines such as engineering and planning are centrally involved in natural resource matters. As a result, our classes have always contained a substantial complement of students from these disciplines. The dilemma is that they have usually been disciplined in their own areas but have had little or no background in economic theory. Since we assume, and hope, that such students will be present in classes in which this book is used, we have provided an extended introduction (Chapters 2 and 3) to the most pertinent concepts of economic theory.

Considerations of student background lead us to the question of prerequisites. The ideal student will have had reasonably advanced courses in micro and macro-economic theory, calculus through differential equations, linear algebra, and probability theory. A student with this level of training should do no more than scan Chapter 2. On the other hand, a student who has taken a survey course in calculus and a good course in intermediate micro-economic theory should be able to work his way through the book with virtually full understanding, especially if he thoroughly grasps the material in Chapter 2.

Now what about the engineer or planner (or other natural or social scientist) who ventures into this course with more or less strong training in mathematics but is for practical purposes innocent of economic theory? First of all, a really careful reading of Chapter 2 should help such a student. But with no previous economic training at all it may not be enough. We suggest he read in addition to Chapter 2 of this text Chapters 1, 3, 11, 9, 13, 14, 16, 18, 19, 5, 6, and 7 (in that order) in William J. Baumol, *Economic Theory and Operations Analysis.*[*] For those inclined toward a more rigorous mathematical presentation of material, a careful reading of James Henderson and Richard E. Quandt, *Microeconomic Theory,*[†] will pay rich dividends.

---

[*] Second edition, Englewood Cliffs, N.J.; Prentice-Hall, Inc., 1965.
[†] New York: McGraw-Hill Book Company, 1958.

In discussing desirable prerequisites, especially those in mathematics, we may have given the idea this is a highly mathematical text. This is certainly not so. On the theory that "a little mathematics goes a long way," we decided against a purely literary treatment, but a dedicated reader with no mathematics whatsoever could understand almost all of the main ideas in the book.

This text concentrates on theoretical aspects of resources economics while providing enough practical applications to show the relevance of the analysis to policy and decision making. Each chapter contains a *highly* selected list of references, most of which emphasize the descriptive and empirical aspects more than the text does. The result, we hope, is a book suitable for a one-semester course focused on theory, or a two-semester course at a more leisurely pace with an opportunity for supplementary reading.

A Brief Overview

As already explained, Chapter 2 reviews the economic theory of resource allocation. This theory deals with how limited resources can be most efficiently allocated to alternative ends. References to natural resources are incidental in this chapter, but they reveal our cumulative approach to theory. The whole book is primarily about theory and it is the authors' intention that the student should progressively gain depth in the subject. Accordingly, insofar as possible we have repeated a theoretical construct or application several times at progressively higher levels of difficulty and sophistication. In Chapter 2 this progression is fast since we start with the most elementary ideas in economics and proceed to a discussion of general equilibrium for the whole economy.

Chapter 3 deals with economic dynamics and is a natural extension of the theory reviewed in Chapter 2. Dynamics involves the explicit introduction of time into the economic analysis, which produces many complexities. The reader may well find this the most difficult part of the book, as it deals with some of the deepest subject matter in economics—but the issues raised and discussed are also some of the most fundamental, so perseverance is warranted. Questions such as "what does contemporary society owe to future generations" cannot be easy even if one is looking only at a specialized aspect of them.

We have called Part II "Social Economics of Private Production from Natural Resoures." In it we examine one of the ways in which the private market fails to deal with resource allocation problems properly both in a static sense and over time. The basic problem here is one of a shortcoming in property rights—economists call it a *common property problem*. Such problems have a much wider significance than commonly has been reflected in the economic literature, at least until recently. This section is developed initially around several types of natural resource activities where the presence of such problems has for a considerable time been recognized and analyzed. Among these activities are petroleum extraction, fishing, and ground-water exploitation.

Part III deals with economic issues surrounding direct government investment and management activities in natural resources. A central focus for our explorations here is *benefit-cost analysis*. This is one of the most important areas of applied economic theory and warrants extended consideration. We also discuss some aspects of the applications of economic theory to systems analysis and planning and to the pricing of outputs from public projects.

In Part IV we turn to a consideration of natural resource common property problems on a much larger and more pervasive scale. The use of natural resources in the production and consumption process results in residual materials roughly equal in mass to the resources originally extracted from the environment. In one way or another these are returned to the environment. A natural resource of great value is used in this process—the waste assimilative capacity of the environment. But this capacity is not infinite as most people seem to have long supposed. Moreover, natural environments like air and water are also common property resources in that they belong, in a sense, to everyone and therefore to no one. Thus private property interest cannot protect them from overuse and misuse with resulting pervasive misallocations of resources. Collective institutions must be developed to conserve and manage them.

In the final section, "Conclusions and Deep Problems," we restate in complete but summary form the conceptual and theoretical structure constructed in the previous parts of the book. We reexamine the broad significance of common property type problems, the relation of these problems to the more traditional conservation issue of the optimal rate of use of natural resource commodities over time, and discuss economic criteria for collective or government action with respect to natural resources development, use and management. Finally we raise some deep issues with respect to the adequacy of our present economic theoretical constructs for analyzing natural resource problems. We do this not to diminish the significance of what has been learned in earlier sections but to suggest the strong, if not urgent, need for deeper understanding of how humanity can use the world's natural endowments to improve its genuine well-being now and in the future.

CHAPTER 2

Review of Topics from Static Micro-Economic Theory

2.1 GENERAL COMMENTS ON THEORY

Perhaps unique among the social sciences, economics shares a common body of theory. While not all parts of this theory are accepted as equally useful or relevant by all economists, almost all of them explicitly or implicitly build their approach to research and public policy problems on its main propositions. In this chapter and the next we select for review particularly salient topics from the economic theory of resources allocation. The body of theory reviewed will apply to such diverse problems as the best time rate of exploitation of an exhaustible mineral, and environmental pollution. Indeed, theory is the conceptual structure and binding force for this book. Descriptive information is introduced to illuminate applications of the theory and not for its own sake.

This book deals with the economic aspects of the natural resource industries, using industry in a broad sense to mean whatever organizational structures are used to produce a good or service. These are public as well as private. Interest in the economic aspects of the functioning of these industries does not imply neglect of other kinds of theory. Physical, chemical, engineering and biological theories need to be understood. They are taken as given for the economic analyses that we might wish to make. However, when aspects of these theories are tightly interlaced with economics, we sometimes introduce them more explicitly. Our development of the theory of synthetic hydrology in Chapter 7 is an example.

If, as we claim, we have a relevant *general* economic theory, this theory should be as applicable to problems involving natural resources as it is to any other economic problem. But, even so, the natural resource industries are not the same as other industries. In some cases, the legal institutions within which economic behavior takes place are different. In a number of natural resource problems, the very long run assumes an importance that is not present in some other industries. In many instances the cost and benefits of resource use are not "internal" to legally separate enterprises. Although the application of general economic theory to the problems of natural resources sometimes is a bit specialized, there is no really special kind of economic theory involved.

2.2   ECONOMIC THEORY—POSITIVE AND PRESCRIPTIVE

On one hand, it is the task of economic theory to explain a certain range of phenomena marked off as being economic in nature. There is another function of economic theory, however—the *prescriptive*, or as it is sometimes called, the *normative function*. Prescription is not really a function of economic *theory*, if by economic theory we mean a body of principles which is supposed to explain economic phenomena in a way that will permit prediction. Economic theory viewed in this way is indispensable to the task of prescription, for it is only with its use that one can even make a beginning at predicting what would happen if various sorts of prescribed acts were undertaken by somebody—say, the Congress—who is in a position to make these decisions. But a complete theory of prescription, or a complete normative theory, or a complete theory of policy—to use ordinary language—involves a range of considerations that goes well beyond those of economic theory as we view it here. It is extremely important to note that this is *not* the same thing as supposing that in dealing with problems of policy one can afford to throw economic theory out the window. Where we use economic theory prescriptively in this book we try to be very clear about the normative assumptions underlying such use.

In one very limited sense, micro-economic theory might be regarded as prescriptive in its own right. Since it deals with how choices should be made to maximize some objective it might be thought of as saying *if* you want to accomplish such and such most efficiently this is how you must do it. But mathematics might be thought of as being prescriptive in the same sense.

We should also explain the use of the term *micro*-economic theory. There are two broad classes of economic theory, micro and macro. Micro-theory deals with the allocation of limited resources to alternative ends and focuses on *relatively* small decision units—individuals, households, business firms and agencies of government. Macro-theory deals with the overall flow of expenditures and income and overall levels of employment. It focuses on broad aggregates like the consumption and saving of consumers as a group and total business and government expenditures. It grew out of concern with business cycles, unemployment, inflation and economic growth. Somewhat like the wave and particle theories of physics, the two theories have not been fully reconciled or integrated but are each individually valuable for explaining certain phenomena. Macro-economic theory will concern us in the next chapter.

The term "static" is also used in the heading of this chapter. It distinguishes that part of economic theory which does not introduce the passage of time as an explicit variable in the analysis. It deals with the process of resource allocation in a static or "steady state" context. While virtually no economic decisions take place without considerations of time being involved, it is much simpler to introduce most of the fundamental ideas of economics in a timeless context. In the following chapter we extend the static analysis by reviewing the implication of an explicit introduction of time into the economic decisions of the natural resources industries.

2.3　CONCEPT OF THE ECONOMIC SYSTEM

Economic theory says that an adequate explanation of economic phenomena within, let us say, a society such as that of one of the western countries must view these phenomena as forming part of a *system*. The most highly developed version of this idea deals with market-type price systems. Communication of information by price changes is very rapid in this "ideal" system. Factors of production move rapidly and in response to small difference in prices, and so on. In this vision of a system, abstraction is made from many of the complicating factors that are actually present to show clearly what the ultimate effect of certain changes would be if these changes could work themselves out with any other variables held constant.

The usefulness of this abstraction of an interrelated economic system may not be immediately obvious, but those who give their full time to explaining economic phenomena do, by and large, regard the idea of an interrelated economic system as an indispensable aid to thinking about what really happens. It is through a roughly similar real system that economic functions come to be performed in societies such as ours. The desires of consumers are communicated to producers by their purchases. Production is organized and takes into account the scarcity of the different productive services through the medium of the price system and the information provided by prices. Rewards for participation in productive activity are determined as a part of this system, although the resulting distribution may be modified through taxation and through the system of transfer payments. Finally, it is through this system that capital formation is regulated, both in quantity and in composition, influenced by governmental action of various kinds, especially those affecting the rate of interest and the structure of interest rates.

How useful is this conception of an economic system? This is a question to which there is no quick or easy answer. As do all theories, the conception of an economic system abstracts from many aspects of the real world which do, in fact, affect economic phenomena. The question is whether the right level of abstraction was achieved for the particular problems we are trying to explain. There can be little doubt, we feel, that this system contains the essential elements required to explain how the fundamental functions enumerated above actually are performed.

One can take specific account of factor after factor from which abstraction has been made—e.g., knowledge is not perfect, the same production function (defined shortly) is not known by all producers, prices are not uniform all over the country (allowing for locational differences), some goods cannot effectively enter into private exchange, and so on. But if one refuses ever to contemplate a system that is not complicated by these factors, he may miss understanding clearly that the real world—in market-type systems, at least—presents a set of economic phenomena which have the kind of coherence in their patterns over time which can be fruitfully characterized as constituting an economic system. Natural resources are a part of this system, and the behavior and problems of natural resource industries can be understood only in the context of a highly interrelated system.

We dwell on the problem of abstraction because so much of this book emphasizes market failures; i.e., breakdowns of the private incentive system. There is danger that the reader may decide that the exceptions to the theory of the functioning of the economic system are so numerous and fundamental that his efforts to learn micro-economic theory were after all futile. We emphasize that this is not so. Micro-economic theory, while built up largely to explain market-type systems, deals fundamentally with the problem of choice given alternatives and scarce resources. The problem of choice is universal, which is the reason why this body of theory has found application in such diverse areas as socialist planning and operations research, as well as the examination of systems operating under private incentives.

2.4   USEFUL IDEAS FROM PRODUCTION THEORY

Opportunity Cost

We begin our review of static micro-economic theory with that part known as the economic theory of production, and with one of its most fundamental ideas—that of opportunity cost. Simply put, the *opportunity cost* of doing something is what has to be given up *because* you do that something. The question is, what is it that you *cannot* do if you do the something under consideration? Obviously, this conception of cost is relevant to making economic decisions, yet it is surprising how many times analysis goes astray because this concept of cost is not considered.

The analyst must make this idea inherent in his thinking about resource allocation problems. Opportunity cost may not be the same as money outlays, although money outlay expressed in the form of price may in many cases be the appropriate measure of opportunity cost, or at least of a component of it. Looking at the system as a whole, we see that productive services ultimately derive their value from their usefulness in the production of goods desired by the ultimate consumers of the system. These may be state planners, but in a system like ours we usually take them to be private consumers. Thus, in the language that once was used more frequently than it is now, the utility possessed by productive services is a derived utility; that is, it is derived from the fact that the goods and services made by these productive services can yield utility to the consumers of the system. For any given production operation, however, the private producer can take the market values of the productive services as a given. He does not need to inquire into the ultimate origin of this market value.

To see what the concept of opportunity cost means and what it does not mean, let us consider a few examples. If you have an automobile and are asking yourself whether you should take a bus across town or drive your automobile, the relevant cost for you is what you have to give up because you go on this particular trip. Thus, there would be included in the opportunity cost of the bus trip the outlay on gasoline, tires, lubrication, and the wear and tear imposed upon the automobile corresponding to this particular trip. The opportunity cost in this case includes *more* than the money outlays that are immediately associated with the trip, for it includes the wear and tear on the automobile caused by this trip (evidenced in principle by the fact that the car will sell for less with more mileage on it), but it does not include all of the money outlays that are associated with the car. Opportunity cost in this case does not include, for example, the interest on the investment of the automobile, for the outlay on the car has already been made and you are foregoing the interest you could have earned on that money whether you make this particular trip or not.

The opportunity cost of something depends on the situation in which the inquiry is made. Suppose you are asking the question, what will it cost me to make a daily trip across the town by automobile rather than by bus? This is a different question, and the opportunity cost involved is consequently different. In this case, making these trips entails the purchase of the automobile, let us say. Hence the costs associated with this purchase—annual depreciation, interest on investment, insurance, license—must be included as a part of the opportunity cost, for they can be avoided by making these trips by bus.

What is the cost to the economy of imposing a tariff and substituting home production of the good in question for a certain quantity of imported goods of the same kind? In this case, which actually is a very complicated problem, the cost is the amount of "real product" that is sacrificed as a result of taking this action of imposing the tariff.

What is the cost of erecting a dam at the foot of Glen Canyon? First of all, it includes the volume of products that could have been produced with the productive services that were used to construct the dam. This may be well represented by the money cost of constructing the dam (see the discussion of welfare economics below). But there is another opportunity that is foregone, namely, the opportunity of viewing Glen Canyon as it was before the construction of the dam. There is no market price for this foregone opportunity, of course, but the foregone opportunity is real, nevertheless.

What is the cost of maintaining a certain area as an untouched wilderness area? The opportunity cost here is the net annual flow of product that could be had from the area if it were not maintained as an untouched wilderness area but were operated in some other way. That is what is given up or foregone because of the decision to maintain the area as a wilderness area.

Production Function

Another fundamental idea or abstraction of production theory is that of the *production function*. In general, a given output can be produced by many different combinations of inputs. Thus a production function is a statement of the functional relation between inputs and output. For the situation in which a single output is being produced, the production function can be written

$$Q = f(x_1, x_2, \ldots, x_n)$$

where Q represents the output and the x's represent the inputs. The production function is a statement of the *best* ways of producing something. If, for example, we are going to use ten units of labor in the production of ten units of product A, the number of units of capital that will be used in the production function at this point will be the *smallest* number of units of capital service that can be used and still produce ten units of product A. That particular combination of inputs which is selected to produce a given output will finally depend on the *relative costs* of the inputs, of course.

One feature of the production function which is relevant for many problems in the natural resource industries (among others) is the fact that while economic theory proceeds on the assumption that the production function is known, in actuality whether the function is "known" or not is a matter of some ambiguity and uncertainty. In the first place, it is clear that different entrepreneurs or managers do not possess the same technical knowledge. Hence the production functions conceived by them will differ. And in many problems involving natural resources (as we shall see in the succeeding chapters) there is a design problem. That is, there is not an agreed best way of achieving the objectives in question. Instead, the best way must be sought out and will be evident only after much calculation and after many comparisons of different ways of proceeding in this particular situation.

Perhaps this problem emerges most clearly if we consider the case of a river basin and set ourselves the task of managing the water resources and other resources of this river basin in such a way as to maximize social product. In this case, and also in many smaller problems which do not involve a unit as large as a river basin, one of the issues should always be whether the best way of managing the resources of the area has been found. This is only common sense. Suppose you give somebody the task of moving a large pile of dirt from one place to another. He then says, "On the basis of my experience I would say that the best way to proceed is to take a spoon and a tin cup and to fill the cup up, carry the cup over to the other pile, and then keep on repeating this operation as long as is necessary." Obviously, this person's vision of the production function is defective. He has failed to generate methods of handling the situation which are possible with current techniques and equipment.

A great deal of design consists of the application of known principles to particular situations. But it is important to realize that the *degree of routine* with which this application can be made varies enormously from case to case. If the task is to put in a sidewalk, the application of known principles and techniques is rather straightforward. Once a decision is made on the precise location and grade of the sidewalk, everything proceeds in a straightforward way. If we ask how a certain part of a national forest should be used, however, the application of the known principles is far from straightforward, and there is room for just as much ingenuity and vision as can be mustered by the people involved. We shall encounter methodological aids for problems like this— linear programming, for example. But the idea of a production function remains a useful conceptual device for summing up the state of technological knowledge.

Maximization

Problems of economizing inherently involve finding maxima or minima of functions expressing economic magnitudes. We may be interested, for example, in *minimum* (opportunity) cost or *maximum* net benefit from some action. Differential calculus is the classic mathematical tool for solving such problems, and all economists use at least a primitive form of calculus to analyze them. In this analysis, *derivatives* are called *marginal* quantities and two- or three-dimensional diagrams are usually used. However, advanced calculus concepts have also been successfully used in connection with economic problems. We will follow the present custom in economics of switching rather freely back and forth between graphic techniques, accompanied by the marginal terminology, and the use of calculus.

Since marginals and derivatives are basically the same thing (although the idea of a marginal is often applied to a non-continuous function), the rules for decision-making in regard to maximization or minimization (or more generally "extremum") problems are the same. For example, if we wish to obtain a maximum total net yield y from some output x, the basic rule of marginal decision making is that the marginal net yield must be zero, for if this condition does not prevail, altering the level of x would increase y. Intuitively, it is easy to grasp this. Say, marginal net yield is greater than zero, this means that a small increase in x would add to total net yield and vice versa if marginal net yield is negative. These relationships are shown in Figure 2-1. Alternatively, we could have defined

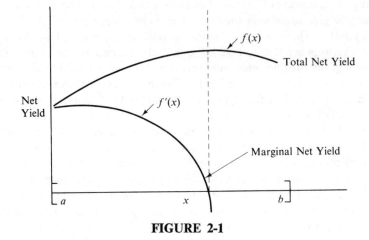

FIGURE 2-1

the total net yield as a function of x; i.e., $y = f(x)$ with domain $[a,b]$. As you will recall from elementary calculus, an extremum of this function is found where $f'(x) = 0$. If the function is nicely behaved in the interval such as the one pictured, and $f''(x) < 0$ (second order condition), the extremum is an absolute maximum. Thus the familiar rule that one finds an extremum of a function by setting its first derivative equal to zero is the same as the marginal decision rule.

The derivative of a function is, of course, itself a function and can therefore be subjected to operations of calculus—taking higher derivatives, for example. We designate the first derivative of $y = f(x)$ as the function $y' = f'(x)$. Since $f'(x)$ is the derivative of $f(x)$, then, by the fundamental theorem of calculus, $f(x)$ must be the indefinite integral (or primitive) of $f'(x)$. Accordingly, the area under the marginal curve up to some point x_0 is the value of the total function at that point x_0.

Other relations of interest concern total, average, and marginal quantities. Let P be the average value of a dependent variable and Q be the number of units. PQ therefore is the total value. As implied above, the marginal value $MV = d(PQ)/dQ$ which in turn equals $P + Q(dP/dQ)$. Thus

$$\frac{dP}{dQ} > 0 \rightarrow MV > P*$$

while

$$\frac{dP}{dQ} < 0 \rightarrow MV < P$$

---

* $\rightarrow$ means "implies that."

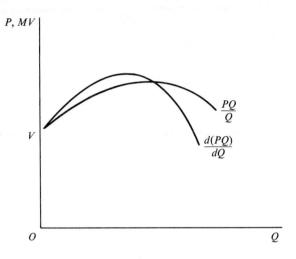

FIGURE 2-2

So we can say that whenever the average value of a function is rising, the marginal value lies above it, and vice versa. The relationship is illustrated in Figure 2-2. This is often encountered in the depiction of cost curves, etc. Figure 2-3 shows the total function and the relationship of average and marginal functions to the total function. In this diagram the average value P at the point, say x_1, is the *slope* of the secant line through the origin and intersecting PQ at the functional value of x_1. This is easily seen when we note that the slope of this

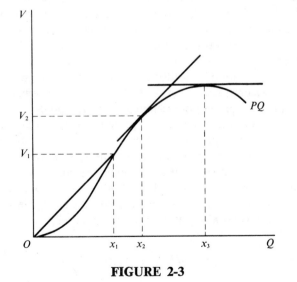

FIGURE 2-3

line is $(V_1 - V_0)/(x_1 - x_0)$ which is simply PQ/Q. The marginal value is the slope of the tangent line at some point, say x_1 or the

$$\lim_{a \to x_1} \frac{f(x_1) - f(a)}{x_1 - a}$$

The limit of this difference quotient as a approaches x_1 is of course the derivative of PQ at x_1.

Substitution

A second marginal rule for optimal decision-making is that a given kind of activity should yield the same marginal returns per unit of effort no matter in what productive effort it is utilized. This raises the matter of substitution possibilities and constrained optimization.

A fundamental aspect of production of all sorts is diminishing returns. In all those cases where more than one productive service is involved, observation indicates that after a certain point is reached, increases in the input of a given productive service with all other inputs held constant are associated with decreasing additions to product. It follows from diminishing returns that a reduction in the price of a productive service will result in an increased use of its productive service in the production process. A corollary is that there must be a decrease in the use of at least some of the other productive services in the production of a given output if we are trying to minimize cost. For a given percentage change in the price of a productive service, the extent of the substitution will vary, depending on the situation. If the service in question is a good substitute for some of the other services that are being used, its use will increase greatly, but if it cannot substitute for the other services easily, the increase in its use will be small.

The concept of the rate of substitution is illustrated in Figure 2-4. We have in this diagram two productive services measured on the respective axes. The curves are isoquants representing combinations of capital services and labor needed to produce the stated amount of product, such as 100 and 200. When we move from point A to point B, with point B being close to (or in calculus terminology, "in a small neighborhood of") point A, we have no change in total output. Therefore, we can say that zero equals the change in the quantity of labor times the marginal physical product of labor, i.e., the increase in product resulting from a small increase in labor input, plus the change in the quantity of capital times the marginal physical product of capital or,

$$0 = \Delta L \times MPP_L + \Delta CS \times MPP_{cs}$$

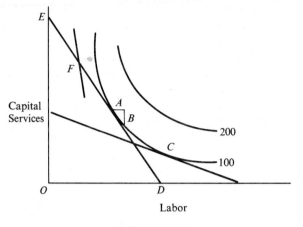

FIGURE 2-4

Thus we see that the slope of this curve between points A and B is equal to the negative reciprocal of the ratio of the marginal physical products of the two productive services, or

$$- \frac{MPP_L}{MPP_{cs}} = \frac{\Delta CS}{\Delta L}$$

You will note that as we move from A to B and further to the right that the slope decreases in absolute value. This is the result of the decrease of the marginal physical product of labor as more labor is used and the simultaneous increase in the marginal physical products of capital services as the quantity of these is decreased. We have drawn a line tangent to the isoquant 100 at point A. The slope of this line represents the ratio of the price of labor to the price of capital services. That is to say, OD units of labor are equal in value to OE units of capital service or

$$\frac{E}{D} = \frac{P_{\text{labor}}}{P_{cs}}$$

Note that if the price of labor goes down—signified by a shift of the price line from ED to the line that is tangent to the 100 isoquant at point C—the point of tangency involves more labor and less capital service.

What is the significance of these two points of tangency? When the price line is ED, given those prices for capital services and labor, the largest amount of product that can be secured for an amount of money equal to OD times the price of labor is 100. Any other point on the price line represents an expenditure of the same amount of money for inputs, but any other combination of the inputs on this line would intersect an isoquant representing a lower output, and instead of 100 units of product we would get only 90 or something less than 100 as at point F. Thus the point of tangency indicates the number of units of labor and capital which will produce the greatest number of units of output given the "budget constraint" represented by the price line. Thus we have illustrated here a production function (all possible isoquants in the production space, of which there are an infinite number), diminishing returns, substitution effects, and the determination of the equilibrium position for maximum production given a budget constraint.

Once more we may develop these same ideas in terms of differential calculus. In the process we will discuss perhaps the most centrally important device ever invented for dealing with problems of constrained or restricted optimization.

Earlier, we introduced a general production function of the form

$$Q = f(x_1, x_2, \ldots, x_n)$$

This says that output is a function of n physical inputs (i.e., materials or services). Now to find a maximum of this function, we could proceed as in our illustration in the section on maximization. We could find n partial derivatives of output with respect to input

$$\frac{\partial Q}{\partial x_1}, \frac{\partial Q}{\partial x_2}, \ldots, \frac{\partial Q}{\partial x_n} *$$

set these equal to zero and solve the system of n simultaneous equations which results. We note in passing (because we need the concept later in the text) that if all these partial derivatives exist and we evaluate them at n prespecified real numbers which we denote **a** (bold means vector in this text), then

$$\text{grad } f(\mathbf{a}) = [f_1(\mathbf{a}), \ldots, f_n(\mathbf{a})]$$

f_1 means the first derivative function with respect to the first variable, and so on for all the variables. This is a simplified notation which we shall use at later points in the text. Read grad $f(\mathbf{a})$ as "the gradient of the function f at **a**." Note that the gradient is itself a vector with n components (a point in n dimensional space). The gradient has important applications in numerical maximum seeking methods, which we shall explore in Chapter 11.

Note that if we were successful in finding the maximum of this function, we

---

* Needless to say, this could turn out to be a very difficult if not impossible task. Moreover, some production functions used in empirical and theoretical work, like the Cobb–Douglas production function, do not have a physical maximum.

would maximize *physical* production.* All marginal physical products (first partial derivatives of the production function) would be driven to zero as required by the earlier discussion of criteria for a maximum. In the marginal terminology this would mean that the marginal physical product (MPP) of each of the inputs is zero. But this implies that we really don't care about costs at all. Certainly this would not be a usual situation in economics. Usually, our objective will be to maximize output *subject to* costs of inputs and a budget restriction. If we look back at Figure 2-4, we will readily see that the price line *ED* is indeed a budget constraint which indicates how much of the two different inputs can be bought for a given amount of money at given prices.

We can solve this problem analytically (at least in simple cases) and in higher dimensions by the method of Lagrange or undetermined multipliers. The concept of the Lagrange multiplier will appear again and again in subsequent discussion. It is the foundation of all modern theory of optimization in the presence of restrictions or side conditions.

In principle, the technique is applicable to any number of variables and restrictions, but for illustrative purposes we will work through a simple production problem involving only two variables and one restriction.

Before we explain the general principles of the method, however, a general comment may help to clarify its rationale. In the unconstrained maximization problem, we proceed by differentiating partially with respect to each variable in turn and setting each of these partial derivative functions equal to zero. This gives as many equations as variables so at least one of the necessary conditions for a solution is met. This method is usually hard to apply when there are constraint *equations* in the problem.† This is because in addition to the partial derivatives equal to zero condition the constraint equations must also be satisfied. Thus we have more equations than unknowns and the system is overdetermined. The Lagrange technique introduces artificial unknowns, as many as constraints, and thereby again brings the number of unknowns into equality with the number of equations.

Let us now turn to a simple example.‡ Consider a simple production function of the form $Q = 5LM$ where Q represents output, L is labor and M raw materials. This function would produce isoquants with slopes similar to those

---

* But Q would not have a maximum unless there is something affecting the production process that is limited in supply.

The second order conditions are complicated in the multiple variable case, involving the determinants of Hessian matrices of second partial derivatives. They can yield theoretical information about the nature of solutions but do not receive much attention in practical work.

† Note that we have emphasized the word *equations*; later we will deal with an important class of constrained optimization problems where the constraints are in the form of *inequalities*. We say that the method is "hard to apply" rather than impossible because it is possible to substitute the constraint equations into the function and then proceed in the usual way. But this method tends to be awkward for large problems.

‡ This example is adapted from William Baumol, *Economic Theory and Operations Analysis*. Prentice-Hall, Inc., Englewood Cliffs, N.J., 1965, Chapter 4.

shown in Figure 2-4. Assume that we have a budget constraint of the form $2L + M = 100$.

A general statement of Lagrange's rule is as follows:

> To find the extreme values of the function $f(x,y)$ subject to the subsidiary condition $\phi(x,y) = 0$ we add to $f(x,y)$ the product of $\phi(x,y)$ and an unknown factor independent of x and y, and write the necessary condition
>
> $$f_x + \lambda\phi_x = 0, \quad f_y + \lambda\phi_y = 0$$
>
> [Note the notation f_x means the partial derivative of f with respect to x]* for an extreme value of $F = f + \lambda\phi$. In conjunction with the subsidiary condition $\phi = 0$ these serve to determine the coordinates of the extreme value and the constant of proportionality λ.†

Now to implement Lagrange's rule with respect to our production problem, we first write the constraint in standard form by taking the 100 to the left-hand side, i.e.,

$$2L + M - 100 = 0$$

We multiply this result by the undetermined multiplier λ and add the result to the production function to obtain the Lagrangian expression:

$$Q_\lambda = 5LM + \lambda(2L + M - 100)$$

We can multiply the second term to make the expression particularly easy to differentiate:

$$Q_\lambda = 5LM + 2L\lambda + M\lambda - 100\lambda$$

As is readily seen, the partial derivatives of Q_λ with respect to each of the variables L, M, and λ are

$$\frac{\partial Q_\lambda}{\partial L} = 5M + 2\lambda = 0$$

$$\frac{\partial Q_\lambda}{\lambda M} = 5L + \lambda = 0$$

$$\frac{\partial Q_\lambda}{\partial \lambda} = 2L + M - 100 = 0$$

---

* We are deliberately using several different types of notation for partial derivatives for two reasons. First, we will find it convenient to use these different notations for various different purposes later in the book and wish to remind the reader of them. Second, they are all found in the supplementary readings.

† P. Courant, *Differential and Integral Calculus*, Vol. II (New York: Interscience Publishers, Inc., 1961). This book contains a good introductory discussion of Lagrange multipliers and a formal proof of Lagrange's rule.

When we set the partial derivative functions equal to zero, we have three equations in three unknowns. Notice that the last one of these, the one which results from differentiating the Lagrangian with respect to the undetermined multiplier and setting the result equal to zero, is simply the budget constraint equation. This always happens when a properly formulated Lagrangian expression is differentiated. Thus, when we set this partial derivative function equal to zero, we automatically assure that the budget constraint is satisfied. We can then proceed to solve the three equations for the three unknowns, L, M, and λ. (The reader may find it a useful exercise to complete the calculation for the budget constraint set at 100.) In the present example, the critical point found by setting the partial derivatives equal to zero is a maximum. But the technique needed for Lagrangian expressions to determine whether an extreme point is a max or min or neither is complex (involving so-called "bordered Hessian determinants") and we will not explain it here.*

For economic theory purposes it is very important to understand that the Lagrange multiplier technique is not only an elegant way to solve a constrained maximum problem involving continuous non-linear functions, but that the multiplier itself has an important economic interpretation. In the present instance, the solution for λ indicates how much production would increase if there were a one dollar relaxation of the budget restriction. Thus, in the neighborhood of Q, corresponding to the solution for L, M, and λ, λ may be interpreted as the marginal productivity of money. More familiarly, it is the reciprocal of the marginal cost of output when factors are combined so as to achieve minimum cost and the prices of labor and capital are 1 and 2, respectively. A simple way to show that λ is the marginal productivity of money is to differentiate the Lagrangian given in the text above with respect to the budget which for slightly greater generality we here designate c.

Thus,

$$Q_\lambda = 5LM + 2L\lambda + M\lambda - c\lambda$$

$$\frac{\partial Q_\lambda}{\partial c} = -\lambda$$

We will see in later applications that this shadow price aspect of λ is very important in connection with the decentralization or decomposition of planning problems. Also, we should note that in modern optimization theory the concept of the Lagrange multiplier has been generalized so that it and the very important "dual" property of linear programming problems, which we shall explain below, are both special cases of the Kuhn–Tucker theorem of non-linear programming.†

---

* For a brief discussion, see James M. Henderson and Richard E. Quandt, *Micro-Economic Theory—A Mathematical Approach* (New York: McGraw-Hill Book Co., 1958), p. 274.

† A statement and proof of this theorem as well as a useful discussion of non-linear optimization in general is found in Clopper Almon, Jr., *Matrix Methods in Economics* (Reading, Mass.: Addison-Wesley Publishing Co., 1967).

We have displayed a graphical and analytical method for determining the least-cost method of producing a given output (or given the amount of money available, maximizing output) once a production function has been specified. It should be apparent that by performing the necessary calculations we could associate minimum production costs with output for as many points as we desire. Thus we can define a function which relates total costs to output. It is this sort of a *minimum function* which we will mean when we speak of *cost functions* throughout this book. By applying the rules relating total, marginal, and average functions indicated above, we can generate a variety of cost functions which are useful for different purposes. Very often in graphical analysis of the firm and industry average and marginal cost, curves are depicted as in Figure 2-5. This

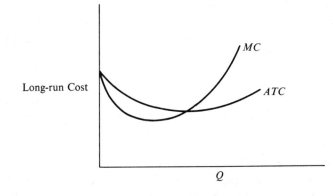

FIGURE 2-5

figure shows the situation in which all factors of production are variable, i.e., can be acquired by the firm in varying quantities and at a fixed price and where eventually decreasing returns prevail. It is necessary for us also to consider situations where such total adjustments of factor use may not be possible and the effect of this on the cost conditions of the firm. The type of cost situation where all factors are variable is conventionally called a "long-run" situation.

Before turning to "short-run" costs, we introduce another general concept from production theory which is necessary for the analysis of many problems in the natural resources industries—as it is for the analysis of problems in all industries. This is the concept of economies of scale.

Economies of Scale

What happens to the cost of producing a product when you change the scale or the size of the firm? If the initial production situation were simply duplicated, there should be no change in the cost of producing the product. Large firms would be just as efficient but no more efficient than small firms. But, of course, one really can't duplicate the initial situation, at least not indefinitely. It is for this reason that the economist expects to find that the cost of producing an article will go down as the size of the production unit increases until forces come into operation that not only stop the downward movement of cost but cause it to rise.

Two factors are involved in this expected behavior of production cost. One is that certain physical relations are such that it is cheaper to use larger sizes. The surface of a 64 gallon container can be only four times that of a similar 8 gallon container and so on. The other general factor involved in economies and diseconomies of scale is entrepreneurship. There is a unitary coordinating function involved in the management of a firm or any economic activity in the real world which cannot be split up or delegated. As we increase the size of a very small enterprise in relation to the quantity of this service of entrepreneurship, there will be increasing returns to this increase in size for a while; that is to say, the cost of production will go down. But after a time, difficulties of coordination, or reporting, and of simply keeping track of what is going on become so great that costs begin to rise. Obviously, the most efficient sizes differ greatly for different industries. It is just as obvious that one entrepreneur is not like another entrepreneur. Some can handle gigantic operations, while the capacity of others is strained by a corner grocery store. The simple functions we used above exhibited rather radical scale economies but no diseconomies of large scale. To reflect eventual diseconomies of large scale, such as depicted in Figure 2-5, we would have had to write a more complicated function.

Although somewhat special in view of our discussion just above, a long-run production function of great theoretical importance is the so-called *linear homogeneous production function* or homogeneous production function of the first degree. A function is defined to be homogeneous of degree γ if multiplication of each of its independent variables (or arguments) by a constant k will change the value of the function by the multiple of k^γ.

For example, if we multiply each variable of the function

$$f(x,y,w) = \frac{x}{y} + \frac{2w}{3x}$$

by k, we get

$$f(kx,ky,kw) = \frac{(kx)}{(ky)} + \frac{2(kw)}{3(kx)}$$

$$= \frac{x}{y} + \frac{2w}{3x}$$

$$= f(x,y,w)$$

$$= k^0 f(x,y,w)$$

The value of this function is unaffected by the multiplication we have performed and so the function is homogeneous of degree 0. On the other hand, the production function we defined in the previous section is homogeneous of degree 2,

$$f(kL,kM) = k^2 f(L,M)$$

i.e., multiplying each of the variables by k would increase the value of the function by k^2. The function

$$g(x,y,w) = \frac{x^2}{y} + \frac{2w^2}{x}$$

is homogeneous of degree one or *linearly* homogeneous as the reader can demonstrate for himself.* An important property of such a production function is that as output is expanded with factors kept in fixed proportions, their average and marginal products do not change. That is, while the production function is homogeneous of degree one, the average and marginal products of the factors are homogeneous of degree zero.† This property is important in relating the linear models we discuss later to conventional production theory.

Another property of linearly homogeneous functions is known as Euler's theorem. Mathematically the theorem says that the value of a linearly homogeneous function can be written as a sum of terms, each of these being the product of one of the first partial derivatives and the corresponding independent variable. Economically, this means that if each input factor is paid the amount of its marginal product the total product will be exhausted exactly by the distributive shares for all the input factors. We will find this theorem of significance in the following chapters.

2.5   SHORT-RUN AND LONG-RUN COST CONCEPTS

Suppose that an enterprise (private or public) is producing the output OA (see Figure 2-6) at a marginal cost of OB per unit. Now suppose we ask what happens

---

* An interesting linearly homogeneous function for economic theory is

$$f(x,y) = \frac{x^a y^b}{px^c + qy^c}$$

If one of the variables in this function is treated as a constant, the function exhibits short-run diminishing returns and has an inflection point and a maximum as the other variable is increased, this being for non-negative inputs x and y and positive coefficients p and q, with $1 < a$, $b < c$ where $a + b = c + 1$. This production function produces "textbook" short-run cost curves if either variable is taken as fixed and the other allowed to vary. See David T. Geithman and Byron S. Stinson, "A Note on Diminishing Returns and Linear Homogeneity," *The American Economist* (Spring 1969).

† A straightforward proof of this property is found in Alpha C. Chiang, *Fundamental Methods of Mathematical Economics* (New York: McGraw-Hill Book Co., 1967), pp. 272–73. Our discussion of linear homogeneous functions is largely based on his development.

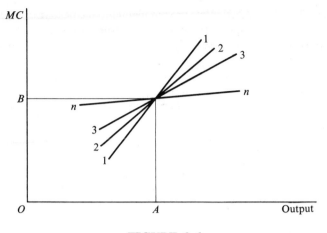

FIGURE 2-6

to total cost as production is increased or decreased from OA. Suppose that the firm is able to change the quantity of only one of the productive services that it uses. In this case, the successive additions to total cost will rise steeply, as is indicated by marginal cost curve 1. Similarly, if output is decreased from OA, the successive decreases in total cost will diminish rapidly, as is indicated by marginal cost curve 1.

Now suppose, however, that the firm is able to change the quantities of two inputs if output is increased beyond OA. Now it won't have to push so far into the diminishing returns area for input 1, since it will be able to substitute some units of input 2 for input 1 as compared with the first situation. Hence, the marginal cost curve will rise less rapidly. If the firm can change the quantities of three inputs, the curve will rise still less rapidly. And if it is free to change the quantity of all of its inputs (as is true in the long run, except for the quantity of entrepreneurship) the marginal cost curve may rise, it may be constant, or it may even fall.

Recall that all marginal cost means is the change in total cost per unit of change in the quantity of output. The concept is a general one. Even though we have related it to the concept of the derivative, which for theoretical purposes is correct, its practical application does not have to be restricted to infinitesimally small changes in output. The definition can be usefully applied even though the change in output is of finite size. However, it is calculated as the change in the total cost *per* unit of change in output. The term "marginal" has a similar meaning in other connections. If one speaks of the marginal cost of labor to the firm, he means the increase in total cost caused by purchasing another unit of labor.

From what we have just said, it is obvious that as many marginal cost curves exist as there are variables. The term "long run" is (as we have already noted) reserved for that situation in which "all" the inputs can be varied in quantity. In particular, the idea of the long run is usually associated with the situation in which the size of the "plant" can be changed. In this way the ideas of short and long-run periods, which in principle are independent of calendar time, come to be associated with calendar time. The short run, in usual usage, refers to a situation in which the size of the plant is not changed but in which the inputs flowing through to the plant can be changed.

Obviously, we have average cost curves which are associated with each of the possible marginal cost curves, but there is no need to stop to explore the relationships between these two different kinds of curves. They follow directly from our previous discussion.

The idea of the marginal quantity is important because, as we have already indicated, the behavior of the marginal quantity is intimately involved in the process of finding the maximum of a function. Suppose we were trying to find out at what output a private firm can make the most money. We have a total cost curve and a total revenue curve, as in Figure 2-7. The addition to total

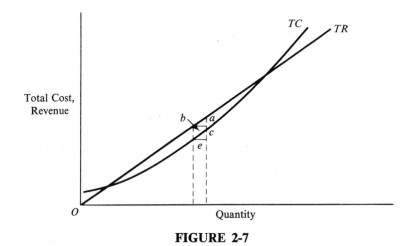

FIGURE 2-7

revenue for each small change in quantity is indicated by the ratio of *a* to *b*. The addition to total cost caused by the small increase in quantity is given by the ratio of *c* to *e*. The first quantity is called marginal revenue and the second quantity is called marginal cost. So long as the addition to total revenue is greater than the addition to total cost, total profit is increased. If one gets into the region where total cost is increasing faster than total revenue, increases in output will decrease total profit. Hence, the maximum profit is to be found at that output where marginal revenue is equal to marginal cost, or where the slopes of the two curves are equal. This will always be true, whether the firm is competitive or monopolistic, and whether we are talking about the short run or the long run, provided we use in each case the cost and revenue curves that are appropriate to the situation. Marginal profit at that output where marginal revenue equals marginal cost, by principles which by now should be familiar, will be zero, as at point *A* in Figure 2-8. If we are dealing with continuous functions, the profit maximizing firm will equate the first derivative of revenue

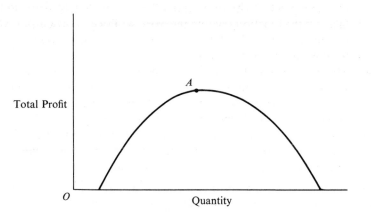

FIGURE 2-8

with respect to output with the first derivative of cost with respect to output. If the firm is competitive (which means by definition that it produces such a small share of industry output that expanding or contracting its output will have an insignificant effect on price), marginal revenue will be a constant. If it is not, the derivative of revenue with respect to output will be diminishing (since the firm produces the whole industry output and therefore must face the fact that price will fall as it extends its output). This must mean, according to our earlier discussion of such relationships, that for the monopolistic firm average revenue, or price, must be above marginal revenue.

It will be highly important for us to explore the properties of a competitive equilibrium for the firm, the industry and the economy. But we will postpone this until we have introduced some important ideas from demand theory.

2.6   SOME USEFUL IDEAS FROM DEMAND THEORY

The Demand Curve

The concept of demand curve is one of the most central in economic theory and we will use it innumerable times in the following chapters. We should, however, be specific about the type of demand we are discussing. As a general concept, the demand curve relates the quantity of a commodity to price, but at least four types of such relationships are commonly found in natural resources literature:

(1)   An individual's demand curve for a commodity or service.
(2)   The collective or aggregate demand of all consumers for the output of an industry.
(3)   The "derived" demand for intermediate goods which will enter into further production. We have already explored the concept of the

marginal productivity of an input factor; the derived demand for the factor is the function relating the MPP $\times$ Price of the output (value of marginal product VMP) to the quantity of the factor used. (This holds for competitive factor markets.)

(4) The demand for the output of a particular firm in the industry. As we have already noted, if the firm is a complete monopolist, this corresponds to the industry demand curve. If the firm is a pure competitor, it is by definition such a small element in the industry's market that any increase in its output has no discernible influence on price. Therefore, price simply remains constant as it expands output, and the firm's demand curve is a horizontal straight line.

Before discussing the maximization theory underlying demand curves, we will explore some general characteristics of demand curves.

(1) *Demand curves are defined "other things being equal."* Thus, we may write the demand functions for commodity A as $Q_A = f(P_n)$ but in fact many other factors than its price can affect the quantity of A demanded. For example, a more complete definition of the function might be $Q_A = f(P_A,I,P_O)$. Thus the quantity some individual is willing to buy of A may be a function of the price of A, his income, and the price of some other commodity O. His (Marshallian) demand function is defined holding these other factors constant. When only the price of A changes so that the quantity Q_A taken changes solely as a result of this, we say there has been a *change in the quantity demanded*. If, however, one of the other variables functionally related to P_A changes, the demand function, as defined, shifts and we say there has been a *change in demand*.

(2) Another characteristic defined for all types of demand functions is the *price elasticity of demand*. The usual definition of the price elasticity of demand is

$$(-1)\,\frac{\%\text{ change in }Q}{\%\text{ change in }P}$$

The minus-one factor makes the resulting elasticity number positive since demand curves will have a negative slope. We can rewrite this definition to read

$$(-1)\,\frac{\Delta Q/Q}{\Delta P/P}$$

which, in turn, can be rewritten

$$(-1)\,\frac{\Delta Q}{\Delta P}\cdot\frac{P}{Q}$$

Now $\Delta Q/\Delta P$ is a difference quotient of the type we use in defining derivatives. Thus, if we let ΔP approach zero we have

$$\frac{dQ}{dP} \cdot \frac{P}{Q}$$

which is the *point* elasticity at the price P_O.

In principle, we can define elasticities for all types of functions; however, two other applications are so frequent that it is important to at least know about them. The concept of price elasticity of *supply* is completely symmetrical with *demand* elasticity and we need discuss it no further. We can explain the concept of *cross elasticity* of demand by referring to our more general expression for the demand function above. Cross elasticity of A with respect to O is

$$\frac{\% \text{ change in } Q_A}{\% \text{ change in } P_O}$$

Point cross elasticity can be derived from this as already explained for price elasticity.

There are some important things to note about elasticity.

a. *A straight line curve on arithmetic paper does not have constant elasticity.* A straight line curve on double log paper does. The latter property often is useful in empirical work. For example, the b coefficients of a linear regression performed on variables transformed to logarithms are the partial elasticities of the dependent variable with respect to these variables.*

b. For any interval along a demand curve where price elasticity is unity, $P \times Q$ (or the total amount paid for the commodity) does not change. The demand curve in this interval will be coincident with a rectangular hyperbola that is asymptotic to the axes. If price elasticity of demand is unity at all points on a demand curve, the curve will be a rectangular hyperbola.

c. If elasticity is less than unity (i.e., the curve is *inelastic*) $P + Q$ will increase as P increases and vice versa where the curve is *elastic*. On a straight line curve plotted on arithmetic paper, elasticity approaches zero as the x-axis is approached, and approaches infinity as the y-axis is approached. Total payments for Q are at a maximum where the curve is just of unitary elasticity.

---

* For a particularly good discussion of this property, see Paul Samuelson, *Foundations of Economic Analysis* (Cambridge: Harvard University Press, 1965).

Demand Curves and Utility Functions

For many purposes we could stop our discussion of demand here but the economic theory of natural resources development, use and conservation is intimately bound up with the subject of *welfare economics*. So we must dig more deeply into the underpinnings of demand theory as related to concepts of consumer welfare.

We begin by visualizing the consumer as having a utility function of the general form

$$U = f(Q_1, Q_2, Q_3, \ldots, Q_n)$$

where the Q's are physical quantities of various goods and services he consumes. (We trust the reader has already noticed that we are starting out in the same way as we discussed production theory. Indeed, both are just special applications of maximizing an n variable function subject to constraints.)

Again, if this function were not otherwise constrained, we would (without here repeating all the problems in doing so) take partial derivatives and set them equal to zero to find a maximum. But this would neglect the fact that the consumer must maximize his utility in the presence of a budget constraint. We may write this constraint in the following form

$$P_1 Q_1 + P_2 Q_2 + \cdots + P_n Q_n = M$$

where the P's and Q's are prices and quantities of goods, and M is the amount of money the consumer has available. We rewrite this expression into the needed form by taking the M over to the left-hand side and then forming the Lagrangian expression

$$U_\lambda = f(Q_1, Q_2, \ldots, Q_n) - \lambda(P_1 Q_1, P_2 Q_2, \ldots, P_n Q_n - M)$$

Now, we find the partial derivatives of this expression and set them equal to zero.

$$\frac{\partial U_\lambda}{\partial Q_1} = \frac{\partial f}{\partial Q_1} - \lambda P_1 = 0$$

$$\frac{\partial U_\lambda}{\partial Q_2} = \frac{\partial f}{\partial Q_2} - \lambda P_2 = 0$$

$$\vdots$$

$$\frac{\partial U_\lambda}{\partial \lambda} = -P_1 Q_1 - \cdots - P_n Q_n + M = 0$$

λ in this case once again has an important economic interpretation. It is the marginal utility of income to the consumer, i.e., it indicates the addition to total utility that would result from an addition of \$1 to the total amount of income available to be spent on goods. This is completely analogous to the situation in the case of production discussed earlier, where λ was the addition to total product to be expected from an increase of \$1 available to spend on inputs.

The above equations imply that

$$\frac{\partial f/\partial Q_1}{\partial f/\partial Q_2} = \frac{P_1}{P_2}$$

etc. for all pairs of goods.

This says that the ratio of the marginal utility of goods must equal the ratio of prices, i.e.,

$$\frac{MU_1}{MU_2} = \frac{P_1}{P_2} = \begin{array}{l} \textit{marginal rate of commodity (or consumer)} \\ \textit{substitution of commodity 1 for commodity 2} \end{array}$$

λ is a scalar or factor of proportionality which indicates that the marginal utility of income should be equal in all uses, i.e., it indicates that the ratio of the marginal utilities of goods to their respective prices should be equal over all goods consumed. The first equation, which is like all the others except the last, says that the rate of increase in utility per unit increase in the consumption of Q_1 must be equal to λ times the price of a unit of Q_1. If λ is regarded as the marginal utility of income, then each one of these equations says that when the last unit of the particular good is purchased, the addition to total utility because of this purchase must be equal to the reduction in total utility occasioned by the expenditure of the money on the good in question. λ, then, is a factor by which the price of each of the goods and services must be multiplied in order to determine the correct quantities of each good so as to maximize total utility subject to the budget restriction.

Since we frequently will find it useful to treat constrained optimization problems in terms of indifference curves (or their production counterparts—isoquants) we will now develop a two dimensional case both in terms of the Lagrangian analysis and indifference curves to show more carefully the equivalence between the calculus and the graphical approach. As an exercise the reader may wish to go back and redevelop the production example on pp. 19–21 in these terms. In addition to the calculus concepts we have used so far this problem will require the use of the *differential*. Differentials will be needed in subsequent parts of the text.*

As a reminder to the reader—when we have the function $y = f(x)$ we know that a given change in x will be related to a given change in y. We use Δ to indicate a finite change and then the difference quotient $\Delta y/\Delta x$ represents the

---

* Our discussion of differentials and total derivatives is based on material in Alpha C. Chiang, *Fundamental Methods of Mathematical Economics, op. cit.*

average rate of change of y with respect to x. It follows then that $\Delta y = (\Delta y/\Delta x)\,\Delta x$. When Δx is infinitesimal Δy will also be and $\Delta y/\Delta x$ is the derivative dy/dx. If we now denote the infinitesimal changes in x and y by dx and dy (replacing Δx and Δy), we can write the above identity:

$$dy \equiv \frac{dy}{dx}\,dx \qquad \text{or} \qquad dy \equiv f'(x)\,dx$$

In these identities dy and dx are called the differentials of y and x respectively. As we will see, it is permissible to manipulate differentials according to algebraic rules in the same way as symbols representing variables and coefficients.

Assume that we wish to maximize a utility function for a consumer who has the choice of two goods x and y each with positive marginal utility; i.e., an additional unit of each good will increase the consumer's utility. The prices of the goods are market-determined and hence not influenced by this individual consumer's decision concerning how much to buy. The available budget of the consumer is designated by M and the problem is thus to maximize

$$U = f(x,y) \qquad \text{where} \qquad \underbrace{\left(\frac{\partial U}{\partial x} > 0, \ \frac{\partial U}{\partial y} > 0 \right)}_{\substack{\text{Both goods have positive} \\ \text{marginal utility.}}}$$

subject to

$$M - xP_x - yP_y = 0$$

We set the problem up in the usual Lagrangian form with the augmented objective function

$$Z^* = f(x,y) + \lambda(M - xP_x - yP_y)$$

Then as the first order condition for an extremum, the following set of simultaneous equations results.

$$\frac{\partial Z}{\partial x} = \frac{\partial U}{\partial x} - \lambda P_x = 0$$

$$\frac{\partial Z}{\partial y} = \frac{\partial U}{\partial y} - \lambda P_y = 0$$

$$\frac{\partial Z}{\partial \lambda} = M - xP_x - yP_y = 0$$

---

* We use this new notation because the symbol Z is frequently used to mean the value of the objective function.

As a bit of algebra will show, the first two equations are equivalent to

$$\frac{\partial U/\partial x}{P_x} = \frac{\partial U/\partial y}{P_y} = \lambda$$

Thus the first order conditions indicate that the above relationship be satisfied subject to the budget constraint. This is the same kind of principle we have found previously in analyzing production and consumption problems. It says that in order to maximize utility the consumer must allocate his budget so that the ratio of marginal utility to price is equal for each good he consumes. Furthermore, this ratio should have the value λ which is the marginal utility of income (i.e., it is the amount his utility would rise if the budget constraint were loosened by $1).

Now we have already seen that an indifference curve is defined as the locus of combinations of x and y that will yield a constant level of U. This means that along an indifference curve the following condition must hold

$$dU = \frac{\partial f}{\partial x} dx + \frac{\partial f}{\partial y} dy = 0$$

As the reader will probably recall,

$$dU = \frac{\partial f}{\partial x} dx + \frac{\partial f}{\partial y} dy$$

in the above equation is the *total differential* of $U = f(x,y)$. The requirement that the total differential equal zero along the indifference curve means that the curve represents a continuous trading off of x and y in such a manner that utility does not change. Again a little algebra will show that an implication of the above equation is

$$\frac{dy}{dx} = -\frac{\partial f/\partial x}{\partial f/\partial y}$$

Thus the slope of an indifference curve such as that shown in Figure 2-9 must be equal to the negative of the marginal-utility ratio.*

Conversely, $(\partial U/\partial x)/(\partial U/\partial y)$ is the negative of the indifference-curve slope and is the rate of commodity substitution between the two goods.

---

* Since $\partial f/\partial x$ and $\partial f/\partial y$ are both assumed positive the slope of the indifference curve must be negative. Note that the marginal utility of x is in the numerator and that of y is in the denominator.

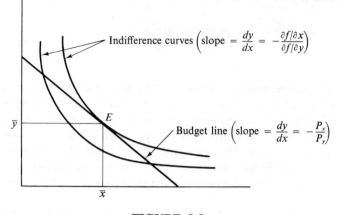

FIGURE 2-9

On the other hand, Px/Py is the negative of the slope of the line representing the budget constraint (or the price line). The previously given budget constraint $M - xP_x - yP_y = 0$ can be written alternatively as

$$y = \frac{M}{P_y} - \frac{P_x}{P_y} x$$

The reader will see quickly that this formula plots as a straight line, and that this line has the vertical intercept M/P_y and the slope $-P_x/P_y$. Thus the condition that the consumer maximizes utility when the highest possible indifference curve is tangent to the budget line (as in E) is equivalent to the condition that

$$\frac{\partial f/\partial x}{\partial f/\partial y} = \frac{P_x}{P_y}$$

which in turn is equivalent to

$$\frac{\partial f/\partial x}{P_x} = \frac{\partial f/\partial y}{P_y}$$

or the condition derived from the Lagrangian formula which says that to maximize utility the ratio of marginal utility to price must be equalized for all goods the consumer buys.

We can use indifference curves to establish an important distinction between two effects of a relative price change on consumption, i.e., the *substitution* effect and the *income* effect. We will use this distinction later in the text.

Assume that the consumer's preference is given by the indifference map in Figure 2-9a. From this diagram we can derive the usual (Marshallian) demand

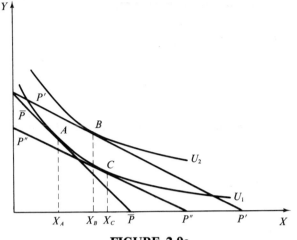

FIGURE 2-9a

function

$$X = X(P_x, P_y, I)$$

by studying the points of tangency between indifference curves and different budget lines as the price of X changes. (The student should illustrate this.)

Assume now that the prices are $\bar{P}_x$, $\bar{P}_y$ and the income is I. That situation is represented by the budget line $\bar{P}\bar{P}$. The consumer chooses the point A, where $\bar{P}\bar{P}$ is tangent to the indifference curve U_1.

Assume now that P_x falls from $\bar{P}_x$ to P'_x and that the new budget line is $P'P'$. The consumer now chooses the point B where $P'P'$ is tangent to U_2. How many dollars can we take from the consumer without him feeling that he is in a worse situation than at point B? In order to answer that question, we draw a new budget line parallel to $P'P'$, but tangent to U_1 at C. At C he is at the same indifference curve as he was at A—that is, neither better nor worse off. We can thus take from him the amount that is represented by the difference between the budget line $P'P'$ and $P''P''$. Can we calculate this amount? Yes, we can, but to do that, we must introduce some notation and develop the theory a bit.

The movement from A to B which is the total movement corresponding to the price change is called the *price effect*. The movement from A to C is called the *substitution effect* and the movement from C to B is called the *income effect*.

We have

$$\underbrace{X_B - X_A}_{\substack{\text{price} \\ \text{effect}}} = \underbrace{X_C - X_A}_{\substack{\text{substitution} \\ \text{effect}}} + \underbrace{X_B - X_C}_{\substack{\text{income} \\ \text{effect}}}$$

Let us start with the *income effect*. When the price of X, P_x changes with $\Delta P_x = P'_x - P_x$, the consumer can still buy the amount represented by A and have $-\$ \, \Delta P_x \cdot X_A$ left over for increasing his consumption. (Note that ΔP_x is negative in our example; that is why there is a minus sign.)

If ΔP_x is small, we can calculate the consumer's increase in X by

$$- \frac{\partial X}{\partial I} \cdot \Delta P_x \cdot X_A \qquad \text{because} \qquad -\partial P_x \cdot X_A$$

is the increase in income due to the price fall and $\partial X/\partial I$ is the increase in consumption of X when income increases by a small amount (say $1). We thus have (approximately)

$$X_B - X_C = - \frac{\partial X}{\partial I} \cdot \Delta P_x \cdot X_A$$

Let us now turn to the substitution effect. If we start at A and then vary the price on X but at the same time adjust the consumer's income I, so that he is always on the same indifference curve U_1, we can find a function

$$X^x(P_x, P_y, U_1)$$

which shows the quantity of X he will demand at various prices P_x. This function is called the *Hicksian compensated demand function*, because it shows the demanded quantity of x when the income effect of a price change is so compensated that the consumer is always on the indifference curve U_1.

If ΔP_x is small, we have (approximately)

$$X_C - X_A = \frac{\partial X^x}{\partial P_x} \cdot \Delta P_x$$

Finally we have

$$X_B - X_A = \frac{\partial X^x}{\partial P_x} \cdot \Delta P_x - \frac{\partial X}{\partial I} \cdot X_A \, \Delta P_x$$

or, if we divide by ΔP_x

$$\frac{X_B - X_A}{\Delta P_x} = \frac{\partial X^x}{\partial P_x} - \frac{\partial X}{\partial I} \cdot X_A$$

or, if we let $\Delta P_x \to 0$

$$\frac{\partial X}{\partial P_x} = \frac{\partial X^x}{\partial P_x} - \frac{\partial X}{\partial I} X_A$$

This famous equation from demand theory is called the *Slutsky equation* ($\partial X/\partial P_x$ is the price effect, $\partial X^x/\partial P_x$ the substitution effect, and $\partial X/\partial I \cdot X_A$ the income effect). From Figure 2-9a, it is clear that

$$\frac{\partial X^x}{\partial P_x} < 0$$

An increase in P_x means the absolute value of the slope of the budget line increases. That increase necessarily implies a decrease in X along the same indifference curve.

If we know the Marshallian demand function

$$X(P_x, P_y, I)$$

we can calculate the Hicksian demand function $X^x(P_x, \bar{P}_y, U_1)$ as follows (we drop the variable $\bar{P}_y$, which is constant):

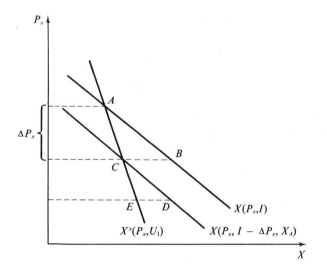

FIGURE 2-9b

We start at the point A in Figure 2-9b. A decrease in P_x by ΔP_x means that the consumer will demand X_B at point B. The income effect is $X_A \cdot \partial X/\partial I \cdot \Delta P_x$. If we subtract this effect from X_B we come to X_C which must be a point on the compensated demand curve. Through C we can draw the Marshallian demand curve corresponding to the income $I - X_A \cdot \Delta P_x$. A decrease in P_x by ΔP_x from the point C now leads to the point D, which shows the price effect. The income effect is $X_C \cdot \partial X/\partial I \cdot \Delta P_x$ and if we subtract this from X_A we come to point E, which must lie on the compensated demand curve. We can continue in this way and plot the whole compensated demand curve.

Let m be the income the consumer must have in order to be at the indifference curve U_1. Obviously, m will be a function of P_x and U_1.

$$m = m(P_x, U_1) \qquad \text{(It is also a function of } P_y.)$$

If P_x changes with ΔP_x, and if ΔP_x is very small, the change in real income associated with the price change is, as we have seen,

$$X \cdot \Delta P_x$$

and we thus have
$$\Delta m = X^x \cdot \Delta P_x$$

From this we see that
$$\frac{\partial m}{\partial P} = X^x$$

and that
$$m(P'_x, U_1) = \int_{\bar{P}_x}^{P'_x} \frac{\partial m}{\partial P_x}\, dP_x + m(\bar{P}_x, U_1)$$

$$= \int_{\bar{P}_x}^{P'_x} X^x\, dP_x + m(\bar{P}_x, U_1)$$

This formula shows that the minimal amount we can take from the individual without his feeling worse off is

$$m(\bar{P}_x, U_1) - m(P'_x, U_1) = -\int_{\bar{P}_x}^{P'_x} X^x\, dP_x$$

or the shaded area in the diagram. This area is called the consumer surplus,

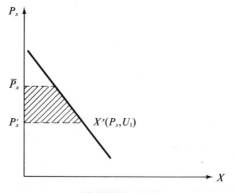

FIGURE 2-10

associated with the fall in P_x from $\bar{P}_x$ to P'_x. In the special case where the income effect $\partial X/\partial I \cdot X_A$ is small, the substitution effect is dominant and the area under the Marshallian demand curve is approximately equal to the area under the Hicksian demand curve. The former is usually used in applied work because consumer "willingness to pay" for a certain quantity of goods is usually easier to estimate than what they would have to be compensated to go without that quantity. The appropriateness of this approach will be discussed at various points later in the text.

2.7 ADJUSTMENT OF THE COMPETITIVE FIRM AND INDUSTRY

For the purpose of the present short discussion, we will assume the industry demand curve is fixed and represented by DD' in Figure 2-11. This is a horizontal

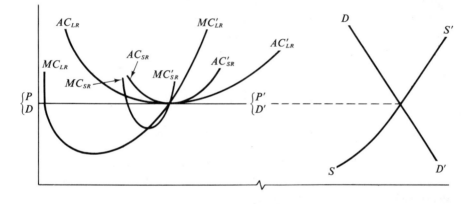

FIGURE 2-11

summation of the individual demand curves of all consumers of this commodity. We also show a short run industry supply curve labeled SS'. This is a horizontal summation of the short-run marginal cost curves of all the firms in the industry. The individual firms are assumed sufficiently small with respect to industry demand that their individual production decisions have no discernible impact upon price; i.e., this is a competitive industry. The price indicated by the intersection of the two curves represents a short-run equilibrium. The long-run supply curve for the industry, on the other hand, is indicated by the horizontal line $PD-P'D'$. In this particular case, the drawing indicates that costs do not rise as the output of the industry expands. Consequently, the long-run supply curve for the industry is a horizontal line at a height indicated by the minimum on the long-run average cost curves for the individual firms in the industry. Thus, the price shown is also a long-run equilibrium.

When this adjustment to long-run equilibrium has been made, the firms in the industry have no incentive to enter or leave since they are making a "normal" return (i.e., price equals average cost which includes a normal profit). Moreover, they have no incentive to change output since price equals marginal cost. If none of the conditions change, this is a long-term equilibrium.

If expansion of the output of the industry causes an increase in the prices of some of the inputs, then the long-run supply curve of the industry will have a positive slope, but this will be smaller than the slope of the short-run supply curve. As output of the industry expands, the cost curves for the individual firm will necessarily be higher, reflecting the higher prices for the inputs. Thus, there may be a succession of short-run industry supply curves each associated with a different position on the long-run supply curve for the industry.

The reader unfamiliar with this mode of analysis should think through for himself what the result of a change in marginal costs or a change in quantity demanded would be and how long-term equilibrium would tend to reestablish itself should conditions then remain stable. It may be noted that in long-term equilibrium several significant equalities prevail, $P = MC_{LR}$, $P = AC_{LR}$, $P = MC_{SR}$, and $P = AC_{SR}$. But to understand the *welfare economics* significance of this we must now bring together a number of elements from our discussion of production theory, demand theory, and maximization.

2.8   FORMAL WELFARE ECONOMICS

The most fundamental concept of modern welfare economics is *Pareto Optimality*. An economy which is Pareto optimal is said to be *efficient*. In this section we shall sketch the theory of Pareto optimality which, among other things, will provide us with an opportunity to bring together the various concepts pertaining to production and consumption in the analysis of the functioning of an economic exchange system. We will only sketch the theory and state its central theorem because its full development is an extended and difficult task. For example, much effort has been devoted by generations of economists to proving that an entire competitive economic system under static conditions will generate a single set of consistent factors and product prices and that these will be consistent with a welfare maximum. There is a large body of literature on the "existence" and "uniqueness" of solutions in a competitive economic system.*

---

* For a discussion of these matters at a relatively accessible level, see James Quirk and Rubin Saposnik, *Introduction to General Equilibrium Theory and Welfare Economics* (New York: McGraw-Hill Book Co., 1968). A concise summary is found in Kenneth J. Arrow, "The Organization of Economic Activity: Issues Pertinent to the Choice of Market vs. Nonmarket Allocation," in *The Analysis and Evaluation of Public Expenditures: The PPB System,* Joint Economic Committee, 1969, Compendium.

To avoid the extreme mathematical complexities associated with a full scale general equilibrium approach to welfare economics we will deal with a very simple economy which has only two goods and two consumers. In a later section, where we need it, we will develop a general equilibrium model in an economy with many commodities and many consumers. The situation analyzed here, while highly simplified, nevertheless can be used to illustrate clearly the central results of welfare economics theory.

The theory of welfare economics discusses such questions as whether a certain tax is a good or bad thing, whether tariffs increase or decrease the welfare or whether a certain public investment should be made or not. The theory is accordingly not only a positive theory which describes the working of an economy, but also a normative theory, which can be used for policy considerations. But whether a thing is good or bad depends upon value judgments, and so the theory of welfare economics must be based upon explicit value judgments. If the theory is to be useful, these value judgments must, however, be such that most people can share them. The value judgments that welfare economics is based on are the following:

(1)   The individual's preferences are important. A person is better (or worse) off, only if he feels that way.

(2)   A change that makes everybody better off means an increase in the total social welfare.

A situation where no one can be made better off without at least one person being worse off is called a Pareto optimum. In an optimum it is not possible to make a change that makes everybody better off.

There is, however, no unique optimum. If we start at an optimum and redistribute the wealth among the individuals, we can reach another different optimum corresponding to the new wealth distribution. There are thus an infinite number of optima. In order to choose between these optima, further value judgments must be introduced; namely, judgments on the distribution of wealth.

We will return to the matter of distribution later, but first we wish to examine the efficiency criteria developed from the theory.

It should be noted that value judgment (2) is very restrictive. There are in fact few changes in the use of society's resources that will satisfy that condition. In spite of this, one can derive some very interesting conclusions from these weak conditions.

In order to do that, we will derive the following conditions for a Pareto optimum:

(1)   Efficiency in production. It is impossible in an optimum to increase the production of one good without decreasing the production of at least one other good.

(2) Efficiency in distribution. It is impossible in an optimum to re-distribute the goods among the consumers, so that one consumer is better off while no other consumer is worse off.

(3) Allocation of resources in accordance with consumer preferences. This condition will be explained later.

We shall now discuss these conditions in a simple model of an economy in which there are constant supplies of two factors of production, two consumer goods and two consumers. As already mentioned, with the use of more advanced mathematics, the same conclusions can be reached with any number of factors, any number of goods and any number of consumers. However, none of the conclusions given here is altered by the more complete analysis. (Of course an increase in dimensions permits the analysis of certain problems, such as complementarity, which are not analyzable with only two.)

Efficiency in Production

Let the given amounts of the factors be A and B and denote the output of the two goods by x and y. We can now draw what is called an Edgeworth box diagram. The sides of the box are the amounts A and B. Let the SW corner be the origin for the isoquant map for good x and let the NE corner be the origin for the isoquant map of good y. The curve connecting the points of tangency between isoquants for x and isoquants for y is called the contract curve. Efficient production can take place only along the contract curve, because if production is at point Q, it is possible to reallocate the inputs, while staying at the isoquant I_x. But this reallocation can be made so that the output of y increases. At point P, no possible reallocation of factors will increase y without decreasing x. At the contract curve, the isoquants have the same slope, and so

$$MRS^x_{AB} = MRS^y_{AB}$$

where MRS^x_{AB} is the marginal rate of substitution of A for B in the production of x and the same for MRS^y_{AB}. But

$$MRS^x_{AB} = \frac{MP^x_B}{MP^x_A}$$

and (where MP^x_B is the marginal physical product of B in the production of x, etc.)

$$MRS^y_{AB} = \frac{MP^y_B}{MP^y_A}$$

and so

$$\frac{MP^x_B}{MP^x_A} = \frac{MP^y_B}{MP^y_A}$$

or

$$\frac{MP^y_A}{MP^x_A} = \frac{MP^y_B}{MP^x_B}$$

The contract curve defines a relationship between x and y which is illustrated in Figure 2-11a.

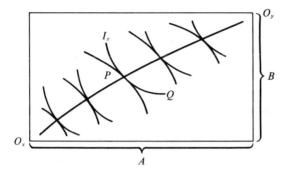

FIGURE 2-11a

The curve TT is called the transformation curve and it shows the maximal output of y for a given production of x. The absolute slope of this curve is called the marginal rate of transformation, MRT_{yx}. If x decreases by one unit, $1/MP_A^x$ units of factor A will be released and can be used in the production of y, which will increase with

$$MP_A^y \cdot \frac{1}{MP_A^x}$$

We thus have shown that

$$MRT_{yx} = \frac{MP_A^y}{MP_A^x} = \frac{MP_B^y}{MP_B^x}$$

MRT_{yx} will increase when x increases because of the law of diminishing returns.

When x is small, only small amounts of A and B will be used in the production of x, and MP_A^x and MP_B^x are large. Moreover, for the same reason MP_A^y and MP_B^y are small.

When x is small, MRT_{yx} must be small. In the same way, when x is big, MRT_{yx} must be large. The above equation expresses the condition for efficient production. It says that for any two goods and for any factors of production the marginal rate of transformation of one good into another must equal the ratio of the marginal physical product of each factor in the production of both goods. Unless this condition holds, a reallocation can increase the production of one good without diminishing the production of another.

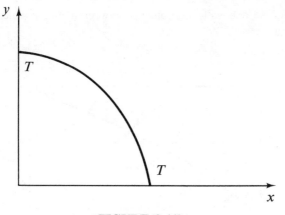

FIGURE 2-11b

Efficiency in Distribution

Let x and y be given.* In exactly the same way as before we can construct an Edgeworth box, with indifference curves instead of isoquants. This is shown in Figure 2-11c. It is clear that efficient distributions of the two commodities among consumer I and consumer II must be at the contract curve. On the contract curve, however, the marginal rates of substitution between the two goods are the same for the two consumers.

$$MRS_{yx}^{I} = MRS_{yx}^{II}$$

If this condition does not hold, both consumers can improve their welfare by trading.

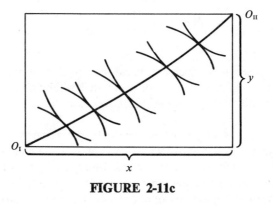

FIGURE 2-11c

---

* They will be a point from the production transformation curve, TT, of Figure 2-11b.

Allocation of Resources for Consumer Preferences

We now assume that conditions (1) and (2) are satisfied. Then we know that

$$MRS_{yx}^{I} = MRS_{yx}^{II}$$

and we denote the common value MRS_{yx}. Furthermore, we know that we are on the transformation curve, so that MRT_{yx} is defined.

Assume now that

$$MRT_{yx} > MRS_{yx}$$

We can now decrease the production of x with one unit and increase the production of y with MRT_{yx} units. But the consumers need only MRS_{yx} more units of y to be compensated for the decrease in x. And so we can give them more; that is, we can make at least one of them better off without causing any harm to the other. This situation cannot be an optimum. With an almost identical argument, one sees that if

$$MRT_{yx} < MRS_{yx}$$

we cannot be at the optimum. Only if $MRT_{yx} = MRS_{yx}$ can we be at the optimum.

We have now derived three necessary conditions for an optimum:

(1) $MRS_{AB}^{x} = MRS_{AB}^{y}$

(2) $MRS_{yx}^{I} = MRS_{yx}^{II} = MRS_{yx}$

(3) $MRT_{yx} = MRS_{yx}$

The Price Mechanism

So far we haven't said anything about institutions that can secure the obtainment of the optimum. If the economy is completely centralized and if the planning agency knows everything about the production functions and the utility functions, it can obviously achieve an optimum by command. But no planning agency has that much information. Is there any other organization of the economy that will achieve an optimum?

Assume that the economy is perfectly competitive and let P_x, P_y, P_A, P_B be the prices on the goods and the factors.

Then we know that in equilibrium, the consumers will have adjusted their demand so that

$$MRS_{yx}^{I} = \frac{P_x}{P_y} = MRS_{yx}^{II}$$

Condition (1) thus is satisfied.

Moreover, the producers will have adjusted their production and their demand for factors so that the profit maximization conditions are satisfied.

$$P_x MP_A^x = P_A = P_y MP_A^y$$
$$P_x MP_B^x = P_B = P_y MP_B^y$$

From these conditions we see that

$$MRS_{AB}^x = \frac{MP_B^x}{MP_A^x} = \frac{P_B}{P_A} = \frac{MP_B^y}{MP_A^y} = MRS_{AB}^y$$

Condition (2) thus is satisfied.

Finally, we see from the profit maximization conditions that

$$MRT_{yx} = \frac{MP_A^y}{MP_A^x} = \frac{P_x}{P_y} = MRS_{yx}^I = MRS_{yx}^{II}$$

Condition (3) is also satisfied.

We have now proved that perfect competition leads to an optimum. This may be regarded as the central theorem of modern welfare economics. Intuitively, this can be seen in the following way. The marginal cost for x, MC_x can be calculated as follows.

An increase in x with one unit decreases y with MRT_{yx} units. This is the real social opportunity cost for x. The value of this cost is

$$P_y MRT_{yx}$$

Profit maximization implies that price equals marginal cost and so

$$P_x = P_y MRT_{yx}$$

The price, P_x, the consumers pay for x reflects the social opportunity cost. The price gives correct information to the consumers on the social costs of their consumption, not only their private costs. When the consumers make a decision, they automatically take into consideration the social costs.

Moreover, the price P_x, reflects consumer preferences for x and so when the producer decides his production volume, he has the correct information on consumer preferences. Information is thus transmitted through the economy via the prices, and there are no distortions in this transmission.

This rather amazing demonstration is based on a highly simplified model which abstracts from many real and serious problems of resource allocations, and much of the rest of the book is concerned with these. Nevertheless, the efficiency criteria developed by the use of this model can be viewed as a standard against which the performance of real economies can be measured. The fundamental criteria for efficiency are applicable to economies in which central planning plays a large role.

2.9 DISTRIBUTION

We have defined the case in which a Pareto optimum may be regarded as a welfare optimum. Clearly, it is only an optimum relative to a given distribution of income or, in the case of pure exchange with no production, given distributions of initial endowments. Since we have no basis for arguing that the distribution of income resulting from private exchange will meet the ethical standards the community might wish to apply to it, we cannot assert that a Pareto optimum is a welfare maximum. This indeterminacy can be removed by assuming that the marginal utility of income is equal for everyone, as is often done in the literature, in which case the Pareto optimum is a welfare maximum. Perhaps more satisfactorily, one can embody a specific distributional value judgment in the form of what is called a *social welfare function*.* Such a function might be determined by a dictator, democratic group decisions, or a legislature. One could regard the distributional legislation embodied in the progressive income tax, welfare legislation, etc., as the implementation by Congress of a social welfare function. If this provides an ethical justification for the distribution of income, one could then regard Pareto optimality as a welfare ideal. There are many problems involved in adequately taking distributional questions into account with respect to policies concerning natural resources development, use, and conservation, but we shall discuss these as they arise in later chapters. Suffice to say here that the economist often finds it useful to introduce artifices which permit him to discuss efficiency independently of distribution.

2.10 MARKET FAILURES

Decreasing Cost

The concept of Pareto optimality is built upon a structure of highly restrictive assumptions. Clearly, all are violated to some degree in reality and some are, at least at times, drastically violated. If there are monopolistic elements in the economy, Pareto optimality conditions may not be met except in special cases. Since this variety of market failure does not enter much into our subsequent discussion, we will not linger over it. We will just point out that the presence of monopoly ordinarily will violate the criterion that producers' marginal transformation rates among goods be equal to consumer transformation rates. Even should they by accident be equal in a monopolistic situation, Pareto optimality

---

* See Henderson and Quandt, *op. cit.,* p. 218.

would be violated as a result of differences between consumers' marginal rates of substitution between goods and labor and the producers' corresponding rate of transformation of labor into commodities. The main way this result enters into natural resources questions is that some natural resources activities involve *decreasing costs*. This means a situation in which scale economies (see section 2.4 above) are so substantial that low cost production requires that the enterprise be large relative to the market so that competition is not possible. Furthermore, under these conditions marginal cost pricing (required for Pareto optimality) will not cover average cost,* so that the enterprise must be run at a deficit if the requirements of Pareto optimality are to be met. This situation is depicted in Figure 2-12.

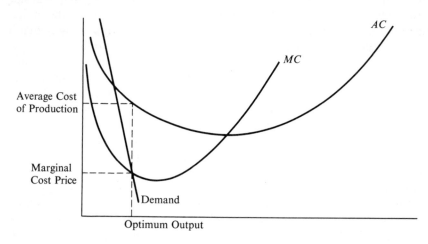

FIGURE 2-12

Public Goods

An extreme case of a decreasing cost situation is what is known as public goods. Much of the recent theoretical discussion of this problem was stimulated by a reexamination of it by Professor Samuelson. In his development he assumed two categories of goods: "... ordinary private consumption goods

$$(X_1,\ldots,X_j,\ldots,X_n),$$

which can be parcelled out among different individuals $(1,2,\ldots,i,\ldots,s)$ according to the relation $X_j = \sum_{i=1}^{s} X_j^i$ and collective consumption goods $(X_{n+1},\ldots,x_{n+m})$ which all enjoy in common in the sense that each individual's consumption of such a good leads to no subtraction from any other individual's

---

* In principle, some form of lump sum extractions plus marginal cost pricing could cover cost. Some form of price discrimination is often used in the case of public utilities.

consumption of that good, so that $X_{n+j} = X^i_{n+j}$ simultaneously for each and every i^{th} individual and each collective consumption good."* For such a good which is characterized by *jointness in supply*, the Pareto optimum condition for private goods requiring equality between marginal rates of substitution and marginal rates of transformation does not hold. Whereas, as we established above, for any two private goods and any two consumers 1 and 2 the condition for optimality is that $MRCS^1 = MRCS^2 = MRPT$ for goods 1 and 2, the requirement where one of the two goods is "public" is equality between the marginal rate of product transformation and the sum of the marginal rates of commodity substitution; i.e., $MRCS^1 + MRCS^2 = MRPT$ of 1 into 2. In the case of the true public good, Pareto optimality requires a zero price since marginal cost is zero. Obviously no private exchange system would result in the production of such a pure public good.

Much of the later discussion of the public goods concept has been confused by the introduction of a separate concept known as *the lack of exclusion* principle as though it were a necessary attribute of a good characterized by jointness in supply. The idea is that if no one can be excluded from participating in the enjoyment of the public good whether he pays for it or not, it will be in the interest of every individual to understate his willingness to pay for the good. As Samuelson himself put it, "It is in the selfish interest of each person to give *false* signals, to pretend to have less interest in a given collective consumption activity than he really has."†

Now jointness in supply (in the sense of being able to serve another consumer at zero marginal cost) and the possibility of exclusion are related but separate matters as can be seen by reference to one of the oldest examples in the literature of such a good. The example is of a bridge across a river connecting two towns.‡ As long as the bridge is not congested (and we will find in later chapters that congestion is a very important matter with respect to public goods), no price should be charged for crossing it. To do so would tend to exclude crossings (which, if made, would yield utility) even though no other person would suffer a loss if the crossing were made. This causes a clear-cut violation of Pareto optimality which requires that every action be taken that can make one person better off without making someone else worse off. Now, the essential point is not the inability to exclude, which could be done simply by putting a toll booth at one end of the bridge, but rather the jointness-in-supply characteristic which dictates that no one should be excluded.§ The complex questions pertaining to

---

* P. A. Samuelson, "The Pure Theory of Public Expenditure," *Review of Economics and Statistics*, Vol. 36 No. 4 (Nov. 1954).

† *Ibid* , pp. 388–389.

‡ The example appears initially to have been used by Jules Dupuit, "On the Measurement of the Utility of Public Works," first published in *Annales des Ponts et Chaussées*, ser. 2, No. 8 (1844); English translation in *International Economic Papers*, No. 2 (London: MacMillan, 1952).

§ A useful clarification of these matters is found in J. G. Head, "Public Goods and Public Policy," *Public Finance*, Vol. XVII, No. 3 (1962). A clear discussion of public goods considerably preceding Samuelson's is found in Howard Bowen, "The Interpretation of Voting in the Allocation of Resources," *Quarterly Journal of Economics*, Vol. LVIII (Nov. 1943), pp. 27–48.

the efficient provision and use of public goods will occupy us considerably at later points in the book.

Such natural resource issues as flood control and air pollution control have major elements of public goodness about them and we will discuss the concept further in connection with such problems. At this point, we wish to make just one further comment.

Since public goods exhibit jointness in supply, individuals' demand curves for them must be summed vertically rather than horizontally as is the case with private goods. This is illustrated in Figure 2-13. Since x_1 is available to D_1 and D_2 simultaneously, the individuals' willingness to pay for this quantity must be summed for that level of production. This is necessary in order that $\sum MRCS = MRPT$.

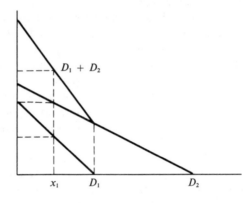

FIGURE 2-13

External Effects

In the prototype economic transaction that we usually think of when we are analyzing economic market phenomena, we have a buyer on one side and a seller on the other side. The buyer may be a household or a business and so also may the producer. While the buyer and the seller are part of the whole complex of market transactions, the effect of any particular transaction is visited upon third parties *only* through the effect of the transaction on market prices. There are only "pecuniary" external effects on other people or other businesses. It is not correct to say that there are no external effects involved, for if this were the case a particular transaction could have no effect on market price whatsoever. While the effect is small in a competitive market, it is *not* zero. But, subject to this understanding, we may say that for all practical purposes a particular transaction involves only the two parties to that transaction and that other people are not affected. When it is said that a competitive market system automatically tends to yield an efficient allocation of resources, a system must be assumed in which this kind of transaction is the only kind that takes place.

While we believe that most of the economic activity in this country can be characterized as involving approximately this kind of transaction, it is perfectly obvious to anyone who cares to look that there are numerous exceptions and that some of them are of great importance. Suppose that a consumer does something—anything—and that this affects some other people in some way other than by the very small and imperceptible effect of this activity on a market price. Suppose he beats his wife, for example, and that this makes her scream and that the scream in turn awakens the neighborhood and makes other wives apprehensive and that they begin to cry and wake the babies, who begin to cry, etc. (The reader can see how closely interrelated the system really is.) Now we have what is called a real external effect, a "technological" effect in contrast with a "pecuniary" effect. That is, in this case the utility function of these other women in the neighborhood involves not only the goods and services that they purchase but also the activities of some other person. That is to say, these utility functions involve the activities of some other person which the individual in question cannot control by buying or refraining from buying something.

At the level of the business firm, many kinds of external effects are involved. Water pollution and other types of pollution are cases in point. Here the operations of a firm produce effects on third parties which are *not* reflected in the revenues or the costs of the firm. It is obvious that there is an opportunity in these cases for a misallocation of resources to occur. The emission of soot from a factory chimney, for example, can increase cleaning bills. It might be that if the firm could be made to bear the extra cost of cleaning the clothes, it would decide to conduct its operations in such a way as to produce less smoke from its chimney. And so on down the list.

Why do "direct" or "technological" externalities occur? In this instance, the ability to exclude is the essential concept. We saw above that jointness in supply (public goods) can exist quite independently of exclusion possibilities. But with respect to externalities, the central problem is "common property." Water and air pollution, for example, occur to unwarranted degrees because the air and water are assets held in common. Hence, market exchanges cannot place a price on them to reflect their scarcity value. In the production of oil there is a "common pool" problem which means that the individual producer has no incentive to consider the costs his pumping imposes on other producers—reduced gas pressure, for example. The natural resource industries exhibit many important external effects.

Externalities, or spillover effects as they are sometimes called, can be either favorable or adverse from the point of view of the recipient. In the one case, they are called external economies and in the other case external diseconomies. They may be produced or received by business firms or by individuals.

Should external effects be eliminated to achieve efficiency? Not necessarily, for the elimination of externally imposed costs or their reduction will, in turn, entail additional costs, and we may be better off *as a group* by continuing to suffer some of the external effect rather than by reducing or eliminating it. In

the case of external economies, it might be desirable to organize in such a way as to increase them.

How can external effects be handled so as to bring about an efficient situation? One way is by "internalizing" the effect, and where the effect is important enough and does not get dispersed too widely, this may be a possible solution. By internalizing the effect, we mean that a single economic unit is created which is large enough to encompass both the operation that produces the effect and also the economic unit that receives the effect. For example, one of the considerations involved in locating a steel-rolling mill close to the steel furnace and in locating the steel furnace close to a blast furnace is that it is possible to capture an external benefit that otherwise would be lost, namely, the heat that is present in the material at various points in the operation. Internalization is not always feasible, of course, for internalization, voluntary or induced, may involve costs so substantial as to outweigh any possible gains to be had from it.

Where the number of recipients of an external effect is not too large and the size of the effect on each recipient can be identified, the economic unit that is producing the external effect and the recipients of the effect may agree on the best way to handle the situation.

Another way of handling an external effect, assuming that something is known about its value, is to impose a tax equal to this value on the economic unit that produces the effect, permitting the economic unit to deal with this tax in whatever way seems best to it. If it is cheaper to eliminate the effect or to reduce it, thereby avoiding a part of the tax, the firm will be stimulated to find a means to do this. If such means are not available, the tax influences the firm in deciding on how much it is going to produce in light of the costs that are imposed on other individuals.

Still another way of handling an external effect, assuming that one has information about the value of the effect and about the cost of alternative ways of dealing with it, is to impose certain standards. One possibility is to ban the output of this external effect. And so on.

We will expand the discussion of external effects in subsequent chapters because they are a large part of the economic theory of natural resources development, use and conservation. In the remainder of this section, we will relate external effects to our earlier discussion.

Assume that any two firms in a competitive industry are linked by technological external economies and diseconomies. Their cost functions can be written as follows:

$$C_1 = C_1(q_1, q_2)$$
$$C_2 = C_2(q_1, q_2)$$

The subscripts refer to the respective firms. Notice that the cost function of the first firm contains the output of the second firm as an argument and vice versa for the second firm. This indicates that externalities exist between the two.

Profit maximization by the firms implies that

(A) $$p = \frac{\partial C_1}{\partial q_1} \quad \text{and} \quad p = \frac{\partial C_2}{\partial q_2}$$

Since both firms are in the same industry, p is equal for the two.*

If we are willing to accept prices as indicators of value (recall the previous discussions of conditions which make this possible), the social benefit from production can be measured by the competitive firms' total revenue, $p(q_1 + q_2)$, and social costs can be measured by the firms' total cost, $c_1(q_1,q_2) + c_2(q_1,q_2)$. To maximize social benefit requires that the joint profits of the firms must be maximized. Let π indicate profit; then

$$\pi = \pi_1 + \pi_2 = p(q_1 + q_2) - C_1(q_1,q_2) - C_2(q_1,q_2)$$

is the total profit of the two firms. The first order condition for maximizing profits is

(B) $$\frac{\partial \pi}{\partial q_1} = p - \frac{\partial C_1}{\partial q_1} - \frac{\partial C_2}{\partial q_1} \overset{\text{set}}{=} 0$$

$$\frac{\partial \pi}{\partial q_2} = p - \frac{\partial C_1}{\partial q_2} - \frac{\partial C_2}{\partial q_2} \overset{\text{set}}{=} 0$$

Second order conditions again involve bordered Hessian determinants which we will not state.

If either $\partial C_2/\partial q_1 \neq 0$ or $\partial C_1/\partial q_2 \neq 0$, then conditions (A) and (B) will not coincide. This shows that in the presence of *either* external economies or diseconomies profit maximization by the individual firm will *not* yield the greatest possible social benefit, except in freak cases where external costs are equal in the relevant sense. Thus to obtain maximum benefit, corrections of the type already described would be necessary, providing departures from optimality are sufficiently large for the possible gain in welfare to outweigh the costs of intervention.†

2.11 "SECOND BEST PROBLEMS"

In recent years a small but significant literature has arisen concerning a set of issues which have come to be known as "second best" problems. The central question this literature addresses is the conditions for Pareto optimality when there are in the system departures from the necessary marginal conditions which

---

* This simplifies exposition slightly but is not necessary for the analysis. We could just as well be considering firms in different competitive industries.

† For the reader who wishes a more detailed treatment of the theory of collective goods and external effects we suggest reading E. J. Mishan, "The Relationship between Joint Products, Collective Goods, and External Effects," *Journal of Political Economy*, Vol. FF, No. 3 (May/June 1969).

by definition cannot be eliminated from the system. One such question, among several we will address in later sections, is what kind of discounting procedure (explained later) the government should use in the analysis of benefits and costs from public projects when private rates of return and rates of time preference differ and the difference cannot be eliminated? Another would be, what is appropriate policy if a market contains uncompensated external diseconomies *and* monopoly elements and one of them cannot be remedied? The general theorem of the second best analysis may be stated as follows:* If there is more than one departure from Pareto optimality, or a particular type is of such a scale that it affects the marginal conditions for more than one consumer and producer, policies inducing a particular marginal condition to be met may increase or reduce welfare in the Pareto sense. An example may help to illuminate this idea. Say a monopolist (whose monopoly position cannot be changed) imposes an uncompensated external diseconomy. If a tax is imposed so that social and private marginal rates of product transformation are made to coincide, price will be increased and consumers' marginal rates of commodity substitution may be pushed even further from marginal rates of product transformation. Second best situations are complicated to analyze.

2.12   LINEAR MODELS FOR SOLVING PRODUCTION PROBLEMS†

Input-Output Models

The general equilibrium model of resources allocation which underlies formal welfare economics represents a general analysis of the interrelationships of markets throughout the economy. Because in principle it involves utility functions for every consumer and production functions for every producer, there is no hope of ever being able to state the system empirically. Furthermore, the functions with which it deals are extremely general and could give rise to a very large system of simultaneous non-linear equations which would defy quantitative solutions. In the last two decades, a drastically simplified inter-dependency system known as the *open Leontief input-output system* has found empirical application. In contrast to the general multimarket equilibrium analysis, the system contains no utility functions, and consumer demands are taken exogenously. Also, the industry rather than the firm is taken to be the unit of production, and the production function of each industry is a constant-coefficient type so that it presents no optimization problem. The return for these

---

* Two articles of particular importance are R. G. Lipsey and K. Lancaster, "The General Theory of the Second Best," *Review of Economic Studies*, Vol. 38, 39 (1956–57) and Otto A. Davis and Andrew E. Whinston, "Welfare Economics and the Theory of Second Best," *Review of Economic Studies*, Vol. 47 (1965).

† Readers who are not familiar with matrices and vectors should pause here and study carefully the first chapter of Clopper Almon, Jr., *Matrix Methods in Economics, op. cit.*

radical assumptions is a model which can be empirically implemented in connection with certain planning problems. We shall illustrate such applications in subsequent chapters.

Here we simply wish to acquaint the reader with the structure of the model.

Input-output analysis for an entire economy is based on a detailed accounting of the flow of goods and services in dollar terms at a particular time. Part of this flow is an inter-industry flow and the remainder flows to an exogenously defined "final demand" sector. This sector generally includes households, government, and foreign trade—often lumped together. For an n-industry economy the inter-industry input coefficients are arranged as a matrix $\mathbf{A} = [a_{ij}]$. We show such an arrangement in Figure 2-14.

$$
\begin{array}{cc}
\text{Input} & \text{Output of Industry} \\
\text{from Industry} & 1 \quad 2 \ldots n
\end{array}
$$

$$
\begin{array}{c}
1 \\ 2 \\ \vdots \\ n
\end{array}
\begin{bmatrix}
a_{11} & a_{12} & a_{1n} \\
a_{21} & a_{22} & a_{2n} \\
& & \\
a_{n1} & a_{n2} & a_{nn}
\end{bmatrix}
$$

FIGURE 2-14

The first column of this matrix says that to produce a dollar's worth of commodity 1, inputs of a_{11} units of commodity 1, a_{21} units of commodity 2, etc., are needed. Frequently the matrix is set up in such a way that no industry uses its own output. In that case, all the elements along the principal diagonal are zero.

If industry 1 is to produce an output just sufficient to meet the input requirements of the n industries as well as final demand of the open exogeneous sector, its total output, which we designate x_1, must satisfy the following equation

$$x_1 = a_{11}x_1 + a_{12}x_2 + \cdots + a_{1n}x_n + d_1$$

where d_1 is the final demand for the output of that industry. We can rewrite the equation as follows:

$$(*) \qquad (1 - a_{11})x_1 - a_{12}x_2 - \cdots - a_{1n}x_n = d_1$$

Except for the first coefficient $(1 - a_{11})$, the others are the same as those in the first row of the $\mathbf{A}$ matrix in Figure 2-14, except they now have negative signs. Similarly, if we wrote the same type of equation for industry 2, it would have the same coefficients as the 2nd row of $\mathbf{A}$ (but with minus signs), except in position a_{22} where the coefficient would be $(1 - a_{22})$. We can produce this same result for the whole matrix $\mathbf{A}$ if we subtract it from the identity matrix $\mathbf{I}$.

Thus we can write

(A) $(\mathbf{I} - \mathbf{A})\mathbf{x} = \mathbf{d}$

where $\mathbf{I}$ is an $n \times n$ identity matrix, $\mathbf{A}$ is the $n \times n$ coefficients matrix, and $\mathbf{x}$ and $\mathbf{d}$ are both n by 1 vectors; $\mathbf{x}$ is the variable vector and $\mathbf{d}$ is the final demand vector. If $(\mathbf{I} - \mathbf{A})$ has the rank n (i.e., is non-singular), its inverse can be found and the system of n simultaneous equations represented by the above matrix equation will have the solution

$$\mathbf{x} = (\mathbf{I} - \mathbf{A})^{-1}\,\mathbf{d}$$

Aside from providing a solution for the n simultaneous equations of which equation (*) is an example, representing commodity and service flows from industries to industries and to final demands, the inverse matrix $(\mathbf{I} - \mathbf{A})^{-}$ has great utility. Once it is available we can pre-multiply any $\mathbf{d}$ by this inverse and produce a new solution vector for the industry outputs $\mathbf{x}$, always on the assumption that the coefficients of the $\mathbf{A}$ matrix have not changed. Since multiplying a matrix by a vector is a simple operation compared with getting new solutions to simultaneous equations, this is a great advantage. Should we have reason to think that the composition or magnitude of final demand could shift, we can easily play through its consequences in terms of inter-industry demands.

Economic circumstances could dictate that the input-output coefficients should remain fixed. Previously, we explained that with fixed input prices and linear homogeneous production function it never pays to change input proportions, no matter what the level of output. Samuelson, in his so-called "non-substitution theorem" demonstrated that this result holds even if there is one scarce factor of production.* Of course, it is doubtful that production functions are in fact linear and homogeneous or that prices of inputs would remain constant over substantial changes in production.

Despite its various restrictive assumptions, input-output analysis has come to be regarded as a basic tool for the analysis of national and regional economic systems.

Linear Programming

Another linear model of production can solve a genuine (and often complicated) problem of optimization. The technique has been used for problems ranging from narrowly defined production problems in particular firms to the analysis of a welfare optimum for an entire economic system. The latter application is known as activity analysis and resembles in general structure the I–O general equilibrium model. It has also found considerable application in regional planning models relating to natural resources use.

---

* See Tjalling C. Koopmans, ed., *Activity Analysis of Production and Allocations* (New York: John Wiley & Sons, Inc., 1951).

Linear programming and its various extensions is basically a post-World War II development, and the growth of its applications has been tremendous. In this chapter we will try to provide a good look at the structure of a linear programming problem and give an intuitive feel for how large problems are solved. In subsequent chapters we will illustrate certain applications to natural resources problems.

To state the mathematical character of the problem in the most general terms, one may say that it involves solving a set of linear equations subject to two side conditions: (1) that no element in the solution vector be negative, and (2) that an auxiliary linear function of the variables has a max (or min) value conferred on it. The auxiliary function is known as the *objective function*. Examine the following typical example of a linear programming problem.*

A manufacturer of ball bearings uses three types of machines—lathes, grinders and presses—in his operation, of which he has 8, 16, and 13 respectively. It is possible for him to make four types of bearings. Each bearing of the first type requires one minute on a lathe, three minutes on a grinder, and two minutes of press time.

These relationships for all the bearings are summarized in Table 2-1.

TABLE 2-1

Time (in min.) required on	Types of bearings			
	1	2	3	4
lathe	1	3	2	2
grinder	3	2	3	1
press	2	3	3	2

The unit profits for the types of bearings are 9, 8, 11, and 6 cents for types 1, 2, 3, and 4 respectively. Thus if we let x_i represent bearing type i, we can write the objective function

$$\max z = 9x_1 + 8x_2 + 11x_3 + 6x_4$$

and the restrictions: subject to

$$1x_1 + 3x_2 + 2x_3 + 2x_4 \leq 8$$
$$3x_1 + 2x_2 + 3x_3 + x_4 \leq 16$$
$$2x_1 + 3x_2 + 3x_3 + 2x_4 \leq 13$$

and finally the non-negativity constraints

$$x_1 \geq 0, \quad x_2 \geq 0, \quad x_3 \geq 0, \quad x_4 \geq 0$$

---

* The numerical example is taken from Clopper Almon, *op. cit.*, p. 59 ff.

Notice that the restrictions are in the form of inequalities rather than the equalities which have characterized the constrained optimization problems we have met previously. The second line, for example, says that the number of grinder minutes used each minute must be less than or equal to sixteen. The inequality is used because we are not required to use all of the grinder time. Economic problems of this type are common. The solution which confers maximum value on the objective function may leave some available grinder time unused.

Non-negativity restrictions give the problem economic or technological meaning. To permit a negative solution would imply running that process backward to make lathe, grinder or press time out of bearings. Mathematically they are necessary for preventing z from tending to infinite size. Any solution of the system which meets the non-negativity restrictions is called a *feasible* solution.

The linear programming problem can now be written in its general form:

$$\max z = c_1 x_1 + c_2 x_2 + \cdots + c_m x_m$$

subject to

$$a_{11} x_1 + a_{12} x_2 + \cdots + a_{1m} x_m = b_1$$

$$\vdots$$

$$a_{n1} x_1 + a_{n2} x_2 + \cdots + a_{nm} x_m = b_n$$

$$x_1 \geq 0, x_2 \geq 0, \ldots, x_m \geq 0$$

where $m > n$. We will shortly show how the equalities in the constraint set were obtained.

In matrix notation the problem may be written compactly as follows:

$$\max z = \mathbf{c\,x}$$

$$\text{subject to } \mathbf{Ax} = \mathbf{b}$$

$$x \geq 0$$

This is an extremely general form and many economic problems can be cast into it. But let us return to the problem we stated earlier. To get rid of the inequalities and at the same time to help us find a first trial solution, we introduce some additional variables which are called slack variables. Their real-world meaning as applied to the example problem is that if a solution assigns positive values to them it means that at least part of the lathe, grinder or press time is idle. They are called slack variables because they take up the "slack" between the time that is used in actual productive activities in the solution and the amount of time available. We now rewrite the linear programming problem with the slack variables included. You will notice that in the first constraint equation, for example, slack variables x_6 and x_7 are assigned coefficients of zero, whereas slack variable x_5, which will indicate unused lathe time in the earlier example, is assigned a coefficient of 1.

$$z = 9x_1 + 8x_2 + 11x_3 + 6x_4 + 0x_5 + 0x_6 + 0x_7$$

subject to

$$1x_1 + 3x_2 + 2x_3 + 2x_4 + 1x_5 + 0x_6 + 0x_7 = 8$$

$$3x_1 + 2x_2 + 3x_3 + 1x_4 + 0x_5 + 1x_6 + 0x_7 = 16$$

$$2x_1 + 3x_2 + 3x_3 + 2x_4 + 0x_5 + 0x_6 + 1x_7 = 13$$

$$x_1 \geq 0, \quad x_2 \geq 0, \quad x_3 \geq 0, \quad x_4 \geq 0, \quad x_5 \geq 0, \quad x_6 \geq 0, \quad x_7 \geq 0$$

We now have the problem in what is called *standard form*. We must now define another term. A *basic* solution to the problem is one which uses only linearly independent vectors. The number of linearly independent vectors possible, as the reader will recall from matrix algebra, depends upon the rank of the **A** matrix. The rank of the above matrix and all its submatrices, containing at least three vectors, is three. The basic solution therefore uses only three activities and assigns a zero value to all others. If the solution is also feasible (in that it meets the non-negativity constraints) it is called a *basic feasible solution*. It is a basic theorem of linear programming that the optimal solution (i.e., the one that confers the highest value on the objective function) is found among the basic feasible solutions of which there is only a finite number.

It is easy to spot a basic feasible solution to the standard form linear programming problem we have written above. A basic feasible solution vector is

$$(x_1 = 0, \ x_2 = 0, \ x_3 = 0, \ x_4 = 0, \ x_5 = 8, \ x_6 = 16, \ x_7 = 13)$$

It is readily seen that this is a solution to the system, that it is feasible, and that it uses only linearly independent vectors and is therefore basic. However, it is a bad solution. Geometrically, it is at the origin of the three-dimensional coordinate system with which we are dealing, and it confers exactly zero value on the objective function. But it is a place to start and from here on the *simplex* method for proceeding toward an optimal solution takes over. (The simplex method is complicated to explain in detail and we will not attempt it here. But what it does is easy to state.) It provides us with rules for taking activities (vectors) out of the basis (the set of vectors comprising a basic solution) and for putting new vectors into the basis in such a way that three conditions are met. (1) The basic solution continues to contain a number of activities (vectors) corresponding to the rank of the **A** matrix, (2) feasibility is retained as vectors are replaced, (3) and for each successive replacement (iteration) the value of the objective function improves (or possibly remains unchanged). Also when set up in an appropriate tableau the method provides a signal when the maximum value of the objective function has been reached and iteration should stop.

An extremely important fact is that the simplex method simultaneously solves a problem called the dual which always accompanies a linear programming problem. If the primal is a maximization problem, the dual is a minimization problem and vice versa. Let us write the dual of the problem given above.

First the restrictions become coefficients in the objective function; thus

$$\min \mu = 8y_1 + 16y_2 + 13y_3$$

Next the $\mathbf{A}$ matrix is transposed (i.e., $\mathbf{A}'$ is formed) and the previous coefficients in the objective function become restrictions; the sense of the inequalities is reversed.

$$1y_1 + 3y_2 + 2y_3 \geq 9$$
$$3y_1 + 2y_2 + 3y_3 \geq 8$$
$$2y_1 + 3y_2 + 3y_3 \geq 11$$
$$2y_1 + 1y_2 + 2y_3 \geq 6$$

Of course, we need the non-negativity restrictions

$$y_1 \geq 0, \quad y_2 \geq 0, \quad y_3 \geq 0$$

What the dual does is assign values to the constraints and these values turn out to have a very important economic interpretation. They are the imputed marginal values or costs of the restrictions; i.e., they indicate how much the objective function of the primal problem would increase in value if the restrictions were loosened by one unit. The maximum value of z (for the solution of the primal problem) is always equal to the minimum value π (for the solution of the dual problem). Total profit from the optimal output combination will just equal the optimum imputed value of the scarce inputs. This result is known as the "duality theorem."

If a slack variable has a positive value in the solution to the primal, the dual assigns zero value to it. This makes good sense since the restriction is not binding and an additional unit could not improve the objective function at all. This result is called the "complementary slackness theorem."

When the proper simplex tableau is used, the dual as well as the primal solutions appear at the optimum stage. Which one is initially chosen as the problem to solve is a matter of computational convenience.

The reader may have noticed that the economic interpretation of the dual is exactly like that of λ, the Lagrange multiplier. The Lagrange multiplier arises from the constrained optimization of a continuous (usually non-linear) function subject to equality constraints (which may also be non-linear). The equality means that the constraint has to be met exactly. The dual arises from the constrained maximization of a linear function subject to linear inequality constraints. As we have mentioned earlier, both are special cases of the Kuhn-Tucker theorem of non-linear programming. Kuhn and Tucker showed that for a wide class of programming problems, including all linear problems and many non-linear ones (convex optimization problems), a Lagrangian expression can be formed just as in the calculus case discussed earlier. This expression always has the property that the solution which maximizes the value of the objective function subject to its constraints will also maximize the value of the Lagrangian expression. In the linear case the dual values *are* the values of the Lagrange multipliers.

Let us look back for a moment to the *I–O* system we discussed in the previous section. Had our constraint set in the linear programming problem been of the form $\mathbf{Ax} = \mathbf{b}$, where $\mathbf{A}$ is $n \times n$ of rank n, $\mathbf{x}$ is $1 \times n$ and $\mathbf{b}$ is $1 \times n$, there would be one solution and one only to the system. This is the mathematical form of the open *I–O* problem. Thus the open *I–O* system can be regarded as a very special case of linear programming where there is one, and only one, solution to the system, and therefore no problem of optimization arises.

Concluding Comment

We now have made a quick pass through a number of the most salient topics in static micro-economic theory. Except for a random mention here and there we have studiously avoided the facts of time and growth in the economic process. To these matters we turn in the next chapter.

PART II

**Social Economics of
Private Production from
Natural Resources**

CHAPTER 3

Dynamics-Capital Theory

3.1 NATURE OF THE PROBLEM

Economic activity involves the production and distribution of goods and services in activities that take place in time. In the various facets of production and distribution theory discussed so far in this book, one aspect of these economic activities is abstracted; namely, the time rates of the outputs and inputs of these activities. The problem under discussion has been *how to allocate given total flows (always per unit time) of various kinds of productive services to different products and to different processes.* Capital goods and land have been in the background, of course, since they provide many of the productive services, but they have not entered into the discussion in any consequential way, since there has been no inquiry into the forces determining the demand for capital goods or governing the behavior of the stock of capital goods over time. The demands for the productive *services* of capital goods have not been taken as independently given, however, but have been viewed as derived from the demands for final goods and services via their marginal productivity in the various production processes. In the analysis of this particular allocation problem, with its fixed total flows of productive services, time does not enter in any essential way. The theoretical system with which such an exchange system is described is therefore called a static system because the solution or equilibrium quantities and values remain unchanged through time and merely repeat themselves indefinitely. Once equilibrium is attained, the system shows no evolution over time.*

As soon as the system under analysis is broadened to include determination of the demands for and the supplies of capital goods, however, the static nature of the equilibrium values is destroyed, and the size of the variables in the system necessarily evolves over time. We can abandon the assumption of a given flow of productive services by introducing the possibility of producing and of wearing out capital goods. Then the stock of capital is subject to change and thereby the available flows of the different types of productive services provided by capital goods. The possibility of enlarging or diminishing the total flows of productive services through capital accumulation implies the possibility of changing total and per capita income and consumption over time. Since the production of capital goods in sufficient quantity to increase the total stock of such goods requires the diversion of productive services from the production of consumer goods and services (in the sense that their outputs could be increased now if it were not for the additions to the capital stock) and since those who forego this possibility of producing more consumer goods are not necessarily those who will control the use of the capital goods, one of the flows in the system will be savings. Savings is the difference between total incomes earned by owners of productive services and the value of the total output of consumer goods and services; that is, the value of the net output of new capital goods.

It is the task of capital theory to develop a coherent view of the forces that determine saving and investment and their rates of return from one period to the next. If this task is fulfilled not only for the next period but for many periods into the future, the theory will also have explained the forces determining the size of the capital stock at any time and any equilibria or quasi-equilibria to which the system is moving. A stationary state without capital accumulation is one of the possibilities.

Capital theory thus purports to analyze the behavior of an economy over time. To concentrate attention on the process of accumulation, it is useful to abstract from the problem of economizing within periods by assuming that an efficient allocation of productive services among processes and products is continuously achieved along the lines discussed in the previous chapter. The process of accumulation can be analyzed from either of two points of view. We may ask how a well-functioning market system would resolve the accumulation problem from period to period *or* we ask how the accumulation process ought to proceed in order to achieve certain specified objectives—such as to "maximize

---

* In this elementary exposition, the problem of how even a static system may be viewed as attaining equilibrium from its initial position is not discussed from a theoretical point of view. Note that this problem requires formulation of a dynamic system, as was emphasized by, for example, Paul Samuelson in his *Foundations of Economic Analysis* (Cambridge: Harvard University Press, 1947). The problem received attention early in the history of economic theory by, among others, Walras and Edgeworth. The rapidity and strength of the movements toward equilibrium values in different parts of the economy are of fundamental importance for the practical application of the notions of welfare economics, which is, after all, the goal to which this book is directed.

welfare." The parallel with static analysis is complete. In that case we asked, on the one hand, how a market exchange system would allocate productive services, and, on the other, what conditions should hold if "welfare" is to be maximized. At least a theoretical possibility exists that the operation of the market system will yield a result which maximizes welfare so far as the allocation of productive services is concerned, depending, obviously, on the definition of welfare and on the constraints imposed on the operation of the market system. Similarly, in the case of capital theory, there is the possibility that the course of investment, capital stock, income, and consumption produced by the market system, if subjected to certain constraints, may coincide with that demanded by welfare considerations. The capital aspects of the market system will be considered first and then some aspects of welfare "over time" will be discussed.

3.2 CONCEPTS

Definition of Capital

At one time, economic theory divided the sources of productive services into three parts—labor, capital, and land. Part of the justification for this division lay in the belief that the supply conditions were quite different, with the supply of labor being adjusted so that wages were at the (conventional) subsistence level, the supply of land fixed because by (David Ricardo's) definition* it consisted of the original and indestructible powers of the soil, and the supply of capital capable of increase according to the level of profits.† With the coming of marginal productivity theory, economists realized that these distinctions were artificial, and that instead of thinking of three sources of productive services it was more useful to think of many different kinds of productive services, each of them homogeneous and having its own marginal productivity. If productive services are thought of in this way, are we then to think of many different kinds of capital goods as being the sources of these services? Clearly this is one way in which the matter can be viewed, but for the purpose of developing a simple overall view of the process of accumulation, it is convenient to think of capital goods as embodying a somewhat mysterious productive power that can be changed in form, with the extent to which the quantity of certain particular types of capital goods can be increased being quite limited. For example, we may as well adopt the view that the quantity of potentially exploitable mineral deposits cannot be increased at all—unless our vision of the economy's future embraces some millions of years.

---

* E. C. K. Gonner, *Ricardo's Political Economy* (London: George Bell and Sons, 1903), p. 44.

† The place of mineral deposits in this classification was never cleared up. The possible explanations are that they were viewed as unimportant or as nonexhausting. Some deposits have been exploited for hundreds of years, perhaps thereby giving an appearance of permanence which they do not possess.

These considerations lead to the general definition of capital as *anything which yields a flow of productive services over time and which is subject to control in production processes*. Notice that this definition does not restrict capital to "man-made durable instruments of production," a definition that enjoys the approval of some writers. Thus land is included, since it meets both of the definition's requirements. Some "inputs" which are involved in certain production processes, such as sunlight, precipitation, and other climatic characteristics, are not included, however, since they are not subject to control in the sense that the entrepreneur in a given location cannot control the rate at which the service which flows from these sources enters his processes. He can, of course, adapt himself to these uncontrolled flows by varying the types and quantities of other inputs.

The view that mineral deposits qualify as capital goods under this definition requires some explanation. The deposit that is actually under exploitation perhaps offers little difficulty, for it is evident that the deposit does provide a service in the production process in that a better deposit may be substituted for other productive services provided by, say, labor and machines. The difficulty appears to come at the stage when the deposit is being "produced," as it were. During the initial stages of the production of the mineral deposit, referring here to economic and not geological production, certain investment outlays may be made for search activities with reference to a certain large area of land but without knowing the specific location of the deposit; indeed, without knowing if there is any deposit in the area being studied. While it doesn't make any sense to try to visualize a possibly nonexistent mineral deposit, it does make sense to regard investment outlays of this type as embodied in an unfinished capital "good" whose tangible evidences of existence take the form of data files, reports, and perhaps knowledge of certain persons. Of course, when the whole process is finished, the capital good may or may not turn out to function properly. The whole process is analogous to the production of a machine or other "conventional" capital good. Even here, some of the early investment outlays may not be evidenced in a tangible form except, for example, in a design. And at the end of the process when the machine is supposedly finished, it may be found that it does not function properly and may have to be abandoned or salvaged—at an overall loss—by additional investment outlays.

As the suggested definition of capital stands, labor is a capital good, for it emits productive services over a period of time, and the quantity of these services used in the productive process is subject to control. This may seem a strange result, for laborers presumably are not bought and sold as are other capital goods. In addition, there is some justification for thinking of certain kinds of labor as being reasonably homogeneous and as not being involved in any kind of investment activity that would make them the source of an increased flow of productive services over the future. However, if it seems convenient to think of some types of labor as capital, there is no bar to doing so. There are many occasions on which it is indispensable to view the laborer (person) as an object in which investment can be embodied, including the analysis of professional education, a considerable part of primary, secondary, and undergraduate college education, apprentice and trainee programs, and on-the-job training.

Historical Notes

Several terms have arisen in the history of capital theory that require brief attention for the student who delves into the literature. First is the notion that *interest* is the reward for *abstinence* or for *waiting*. While abstinence may seem an odd word to use in this connection, if this is taken to mean that interest is the payment that must be made in order to induce and maintain *continued* surrender of control over productive services represented by the price of a capital good,* the use of the term is harmless but not necessary. Historically the term arose as an analogue to the "pain" of labor.

Similarly, if *interest* is viewed as the payment for *waiting* (to make and consume goods that could have been produced earlier), no confusion is introduced. It is an easy step, though, from the term "waiting" to other related terms that can be the source of considerable confusion. For example, while time obviously enters into the production process, it is not useful to think of time as a factor of production. Rather, production takes place in time, with the result that the exploitation of investment opportunities, which requires control over a quantity of productive services for some period of time, comes to be tied up with the passage of time in a systematic manner that receives expression in the interest rate.

Time, in the form of the period of production, had a strategic role in the theories of capital associated mainly with the "Austrian" school. Here the concepts of "roundaboutness" and "period of production" were regarded as playing a central role. Except for special cases, however, there is no readily discernible period of production for capital goods, and if the definition of capital suggested here is adopted, it is difficult to imagine what the period of production would be in the case, for example, of land. The concept of "roundaboutness" is similarly hazy. Certainly it is erroneous to think of capital as being productive *because* its use represents a production process that is more roundabout—in some sense—than some other. These two concepts are not needed for the purposes of this text.†

---

* If the notation of abstinence is to be used at all, it cannot be applied only to the initial saving but must refer to the continued foregoing of use for production of consumption goods of the productive services "congealed" in the capital good.

† Frank H. Knight discussed Austrian capital theory in an article appearing in the *Journal of Political Economy*, 1936, Vol. 44, No. 4, pp. 433–63 and No. 5, pp. 612–42. Apart from the critique of Austrian capital theory, this article, "The Quantity of Capital and the Rate of Interest," is of fundamental importance for the student of capital theory. The controversy over the period of production was reopened by Nicholas Kaldor in his "Annual Survey of Economic Theory: The Recent Controversy on the Theory of Capital," *Econometrica*, Vol. 5, July 1937, pp. 201–33. Frank Knight replied in "On the Theory of Capital: In Reply to Mr. Kaldor," *Econometrica*, Vol. 6, No. 1, January 1938, pp. 63–82.

3.3 INDIVIDUAL SAVINGS AND CONSUMPTION OVER TIME

A large part of the savings in a market economy is the result of decisions of individuals on the management of the income they receive from their own work and assets. The whole system by which the total savings of the economy is determined is complicated and has a number of parts whose connection with individual preferences is indirect. Some savings are made by institutions whose decisions are made by individuals. They may be acting as agents for individual investors, as with corporate management, for example. As agents, their decisions may involve considerations quite different from those with which some of their principals are mainly concerned; for example, the size of the institution, its prestige, etc. At the least, however, the decisions of the agents are accepted by the individual principals. The one exception is that of government, where the decision to save or not to save may be enforced by coercion of those who do not agree. Nevertheless, the point of view of the individual as individual appears to provide the fundamental base for understanding the main forces at play in determining the quantity of savings over time. Individual motives are not changed because their execution is not "direct" but takes place through a network of institutions, both profit and nonprofit.

Let us consider the problem of an individual who has just reached the age where he is responsible for his own financial decisions and who is making a financial plan for the rest of his life. For simplicity, we will assume that he knows the future course of his needs and income. If the time patterns of his income and needs are different, the individual will have reason to save and dissave at various times during his life. The problem to be considered is how to analyze and describe the process by which he reconciles the different flows of income and needs. Before turning to this problem, we need at least a preliminary understanding of the concept of *present value*. This concept plays a central role in applications of economic theory to natural resource problems because they so often involve variable flows of receipts and outlays, just as in the case of the individual.

To develop the meaning of "present value," let us suppose that certain individuals in the economy wish to gain a present command over more productive services than they now have. They may want to consume more now, or they may want to use the funds to buy (i.e., produce) a piece of capital equipment. Other individuals are willing to lend a part of their present command over productive services. If these transactions take place on a market, *one* price can be expected to emerge, and this price will be called the rate of interest. It is *the price*—read again the description of the two types of transactions—that relates present and future values. These values represent command over productive services. This price is expressed as a pure number which relates the two sums for a specified period of time.

The single return, or price, that will tend to emerge for all lines of investment will have a special meaning. The longer the period between the investment and the return, the greater must be the return, and it must be greater in a special way if the following two situations are to be equivalent:

Now	One year from now	Two years from now
Situation A: Invest \$1		Receive \$1 plus return . for 2 years $= S_2$
Situation B: Invest \$1	Receive \$1 plus return for 1 year $= S_1$. Invest S_1.	Receive S_1 plus return on S_1 for one year at the rate of $(S_1 - \$1)$ per dollar invested $= S_1 + (S_1 - \$1)S_1$

The initial investment is the same in both situations. Hence, competition in the market should insure that the sum of money available two years from now should be the same in both situations:

$$S_2 = S_1 + (S_1 - \$1)S_1$$

$$= S_1 + S_1^2 - S_1 = S_1^2$$

Now substitute $(1 + r)$ for S_1. We have:

$$S_2 = (1 + r)^2$$

For equivalence among investments of different periods, this relationship must hold not only for two periods as compared with one, but for any pair of periods. That is, $S_n = (1 + r)^n$.*

Because of the existence of the opportunity to invest now and to secure a return on this investment later, a dollar spent or received now should not be regarded as having the same value *as of now* as a dollar spent or received at some other time. As we have just seen, a dollar spent now should be regarded as equivalent (in terms of present value as of now) to $\$(1 + r)$ spent one year from now and as equivalent to $\$(1 + r)^2$ spent two years from now, and as equivalent to $\$(1 + r)^n$ spent n years from now.

This process by which dollars spent or received at different times are made comparable by converting them to "present value" as of a *given date* is called

---

* In order to facilitate explanation of basic ideas, it has been assumed that the one-year return to investment is the same in both years. This need not be the case. If change in the return to investment can be foreseen, this should receive recognition in the discounting process. For example, the discount "factor," $(1 + {}_0r_2)$, for a two-year period from $t = 0$ to $t = 2$ should be the geometric mean of the discount factors for the separate years, $(1 + {}_0r_1)$ and $(1 + {}_1r_2)$. That is, $(1 + {}_0r_2)^2 = (1 + {}_0r_1)(1 + {}_1r_2)$.

discounting. For example, to convert $10 to be received in 1976 to dollars of present value of 1973, we divide $10 by $(1 + r)^3$.

$10 received in 1976 has a present value (P.V.) as of 1973 of:

$$\frac{\$10}{(1 + r)^{76-73}} = \frac{\$10}{(1 + r)^3}$$

For example, if the rate of interest is 20 percent per year, then,

$$\frac{\$10}{(1 + .20)^3} = \frac{\$10}{1.728} = \$5.79$$

to the nearest cent.

On the other hand, $10 received in 1973 has a P.V. *as of 1976* of $10 *multiplied by* $(1 + r)^3$

$$= \$10(1 + r)^3 = \$10(1.728) = \$17.28$$

Now let us return to the problem of the individual who wishes to reconcile differences in the time patterns of his income and consumption. If the capital market and foresight were perfect, he could calculate the present value of his lifetime income and, by investing and/or borrowing, could enjoy a flow of cash to match any consumption stream whatsoever—provided the present value of this stream did not exceed the present value of his lifetime income. Most individuals, for example, probably find their initial earnings to be lower than they will be in the middle or later period of their working lives. Depending on the particular occupation, the peak earnings may come at the end of the working life, or for others, earlier. Professional athletes, for example, have early peak earnings from their athletic activity. In most cases, income drops precipitously at retirement. The demands of the individual may follow a radically different time pattern. At the outset of the working career, the worker may be single, with no demands for goods required to support wife or children, a more elaborate household, or college education, but the period of little responsibility usually does not last very long. In later life, certain demands will have diminished or vanished, perhaps because of physical or psychological change, and demands which arose because of children will have declined.

Rational adjustment to this presumably typical life cycle of earnings and demands would call for increasingly heavy borrowing (at least on the net) so long as demands are "ahead" of income, to be followed by a paying off of debt and still later by saving. During retirement, or during the later years of low earnings, in the case of those with early peaks these savings will be drawn down to enable consumption to remain above the low or zero level income. This pattern would be followed even if the market rate of interest confronting the individual were close to zero. A positive rate of interest can alter this adjustment substantially, however, as can be illustrated by Figure 3-1, in which this adjust-

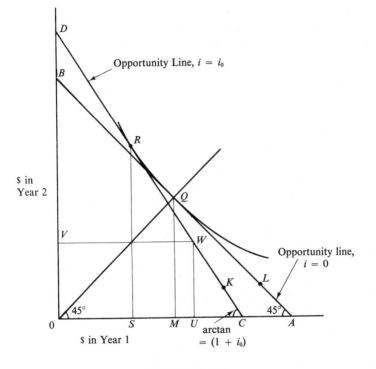

FIGURE 3-1

ment of the individual between two "years" is examined. The two "years" can be thought of as being any pair of actual years (including adjacent years) with quantities for other years held constant, or the two "years" might be thought of as dividing a working lifetime into two parts.

In the figure, the opportunity line AB with a slope of 45 degrees represents the possibilities for moving income from one year to the other (assuming $i = 0$) for an individual whose initial incomes in the two years are represented by a point somewhere on this line. Point A, for example, would represent a situation in which all income is received in the first year and none in the second. By lending, the person could attain any position on the line AB.

Line OQ also has a slope of 45 degrees. The indifference curve tangent at Q is symmetrical around the line OQ. By principles explained in the preceding chapter, we see that the absolute value of the slope of the indifference curve is equal to the ratio of the marginal utilities of consumption in the two years,

$$\frac{MU_{C_1}}{MU_{C_2}} *$$

---

* In this discussion, it is assumed that income is completely converted to consumption in one or the other of the two periods.

It is customary to say that symmetry of the indifference curve system around OQ indicates that this particular person has no *intrinsic time preference*. That is, given the opportunity to shift income between the two years dollar for dollar, which is what the slope of 45 degrees of line AB means, he will prefer to divide his initial incomes equally between the two years, as at point Q. If he moves away from point Q in such a way as to feel just as well off as before, each dollar by which C_1 is reduced requires increasing amounts of C_2. If the movement is in the other direction, the rate at which consumption must increase to maintain indifference will be exactly the same.

But how can the situation of a person with no intrinsic time preference be distinguished from that of a person with intrinsic time preference which is offset by differences in the structure of demand for the various goods and services in the two years (i.e., "needs" are different)? The answer to this question will not be attempted here. The assumption of identity of the structure of demand in the two years is used here simply as a way to give meaning to the concept of intrinsic time preference. If the indifference curve were tangent to AB at point L, say, and demand structure was the same in both years, the person would be exhibiting a positive intrinsic time preference. That is, he has chosen to spend earlier rather than later even though demand structure is the same in the two years. If when year 2 comes along he does not regret the time pattern of expenditure that he chose, his time preference may be said to be consistent through time. But if in year 2 he wishes he had spent less in year 1 than in year 2, his intrinsic time preference has switched direction. It is plain that any such inconsistency would pose serious difficulties for a theory of welfare over time.*

If the market provides the individual with the opportunity to convert income between the two years at a positive rate of interest, his behavior will be different even though he begins with the same initial incomes and has *no* intrinsic time preference. Suppose that initial incomes are indicated by point W, that is, $Y_1 = OU$ and $Y_2 = OV$. The absolute value of the slope of the line CD with respect to C_1 axis is $(1 + i)$, reflecting the opportunity now open to the individual to lend a dollar and receive a dollar plus i a year later. Thus all points on the line CD are attainable from a pair of initial incomes represented by any point on the line, either by lending or borrowing.

In this particular case, the highest indifference curve that can be attained is the one drawn on the figure as tangent to CD at point R. He lends a sum equal to the horizontal distance between W and R, reaping $(1 + i)$ times this amount in year 2, equal to $US(1 + i)$.

Point R, which indicates the consumption levels of the two years, can be interpreted in terms of c, the relative change in consumption from year 1 to year 2, the rate of interest, i, and δ, the elasticity of substitution of the indifference curve at this point.

---

* See the excellent discussion of this problem by R. H. Strotz, "Myopia and Inconsistency in Dynamic Utility Maximization," *Review of Economic Studies*, Vol. XXIII, 1955–56, pp. 165–80.

In deriving the expression for δ, it is convenient to imagine a movement to R on the same indifference curve from a point at which the ratio of the prices of C_1 and C_2 is $1/(1 + i)$ times the ratio at R. Since the ratio at R is $(1 + i)/1$, the point required has a price ratio of

$$\frac{1}{1 + i} \cdot \frac{1 + i}{1}$$

or 1. By the diagram, this is point Q.

Recall that the elasticity of substitution is defined as the relative change in the ratio of the two quantities on the isoquant (here C_2/C_1) divided by the relative change in the marginal rate of substitution of C_2 for C_1; then:*

$$\delta = \frac{\dfrac{(RS/OS) - (QM/OM)}{QM/OM}}{\dfrac{1}{1/(1 + i)} - 1} = \frac{(RS - OS)/OS}{i} = \frac{c}{i}$$

Observing that $(RS - OS)/OS = c$ is the relative amount by which consumption has grown from period one to period two, we conclude that the individual's consumption should grow at a relative rate per year equal to $i\sigma$. If the elasticity of substitution is $\frac{1}{2}$ and i is 8 percent, consumption should grow at 4 percent per year—assuming that δ and i remain unchanged.

δ is inversely related to the second derivative of the indifference curve, which is to say that δ reflects the ease with which consumption in one year may be substituted for consumption in another while leaving the individual in the same total utility position. δ may be expected to approach zero as income declines since at some point it clearly becomes inadvisable to reduce present income even for a large increase in future income. Similarly, with very high income δ may again be very low since there is little or nothing to be gained by shifting consumption for the sake of greater gain later on.

The individual's adaptation to a change in the rate of interest confronting him involves the usual *substitution* and *income effects* of demand theory.† Again

---

* Recall that if total utility $= U(C_1, C_2)$, then the marginal rate of substitution at U_0 between C_2 and $C_1 = -\dfrac{dC_2}{dC_1} = \dfrac{U_{C_1}}{U_{C_2}} = \dfrac{P_{C_1}}{P_{C_2}}$

The last equation requires that the person take the prices at which the two goods can be converted as given. With the opportunity to lend and borrow at i, $(1 + i)$ units of consumption in the second period are required to be equal in value to one unit in period one. That is, the price of a unit of C_2 in terms of C_1 is $1/(1 + i)$. The price of C_1 is taken as one, of course. Here we use the arc between R and Q for convenient illustration, QM/OM being equal to one. [See J. E. Meade, *The Growing Economy* (Chicago: Aldine Publishing Co., 1968), p. 204, for further discussion.] For an analysis of the concept of elasticity of substitution, see R. G. D. Allen, *Mathematical Analysis for Economists* (London: MacMillan & Co. Ltd., 1938), pp. 340–45.

† Recall the explanation of these in Chapter 2.

let us view consumption in years 1 and 2 as two separate commodities. The individual's indifference map is symmetrical around a line at 45 degrees to the axes. If the initial incomes are indicated by point A in Figure 3-2 and the rate

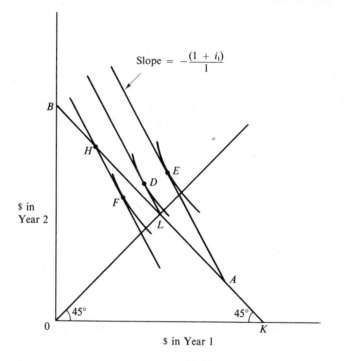

Slope $= -\dfrac{(1 + i_1)}{1}$

$ in Year 2

$ in Year 1

FIGURE 3-2

of interest is zero, as indicated by opportunity line KB at 45 degrees to the axes, the best that can be done is to move to point L.

Now suppose that the rate of interest moves from zero to i_1 as indicated by the greater slope of AE, which is now the opportunity line instead of AB as before. The individual's position now can be improved by moving from point L to point E. This movement may be broken into two steps, a substitution effect from L to D^* resulting from the change in relative prices only, and an income effect from D to E. Since the price of C_2 in terms of C_1 has been reduced, the substitution effect, always in favor of the commodity whose relative price has fallen, involves an increase in C_2, that is, an increase in savings in this case.

---

* The description of the substitution effect as involving a movement from L to D implies that the unchanged income position is defined as one from which the former equilibrium could be attained. That is, at the new prices, point L would be attainable from point D. The alternative would be to describe the substitution effect as involving a movement on the same indifference curve containing point L to a point below and to the left of point D. The former is the Slutsky and the latter the Hicks view of the substitution effect. See Milton Friedman, *Price Theory: A Provisional Text* (Chicago: Aldine Publishing Co., 1962), p. 53, for further explanation.

The income effect, which is favorable for a saver, partially offsets the substitution effect and tends to increase the consumption of both commodities. The total effect as shown here involves an increase in C_1, that is, a decrease in saving.

The total effect on C_1 may be negative. Suppose, for example, that the initial position is at L instead of A and that the rate of interest is zero. There would be no reason to save or invest. If i now increases to i_1 as before, the best that can be done is to move to D. C_1 decreases and savings are now positive. Now only the substitution effect is operative, for there are no savings on which the income effect can operate.

Now consider the case in which the individual is a borrower, with his initial position at H. With the interest rate at zero, the individual will now move to L, borrowing a sum equal to the horizontal distance between H and L in order to increase current consumption. If now the interest rate rises to i, he will move from L to F, a movement that may be thought of as involving a substitution movement from L to D plus an income effect movement (negative, for the situation at L is one of borrowing) from D to F. The substitution effect operates to reduce C_1 and the income effect now operates in the same direction, reducing both C_1 and C_2. Borrowing must decrease.*

3.4   SAVINGS BY ALL INDIVIDUALS

The fact that persons find it advisable to adapt their consumption to a positive interest rate does not imply positive savings for the society. Let us assume a society with a stable age distribution and stable labor force in which there is no technological progress. If, on the average, people try to leave estates of a certain size and succeed in this endeavor by an error that remains constant, there will be no net savings over the lifetime of the average person and no net capital formation. During parts of his life the individual may have a positive net worth. Indeed, his average net worth over his adulthood would represent his aliquot portion of the economy's capital. Consumption streams could be rising over a lifetime, reflecting adjustment to a positive rate of interest, but all lending and borrowing would be for the purpose of adjusting for discrepancies between income and the desired consumption stream selected in view of the rate of interest available. For the society as a whole, the situation would be one in which the desired quantity of savings in relation to wealth and income is zero.

Changes in any one or more of the characteristics of this situation could result in capital accumulation. Technological progress, bringing an increase in real income, would be likely to increase the desired net worth of the individual over his adulthood. Suppose, for example, that there is no discrepancy between the general course of the earnings and desired consumption streams during working years but that there is a period of retirement with expenditures to be

---

* For further discussion, see William S. Vickrey, *Metastatics and Macroeconomics* (New York: Harcourt, Brace & World, Inc., 1964), pp. 10–16.

covered only from interest and liquidation of investments. If the rate of interest has not declined too much as a result of the particular type of technological progress (that is, if it has not been too capital saving in nature), an individual will save more during the working years in order to permit retirement consumption to rise along with consumption during working years.

Up to this point it has been assumed that the average estate actually left is constant even though different from the average intended estate.* If the desired estate instead is related to the level of real income, then any factor causing real income to rise will lead to net investment over a lifetime, assuming attempts to save more get translated into investment, and the stock of capital will increase. There are various motives that might be expected to lead to a positive relation between the size of desired estate and the level of income. Certainly many of the rationales guiding provision for heirs† have the result of wishing to leave a larger estate the higher the income. Perhaps even more important is the fact that wealth is an important source of power and prestige. But even if wealth is viewed in this way, it is unlikely that it will be liquidated during the person's lifetime for consumption purposes, unless a person accustomed to the attention that wealth can bring is willing to spend his later years in an even greater obscurity than that which comes to wealthy persons. Setting up a permanent foundation does not constitute liquidation but instead is a way of calling to public attention the size of one's accumulation, as is also the purchase of the privilege of leaving one's name carved in the stone of a university building. And liquidation during life is out of the question for the type of person who contemplates with keen anticipation his obituary headline, "Distinguished Industrialist Leaves Estate of $X Million."

3.5 INVESTMENT AND THE INDIVIDUAL ADJUSTMENT‡

If an individual has real investment opportunities, he may be able to attain a much better position, depending on how good the opportunities are. Suppose the person's initial incomes are as indicated by the coordinates of point A in Figure 3-3. If there are no real investment opportunities and the market rate of

---

* If insurance operations were costless, it would be an easy matter to reduce the discrepancies between the actual estate left and the desired estate.

† For example, some of these might be characterized as wanting to give the heir a good start in life; not wanting the heir to have to work so hard as his father; wanting the heir to be distinguished (by his wealth); not wanting to consume more; and being unable to think of a better recipient of the wealth than one's heir, etc. Natural heirs are usually the objects of such rationales, although some of them are applicable to other heirs, too.

‡ The standard reference on the subject matter of this section is J. Hirshleifer, "On the Theory of Optimal Investment Decision," *Journal of Political Economy*, August 1958, Vol. LXVI, No. 4, pp. 329–52.

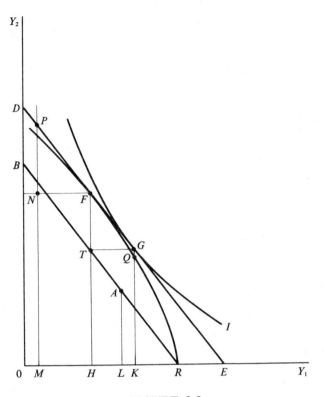

FIGURE 3-3

interest for consumption loans is that indicated by the absolute value of the slope of BR,* the individual would move from position A to the point on the line which is tangent to an indifference curve for the two years' consumption. Some individuals, however, will have real investment opportunities. In this case, attainment of the final optimum involves two stages: first, attaining the investment optimum and, second, the consumption optimum.

Let us suppose that the individual plans a series of investment programs, first for the investment of a small sum, and then for larger sums, always with the objective of maximizing the return in year 2 from the sum in question. As the size of the program is increased, new projects may be added and the size of the earlier projects probably will be increased. That is, there will be both an extensive and intensive margin for investment in projects. To represent this series of programs on the diagram, point R, which is the present value equivalent (at the given rate of interest) of the initial endowment of incomes at A, can be regarded as an origin from which the size of each investment program is measured with

---

* That is, by moving k dollars to the left of point A (lending them), $k(1 + i)$ can be obtained in year 2. Thus the slope of BR (and DE) is $-[(1 + i)/1]$.

the return of funds the second year measured vertically from this year. Thus one of the programs (not just one project) has initial investment of RK, with a second year return of funds equal to KQ. Another specific program has initial investment RH with second year return of funds HF. When these returns and those from other investment programs are ordered by size of return, measuring investment in each case from point R to the left, an investment program curve, FQR, will be traced out showing second year total return as a function of the amount invested. As the amount invested in the program increases, optimum investment in opportunities or projects already in the program will increase and new opportunities will be added.

The larger optimum scale of project associated with lower rates of discount is a consequence of diminishing returns to the application of capital to a given investment opportunity. With "natural resource" investments, for example, a dam site at which water will be stored for irrigation, the reasons for (ultimately) diminishing returns are rather obvious.

When the market interest rate confronting the individual changes, the opportunity line, BR, pivots around point A, which indicates incomes in the two years. The new investment program function will shift horizontally by the amount by which point R, indicating present value equivalent of $Y_1 + Y_2$, has shifted. Recall that the only role played by the actual market rate of interest in the derivation of the investment program function was to locate the origin from which size of investment program is measured.

Since the individual can borrow or lend at the market rate, i, it will be profitable for him to undertake real investment so long as the marginal return, indicated by the absolute value of the slope of $FQR - 1$, is greater than i (indicated by the absolute value of the slope of $BR - 1$). His optimum investment program is RH with marginal return of i at point F.

Next, he proceeds to determine his consumption pattern. If he finances himself, his first year's consumption will be only $(OL - RH)$, or OM. His second year's consumption will be much greater than AL, being equal to $(HF + AL)$. If he is willing to borrow, however, he can easily attain a higher indifference curve than the one that passes through P. For example, by borrowing LR, thus giving him first year funds of OR, he can have first year consumption of OH and invest HR. The second year income (AL), will necessarily just cover repayment of the loan, LR, leaving the whole return from investment, HF, available for year 2 consumption. The two year consumption position would be indicated by point F.

Since this person appears to have a preference for year 1 income, however, he can improve his position even more by borrowing in addition the sum HK, thus moving along the opportunity line DE to a point tangent with an indifference curve. Consumption and investment in the first year, $OK + HR$, are financed by first year income, $Y_1 = OL + $ loans LR and HK. Initial income in the second year, $Y_2 = LA$, is just sufficient to pay off the investment loan of LR. TF of the total investment return of HF is used to pay off the consumption loan of $HK(=TG)$, leaving KG for C_2.

3.6 TREES, WINE, HAIR, ETC.

The problem of how long to let trees grow before trimming, wine age before selling, and hair grow before cutting can be analyzed with a diagram somewhat similar to the preceding one. Suppose that a certain tract of newly planted trees has been acquired for k. Time is measured on the horizontal axis of Figure 3-4

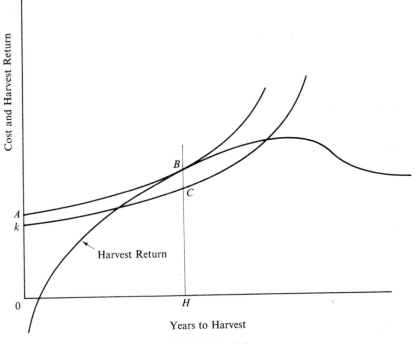

FIGURE 3-4

and the return (receipts less harvest cost) from harvesting on the vertical axis. The curve showing return at harvest no doubt will have a maximum, but at some point will level off since factors reducing the return, such as debris on the forest floor and dispersion in the ages of the trees in the tract, will have reached a steady state. The behavior of the return curve to the right of the maximum is of no interest to the profit maximizer, however.

The objective here is to maximize the positive difference between return at harvest and the cost of the tract, k. To be comparable, the return and cost must be expressed in dollars as of the same date. To do this, we put a constant present value curve on the figure so that it is tangent to the return curve at B and has a present value of A at $t = 0$.* Because of the opposite curvatures of this curve and the return curve, no other constant present value curve that touches the harvest return curve can have a larger present value than A.

---

* That is, $V_t = Ae^{it}$. In particular, $B_H = Ae^{iH}$.

The constant present value curve has the same relative slope at every point; namely, the rate of interest.* Thus we can conclude that maximization of harvest return over initial cost of $k occurs where the harvest return curve also has a relative slope equal to the rate of interest.† The initial cost of $k is not present in this necessary condition, of course, since it is not a function of time but is fixed.

Suppose, however, that we are considering not one stand of trees of the same age but a systematically rotated large forest. If trees are planted at a steady rate, a per unit time, beginning at $t = 0$ at a cost of k per tree, then for an optimum tree life of t, we shall have a steady rate of timber available at t_1 of $Q = af(t)$ [$f(t)$ is the growth function for one tree]. Once the optimum t has been selected and the first trees planted have reached this age, a trees per year will be harvested

---

* That is, $(1/y)(dy/dt) = i$ where $y = Ae^{it}$. With annual instead of continuous compounding (see below), if $y = A(1 + i)^t$ the slope is a constant, $\ln (1 + i)$, which is approximately equal to i for small i. If the vertical axis is expressed in logarithmic instead of natural values, the constant present value curves would be parallel straight lines with $\ln y = \ln A + it$ or $\ln y = \ln A + t \ln (1 + i)$.

Continuous compounding

To show the nature of continuous compounding, start with the expression for annual compounding:

$$y = (1 + i)^t$$

If compounding is n times per year, then

$$y = \left(1 + \frac{i}{n}\right)^{nt} = \left[\left(1 + \frac{i}{n}\right)^{n/i}\right]^{it}$$

Substituting m for n/i,

$$\lim_{m \to \infty} y = \left[\left(1 + \frac{1}{m}\right)^m\right]^{it} = e^{it}$$

(and therefore as $n \to \infty$ since $n = im$). That is, the expression in the square brackets approaches a limit $e = 2.71828...$, which is the base of the natural (Napierian) log system.

† It is often said, incorrectly, that the optimum period of harvest is that for which the rate of growth of the tree is equal to the rate of interest, but this could be the case only if harvest costs for the tract are strictly proportional to sales. Suppose that:

$$Q = af(t) \quad \text{is salable volume}$$
$$P \quad \text{is price of product}$$
$$h(Q) \quad \text{is harvest cost per unit volume sold}$$
$$k \quad \text{is initial cost of tract.}$$

Then the present value of total net return is

$$NR = e^{-it}[Paf(t) - h(Q)af(t)] - k$$
$$\frac{dNR}{dt} = ae^{-it}[Pf'(t) - h(Q)f'(t) - f(t)h'(Q)f'(t)] - aie^{-it}[Pf(t) - h(Q)f(t)] = 0$$

or $$i = \frac{f'(t)[P - h(Q) - f(t)h'(Q)]}{f(t)[P - h(Q)]}$$

This reduces to $i = f'(t)/f(t)$, the relative rate of growth of volume, only if $h'(Q) = 0$, that si, if $h(Q) = c$, with $c \geq 0$. In this case, total harvest costs at t are cQ.

and planted. If P is the net price after constant per unit harvest cost, then a perpetual cost stream of a k per unit time begins at $t = 0$ and a perpetual revenue stream of $PQ = Paf(t)$ begins at t_1. What should t_1 be to maximize the P.V. of the whole operation?

P.V., as of $t = 0$, of the revenue stream is P.V. as of t_1 discounted to $t = 0$,

$$e^{-it_1} \cdot \frac{Paf(t)}{i}$$

That is, the right factor is the P.V. of the perpetual revenue stream at the time it begins (t_1). The left factor discounts this P.V. to P.V. as of $t = 0$. P.V. of the perpetual cost stream is ak/i. The net P.V. is

$$NR = \frac{e^{-it_1}Paf(t_1) - ak}{i}$$

Setting

$$\frac{dNR}{dt_1} = a \frac{[e^{-it_1}Pf'(t_1) - iPf(t_1)e^{-it_1}]}{i} = 0$$

or

$$\frac{f'(t_1)}{f(t_1)} = \frac{1}{Q}\frac{dQ}{dt} = i$$

the result is the same as for the single tree considered in isolation.

The simple form of this problem conceals some important elements, however. This is a result of assuming that perpetual planting took place at a constant given rate. But how much land was to be used? The implicit assumptions were that the total quantity used would be such as to maintain the same ratio of land per tree, thus maintaining the validity of $f(t)$, and that land is free. Suppose that the quantity of land is limited, however, and that it is desired to maximize the return to a given tract. A proper analysis of this problem requires knowledge of the production function for lumber with land as one of the inputs. To simplify matters, we take the view here that the amount of land required per tree is constant. We assume that the planting rate is indeed constant and continuous, once chosen, but that it is chosen simultaneously with determining the age at which trees are harvested. Thus we start planting at $t = 0$ and continue. Harvesting begins at t_1 and continues at a constant rate. After this point the number of trees harvested is equal to the number planted per unit time.

K	total acres in tract
k	acres required per growing tree
$f(t_1)$	salable volume of wood in a single tree as of t_1
c	cost of planting one tree.

If harvest rate is $f(t_1)$ per tree, kt acres are required per tree harvested since it takes t_1 years for a tree to mature to size $f(t_1)$. Thus from a tract of K acres, we can harvest K/kt_1 trees per unit time, giving a total continuous harvest rate in volume of wood of $Kf(t_1)/kt$ per unit time. The permanent revenue stream, assuming a price of $\$P$ per unit of product, will have a present value as of time t_1 (measured from $t = 0$) of $PKf(t_1)/ikt_1$ and as of $t = 0$ the same quantity discounted to $t = 0$, i.e.,

$$e^{-it_1} \frac{PKf(t_1)}{ikt_1}$$

The planting rate is also K/kt_1 trees per unit time. The cost flow is $\$c$ times this, giving a present value as of $t = 0$ of cK/ikt_1.

The present value of the opportunity as of $t = 0$ is (t in this and the immediately following equations is to be understood as t_1):

$$\text{P.V.} = \frac{PKf e^{-it}}{ikt} - \frac{cK}{ikt}$$

$$\frac{dPV}{dt} = \frac{K}{ik}\left[\frac{P(t\{-ie^{-it}f + e^{-it}f'\} - fe^{-it})}{t^2} + \frac{c}{t^2}\right] = 0$$

The expression in square brackets must equal zero. Changing the order of terms,

$$P\left[\frac{tf' - f}{t^2} - \frac{if}{t}\right] + \frac{ce^{it}}{t^2} = 0$$

Since

$$\frac{d(f/t)}{dt} = \frac{tf' - f}{t^2}$$

$$P\left[\frac{d(f/t)}{dt}\right] = iP\left(\frac{f}{t}\right) - \frac{ce^{it}}{t^2}$$

What does this equation mean? If there is no cost of planting and the rate of interest is zero, the operator should maximize product of the tree per unit time required to grow the tree. That is, $[d(f/t)]/dt$ is zero. Product per unit time may be interpreted, however, as product per unit land required per growing tree provided we take k as the unit of land.* With c zero and i positive, the relative rate of growth in product per tree per year of tree life should equal the rate of interest.

With both c and i positive, the gain from increasing product per tree per year of tree life should be equated to interest on the receipts per tree harvested per

---

* That is, if k is the unit in which land is measured, land in use per tree harvested is $kt_1 = t_1$.

year of tree life minus the marginal saving in planting cost resulting from extension of tree life.*

The tree and wine problem has received a good deal of attention in the history of capital theory and is still useful in this very general form to show how production involving natural processes necessarily operating through considerable periods of time must be adapted to the fact of a positive market rate of interest which indicates the presence of real investment opportunities in our world. It should be realized, of course, that the problem of forest management is vastly more complex than this very general formulation. In its full complexity, the problem involves not only effects on costs and revenues connected with time of harvest and size distribution of trees but also the pattern or configuration of harvesting and culture activities over large areas as well as within particular tracts. It takes more than a knowledge of elementary—or even advanced—calculus to make a competent forest manager. But no one can be a competent forest manager without understanding—not necessarily in terms of calculus—the general problem analyzed here.

3.7 A SIMPLE COMPLETE SYSTEM

The various themes that have been discussed can now be brought together into a simple system in the neoclassical tradition to illustrate the balance of forces at any one time and the direction of movement of the system through time. A compact system that satisfies these needs has been provided by Milton Friedman.†

It is assumed that there is no technological progress in the economy and no growth of population. Capital, which is viewed as being made up of various kinds of concrete instruments which yield permanent income streams, is measured by its value. This value, W, clearly will vary inversely with the rate of interest with $W = Y_w/i$, where Y_w is the income per unit time from capital.

---

* You may wish to try to portray this problem graphically. Try first f/t_1 as a function of t_1; then $f/t_1 e^{-it_1}$ as a function of t_1. And then c/t_1.

There are as many ways to formulate these semi-static problems as there are production functions and paths to a steady state. Clearly the problem in a real context is a very complicated dynamic problem since dX/dt, where X is the mass of wood in the forest, is *not* a function of X but depends on the path that was taken to get to the particular X. That is, dX/dt depends on the age distribution of the trees and their spacing, and this depends on the path to X.

Another simple problem is that in which planting is not continuous but in which the whole tract is planted at one time with periodic harvests, with this sequence being continued indefinitely.

Although models of this type abstract an important and fundamental economic element of the management problem, they clearly are naive from an ecological point of view. This becomes evident on describing their growth regimens in terms of a transition matrix which, when post-multiplied by an age distribution vector for a given period, will yield the age distribution for the succeeding period. The elements of the transition matrix are birth rates (planting rates in this case) and survival rates (equal to zero or one in this case).

See E. C. Pielou, *An Introduction to Mathematical Ecology* (New York: Wiley-Interscience, 1969), pp. 33ff., for a discussion of discrete population matrices.

† Friedman, *Price Theory: A Provisional Text, op. cit.*, pp. 257–63.

The final equilibrium toward which this system moves will be a stationary equilibrium in the sense that all flows per unit time will repeat themselves. This implies that there will be no saving and investment at this final equilibrium. The final equilibrium is the result of balance between the demand for capital instruments, measured by value, and the supply of capital. The price that brings about this balance is the rate of interest.

The demand curve in Figure 3-5 shows the combinations of i and W for

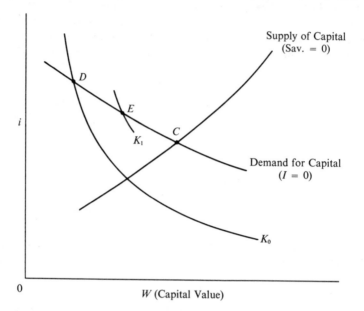

FIGURE 3-5

which I (investment per unit time) is zero. Each point on the demand curve refers to a different stock of physical capital instruments. Point D, for example, refers to a stock of capital which has a value equal to the abscissa of D and yields an income of $i_D W_D$.

Various combinations of i and W for given real capital stock will yield the same income, however, as indicated by the rectangular hyperbola, $V_{w_D} = iW$, which is labeled K_0. However, there is only one interest rate at which, given an actual stock of K_0, there is no desire on the part of capital users to increase or decrease this stock, and that is the rate of interest indicated by D. If there were no desire to change the capital stock from K_0 at higher or lower rates of interest, the demand curve for $I = 0$ would in fact be represented by the curve K_0. With i at i_D, however, opportunities for investment will exist which will pay at a lower rate of interest. If the rate were lowered a small amount, users of capital would wish to invest in a larger stock, this desire being satisfied when they find themselves on the demand curve shown, say, at point E. The larger stock of capital goods associated with point E may be represented by another rectangular hyperbola, K_1, through point E.

The supply of capital is to be thought of as a demand for claims on capital instruments; that is, willingness to hold the financial instruments entitling the holder to permanent income streams. The particular curve relevant to determination of the final equilibrium is that for zero savings (where savings is defined, as usual, as income minus consumption per unit time). At point C, the total capital value demanded is equal to that supplied *and* savings are equal to investment at a level of zero. Thus a stationary equilibrium has been reached. If investment opportunities have not been exhausted, the associated stock of capital goods can again be represented by a rectangular hyperbola through point C once more with steeper slope than the demand curve for capital. Capital users would be willing to enlarge this stock if i were lower, but there is no force in the system that will lower the rate of interest.

The progress of the system toward final equilibrium is illustrated in Figure 3-6, which contains the preceding figure plus additions to show savings and investment. Suppose the initial stock of capital is K_0. The interest rate cannot be as indicated by i_D, for savings would be greater than desired investment, which would be zero. As the interest rate moves down from i_D on K_0, investment increases from 0, and as the interest rate moves up from the intersection of the capital supply curve (Sav. $= 0$) and K_0 the savings rate increases from zero. Saving and investment are equalized at, say, 20 percent of income at point A. The two curves through point A are, however, curves of demand for and supply of *capital* as they are with savings equal to investment at 20 percent of national income and with present capital stock of K_0. The related functions showing the relation among i and investment and saving, with each measured as a percent of income, are shown in the diagram to the left, with point A' corresponding to point A in the capital diagram and B' to point B. The sequence through time is from point A to B and finally to C, corresponding to A', B' and C'.

In this system with no technological progress, the accumulation of capital through saving and investment results in a fall in the rate of interest as time goes on. The rapidity of this fall and its ultimate limit will depend on the particular characteristics of the functions that describe and govern the system. In the most general terms, one of these factors would seem to be what may be described as the rate at which the range or scope for investment enlarges as the interest rate falls. This factor is summed up in the demand curve for capital (say, with zero savings), in particular, in the rate at which it falls. A second and fundamental factor is summed up in the position and rate of rise in the supply of capital function (say, with zero savings). Behind this function is a utility function relating total utility to income. By imposing particular characteristics on these functions, systems could be concocted whose final equilibrium is with a zero or positive rate of interest and with this equilibrium reached in finite time or only approached asymptotically.

Suppose that the present status of the system in Figure 3-6 is that of point A. Now suppose that there is a burst of technical progress. This will have the effect of raising all of the demand curves for capital, such as the demand curves for $I = .2$ and $I = .1$ (each associated with a different level of annual investment). Thus the new demand curve crossing point A might be one associated with

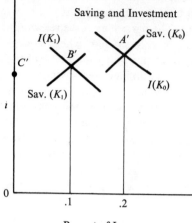

Saving and Investment

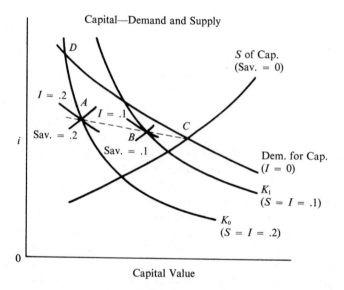

Capital—Demand and Supply

FIGURE 3-6

investment equal to 30 percent of income. The new equilibrium point associated with capital stock K_0 will be above point A on curve K_0 with savings and investment somewhere between 20 and 30 percent, and the interest rate will be higher than before.

The system above may be expressed in mathematical form as follows.

Variables:

W   wealth (measured in value)
i   rate of interest
Y_w income from wealth
I   investment per unit time
S   saving per unit time

The first equation of the system relates wealth and the level of investment to the rate of interest.

(3-1)
$$i = f(W,I)$$

For a given level of investment, this function shows the quantity of permanent income streams entrepreneurs wish to hold in real form (but measured here in value) at various levels of interest rate.

The second equation relates the rate of interest to wealth and savings per unit time:

(3-2)
$$i = g(W,S)$$

and expresses the willingness of savers to hold claims to permanent income streams at different rates of interest, given the level of saving per year.

In the "short" run, by which is meant simply a period so short that the real stock of capital (and hence income from capital) can be regarded as constant, three more equations complete the system:

(3-3)
$$S = I$$

(3-4)
$$Y_w = iW$$

(3-5)
$$Y_w = Y_{w_0}$$

The final equilibrium of the system when it has come to rest is expressed by the first two equations plus the following:

(3-6)
$$S = 0$$

(3-7)
$$I = 0$$

(3-8)
$$Y_w = iW$$

To set the stage for later consideration of the role of natural resources in the progress of the system over time with growth in the labor force (assumed to be zero up to now), we turn now to a brief examination of various versions of steady growth systems, first without and then with technological progress. This examination will be followed by a discussion of some of the possible ways by which steady growth can be slowed down and brought to a halt apart from the combined forces of diminishing returns to investment in abstraction from natural resources and a declining propensity to save with rising income and wealth as were present in the system just discussed.

3.8　STEADY GROWTH SYSTEMS

One Product, Two Factors, No Technological Progress*

One of the simplest systems is one in which the same product is usable both as a consumption or a capital good, in which there are two factors of production, labor and capital, and in which there is no technological progress. The single product assumption is not so unrealistic as it may sound, because in the long run particular forms of capital can be converted into consumer goods and other forms of capital with little or no loss.

Let us assume that there are constant returns to scale and that the elasticity of substitution between the two factors is one. For our purposes, the important consequences of these two assumptions are the following:

a.　With constant returns to scale, total product is exactly exhausted if factors are paid according to their marginal productivities.†

b.　In the absence of technological progress, the share of each factor in total product will remain constant if they are paid according to marginal productivities.

The only production function with constant returns to scale (homogeneous in the first degree) and with elasticities of substitution between the pairs of factors equal to one at all points is the Cobb–Douglas function expressed as $Q = AK^{\alpha}N^{(1-\alpha)}$ for two factors, where $0 < \alpha < 1$.

---

* Symbols in this section are as follows:

$$Q = Y = \text{product}$$
$$N = \text{labor}$$
$$R = \text{natural resources}$$
$$P = \text{progress}$$
$$K = \text{capital}$$
$$k = K/N, \text{ capital per capita}$$
$$r = R/N, \text{ natural resources per capita}$$
$$q = y = Q/N = Y/N, \text{ output or income per capita}$$

An asterisk indicates the *relative* (i.e., percentage/100) rate of change of a variable with respect to time. Thus

$$\overset{*}{K} = \frac{1}{K}\frac{dK}{dt} = \frac{d \log K}{dt}$$

$\overset{*}{k}$ indicates $\dfrac{1}{k}\dfrac{dk}{dt} = \dfrac{1}{(K/N)}\dfrac{d(K/N)}{dt} = \dfrac{d \log k}{dt}$

A dot above a letter will indicate the *absolute* rate of change of a variable with respect to time. Thus

$$\dot{K} = \frac{dK}{dt} \quad \text{and} \quad \dot{k} = \frac{dk}{dt} = \frac{dK/N}{dt}$$

A good general reference for this section is J. E. Meade, *The Growing Economy* (Chicago: Aldine Publishing Co., 1968). Our indebtedness to this work is apparent.

† Recall the discussion of Euler's theorem in Chapter 2.

Since it is useful to build our discussion around a particular production function, the Cobb–Douglas has been chosen as the simplest function which contains the economic factors essential to the discussion. It is worth pausing a bit to become better acquainted with it.

Let us start with the formulation, $Q_1 = AF(K,N) = AK^{\alpha}N^{(1-\alpha)}$ with

$$Q = \text{output}$$

$$K = \text{capital}$$

$$N = \text{labor}$$

This can be simplified by changing the unit in which Q is measured. Setting $Q_2 = (Q_1/A)$,

$$Q_2 = K^{\alpha}N^{(1-\alpha)}$$

Note that there are constant returns to scale; that is, increasing each factor by the same proportion increases product in the same manner:

$$F(\lambda K, \lambda N) = (\lambda K)^{\alpha}(\lambda N)^{(1-\alpha)} = \lambda K^{\alpha}N^{(1-\alpha)} = \lambda Q_2$$

If factors are paid according to their marginal productivities, the share of each factor in total product is constant and equal to the exponent attached to it regardless of the proportion between the factors:

$$\frac{K(\partial Q/\partial K)}{Q_2} = \frac{K\alpha K^{(\alpha-1)}N^{(1-\alpha)}}{Q_2} = \frac{\alpha K^{\alpha}N^{(1-\alpha)}}{Q_2} = \alpha$$

and similarly for N. Relative shares sum to 1, as with any production function homogeneous in the first degree (i.e., $\alpha + (1-\alpha) = 1$).

To simplify the function even further, divide both sides by N:

$$\frac{Q_2}{N} = \frac{K^{\alpha}N^{(1-\alpha)}}{N} = \frac{K^{\alpha}}{N^{\alpha}} = \left(\frac{K}{N}\right)^{\alpha}$$

With $q = Q_2/N$, and $k = K/N$, we have:

$$q = k\alpha$$

which could hardly be more compact. That is, the properties of this function in the constant returns form involve *only* the proportion between the factors and *not* their absolute values.

The per capita marginal product of capital, dq/dK, is equal to $\partial Q/\partial K$ at the corresponding points on the functions:

$$\frac{dq}{dk} = \alpha k^{(\alpha-1)} = \alpha \left(\frac{K}{N}\right)^{(\alpha-1)}$$

$$= \alpha K^{(\alpha-1)} N^{(1-\alpha)} = \frac{\partial Q}{\partial K}$$

The marginal product of labor is

$$\frac{\partial Q}{\partial N} = \frac{\partial(Nq)}{\partial N} = q + Nq' \frac{dk}{dN} = q - kq'$$

Diminishing returns in this function depend only on the proportion between the factors in view of constant returns to scale. That is, the derivative of marginal product is negative:

$$\frac{d(dq/dk)}{dk} = \frac{d(\alpha k^{(\alpha-1)})}{dk} = \alpha(\alpha - 1)k^{(\alpha-2)}$$

which is negative since $0 < \alpha < 1$.*

The same properties are preserved for functions with more than two factors if exponents sum to one.

For the general production function with constant returns, $Q = F(K,N)$,

$$dQ = \frac{\partial Q}{\partial K} dK + \frac{\partial Q}{\partial N} dN$$

From this

$$\frac{dQ}{Q} = \left(\frac{K}{Q} \cdot \frac{\partial Q}{\partial K}\right) \frac{dK}{K} + \left(\frac{N}{Q} \cdot \frac{\partial Q}{\partial N}\right) \frac{dN}{N}$$

The first parenthetical expression is the marginal product of capital multiplied by the quantity of capital and divided by total output, and similarly for labor. These are, therefore, the relative shares of capital and labor in total output, and are equal to α and $(1 - \alpha)$, respectively, where these are the exponents in the function used above. These factors may be called the proportional marginal products.

Let us label these factors U and W, respectively. If Q is viewed as a function of time, division by dt gives:

$$\frac{1}{Q} \frac{dQ}{dt} = U \frac{1}{K} \frac{dK}{dt} + W \frac{1}{N} \frac{dN}{dt}$$

Since there is no need to distinguish between output and income, $Y = Q$. Using letters with asterisks to indicate the *relative* rate of change in these variables per unit time, the equation expressing the relative movement of income

---

* See R. G. D. Allen, *Macro-Economic Theory* (New York: St. Martin's Press, 1968), pp. 43–52; and his *Mathematical Analysis for Economists* (New York: MacMillan & Co., 1939), p. 317.

per unit time, in response to the relative changes in capital and labor is

$$\overset{*}{Y} = U\overset{*}{K} + W\overset{*}{N}$$

Now let us ask what relations will hold if growth is steady in the sense that $\overset{*}{Y} = \overset{*}{K} = \overset{*}{N}$. If $\overset{*}{K}$ is the relative rate of increase in capital which will permit this steady growth, then, taking $\overset{*}{N}$ as exogeneous,

$$\overset{*}{K} = U\overset{*}{K} + W\overset{*}{N} \quad \text{or} \quad \overset{*}{K} = \frac{W\overset{*}{N}}{1 - U}$$

In the case of constant returns, this is equal to $\overset{*}{N}$.†

If $\overset{*}{K} = \overset{*}{N}$, then in steady growth with constant returns

$$\overset{*}{Y} = U\overset{*}{N} + W\overset{*}{N} = \overset{*}{N}(U + W) = \overset{*}{N}$$

That is, per capita income does *not* grow.

Note that steady growth does not involve directly the propensity to save nor the quantity of capital in absolute value, but $\overset{*}{K}$ must be equal to sY/K, or $\overset{*}{K}K = sY$, where s is the fraction of income saved. This simply says that total savings = investment. If we regard s as fixed, $\overset{*}{K} = \overset{*}{K}$ only if the initial quantity of capital is at the right level initially to give $\overset{*}{K}$.‡

Although s does not affect the rate of uniform growth, it does affect the *level* (with respect to a given N) at which this growth can take place. Suppose that s suddenly rises from a level associated with steady growth. Both k and y will now rise. The absolute values of capital and income will now grow, but with Y

---

† Recall that with constant returns, $(1 - U) = W$. From the exhaustion of product theorem for constant returns,

$$\frac{\overset{*}{Q}}{Q} = \frac{K}{Q}\frac{\partial Q}{\partial K} + \frac{N}{Q}\frac{\partial Q}{\partial N}$$

or $1 = U + W$.

‡ Suppose capital is below this level. Because of diminishing returns and homogeneity, Y_0/K_0 will be greater than the $\overline{Y}/\overline{K}$ that would be associated with $\overset{*}{K}$. This is so because, with $Y = K^\alpha N^{(1-\alpha)}$,

$$\frac{\partial(Y/K)}{\partial K} = (\alpha - 1)K^{(\alpha-2)}N^{(1-\alpha)} < 0$$

Thus
$$\overset{*}{K_0} = \frac{sY_0}{K_0} > \frac{s\overline{Y}}{\overline{K}} = \overset{*}{K}$$

and therefore $\overset{*}{K_0} > \overset{*}{K}$.

As $\overset{*}{K_0}$ approaches $\overset{*}{K}$, so also will $\overset{*}{Y}$. (Recall that $\overset{*}{Y} = U\overset{*}{K} + W\overset{*}{N}$). This approach probably would be asymptotic in many systems that might be specified.

rising slower because of diminishing returns, thus reducing sY/K to the point at which $\overset{*}{K}$ is equal to $\overset{*}{N}$.

Growth with all variables increasing at the same relative rate through time has been dubbed "Golden Age growth" by Joan Robinson because of its improbability of occurrence.* There are, of course, many such paths, as we just pointed out for the simple model under discussion here. But which of these paths will yield the highest rate of consumption at any moment of time? Since we are dealing with uniform rates of growth, this is a simple problem.

Given the initial size of the labor force, N_0, total output will depend on the initial $k = K/N$ that is "chosen," and consumption in period t will be total output less investment. Investment, as well as output and capital, will increase at the steady rate, $\overset{*}{N}$ (there is no depreciation). With $K_t = k_0 N_0 e^{\overset{*}{N}t}$,

$$I = \frac{dK_t}{dt} = \overset{*}{N}k_0 N_0 e^{\overset{*}{N}t}$$

Since $Q_t = f(k_0)N_0 e^{\overset{*}{N}t}$ in steady state growth, consumption at t is

$$C_t = Q_t - I_t = f(k_0)N_0 e^{\overset{*}{N}t} - \overset{*}{N}k_0 N_0 e^{\overset{*}{N}t} = [f(k_0) - \overset{*}{N}k_0]N_0 e^{\overset{*}{N}t}$$

To find the initial (and therefore subsequent) levels of capital to yield the highest stream of consumption, set equal to zero the derivative

$$\frac{\partial C_t}{\partial k} = (f' - \overset{*}{N})N_0 e^{\overset{*}{N}t} = 0 \qquad \text{or} \qquad f' = \overset{*}{N}$$

That is, choose k so that the marginal product of capital is equal to the steady rate of growth of the system, which is the rate of growth of the labor force. Because of the convexity of f and the assumption that $\overset{*}{N}$ is constant, there is only one such point on f.

All of this implies that only one certain savings ratio, $s = S/Y$, will result in this highest consumption path. Starting from $\overset{*}{N} = f'$, and multiplying each side by equal factors:

$$\frac{\overset{*}{N}(K/N)}{Q/N} = \frac{f'(k)k}{f(k)}$$

$$\overset{*}{K}\frac{K}{Q} = \frac{f'(k)k}{f(k)}$$

$$\frac{I}{Q} = s = \frac{f'(k)k}{f(k)}$$

(Recall that $\overset{*}{N} = \overset{*}{K}$. Thus $\overset{*}{N}K = \overset{*}{K}K = I$.)

---

* Joan Robinson, *The Accumulation of Capital* (Homewood, Illinois: Richard D. Irwin, 1956), p. 99.

Note that savings and investment* are equal to the earnings of capital on this path:

$$S = I = N\overset{*}{k_0}N_0 e^{\overset{*}{N}t} = f'K_t$$

This savings function—wages spent entirely on consumption and all "profits" saved—is known as the classical saving function by virtue of its use in some classical economic theory.

If the savings function does not permit this result (for example, suppose s is a constant at some other level or is a weighted average of constant savings propensities for wages and property income), then this optimum path is not attainable.

Note that this is only the optimum of the steady growth consumption paths. Some nonsteady growth paths may be preferable in some cases.†

Technological Progress

Now let us change the previous assumptions in one respect by allowing technological progress. But how is technological progress to be described? How might it change the production function? In general terms, we have a production function, $Q = F(K,N,t)$. Progress may be thought of as being equivalent to the effective augmentation of labor, capital, or both:

(i) $Q_t = F[K,P(t)N]$. If $P(t) = e^{\overset{*}{P}t}$, $N_t = N_0 e^{\overset{*}{P}t}$ would be the effective supply of labor if labor in natural units does not grow.

(ii) $Q_t = F[P(t)K,N]$, or

(iii) $Q_t = F[P(t)K,P(t)N]$. (This is equal to $Q_t = P(t)F(K,N)$ in the case of constant returns).

The first type of progress is known as Harrod neutral‡ in the sense that steady growth (y/k unchanged) leaves the marginal product of capital unchanged with constant returns.

The second type of progress is known as Solow neutral§ and is entirely analogous to Harrod neutrality with an interchange of K and N.

---

* See pp. 93–94.

† The particular path which yields the highest consumption path of all Golden Age paths has been dubbed the Golden Rule Accumulation path by E. S. Phelps because the saving pattern it yields for different generations constitutes an application of the golden rule of conduct to the savings problem in this particular formulation. For a clear discussion of this and other "golden rule" problems, see his *Golden Rules of Economic Growth* (New York: Norton Publishing Co., 1966).

‡ For a more detailed discussion, see Allen, *Macro-Economic Theory, op. cit.*, p. 242.

§ See R. M. Solow, *Capital Theory and the Rate of Return* (Amsterdam: North-Holland, 1963).

The third expression embodies what is known as Hicks neutrality* in that progress increases the marginal productivities of inputs by the same percentage for a given input combination. Thus the relative shares of the factors remain the same if payment is proportional to marginal productivities. If the nature of the advance increased the marginal productivity of labor less than that of capital, the progress usually would be said to be labor saving (equals capital using).†

Because Harrod neutrality involves progress that has the same effect as an increase in the supply of labor without progress, the analysis of the previous case (increase in labor force in natural units with no technical progress) can be applied without change except that the steady growth rate now is $m = \overset{*}{P} + \overset{*}{N}$, where $\overset{*}{P}$ is a constant relative rate of (Harrod) progress per year. Product per capita grows at $\overset{*}{P}$. The golden rule path now would require $f' = \overset{*}{P} + \overset{*}{N}$.

Progress that is universally labor augmenting in effect clearly is an unlikely possibility. Hicks neutrality, with a multiplicative effect on output, would seem to many to come closer to representing real change. If this type of progress is not simultaneously Harrod neutral, however, steady growth, with capital and output growing at the same rate, is not possible except with the linearly homogeneous Cobb–Douglas.

Before going on to consider the role of natural resources in growth, let us summarize what has just been covered.

First, in the absence of technological progress, steady growth of capital and income at the same rate is possible with a constant returns function. This rate is the exogenously given rate of growth of the labor force. The rate of savings affects the rate but not the level of growth. There is no growth in per capita income.

Second, of all the possible steady growth paths, that one will have the highest consumption path on which the marginal product of capital is equal to the relative rate of growth in the labor force. Savings will be equal to earnings on capital.

Technological progress can be regarded as equivalent to factor expansion. Under progress that is the equivalent of labor augmenting, the steady growth rate of capital and income is equal to the relative rate of growth in the labor force plus the rate of progress. The steady growth path with the highest consumption path requires that this sum be equal to the marginal product of capital.

The linearly homogeneous Cobb–Douglas function has the unusual property of characterizing simultaneously each of the three types of factor augmenting progress (Harrod-labor; Solow-capital; Hicks-both). The indicated rates of progress are different, of course.

---

* This is known as Hicks neutrality since the definition was first suggested by J. R. Hicks in his *Theory of Wages* (New York: St. Martin's, 1932).

† If all inputs were reduced by the same proportion so as to produce the same output as before, since the marginal product of labor increased relatively less than that of capital, total cost could be lowered by substituting capital for labor. The progress is therefore called labor saving.

Natural Resources

If natural resources are incorporated in the production function as are capital and labor, the implicit assumption is that some unit has been found in which the quantity of natural resources entering into production can be expressed. To do this in application necessarily would involve an index number problem of the same degree of complexity as a similar attempt for capital.

Waiving this problem, let us first consider the case in which the quantity of natural resources is rigidly limited—they are all in use and are not deteriorating in quality.* In terms of a Cobb–Douglas function, $Q = K^\alpha N^\beta R_0^\gamma$, with R for productive services of resources.†

The effect of resource limitation can be seen by expressing returns to scale as:

$$\lambda^{(\alpha+\beta)}Q = A(\lambda K)^\alpha (\lambda N)^\beta$$

where A is simply R_0^γ. The nominally constant returns situation with

$$\alpha + \beta + \gamma = 1$$

can be viewed as one of *decreasing* returns to scale if R_0 cannot be increased along with K and N. $(\alpha + \beta)$ is less than one.

What if resources are deteriorating in quality? This is equivalent to a decrease in R. The nondated production function is not changed by this deterioration—Q still is equal to $K^\alpha N^\beta R^\gamma$—but the dated function is changed. Incorporating $e^{\overset{*}{P}t}$ for Hicks-neutral progress we have, say,

$$Q_t = e^{\overset{*}{P}t}K_t^\alpha N_t^\beta [G(t)R_0]^\gamma$$

where $G(t)$ is a decreasing function of t and dependent on past production such as $G(t) = G(\int_0^t Q \, dt)$.

In general, at a particular t, we can think of (small) relative rates of increase per unit time in product and inputs as

$$\frac{1}{Q}\frac{dQ}{dt} = \overset{*}{Q} = \overset{*}{P} + \alpha\overset{*}{K} + \beta\overset{*}{N} + \gamma\overset{*}{R}$$

---

* This is a very imprecise statement for resources whose quality can be controlled within limits. Soil is a good example.

† With this particular function, all of each input is used no matter how low its price since the marginal product of an input is always positive, regardless of quantity used.

If the production function were such that the marginal product of resources declined to zero before all R_0 was in use, then the limitation on R would have no effect up to certain outputs since R actually in use could be increased *pari passu* with K and N up to R_0.

where $G(t) = e^{\overset{*}{R}t}$ in the production function immediately above.* Per capita growth in output then equals

$$\overset{*}{Q} - \overset{*}{N} = \overset{*}{P} + \alpha\overset{*}{K} - (1 - \beta)\overset{*}{N} + \gamma\overset{*}{R}$$

The depressive effects of population growth and resource deterioration on growth of per capita output are additive with weights $(1 - \beta)$ and γ, respectively.

If there are constant returns to scale with $\alpha + \beta + \gamma = 1$, the weight $(1 - \beta)$ is equal to $(\alpha + \gamma)$:

$$\overset{*}{Q} - \overset{*}{N} = \overset{*}{P} + \alpha\overset{*}{K} - (\alpha + \gamma)\overset{*}{N} + \gamma\overset{*}{R}$$

If there is growth with $\overset{*}{K} = \overset{*}{N}$, the growth of per capita income turns on $\overset{*}{P}$ in relation to $\gamma(\overset{*}{N} - \overset{*}{R})$.

Per capita income growth is positive or negative depending on whether

$$[\overset{*}{P} + \alpha\overset{*}{K}] \gtrless (\alpha + \gamma)\overset{*}{N} - \gamma\overset{*}{R}$$

If $\overset{*}{K} = \overset{*}{N}$, this inequality reduces to $\overset{*}{P} \gtrless - \gamma(\overset{*}{R} - \overset{*}{N})$. Under the assumptions made, whether output per worker rises or falls depends on whether the rate of technological progress is high enough to offset the depressive effect of decline in the per capita quantity of natural resource services available. The impact of this decline depends on the importance of natural resources in the production function. For a constant returns Cobb–Douglas function, this is measured by γ, the exponent attached to natural resources.†

The expression of deterioration in natural resources as a reduction in R is appropriate not only for exhausting resources such as minerals but also for production activities having adverse effects on the productivity of natural resources owned by others via resources owned in common. Our practice of expressing the services of natural resources as a flow of services per unit time of "land" or surface of a certain type already incorporates the services of the environment (sunlight, the many dimensions of climate, water regimen, etc.) into a unit that can be appropriated—such as an acre of land. However, from a conceptual point of view R can be thought of in a more general way as providing

---

* Take logs and differentiate.

† The role of a productive factor of fixed quantity (no deterioration in quality) such as land in a system with labor and capital has been examined by Donald A. Nichols ("Land and Economic Growth," *American Economic Review*, Vol. LX, June 1970, pp. 332–40). He finds that if technological change is simultaneously labor and land augmenting at a constant relative rate, a balanced growth path is possible with the price of land increasing at the rate of growth of output (production function assumed to be linearly homogeneous). Capital gains from the increase in land price can satisfy desires for increased wealth.

a group of specific "physical" services, some of which can be preclusively appropriated by ownership of a piece of surface or earth but others of which are in common ownership, such as the assimilative capacity of the atmosphere, the energy transmitting characteristics of the atmosphere, and individuals' perceptions of rural and urban "landscape" that cannot be owned preclusively. Common ownership or failure of the "owner" to act responsibly is likely to be associated with uneconomic deterioration of quality, as exemplified by recent changes in the assimilative capacity of the air in many locations and some water bodies.

Note that this whole discussion implies that all "bads" as perceived by consumers or which result in the deterioration of natural resources should be included, in principle, in the reckoning of net final real product of the economy. Those which increase current costs of enterprises do get reflected in the reckoning of real net product in the official income accounts. This is not true of pollution treatment costs incurred by government, however, if they are treated as general government expenditures.

* * * * *

Because natural resources are capital for the purpose of economic analysis, the role of capital in the analysis of an economic system has been given considerable attention. The first system examined focused on the relations between income, savings, investment, and capital accumulation with a constant population and no technological progress. We then proceed to examine relations among these variables in a system with population growth, later showing how to introduce technological progress and how it would affect growth. Population growth and technological progress were examined in the rather restricted domain of steady growth. This restriction was useful for explaining certain relations between time rates of change, but hardly permits coming to grips with the more fundamental, interesting, and difficult problems involving capital accumulation and natural resources. A slight beginning was made, however, in fitting natural resources into the analysis up to this point.

The next task is to examine the general problem of the optimum course of capital accumulation without restriction to cases of uniform growth. Somewhat paradoxically, perhaps, our views on this subject turn out to clear the way for the application of conventional economic theory to natural resource problems with a comparatively short horizon—say decades. The grander problems associated with longer horizons and the accompanying possibilities for catastrophic developments are postponed for brief discussion at the end of the book.

3.9 WHAT IS THE PROPER COURSE OF CAPITAL ACCUMULATION OVER TIME?

So far we have been discussing the course that capital and output would follow in a market economy in various simple cases of steady growth. If the initial values of the variables were not such as to permit this steady growth, we have limited ourselves to pointing out the direction of movement that would be taken by the variables. With the systems we have been considering, this movement would proceed to a state of steady growth (which includes the static steady state case if there is neither population growth nor technical progress) if the growth determining parameters remained unchanged. Now we ask what might be said about the desirability of all the various paths of growth which are feasible for an economy subject only to the contraints of factor supplies at each point in time and the state of technology. That is to say, consumption per capita depends on the course of investment and technological progress, if any. Different consumption paths may cross each other, for if more is saved now, consumption can be higher later, and vice versa.

Rate of Accumulating Capital

As pointed out earlier in the discussion of static allocation, a competitive system with no external effects flowing from the decisions of the economic units will be efficient in the sense that no unit will be able to improve its position without making some other unit worse off. The conditions necessary for efficiency are expressed as equalities between the different marginal rates of transformation or substitution—among consumers, producers, inputs, and outputs. These equalities are achieved if producers and consumers confront the same prices for outputs and inputs and if each member of the two groups succeeds in maximizing profit and utility respectively.

If the same underlying assumptions are made for a system accumulating capital through time, including that of no technological progress, it is clear that similar efficiency conditions can be derived in precisely the same manner by simply viewing as different commodities the output of a nominally identical commodity at different times. In addition to the contemporaneous marginal equalities, there will now be marginal equalities between goods produced and consumed at different points in time. In particular, consumers and producers will adjust all of their intertemporal transactions to the (correctly) anticipated rates at which present inputs can be converted into future outputs through the process known as investment.

It is clear that in the real world the obstacles to a practical approximation to ideal efficiency conditions are greater in the dynamic case than in the static. One has but to think of the implications of knowledge of prices, of technological change, and fluctuations in the general level of business activity. On the structural side, the presence of a very sizable corporation income tax prevents any close approximation of equality between intertemporal transformation possibilities confronting consumers and corporate enterprises investing in capital goods.

Despite these differences of degree, the two situations—static and "dynamic"—are similar in another important respect. In the case of static allocation, the efficient result does possess the property that any economic unit, given its initial resources, can better its position only at the expense of at least one other unit, but this is not the same thing as saying that this particular efficient outcome represents a position of maximum social welfare. There are many possible efficient outcomes, differing from each other in the distribution of initial resources. Thus the society may decide, for example, to modify the operation of the system in order to obtain what is viewed as a better social state.

One of the major modifications in societies with private ownership of productive assets, which means all societies if human capabilities are viewed as a productive asset, is in the distribution of income that would otherwise result. A number of years ago the analysis of this problem took the form of asking how taxes should be imposed to finance the activities of government and was analyzed in terms of utility. The problem was viewed as one of analyzing the implications for the type of taxation of various possible principles of sacrifice stated in terms of utility. Thus some of the possibilities considered were those of proportional sacrifice, equal sacrifice, minimization of total sacrifice, and so on.

In recent years the analysis of the problem of modifying the distribution of income has become more comprehensive in a number of ways. The fact that the products produced by government produce flows of satisfaction now receives very explicit recognition, and we have even come to recognize that the distribution of income can be modified by money payments to individuals as well as by variations in the amount of taxes they pay to government. In addition, there probably is a keener appreciation of the importance of understanding the relation between taxes—positive or negative—and economic incentives, if only because of the higher level of taxes now than formerly. No doubt much of the present-day discussion of these problems could be cast in utility terms, but the fact is that to a considerable degree it is not. The question raised by this change is whether utility is the appropriate language in which to discuss problems of distribution. Indeed, something of an answer has been given to this question in the emphasis placed on the incommensurability of utility between different individuals.

Analysis of the problem of the rate at which capital ought to be accumulated also has been carried out in terms of utility, with this type of analysis enjoying a strong resurgence after World War II. In view of the parallels between the two problems, the distribution of income and the problem of the rate of capital accumulation, the question naturally arises whether discussion of the latter problem may not in the future experience the same type of development as has the discussion of modification in the distribution of income.

One important reason why an efficient result ground out by competitive market forces may not constitute a social optimum is that many people have an interest in the overall distribution of income that results. It is hard to conceive that a person could be interested in the quantities of goods and services he consumes personally without also being interested in the overall distribution of income, since it surely will affect his income. In addition, many people have an interest in the levels of income of others, some of them known, but in many cases not. Thus the overall distribution of income comes to be a factor, along with his own consumption, in an individual's evaluation of a social state.

Although any individual is free to make partial changes in the distribution of income by giving money or other property to other individuals, there are only a few persons whose own acts of redistribution could significantly affect the nature of the distribution of income.* Consequently, we may decide collectively, and have so decided in the United States, to modify profoundly the distribution of income that would exist in the absence of modifying measures in the belief that a higher level of social welfare is attained.

The situation with respect to the accumulation of capital is closely analogous. Many people may feel that the overall rate of capital accumulation resulting from individual adaptation to market prices, including the rate of interest, ought to be modified, not to modify the contemporaneous distribution of income but to modify the distribution of income through time. There is nothing paradoxical here. In any case where the individuals of a society are interested in an overall aspect of the results of a system which are the consequence of individual adaptation to the actions of others, there is a possibility that the collective view will be to alter the operation of the system that has produced these results.

The modern analysis of the problem of determining the socially optimum rate of accumulation dates back to Frank Ramsey's seminal article of 1928.† Fortunately, one version of the savings problem considered by Ramsey can be explained in a simple way and can provide some insight not only into Ramsey's solution but also an indication of the spirit that has animated the recent resurgence of interest in this problem.

Ramsey, along with A. C. Pigou and others, was of the view that utility was additive over the persons in a society at a given time and over persons at different times, no matter how widely separated. In the view of the former, the discounting of later utility was regarded as ethically indefensible, arising from a weakness of the imagination. The latter ascribed the discounting view to a weakness in our telescopic faculty, by means of which we see "future pleasures, as it were, on a diminished scale."‡

On the assumption of no discounting of future utilities, Ramsey then asked how fast capital should be accumulated in a society with a constant population and with no technological progress. He did not specify that the society have a terminal date or that the problem be viewed as one of maximizing the stream of consumption between now and T with a specified stock of capital at T. (These

---

* Although it is true that almost any change made to improve efficiency will have some distributional consequences, it in no way follows that each decision on whether to undertake an action affecting the allocation of resources should rest in part on its distributional as well as its efficiency consequences. If our interest is in the overall distribution of total personal incomes, it would seem rather myopic to applaud a particular change in government action because it moves a few incomes in a "correct" direction. If the "correct" direction is always toward, say, average income, the implicit ethical criterion for determining relative incomes would seem to be equality of money income. This is a possible criterion, but certainly is not espoused as a complete criterion by very many people in the United States or any Western country. This matter is discussed further in Chapter 6.

† Frank P. Ramsey, "A Mathematical Theory of Saving," *Economic Journal*, Vol. 38, No. 152, December 1928, pp. 543–59.

‡ A. C. Pigou, *The Economics of Welfare*, 1st ed. (London: MacMillan & Co. Ltd., 1920), pp. 24–25. Another possible explanation is that he was looking through the wrong end of the telescope (so to speak).

are ways to simplify the problem that are currently popular, on occasion seeming to suggest that a technique is looking for a problem).

Obviously, the very idea of a maximum with neither of these simplifying devices is something of a challenge, a challenge that was met in an ingenious manner. Ultimately, Ramsey said, the economy will reach a state of Bliss which will involve either marginal utility of consumption of zero or marginal productivity of capital of zero. If it is assumed that one of these states is reached within a finite period, we can define the optimum consumption stream as that which maximizes the utility of consumption between now and Bliss since it is clear that there is no improving on Bliss.* It turns out to be more convenient, as will be evident in a moment, to minimize the difference between the Bliss total utility level and the utility of the stream of consumption.

J. M. Keynes, according to Ramsey, perceived a simple solution to this problem, which may be described in the following way. Suppose that a certain feasible schedule of consumption is specified. What is the condition that would just make it worthwhile to increase saving a small amount in the first year of this schedule in order to permit a little more capital formation now and a little more consumption later? Suppose that the first year's saving is increased by one day's consumption. Then we may view the old and the new schedules of consumption as follows:

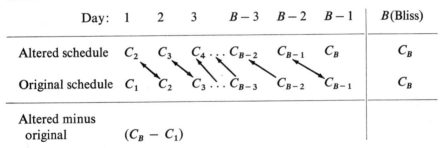

Day:	1	2	3		$B-3$	$B-2$	$B-1$	B(Bliss)
Altered schedule	C_2	C_3	C_4	$\dots$	C_{B-2}	C_{B-1}	C_B	C_B
Original schedule	C_1	C_2	C_3	$\dots$	C_{B-3}	C_{B-2}	C_{B-1}	C_B
Altered minus original	$(C_B - C_1)$							

Since the relation between total utility and the societal rate of consumption is viewed as independent of time, the original consumption schedule may be subtracted from the altered as indicated in the schematic. $(C_B - C_1)$ then is the gain in consumption units from increasing the first year's saving by a small amount (one day's saving here). The utility associated with this gain must be balanced against the sacrifice. That is, the gain is the total rate of flow of utility per day (TU) for the society at Bliss minus the total rate of flow of utility for the society *now* at $t = 1$. In equilibrium, this gain must be equal to the rate of saving per day times the marginal utility of consumption:

$$TU_B - TU_1 = S \cdot MU_{C_1}$$

This condition must hold at all points in time.

---

* James E. Meade, *Trade and Welfare* (London: Oxford University Press, 1955), p. 94, suggests that Bliss might better be called a state of glut. The assumption that Bliss will be reached in a finite time seems not to have been made by Ramsey.

The rate of saving as of now is independent of the rate of interest in the sense that it does not appear explicitly. It cannot be independent of the production function, of course, for this determines total utility at Bliss (as Ramsey noted) and, together with the choice of S, determines total and marginal utility now (as Ramsey did not note).

The rate at which savings progress through time is expressed in the condition that the gain from postponing a unit of consumption a small bit of time must be equal to the sacrifice:

$$MU_{C_t} = \left(1 + \frac{\partial F}{\partial K} \Delta t\right) \ (MU_{C_{(t+\Delta t)}})$$

| Present MU of sacrifice of one unit of consumption | Return on one unit of capital invested for the period, Δt | MU of one unit of consumption at time $(t + \Delta t)$ |

$$MU_{C_t} = MU_{C_{(t+\Delta t)}} + \frac{\partial F}{\partial K} \Delta t \, MU_{C_{(t+\Delta t)}}$$

$$\frac{MU_{C_{(t+\Delta t)}} - MU_{C_t}}{\Delta t} = -\frac{\partial F}{\partial K} MU_{C_{(t+\Delta t)}}$$

or, as $\Delta t \to 0$,

$$-\frac{1}{MU_{C_t}} \frac{dMU_{C_t}}{dt} = \frac{\partial F}{\partial K} = r$$

where K is capital and F is the production function $F(K,N)$. That is, the relative rate at which marginal utility declines through time is equal to the rate of interest.

After World War II, study of the problem of the optimum rate of capital accumulation acquired new life, partly because it was and continues to be an issue of pressing practical importance for poor countries and partly because of the increasing level of mathematical sophistication of economists. This literature has continued to develop in the directions first indicated by Ramsey, who considered several cases considerably more complex than the one just analyzed.*

---

* An idea of the literature can be conveyed by stating, without discussion, some of the results developed and summarized by Phelps, *op. cit.*, pp. 86ff.

Consider a problem similar to the simple Ramsey problem in which there is population growth but in which the utility function to be "maximized" over time depends on the average consumption and not on the number of people. By having the Golden Rule path play a role analogous to Bliss, the problem can be handled in the same way with the result that the optimum consumption path (optimum in the sense of minimizing the difference between actual and Golden Rule consumption) gradually approaches the Golden Rule path, but with the return on capital equal to the rate of population growth rather than being zero as in the case of the problem considered earlier.

If the preceding conditions are modified by imposing a discount rate on future utility (again

Utility Models of Optimum Capital Accumulation

It would be rash to claim that any of the utility models of optimum capital accumulation has practical significance for our decisions on savings. Here we wish to indicate some of the problems and ambiguities inherent in the approach, not, unfortunately, with the result of preparing the way for a clearly more satisfactory approach, but to place the problem in a broader and less artificial context than that of the language of utility.

First, it should be noted that any approach to the problem that gives importance to the comparison of widely differing incomes at widely different periods of time will be difficult of implementation because of the difficulty of predicting the rate and nature of technical progress and of population growth.

Leaving aside such practical matters as the difficulty of foreseeing the future, we find ourselves asking whether use of the language of utility has not diverted attention from and forestalled discussion of relevant ethical aspects of the accumulation problem. This feeling is far from constituting an attack on the usefulness of the language of utility for other problems, namely, the economizing actions of the individual and also for problems of contemporaneous allocation involving different individuals.

Average Utility vs. Numbers

The language of utility has some advantages in considering the accumulation problem. For example, it forces explicit consideration of the following fundamental question: Is our concern for future generations to be directed toward per capita income and utility or is it to be directed to per capita utility multiplied by the number of people? If the latter, then—on the assumption that total utility is an increasing function of income*—the view is being taken that the

---

based on average consumption), the consumption path no longer approaches the Golden Rule path in which the rate of interest and growth are equal to the rate of population growth but rather to a Golden Age path in which the rate of interest (marginal product of capital) is equal to the rate of population growth *plus* the discount rate on future utility.

If labor augmenting technical progress is introduced into the problem, matters are considerably complicated. For a finite period with a required ending capital stock, the Golden Rule path is not optimal for all utility functions.

For unbounded periods with a utility function possessing constant elasticity of marginal utility, the situation is still more complicated. The existence of an optimum depends on the rate of discount of future utilities (which could be zero) being sufficiently high to balance the rate of labor augmenting progress and the inelasticity of the utility function. (Defined in the usual way as the elasticity of marginal utility with respect to consumption. The optimal path approaches the Golden Age path or the Golden Rule path according as the discount rate, $d, \geq \lambda(1 - E)$, where E is the elasticity of marginal utility. See Phelps, *op. cit.*, p. 95.) In one special case, the optimal path approaches the Golden Rule path with the rate of interest equal to the rate of labor augmenting progress plus the rate of population growth. In the other cases where an optimum exists, a Golden Age path is approached. In general terms, it appears that a rapid falling off of marginal utility with increasing consumption is favorable to the existence of an optimum.

* To make this assumption is not mere pedantry, as the subsequent discussion and your own reflection will show.

society with low income and many people at a certain time may be just as well off as the same society with higher incomes and fewer people at some other time. Would this imply the possibility that India, viewed as a society, is now as well or better off than Denmark? On the other hand, as Meade suggests,* maximization of per capita utility carries the strange implication that in a group of static economies considered as a whole, welfare will be increased by destroying those with per capita incomes below the maximum.† Although it may seem that the per capita view comes off better in a dynamic planning context, we shall see later that a similar or related difficulty is involved.

Each of these points of view has been espoused by workers in this field. Phelps is of the opinion that recent work tends to favor the strictly per capita view, that is, that numbers cannot make up for low per capita utility.

An ingenious way of expressing one aspect of the difference between the two points of view has been formulated by T. Koopmans.‡ Suppose that the individual total utility function is the same whether the societal calculation of the optimal course involves only per capita utility or per capita utility times number of people. For the ith individual, call this $u_i(c)$. If numbers are to count, then total utility of the society over the period 0 to T is equal to the integral from 0 to T of the sum of all the individual rates of utility flow at time t:

$$\int_0^T \sum_{i=1}^{L_t} u_i(c)\, dt$$

where L_t is number of people at time t. If population is increasing at a percent per year, then if we set the initial population L_0 equal to one§ and view $u_i(c)$ as average utility flow per person, total utility of the society may be expressed as:

$$\int_0^T e^{at} u_i(c)\, dt$$

On the other hand, if total utility of the society is to depend only on per capita utility, then from period 0 to T it is equal to

$$\int_0^T u_i(c)\, dt$$

---

* Meade, *op. cit.*, p. 87.

† Or, considering an isolated economy or economic "group," how many people of low marginal productivity should be eliminated in order to maximize per capita income?

‡ As discussed in Phelps, *op. cit.*, p. 83.

§ This is permissible for our purpose since the question is: How do the two criteria rank different streams of societal consumption? We are not interested in finding out whether the sum of individuals' total utilities over a period of time is greater than the sum over the period of average annual total utility per person in a society. We already know that.

From the point of view of someone who believes that numbers should count—that the first expression is the one that should be used—the second criterion is equivalent to using the first but discounting the sum of individual utilities in year t at the rate of a percent per year:

$$\int_0^T e^{-at}\left[e^{at}u_i(c)\right] dt = \int_0^T u_i(c)\, dt$$

If population is not increasing, the two criteria come to the same thing so far as the optimum course of saving is concerned. In the Ramsey condition for the simple case analyzed above, for example, savings and the levels for Bliss and present total utility could be interpreted either as societal or individual. If population is increasing exogenously, however, the two criteria will yield a different course of consumption, for the per capita utility criterion gives more weight to nearer utilities. This would be true whether population continues to grow at a uniform rate, which actually could not continue indefinitely, or if it is regarded as growing to a higher but fixed level.

The conflict between the two criteria—which has been characterized here as one between numbers vs. per capita utility—becomes obvious if population in fact can be controlled,* a situation in which some countries may find themselves in the future. The difference between the two criteria has been most clearly explained by Meade,† and can be formalized with the following model:

	p	population
	C	total consumption of society
$c = C/p$		per capita consumption
$g(p) = C + S$		output
	S	total savings (constant)
	TU	total utility of society
$u = f(c) = f\dfrac{C}{p} = f\left(\dfrac{g(p) - S}{p}\right)$		total utility per person

If the goal is to maximize per capita income and utility, then population should be managed so as to avoid penalties because of economies or diseconomies of scale (think of natural resources as being involved in addition to produced capital goods), regardless of the amount that is saved at each moment:

$$\frac{du}{dp} = f'\frac{dc}{dp} = f'\frac{pg' - C}{p^2} = 0$$

or

$$g' = \frac{C}{p}$$

---

* That is, if population can be made to move up or down over a fairly short period in response to deliberate governmental policy. The "short period" would be several decades long.
† Meade, *Trade and Welfare*, op. cit., p. 91.

That is, choose that population for which the marginal product of labor equals average consumption. This maximizes average consumption.

In contrast, suppose the goal is to maximize the (summated) total utility of the society. The problem may be viewed as one of adjusting population in an otherwise constant situation, including constant savings. Alternatively—and still abstracting from the problem of the time path of savings and capital—we may suppose that population can be adjusted to optimum size for the stock of capital and natural resources at each point in time. Redistribution to achieve equal consumption is assumed. Then,

$$TU = pu = pf$$

$$\frac{dTU}{dp} = pf' \frac{dc}{dp} + f$$

$$= pf' \left[\frac{pg' - g + S}{p^2} \right] + f$$

$$= f' \left[g' - \frac{C}{p} \right] + f = 0$$

for necessary maximum condition, or

$$u = \begin{matrix} \text{(marginal utility} \\ \text{of consumption)} \end{matrix} \left[\begin{matrix} \text{(average consumption} \\ \text{per person)} \end{matrix} - \begin{matrix} \text{(marginal product} \\ \text{per person)} \end{matrix} \right]$$

That is, adding one more person who consumes at the average rate increases utility by u. However, he adds only his marginal product, and to bring his consumption up to the average, some product must be taken from the other people, and this is valued (in units of utility) at the marginal utility of consumption per unit. The objective is to find the point at which the additional gain and loss are in balance.

Note that maximization of total utility requires that labor be increased to the point where

$$g' = \frac{C}{p} = \frac{u}{f'}$$

in contrast to

$$g' = \frac{C}{p}$$

when per capita utility is maximized.

Invariance of the Utility Function

Study of the optimal accumulation problem in the Ramsey tradition has proceeded on the often tacit assumption that the utility function relevant for this problem is invariant. The same function is presumed to apply to the people in this economy now and at any time in the future, which would seem to imply the view that the same function is applicable to people in different economies at the same time in view of the fact that differences over time in the same society may well be greater than differences among societies at a given time. So far as formal analysis of the accumulation problem along Ramseyan lines is concerned, there is no reason why the utility function must be regarded as invariant. Workers in this field seem to have little taste for considering the changes that ought to be made in it over time, however. No doubt Ramsey was right when he observed that without this simplifying assumption the results would appear to be special and even more complicated.

One possible objection to the assumption of invariance may be put in this way. So long as the economic aspects of the individual's life unfold in a way that is reasonably consistent with his past expectations, he does seem to behave in a way not only consistent with diminishing marginal utility, but in a way that suggests a rather high marginal utility over a wide range of income in the sense that size of income clearly matters for most people and that considerable effort is expended to economize. But if persons are asked if they will enjoy a larger flow of satisfaction with an income distinctly higher than the levels within their expectations, some may well reply—with a frequency unknown to us—that they have their doubts. Indeed, if the contemplated change is large enough, some will reply that the flow of satisfaction will be less. Or consider reversibility. Imagine a substantial increase in income with adaptation to the new level with a later fall to the old level. There seems to be a real possibility that the initial feeling of increase in satisfaction consequent on the rise will be less than the feeling of decline in satisfaction consequent on the fall. But the feeling of satisfaction may be the same at the two levels after adaptation to the level in each case.

If we ask whether the flow of satisfaction enjoyed by different persons with different incomes varies directly and substantially with income, the answer cannot be a simple yes. It seems obvious that there are many pairs of individuals with greatly differing incomes whose total utility flows—if this notion has any meaning at all—are similar to the external observer. An illustration of this assertion is provided by those cases in which persons did not know that they were poor until told that their incomes were below the official "poverty line." On the other hand, it is clear that some low incomes are combined with circumstances, among which must be included the envy that often accompanies the knowledge that there are other incomes much higher, such that a higher income leads to a clearly felt improved position.

Finally, it may be observed that people in different stable, well-integrated societies—and perhaps even these conditions are not necessary—appear to many to be equally happy with widely differing incomes.

Some writers would differentiate between happiness and the flow of utility* on the ground that happiness depends on factors in addition to the economic,

---

* For example, Meade, *op. cit.*, p. 94.

whose contribution to happiness depends on consumption. But it is precisely this latter assertion that observation of different societies and different people calls into question. That is, happiness or welfare may not be increased by increasing incomes and consumption beyond some ill-defined level at which misery ceases and happiness begins. In some circumstances welfare may be diminished by an increase in consumption as usually measured. The reader can decide for himself whether this characterizes our society now.

If these possibilities are indeed close to the mark, it would seem doubtful that precepts for action can come out of analysis based on the assumption of ever-increasing total utility as consumption rises.

Should the Poor Help the Rich?

The question of whether the poor should help the rich is a good deal more subtle than it may appear to be on its face and may even be meaningless unless careful attention is given to the definition of help. The principle which seems to be implicit in much of our thought and action about the contemporaneous problem of distribution seems to be something like this—no, the poor should not help the rich unless the poor can thereby be made better off. And of course it is very easy to imagine a situation in which in a sense it pays the poor to help those who are already better off than they are. Suppose, for example, that in the name of equity a system of taxes and transfers had been instituted which left incomes approximately equal, say, with a gap of only 10 percent between the lowest and the highest income recipients. It may be that the people who have the capability of contributing greatly to the efficiency with which production is organized are constituted in such a way that they would do this work only if able to enjoy the things associated with having a considerably higher income than others. In this case what would amount to a transfer of money from the poor to the rich with respect to the former total income for the society would turn out in fact to benefit the poor in absolute terms.

In fact, in a world where material incentives are important, a simple answer of no to the question of whether the poor should help the rich, if coupled with yes to the reverse question, would be absurd. Indeed, the acceptance of the distribution of income as of a given moment implies a qualified answer of no by society to each of the questions—no more shifting of the distribution is desirable.

The most general and probably most important justification for some degree of inequality in the distribution of incomes is that of incentive. We want the productively able to work, both for themselves and for the rest of society. Without adequate incentive, they may not contribute to production and may resort to violence.

Incentive considerations in relation to equity is a matter that relates to a simultaneously existing group of people. If the poor are given too much, incentives may suffer. If incentives to work are made too strong, many will suffer from hunger or worse. Thus the "transfers," however they might be measured, conceivably may affect all incomes favorably or unfavorably. The distribution "chosen" can be viewed as the result of balancing considerations of egalitarianism, compassion, incentive, and social stability.

In contrast, there seems to be no similar way of justifying an increase in the rate of capital accumulation for the benefit of future generations. Income transfers between generations made by increasing net saving or by consuming capital always have the effect of reducing the income of one of the groups from what it otherwise would have been. An increase in saving now undertaken for the benefit of future generations cannot be justified by a claim that contemporary consumption will thereby be raised. In the face of this, the business of adding the utilities of people in different generations begins to look like a different kind of operation from that of adding the utilities of contemporary persons with different incomes. In the latter case, we are willing to add (which is a way of saying that advantages were equalized at the margin as between the different people) *because the distribution actually in effect is grounded in an agreed ethical solution of the problem. In the intergeneration case, there is nothing comparable.*

Once the general distributional problem has been solved in our society, we do not feel that person *A* should give a part of his income to person *B* with a higher income. The situation is not quite analogous to the intergenerational savings problem because of the productivity of capital, but it can be brought close to it. Suppose person *C* said to person *A*, "If you will give $X to person *B*, whose income is admittedly higher than yours, I, too, will give $X to person *B*." Person *A* no doubt would refuse to join this game, and it seems doubtful that very many people would fault him for this refusal on the ground that he had violated some ethical principle. What that principle would be is difficult to imagine. All this is not to say that person *A* should never give anything to person *B*, for it is within the power of person *A* to bestow gifts other than money, some of which are not limited in quantity in the way that money is— love, for example.

If we view the Ramsey-like analysis of the savings problem as aimed at practical decision rather than as an intriguing problem in mathematical economics, the objection that we have difficulty in agreeing on the nature of the utility function comes as something of an anti-climax in view of the preceding discussion. If it doesn't make sense to add the utilities of different generations, it makes little difference that we can't even determine the function for a single generation beyond the property of diminishing utility.

Alternatives to Utility Maximization Over Generations

The line of thought that has been pursued here can be summarized in two statements: one, that there is no solution to the problem of our capital accumulation obligations to future generations along the usual utility lines that will be more than a means of diversion, and two, that a brief examination of the ethical aspects of the problem suggests that earlier generations have no obligation to accumulate capital, for even if the stock of capital per person were to remain constant, it is almost a certainty that future generations would have the potentiality of being better off than we are because of technological advance.

The view that the problem of our obligations to future generations is only or mainly a problem of the rate of capital accumulation ignores other serious problems that may result in seriously damaging consequences to them. The particular composition of the bill of final goods, the production processes used, and the availability of the technology and institution for dealing with undesirable effects of consumption and production presently not taken care of by market forces or governmental action, size of population—these are the things that carry a threat to our successors. The potential threat goes far beyond the possibility that some future generation may have an income only 200 percent higher than ours rather than the 300 percent that would be possible if we were to save more. If the problems reflected in the composition of product and processes are not dealt with adequately, the threat is not one of a smaller increase in income than that attainable with more saving now but one of an absolute and conceivably catastrophic fall in real income, viewed comprehensively. If exclusive emphasis were placed on increasing income as conventionally measured, these penalties would be realized in substantial degree.

The discussion so far has been carried on as if there were only one society in the world and one government. When the problem is extended to one of capital accumulation in a world of separate nations, it appears to be complicated considerably, and little attention seems to have been given to these complications.

If our society is considered in isolation and the "environmental" problems just mentioned are handled reasonably well, the capital accumulation problem does seem to come down to a question of why we should stint to make future generations even better off than we are. If the welfare of future generations in other nations can be affected by our decision on savings and this is to count in this decision, this argument may not apply because they are not now so well off as we are now and may not be in the future (by conventional economic measures!). This does indeed seem to be the case, but to say this is merely to begin the discussion.

First, there are formidable difficulties in transferring product from one government to another. That a transfer now would result in a higher capital stock in the receiving country such that future income, per capita or total, would be significantly higher is doubtful. That later transfers for consumption abroad resulting from a higher present savings rate here would be desirable is certainly debatable and would be regarded by many—including some in the recipient countries—as productive of highly undesirable consequences.

Alteration of our savings rate for the purpose of improving the welfare of future generations abroad is a weak instrument and possibly one that would have results counter to those intended. Other elements in the situation of other societies less fortunate than ours are of far greater importance for their future welfare. For good or for ill, nationalism ensures that the major responsibility for manipulating these elements lies within each nation.

Finally, recall the discussion of the relation between income and happiness. This line of thought is applicable as much to the case of raising incomes of future generations up to our income level as to raising their incomes above our level, as in the domestic case.

Society cannot avoid an implicit choice of the rate of capital accumulation, of course, nor do our comments mean that there is no solution to this problem of choice. In view of our discussion, the possibility of choosing to let the market express individual preferences for lifetime savings is quite attractive. This would probably be the best way to characterize the choice we seem to have made. In view of our past experience with capital accumulation under market forces, it would be difficult to contend that the interests of future generations are suffering. Market forces have not taken and probably cannot take care of all our obligations to future generations. Some of these will require very careful handling entirely apart from any tinkering with the overall rate of capital accumulation.

So far as capital accumulation is concerned, market forces have indeed provided us with a large and increasing stock of capital per capita. Market forces permit the adjustment of savings (and consumption) plans to investment productivity prospects, with each participant acting on the basis of his own horizon, of course, as discussed earlier in the chapter.

If the market is to be the instrument, however, its operation ought to be efficient. There are many obstacles to this, several of which have been touched on already and some of which cannot be eliminated. Included are all the imperfections with which we are familiar from the discussion of static allocation. In the case of investment, a major barrier to efficiency is the presence of a corporation income tax of approximately 50 percent, which makes impossible an equation at the margin of rates of return facing individuals and those deciding on corporation investments. The elimination of this and other barriers or a reduction in their importance would have important effects on the allocation of investment (imagine the effects of requiring government investments to meet a 10 percent or higher standard!) and possibly on the quantity of savings.*†

---

* For a discussion of the difficulties in achieving a governmental neutrality toward savings, see E. S. Phelps, *Fiscal Neutrality Toward Economic Growth* (New York: McGraw-Hill, 1965).

† The literature on the subject matter of this chapter is extensive. A few references in addition to those cited in the text that might be useful to the general reader are the following:

Baumol, William J., *Welfare Economics and the Theory of the State* (2nd ed.) (Cambridge: Harvard University Press, 1965).

Denison, Edward F., *The Sources of Economic Growth in the United States and the Alternatives Before Us* (New York: Committee for Economic Development, 1962).

Dewey, Donald, *Modern Capital Theory* (New York: Columbia University Press, 1965).

Hicks, John R., *Capital and Growth* (New York: Oxford, 1965).

CHAPTER 4

Natural Resource Problems
Involving Change Over Time

The role of time in economic analysis was discussed in a general way in the previous chapter. The role of time in economic analysis can now be extended by showing how two particular types of natural resource productivity may be managed as a part of a system in which output is maximized in the efficiency sense.

The two types of natural resource productivity to be examined are mineral deposits and components of a biological system, that is, mineral resources and all other natural resources.* The discussion will be far from comprehensive, however. We will attempt to select a few of the general aspects of the exploitation of natural resources which either cannot be analyzed in static terms, or which require some consideration of the path that ought to be taken in getting to a situation that can be characterized in static terms.

Single firms confront many problems which involve the selection of a path through time for a group of variables (for example, investment and output) because of certain restrictions on the possible behavior through time of some of the variables involved. These restrictions arise from a wide variety of sources such as the physically necessary sequencing of certain activities, natural growth or replacement processes, etc.

Similar problems face industries and groups of economic units operating in a limited area, including, for example, such seemingly diverse activities as ground-

---

* Even this boundary is not sharp. For example, some metals are concentrated by certain bacteria.

water management, lumbering, and fishing. Although the discussion will tend toward analyses of problems facing single firms, the fact that a group of firms is involved and that the relevant time horizon may be quite long leads us to select and concentrate on certain aspects of these problems which seem to be of special relevance for behavior of the industry group and thus for the assessment and possible modification of the governing institutional arrangements.

4.1 THE MEANING AND SIGNIFICANCE OF EXHAUSTION

The exploitation of minerals cannot be analyzed exclusively in static terms because the assumption of indefinite repetition of flows per unit time is an inadequate basis for explaining certain situations that inevitably occur. The exploitation of mineral deposits leads steadily to their "exhaustion," which may be defined as a rise, gradual or sudden, in the cost of exploitation caused by exploitation. One of the limiting cases is that of constant cost of exploitation up to the point at which the mineral is either literally exhausted or cost jumps so high that quantity demanded is zero. Obviously, this does not describe reality, but the idea of actual and complete physical exhaustion proves to be useful for explaining the relevant theory because of its simplicity.

A more sophisticated view of exhaustion as constituting a gradual rise in the cost of exploitation requires that exhaustion be viewed as a process taking place over time. The only point at which exhaustion could be said to occur would be that at which cost rises to the point at which none of the mineral product is demanded. This point is not characterized by a single physical situation but is dependent on the demand for the product (that is, on what can be done with the product and the prices of substitutes) and the cost of exploitation, which in turn depends on technology and prices of inputs.

4.2 EXPLOITATION OF A MINERAL DEPOSIT

Neglected Factors

The purpose here is not to analyze the problems involved in planning the whole complex of operations involved in exploiting a mineral deposit—necessarily over a considerable period of time—but to abstract certain basic features of this problem that also are of fundamental importance in forming a theory of the operation of a mineral industry over time. So far as the problem of the firm is concerned, however, the economist should be aware of the major role played by the form and other characteristics of the deposit in planning operations in a practical setting.

Consider, for example, the rich variety of forms that a deposit may take. It may be superficial or deep. It may approximate many different geometric shapes, such as a cylinder or sections of a cylinder at various inclinations, spherical or conical sections, lenses, and so on. The density of ore can be distributed within the deposit in an infinity of ways. It may be uniform within the deposit with rather sudden declines at the surfaces. It may be distributed randomly in two or three dimensions. In other cases, the density may be uniform locally but decline systematically from the inner to the outer portions of the deposit. The density distribution of a mineral and the configuration of the deposit are important elements in determining the extent to which all of the mineral in a deposit is going to be mined. Other considerations are the technologies available and the prices of the inputs associated with them.

There is always a "cut-off grade" in every direction higher than that of the mineral content of the country rock. Although there are a few unusual situations in which a large fraction of the mineral with density of distribution greater than that of country rock will actually be mined, the best course of action for society as well as the firm is almost always to leave a substantial quantity of the mineral behind. There is an analogous problem at the later processing stages, for example, in milling, smelting, and refining. It is always desirable to leave some metal in the dump or on the slag heap, or oil in the ground, for it does not pay society to recover metal at a cost greater than its value.

This complex of conditions associated with the deposit has its expression for economic analysis in the *production function*, which will be considerably complicated by intertemporal relations between various activities. In certain ways, these physical constraints simplify the problem of planning operations over time because certain sequences of operation are either impossible or so costly as to be obviously undesirable. On the other hand, the very complexity of the physical situation opens the possibility that solutions thought to be near optimum may be revealed to be deficient by adequate analysis.

The Problem of the Mining Firm

Let us radically simplify the problem of producing metal from a mine by neglecting many of the complications just described, and concentrating on a few basic economic aspects of the problem. Assume that (1) the mining firm sells metal in a competitive market (constant price); (2) exploitation of its mineral deposit is technologically independent of its other holdings and is subject to exhaustion; (3) the firm has a long-run average cost curve reflecting outlays actually made which include expenditure for mining and recovery of metal for ore but which does not include any rent on the deposit; (4) the rate of discount is positive.

The cost curve implied by assumption (3) depends only on the current and not the cumulated rate of output, does not change over the life of the mine, and has a minimum. We are assuming here that "plant" is adjusted year by year to the optimum size. If this is not possible, some obvious modifications will have to be made in the necessary conditions. A physical situation which would yield this result would be that of a deposit with a long shape of uniform cross section, for example, a horizontal half cylinder either above or below the ground. That is, long-run average cost would be a function of output per unit time but not of cumulated output.

How much should the firm produce in each period of time until exhaustion of the deposit? Consider first some of the bounds of the problem. If the quantity of mineral in the deposit were large, so that exhaustion would be far into the future and the deposit *cannot* be sold in part, the situation would be the same as that of agricultural land viewed as providing a productive service in perpetuity. The firm would produce that output at which long-run marginal cost is equal to price, here assumed to remain constant.* The essential point is that the decision on this year's output has no repercussions on the cost of output in any other year—or, in different but equivalent language, the production of a ton of ore now does not affect ability to produce a ton of ore at some other time.

Suppose that exhaustion is not in the indefinite future, however. If the investment opportunities available are reflected in a positive interest rate and, contrary to our assumption, the long-run cost curve is horizontal, the whole deposit would be produced instantly in order to maximize the present value of the excess of revenue over cost.

On the other hand, if the long-run cost curve has a minimum but the rate of discount is zero, the firm would choose to produce in each year that output at which average cost is at a minimum until the deposit was exhausted.

The correct solution of the problem under the conditions initially specified is easy. *The optimum sequence of outputs will reflect the impossibility of increasing the present value of total revenue minus outlays by transferring a unit of output from one period to another.*† This will be the case only if the *present value of price minus long-run marginal cost is equal in all periods with production.*

The problem can be analyzed with the aid of Figure 4-1. It consists of a series of juxtaposed diagrams showing, for each period in which there is production, price and cost per unit of metal output as a function of rate of output per unit time. The diagrams differ from those of purely static analysis in two respects, however. First, instead of measuring price and cost upward from a common zero level, we measure discounted price (price − cost) downward from a common zero level. Thus the usual abscissa is represented by a different line for each year. The distance of this line from the common zero level is equal to discounted price, or $P/(1 + r)^t$. The cost curves can be viewed as being measured up from these changing abscissae or, alternatively, as located by measuring discounted (P − cost) downward from the zero line common to all the years. Cost curves are shown here schematically, with only small segments of the marginal and average cost curves shown in the vicinity of the minima of the average cost curves.

Now how may the mine owner determine his schedule of production? First, we can be sure that the discounted value of price minus marginal cost will be the same in all years.

---

* What would happen if this and other deposits could be sold in part?
† The outputs will be positive, of course, only if this present value is positive.

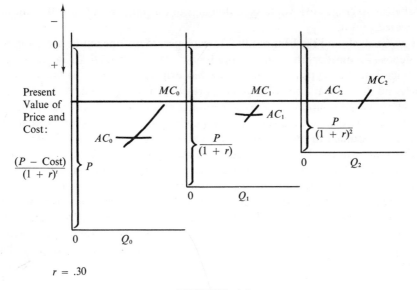

FIGURE 4-1

Second, and perhaps not quite so obvious, output in the last period in which there is production will be at the rate associated with average cost.* To see this, suppose the P.V.† of price minus marginal cost is equal in all years, but in the last period immediately preceding exhaustion, this quantity corresponds to an output larger than that at which average cost is minimized. It would now pay to take a little output from each of the years over this period of production (sacrificing net revenue at the rate of P.V. of price minus marginal cost for each period) and extend the whole period of production by producing at the rate which minimizes average cost in the next later period. The gain in this period would be at the rate or P.V. of price minus minimum average cost, a sum per unit that is larger than that sacrificed by reducing outputs in the earlier periods.

On the other hand, suppose the P.V. of price minus cost is equal among the years of the production period at such a level that output in the last period (n) is less than that associated with minimum average cost. If this is also true in the immediately preceding periods, it will pay to eliminate output of period n, losing this output times price minus *average* cost (higher than minimum average cost) and gaining a larger ($P - C$) relevant for the addition multiplied by $(1 + r)$ because the receipts and outlays come one year earlier.

If the same argument applies to period ($n - 2$) as to ($n - 1$), it will pay to continue moving output toward the present. Clearly, when it no longer pays to compress or extend output in time, the last bit of output produced will be at the rate at which average cost is minimized and earlier outputs will be at higher rates.

---

* Production at this rate could be for only a part of the unit time period, say a year, if necessary.

† Present value

The final result is a series of outputs which diminishes over time at a rate which depends on the rapidity with which marginal cost rises and on the rate of discount. That is, although near net revenues are worth more than distant net revenues, concentration of production in a short period of time would penalize the firm because of the diseconomies of large scale (very intensive) exploitation.* Consequently, output is shifted to the future until the marginal gains from shifting the scale and the operation of the discount factor are in balance. The resulting output stream declines over time because the discount factor makes it profitable to have higher near outputs in spite of the diseconomies of scale that are suffered.

If the rate of discount had been higher, the later cost curves would be closer to the zero line and production would be moved closer to the present to reduce the impact of the higher discount rate on net revenues with the later cost curves being affected more than the earlier ones. The life of the mine would be reduced.

A cost reduction that lowers the undiscounted cost curves uniformly will be translated by the discount rate into smaller increases in price minus cost for later than for earlier years, thus leading to a shift of output toward the present and a shortening of life of the mine just as did a higher discount rate. A rise in price will have the same effect, of course.

This analysis shows that the onset of diseconomies of scale in mine operation and the rapidity with which they are experienced, often attributable to the characteristics of the deposit rather than to diminishing returns to entrepreneurship, is one of the principal determinants of mine life. Consequently, if "proved reserves" are reasonably well estimated at the beginning of a deposit's exploitation, the ratio of reserves to production for the industry will have *no* relation to the prospective life of the industry. That is, they will indicate nothing about the time when the industry will "run out" of a mineral. On the contrary, a decline in this ratio that reflects technological developments that have made possible the more rapid exploitation of a deposit is something to be welcomed rather than an occasion for viewing with alarm because less capital (productive power) is tied up during long periods of exploitation. The only reason why substantial parts of good deposits remain unexploited at any particular time is because no economical way can be found to exploit them quickly.

4.3 THE MINERAL INDUSTRY—CONSTANT COST

Constant Cost Forever

Suppose it is anticipated that the cost of producing a mineral product will remain constant into the *indefinite future*. Clearly there is nothing to be gained by withholding exploitation of deposits for later higher prices. Deposits will be

---

* An easy way to appreciate the force of these diseconomies is to imagine what would happen to total cost if a given earth-moving job—stripping, tunneling, or whatever—were speeded up by increasing multiples. In many cases technological and even ultimate physical limits will be approached very rapidly whether the job is being done by a large or small firm.

brought into production until price has been driven down to the cost of producing the mineral product.

If the precise location of particular deposits is not known but it is anticipated that the cost of exploration will remain constant along with other costs, the conclusion is not altered. Price will be driven down to the level of all costs. This will be true whether the deposits discovered are of uniform quality or if only the average quality remains uniform. *In either case, the "rent" on the deposits exploited will be completely absorbed by the cost of exploration.* Where deposits are not of uniform quality, sub-marginal deposits will remain unexploited and marginal deposits will earn no "rent" to contribute to exploration cost.*

Constant Cost Up to Rigid Limit

Now suppose the cost of producing a mineral is constant up to a known fixed cumulated quantity, which is equivalent to saying that at a certain cumulated output, cost jumps to a point so high that there is no demand. As in the preceding case, the assumption of constant cost still leaves the problem very simple even though exploration is necessary. It is assumed that the demand curve has a finite intercept.

In these circumstances, competitive forces will ensure that there is an initial price above cost such that with price minus cost (i.e., net price) rising through time at the rate of discount, the maximum price for zero demand will be reached at the moment of exhaustion.

The situation of constant cost up to a fixed quantity of production is illustrated in Figure 4-2. *OB* is cost per unit, which remains constant over time. *CD* is the equilibrium course of price over time. The demand curve at each moment of time is represented by the right side of the figure.

If a sufficient number of people in the market perceive the future equilibrium course of the industry correctly, any deviations from this course will induce some of them to advance or retard the time of production from deposits already held by someone or which can be found by someone. The final result will be a course of price over time such that no owner will regret the time at which he actually produces from a deposit. It will be a matter of indifference when outlays are actually made on potential mineral producing land to find and actually produce a deposit. All this is possible only if price starts out at *OC* with Q_0 as indicated on the demand curve, with net price, *CB*, rising at the rate of discount. The quantity produced and demanded declines as price moves up the demand curve, with maximum price, *OA*, being reached as the last deposit is exploited at time *T*. The essential conditions are (1) that discounted net price be equal for all periods:

$$\frac{P_j - C}{(1 + r)^j} = \frac{P_i - C}{(1 + r)^i}$$

---

* Results will be somewhat different if exploration efforts can be directed toward the better or poorer deposits; that is, if the function of exploration produces joint products in variable rather than fixed proportions.

Price and Cost Over Time   Demand Per Unit Time

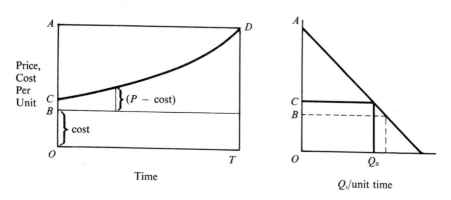

FIGURE 4-2

or in particular, that $P_t - C = (P_0 - C)(1 + r)^t$; and (2) that deposits be exhausted when price brings quantity demanded to zero (OA in the diagram).

From this simple diagram, we see the effects of changes in the various parameters of the problem on the course of price over time and on the period of exploitation. Bearing in mind that the course of prices must be such that the initial net price grows at the rate of discount and that the exhaustion is reached as price reaches OA, we realize that a *higher rate of discount* with initial price of OC would result in a higher price at each point in time than before with some deposits unexploited when price OA is reached. Initial prices will, therefore, have to be *lower* (with larger Q_t's) and later prices higher (with offsetting smaller Q_t's). The life of the industry, T, will be reduced.

If *cost* were lower but initial price maintained at OC, the larger absolute initial net price (OC minus cost) would follow a course steadily rising above the curve, CD, a schedule of prices which again would fail to attain exhaustion. The proper adjustment is similar to that for an increase in the rate of discount. Initial price will fall less than the decrease in cost, however, for the new price curve must cross the old in order to secure exhaustion at the proper time, which will necessarily be earlier than the original T because of lower initial prices.

A constant absolute tax on each unit of output would be equivalent to a uniform increase in cost. A constant percentage tax on the net price, however, would require no change in prices or outputs.*

It appears that increases in demand (that is, higher quantity for each price or higher price for each quantity) must result in a shift of consumption toward the present and shortening of the life of the industry. That is, if demand is such that

---

* If the course of market price over time is unchanged, exhaustion will occur at the same time as before and the present value of net price after tax will *still* be the same in all periods, although smaller by the amount of the constant percentage tax. If the p.v. of net prices in different periods before the tax is imposed is equal as in $_1P_t = P_0e^{rt}$, multiplying each side by $(1 - t)$, where $100t$ is the percentage tax rate, will still leave them equal.

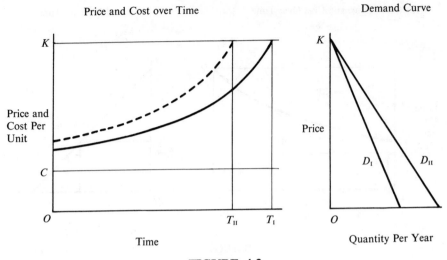

FIGURE 4-3

we are willing to have exhaustion in the comparatively near future (the demand curve has a finite price intercept), an increase in the value of the product to us in every period carries the implication that we should consume it more rapidly. Consider three cases of simple shifts in linear demand curves. First, suppose that q_t increases by a constant percentage for each price (i.e., price elasticity remains constant at each price) as on the right side of Figure 4-3. If the course of price over time were unchanged after the shift of demand, exhaustion would

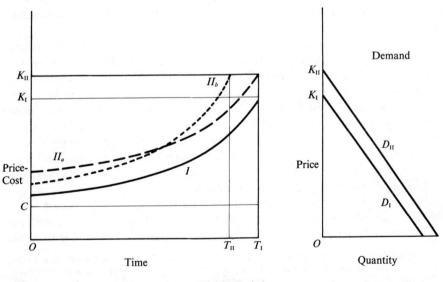

FIGURE 4-4

be premature. If prices are to be higher to prevent this, net price still will have to rise at the rate of discount. A higher initial price and net price will therefore result in earlier exhaustion, as at T_{II}.

If the demand curve shifts vertically by a constant amount, as in Figure 4-4, a rise in price by this amount at each point in time would leave T unchanged (see curve II_a). This cannot be, however, since the net price would now be rising more slowly than the rate of discount (since the net price associated with curve I was rising at the rate of discount). Curve II_b, with a lower initial net price which rises at the rate of discount and crosses curve II_a, will supply the two necessary conditions. T will be reduced, as at T_{II}.

Finally, suppose the demand curve shifts so that price is higher by a constant percentage for each quantity. The argument is similar to the preceding one, and is illustrated by Figure 4-5.

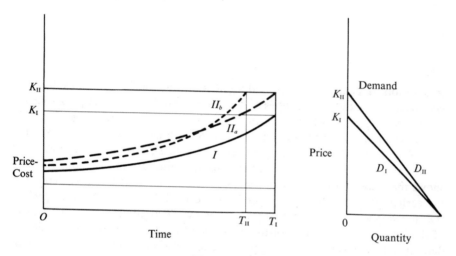

FIGURE 4-5

4.4 THE MINERAL INDUSTRY—QUALITY, COST, QUANTITY

Let us complicate the preceding problem by introducing variation in the quality of the deposits, but still assuming constant cost within each quality. Assume that the total quantity which can be produced from each quality is known. The simplest case, depicted in Figure 4-6, is that of two different qualities. Cost of the mineral from the better deposits is OC_b and from the worse is OC_w.

The owners of the better deposits (or of potential mineral-bearing land if precise locations of deposits are not known) can always outbid the owners of the poorer for the privilege of producing in the nearer periods. That is, the better deposits will be produced first and at prices *low enough relative to later prices to make it unprofitable for poorer deposits to be produced in the earlier periods.*

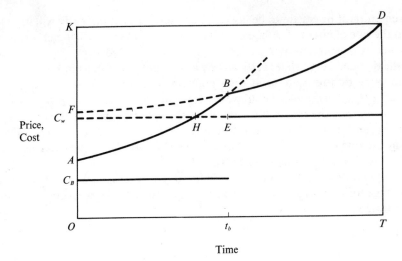

Time

FIGURE 4-6

In addition, if there is to be no inducement to shift output *within* each of the periods in which the two qualities of deposit are produced, the net price (market price minus cost) must be increasing at the rate of discount within each.

The result is that price moves from A to B, with net price, AC_b, rising at the rate of discount. Market price then rises from B to D, with net price, BE, rising at the rate of discount. If BE is carried back at the rate of discount, FB then shows the price that would be necessary for exploitation of a poorer deposit in the earlier period to be equally profitable to exploitation in the later period. AB, showing the course of actual price, is below FB at all times up to t_b, the end of the period of exploitation of the better deposits. Contents of both grades of deposit are exhausted at T when price reaches the maximum at zero demand, OK. Output per unit time diminishes as price moves up. With the periods of exploitation equal as drawn, the contents of the better deposits would be considerably greater than that of the poorer deposits because prices are lower while the better deposits are being exploited.

If the percentage of mineral in the poorer deposits were higher, with the total in both grades constant, the total period of exploitation would be extended and that for the higher grade would be reduced. Early prices will be raised and later prices lowered with corresponding effects on the net prices of the two grades.

To see this, suppose that the initial price remained at OA. The poorer deposits would come into play before price B is reached. If this new initial net price for the poorer deposits then increased at the rate of discount, exhaustion would be reached before price has reached OK. Consequently, initial price must be above OA. On the other hand, if the initial price were such that the better deposits are exhausted as price reaches curve FB to the left of B, some deposits would remain unexploited when price reached OK since in each period price would be the same or higher than in the original situation. Hence the new price segment for the poorer deposits will have to be below BD and the total period of exploitation will be extended.

Assume a reduction in the cost, OC_w, or production from the poorer deposits, with the quantity of mineral in these remaining the same. This will result in lower initial prices for the better deposits and for a part of the period when the poorer deposits are produced but with higher later prices. The period of exploitation for the better deposits and for both grades together will be reduced.

To see this, suppose that initial price remained at OA. Then the new higher net price starting at B and increasing at the rate of discount would yield a price curve above BD since C_w is now lower and BE, which rises at the rate of discount, would then be larger. The result would be that some deposits are unexploited when price OK is reached. Initial price must therefore be below OA with consequent exhaustion of the better deposits before t_b. To avoid premature exhaustion of the poorer deposits, the initial royalty for them must be such as to yield a price curve crossing BD so that the increased earlier consumption is offset by reduced later consumption as price moves up to OK.

An increase in the quantity of poorer deposits, with costs remaining the same, would result in lower prices at all times. The better deposits would be exploited more quickly, and both the period over which the poorer deposits are exploited and the total period of exploitation would be lengthened. This follows immediately from observation that curve BD would now leave deposits unexploited as price reaches OK. Hence the initial price must be lower than OA to result in a transition price at a point like B that is lower than B and below the curve AB. The point like B will be somewhere in the triangle HBE with the new price curve for the poorer deposits below the old one.

4.5 MANY GRADES OF DEPOSITS—QUANTITY AND COST KNOWN

If the number of grades of deposits in the analysis is increased, the limiting case is that of continuous increase in cost as cumulated production rises. If cumulated production has a limit and cost at this maximum is at a level for which demand is greater than zero, the terminal situation is one of zero demand, cumulated production at the maximum, and a positive net price.

On the other hand, if the cumulative cost curve rises to or beyond the maximum price permitted by the demand function, net price must eventually decline and approach zero as both the market price and cost approach the maximum price associated with zero demand.

Graphic Derivation of the Basic Condition

By suitable manipulation of a diagram similar to that for deposits of two grades, some insight into the progression of net price through time can be gained.

Surprisingly, we can derive the fundamental result from applying the calculus of variations to the problem. Figure 4-7 is similar to Figure 4-6 except that we now

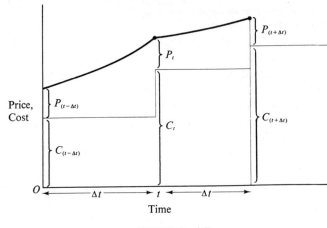

FIGURE 4-7

envision cost rises between short periods, Δt. From the preceding discussion, it is clear that the following equation must hold (p refers to *net* price):

$$p(t)(1 + r\,\Delta t) + C(t) = p(t + \Delta t) + C(t + \Delta t)$$

$$rp(t)\,\Delta t = p(t + \Delta t) - p(t) + C(t + \Delta t) - C(t)$$

$$\lim_{\Delta t \to 0} \frac{rp(t)\,\Delta t}{\Delta t} = \lim_{\Delta t \to 0} \frac{p(t + \Delta t) - p(t)}{\Delta t} + \lim_{\Delta t \to 0} \frac{C(t + \Delta t) - C(t)}{\Delta t}$$

$$rp = \frac{dp}{dt} + \frac{dC}{dt}$$

With x as cumulated output and $q = (dx/dt)$, the rate of output per unit time, this may be rewritten as

$$rp = \frac{dx}{dt} \cdot \frac{dC}{dx} + \frac{dp}{dt}$$

$$= q \cdot \frac{dC}{dx} + \frac{dp}{dt}$$

$$r = \frac{q}{p} \cdot \frac{dC}{dx} + \frac{1}{p}\frac{dp}{dt}$$

If cost does not rise with cumulated output, net price then increases relatively at the rate of discount unless deposits are in effect limitless, in which case p is zero and so is dp/dt. If cost is rising with cumulated output, however, the relative rate of increase in net price $[(1/p)(dp/dt)]$ will be less than the rate of interest by the rate of cost increase per unit of cumulated output relative to net price times the rate of output per unit time. In the case where cumulated cost can rise as high as the price associated with zero demand ($q = 0$), both q and p approach zero as this market price is approached, thus opening the possibility of an asymptotic approach to this market price.

The above expression is the same as the general necessary condition for optimizing the exploitation of a mineral resource over time, which is reproduced here with some modifications to show the relation. Before doing this, it will be worthwhile pausing to examine the general nature of the problem under consideration.

The problems considered earlier for which differential calculus was used or could have been used included an objective function involving a finite set of variables whose maximum was sought, perhaps subject to one or more side conditions expressed as equations. That is, the objective was the maximization of, say, $F(x,y,z)$ subject to side conditions $\phi_1(x,y,z) = 0$, $\phi_2(x,y,z) = 0$, etc.

In problems of the type to be considered now (for example, with cost dependent on cumulated output) the task is to find a path for the variables through time which will maximize the value of an *integral*. This type of problem is one in the calculus of variations, so called because it involves analysis of the possible variations in a function expressing this time path so as to maximize (or minimize) the value of the objective integral.*

The general problem may be visualized as that of finding a path for a variable between two fixed points which will maximize the objective integral. The conditions of the problem determine the general form that the function may take. Now imagine a series of variations in the tentatively chosen function directed toward finally locating the optimum function. As in Figure 4-8, each of the

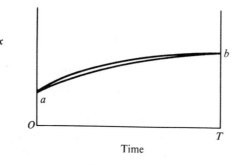

FIGURE 4-8

tentatively chosen functions must go through the specified end points. The question to be investigated is: What condition must be satisfied if it is impossible

---

* Of course, time does not have to be a variable in variational problems. Because it often is in economics problems, however, we shall speak of it as one of the variables.

to increase the value of the objective integral by further permissible variation of the function?

This question is analogous to one that could be asked about a given function, $y = f(x)$: Suppose in this case that we change the value of x by a small amount and compare this with the corresponding change in the value of the function, y. What condition involving this variation must hold in order that the value of the function, y, be at a maximum? $(dy/dx) = 0$ is the answer, of course. Here we are moving from point to point on a given function, but in the variational problem we are moving from function to function in a restricted way. In general terms, the questions are similar: What conditions must hold if the objective function is to be a maximum?

Suppose the objective function is

$$V = \int_a^b F(\mathbf{x},\dot{\mathbf{x}},t)\, dt \qquad \left(\text{where } \dot{\mathbf{x}} = \frac{dx}{dt}\right)$$

We seek a function $x = \phi(t)$ to maximize V.

The solution of this problem was one of the many great achievements of Leonard Euler (1707–1783). The required necessary condition, which provides the foundation for the calculus of variations, is:

$$\frac{\partial F}{\partial \mathbf{x}} - \frac{d(\partial F/\partial q)}{dt} = 0 \qquad \text{where} \quad q = \dot{\mathbf{x}} = \frac{dx}{dt}$$

This must hold at each moment in time. It is important to note that the second term is a *total* and not a partial derivative.* The required function will be the solution of this differential equation, $\mathbf{x} = \phi(t)$. This is called a differential equation because it involves derivatives (i.e., differentials).

The solution to a differential equation is simply an equation whose various derivatives will satisfy the differential equation when inserted into it. The procedures for finding solutions are simple in some cases but complex in others. The reader should see a text in differential equations for details.

The solutions of differential equations in economics involving time may take a variety of forms. The path of the variable of interest may approach a limit monotonically (no change in sign of first derivative), it may increase or decrease without limit (usually indicating that something was wrong with the formulation of the problem), it may oscillate with increasing, decreasing, or unchanging

---

* Calling $\partial F/\partial q = p$, since p may be a function of $\mathbf{x}$, $\dot{\mathbf{x}}$, and t,

$$\frac{dp}{dt} = \frac{\partial p}{\partial \mathbf{x}}\frac{dx}{dt} + \frac{\partial p}{\partial \dot{\mathbf{x}}}\frac{d\dot{\mathbf{x}}}{dt} + \frac{\partial p}{\partial t}$$

Note that
$$\frac{d\dot{\mathbf{x}}}{dt} = \frac{d^2\mathbf{x}}{dt^2}$$

amplitude (and similarly for periods) as a limit is approached, and approaches to limits may be asymptotic or not. Thus the variety of solutions is rich, although not rich enough to go very far in handling discontinuous elements, for which other tools are needed.

The Problem of Maximizing Societal Return—
Cost Rising with Cumulated Production

With this digression, let us turn to the analysis of the optimum time schedule of production and consumption of a mineral, the cost of which rises with past production.

Assume a demand curve that does not change over time. It has a finite intercept on the price axis. At a given time, t, the flow of utility from consuming at the rate of $q = dx/dt$ (x is cumulated output) is the area under the demand curve.

At the same time, the flow of total cost can be viewed as the area under a rising marginal cost curve that is a function of (1) the rate of output, q (we assume supply equals demand at all times); (2) cumulated output; and (3) time. If we wish to view exploration as involved in the problem, the deposits discovered at any given time must be viewed as being of uniform quality (as measured by the sum of exploration plus other costs per unit of product) if this simple treatment of the problem is to be adequate. Thus as production takes place and time proceeds, cost will rise, and we assume that it can rise beyond the price intercept of the demand curve.

The flow of net social return will be the difference between the area under the demand curve and that under the cost curve. That is, it will be equal to the shaded area in the figure below.

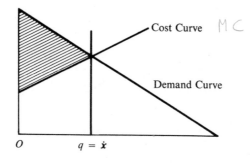

FIGURE 4-9

Calling this net social flow u and the difference between market price and cost p,

$$u_t = \int_0^q p(\mathbf{x},q,t)\, dq$$

The present value of u_t is $F = ue^{-rt}$. The objective is to maximize

$$V = \int_0^T F dt$$

where T is not fixed.

Euler's equation provides the necessary condition for solving this problem, and this is done in general terms in the latter part of this chapter.

Here we content ourselves with some numerical examples which can illustrate the way various factors in the problem are related.

Consider the following case:

$$\text{unchanging demand curve } P = a - bq = 10 - 1 \cdot q$$

$$\text{cumulative cost curve } L = c + \beta\chi = 2 + .08\chi$$

where P is market (not net) price, L is marginal cost per unit, and χ is output cumulated from $t = 0$.

As we saw earlier, if β was zero, net price $p = P - L$ would grow at the rate of interest. Here the same force—that is, the necessity of discounting each period's net returns because of the existence of other investment opportunities yielding the market rate of interest—is at work, but as the earlier derivation showed this is offset by the rising cost of production. Note that no independent influence of time on cost is included in this example.

This can be clarified with the basic relationship derived earlier:

$$\frac{dp}{dt} = rp - \frac{dC}{dt} *$$

The significance of dC/dt can be clarified with the aid of Figure 4-10. If dC/dt

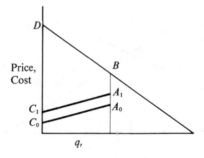

FIGURE 4-10

is zero, then net price rises at the rate of interest $[(dp/dt) = rp]$. If it is not zero, then we may visualize the cost of the last unit produced at time t as represented by A_0 with price at point B.

---

* Observe also that since $dp/dt = (dP/dt) - (dC/dt)$ (p is net price and P is market price), we have $dP/dt = rp$. This does *not* say that market price rises at the rate of interest.

If cumulated output had been one unit higher at the beginning of the period, however, the cost of each unit produced during the period would be higher by approximately dC/dx, represented by $C_1 - C_0 = A_1 - A_0$, the rate at which cost rises with cumulated output. The total reduction in u for the whole period as a result of the fact that cost rises with cumulated output would be $-q(dC/dx)$, or $-(dx/dt) \cdot (dC/dx) = (-dC/dt)$.

With the objective the maximization of net social gain from exploiting this mineral, the solution of the numerical example set forth above, using a discount rate of 10 percent, results in a rising market price and cost, at first rapid and then with an asymptotic approach to the maximum price of 10 permitted by the demand curve. The rate of production is initially high but falls off rapidly as it approaches zero. The net price (the social gain on each unit produced) falls rapidly at first and approaches zero. These results are portrayed as Case I in Figure 4-11.

Now suppose the situation is changed by adding another source of material, such as seawater, with indefinitely constant cost of 6 per unit. (This is represented

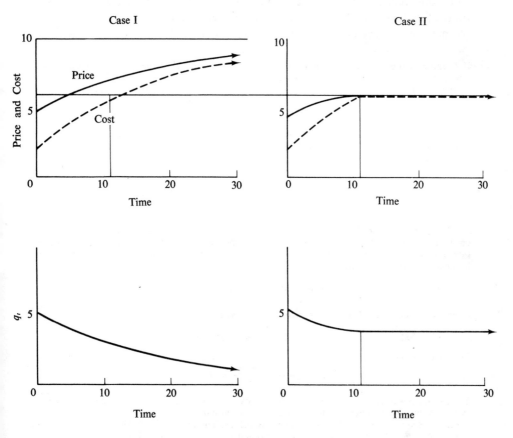

FIGURE 4-11

as Case II on the right side of Figure 4-11.) The lower cost source is now exploited first and more rapidly than before and is abandoned after about 11.1 years when its cumulated cost per unit reaches the cost level of the "inexhaustible" source. In contrast, the cost level of 6 was not reached until 13.2 years in the preceding case in which no constant cost source was available.*

If civilization something like the present one survives for a long period, Case II or approximations thereto will almost necessarily represent the situation of many actual mineral products.

4.6   EXPLORATION

Exploration has been incorporated into the cases considered so far by the use of simplifying assumptions that in effect made outlays on exploration entirely similar to those on mining and subsequent processing. These simplifying assumptions have the virtue of making clear that exploration activity is not to be encouraged, *per se*, any more than one would want to encourage expenditure on the function of milling ores or of shelling peanuts. It would seem a little odd to imagine the sellers of Planters Peanuts arguing that incentives should be

---

* Some of the details of Case II are as follows: Let time T be the time when cumulated cost per unit reaches the level of 6 at which a constant cost source is available. In a year before T, the quantity entering the summed social utility is the integral of price minus cost over the

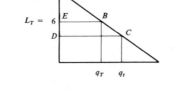

interval of 0 to q_t, or ACD. For a year after T it is the same integral between the demand curve and cumulated cost curve $L = 6$. ABE is present for each year regardless of the T selected. Hence we need be concerned only with the quantity for time T of $ACD - ABE$, the latter term being a constant. That is,

$$M = u_t - W = \int_0^q p(x,q,t)\, dq - W$$

where W is a constant ABE. $F = e^{-rt}(u_t = W)$. We seek to maximize

$$V = \int_0^T e^{-rt}(u_t - W)\, dt$$

The necessary condition

$$\frac{\partial F}{\partial x} - \frac{d(\partial F/\partial q)}{dt} = 0$$

is the same as before, and the general solution, expressing χ as a function of time, is the same as before, but the terminal conditions are different, in part.

The consequence is that T is not infinite as before. The approach of price and cost to the level of 6 is not asymptotic, as was the approach to 10 before, but takes place in the short space of about 11.1 years.

provided to encourage more peanut shelling, yet it is often argued that exploration for minerals ought to be encouraged and stimulated by subsidies or their equivalent. As a general matter, the one is as uneconomic as the other. Outlays on exploration are like any others: The object is to spend as little and as late as possible, making appropriate adjustments at the margins where inputs can be substituted. These adjustments refer to the composition and timing of different *types* of expenditures on exploration, a complication in the problem that will be discussed shortly. Given the composition of expenditures on exploration, however, it still remains true that they should be as little and as late as possible.

Classification of Cases

The first cases considered were those of constant cost over time, viewed as continuing indefinitely or up to a fixed limit of cumulated production. If these cases are viewed as involving exploration, the constancy of cost derives from a belief that there are not any differences between areas with respect to the expected present values of deposits that are found.

The belief may or may not reflect the real situation, but if it does not, the error is not discovered. Looking backward, there may be differences among areas, but if no one can explain these differences so as properly to separate a good area from a poorer one, selection of areas for exploration may as well be based on the assumption of no differences among areas.

There are two cases to be distinguished. First, if deposits found are of uniform quality, they all are exploited as they are found. Second, if deposits found show variation in quality, there may be a cutoff point established, with deposits of a quality below this level never being exploited if the constant cost situation is viewed as continuing indefinitely. In this case, mining and processing expenditure can be reduced by exploring sufficiently to find a larger number of better deposits and vice versa. The objective would be to minimize the sum of the two per unit of mineral product produced.

The situation is quite different, however, if exploration effort is viewed as finding deposits of variable quality but only up to a fixed limit. Substitution between exploration and subsequent processing costs is still possible, but now deposits that are not immediately exploited will be exploited later. Exploitation of the resource will have two stages. In the first, exploration will take place and there will be a fixed cutoff point characterized by the condition that a unit of product can be produced more cheaply by exploring and exploiting deposits above the cutoff point than by exploiting those previously found that are below this point. When all deposits have been found the industry will begin to exploit, in sequence of quality, those deposits below the previous cutoff point.

The constant cost cases represent a polar position in that there is no information that can be developed that will permit different areas to be distinguished in such a way as to lower the cost of finding and producing mineral product. The other extreme hypothetical case is that in which information exists which permits the arranging of different areas in an ascending cost sequence. We may imagine exploration as still being necessary but deposits discovered within a region are of uniform quality. At the extreme, all deposits are known and no exploration is necessary. This case has already been analyzed.

In between these two polar cases are those in which it is possible to distinguish between areas, but in which the discrimination, though better than chance, is less than perfect. Exploration outlays may be of a number of different types, some coming early in a sequence of sifting activities, designed to make gross distinctions among areas; and others designed to make finer distinctions down to identifying particular deposits and determining their detailed characteristics.

If the volume of mineral production is small relative to the quantity of potential mineral-bearing lands, this situation would be essentially the same as the constant cost situation described above. One could think of the development of an optimum sequence and mix of exploration activities which would be repeated many times. Each repetition of the sequence would result in the discovery of deposits of different qualities and the establishment of a cutoff point, with some of the deposits being exploited and some not.

Suppose, however, that the volume of mineral production is not small relative to the quantity of potential mineral-bearing lands and that some of the exploration activities are of such a nature as to be cheaper when performed on a large scale and/or to have important external effects when applied to small tracts. For example, information that you develop about your potential mineral-bearing land may be useful to your neighbor, or, in the case of private bidders for concessions on government-owned land, the same information could be used by all bidders. In such a case the optimum sequence and mix of exploration activities must be solved as a whole with an attempt to foresee developments over time, for it may be inappropriate to think of sequences of exploration activity as being repeated. It may be that the appropriate way to view the problem is as one of progressive modification of the quantity and type of information available about mineral potentialities.

An Extreme Proposal

The nature of the problem can be sharply posed by considering a proposal that is made recurrently: To make subsequent search for minerals more rational, drill (taking core samples where appropriate) the whole of the United States (and more?) on, say, five-mile centers.

Such a proposal cannot be rejected out of hand, that is, on an *a priori* basis. While it is possible that the cost involved could not possibly be offset by later savings in exploration expenditures, the only way to demonstrate this or to evaluate the proposal in case this is not true is to try to develop estimates of the quantities that are involved in the problem. The cost of such a program can be estimated reasonably well—within very broad limits!—but the difficult part of the problem is to assess the worth of the additional information. That is, what would be the saving in subsequent exploration expenditure? Fortunately, some light can be thrown on these questions by sample investigations. Careful quantitative study of these questions which can produce satisfactory statistics is lacking.

Drilling on five-mile centers is an extreme program, of course. Without going to this length, many governments have spent and are spending large amounts of money in other ways in an attempt to provide information that will permit the differentiation of regions with respect to their mineral potential. The Canadian government has conducted series of regional geological studies and electro-magnetic surveys covering most of the country directed to this end. The U.S. government is involved in a similar program, although coverage is more variable (some areas very intensively studied and others not), with a larger percentage of its area not studied at all or at a very low level of intensity. In the case of both countries the justification for these programs rests on "judgment" and hunch rather than on any solid statistical demonstration of their worth.

A "Location System" Problem

The "location system" of the United States gives free access to potential mineral-bearing public lands. In the case of the so-called "hard-rock" minerals, a person can get exclusive mineral (and other) rights in the form of a claim or a patent by asserting, and to a degree establishing, that he has discovered a valuable mineral. Mineral rights are given to anyone meeting certain conditions, the principal of which is the alleged discovery of an eligible valuable mineral.

Suppose all deposits discovered at a given time are of uniform quality but costs are rising. In this case the better lands will be explored first and the poorer later as prices rise. If mineral rights are privately owned, there will be no incentive to undertake early exploration on land of a given quality, the proper time being immediately before the time at which it is exploited in the quality sequence. This situation is portrayed in Figure 4-12 but with exploration costs *not* included in the curve showing cost over time.

At time AB deposits of a certain grade are produced, yielding a net price FE (equal to market price FH minus production cost BH and exploration cost BE).

Now suppose mineral rights can be acquired merely by discovery, as is presently the case with "hard-rock" minerals in the United States. By discounting the quantity FB, its P.V. can be expressed as of any time, t, between $t = 0$ and $t = AB$. Before time AC, this value is below the cost of exploration, $EB (= DC)$. But *at* time AC it will just pay to explore and gain the mineral rights even though the deposit will not be exploited until CB years later. Note that the *accumulated* exploration outlay made at time AC has now *entirely* eliminated the social net return on the deposit of FE as of time AB. This return has been entirely dissipated by premature exploration outlays.

This unfortunate outcome could be avoided by the sale or lease of mineral rights by competitive bidding, assuming well-functioning markets. A competitive auction of rights is currently the practice with offshore oil of the 48 contiguous

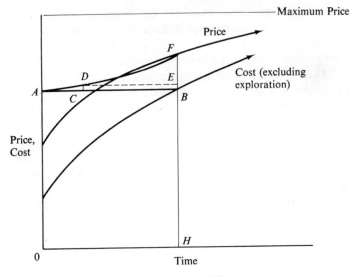

FIGURE 4-12

states and with Alaskan state-owned oil lands. Rights to a rather lengthy list of other minerals on certain federal lands are subject to lease, but for various reasons the approximation to a competitive result is poorer.

Once again we see illustrated the principle that poorer economization in the use of a resource requires that *someone have an interest in economizing*. Ownership of the resource or of the right to use it by someone interested in maximizing the return from it is perhaps the most effective way to avoid the wastes that accompany free access to the services of a resource.

4.7 IDENTIFICATION OF AN EXHAUSTING SITUATION

How can we know if we are "running out" of a mineral? First, consider what can be learned by looking at royalties. The most important point here is that a royalty is not the same thing as the net price of a mineral in the sense used here. A royalty is a payment made for the privilege of removing mineral from the earth, but there is no reason to suppose that this is equal to the net price—in ground— of mineral-bearing land, since information about this price is at "zero" base level.

Royalties can be generated by *any* increase in information as well as by anticipation of future price rise, that is, impending "exhaustion." For example, long-run equilibrium will require that outlays by former holders of mineral rights to acquire more information be covered by royalties if the rights are sold or leased, but this is compatible with a situation in which costs are anticipated to remain constant indefinitely. Similarly, royalties can be generated by other activities that increase the level of information, such as government geological survey activities, academic investigations (whether theoretical, laboratory, or field) as well as by accidental accretions to knowledge resulting from activities *not* undertaken in response to mineral price incentives. Similarly, expenditures on development made before lease of rights may end up being covered by a royalty.

The approach of exhaustion would be signalled by a rise in the price of rights to potential mineral land of given probable physical characteristics and level of information, or (what is the same) a deterioration in the physical characteristics and level of information that can be had for a given outlay, with other factors remaining unchanged.

Clearly the detection of this situation is no easy matter. First, there is great difficulty in determining changes in the quality of mineral-bearing land. Second, technology is changing constantly and offsetting to some degree any tendency to rising cost. It may even reverse the rankings of the quality of deposits, as has indeed happened in those cases where the economies of scale associated with open-pit mining plus sink-and-float techniques for separation of mineral from gangue have made large deposits with ore of low mineral content cheaper to exploit than smaller deposits with ore of far higher mineral content.

Third, royalties, and possibly a rise in them, can result from monopoly. Suppose, for example, that a country's deposits of a certain mineral are so poor that they cannot compete against the imported mineral product. If imports are now barred by governmental action, royalties may suddenly appear. Product price may be constant over time if there is a large number of these poor deposits, the royalties in this case reflecting costs incurred before lease. If the quantity is limited, a pseudo approach to exhaustion will result, with product price and royalties for land of a given quality rising. The reader may wish to consider the degree to which this model is applicable to the U.S. oil industry.

The cases of long-persistent price increases for mineral products are very few, if any. It is not surprising that this should be so, for any tendency to price rise comes to be tempered in various ways. First, rise in cost and the associated fall in net price plus the diminution of quantity demanded as price rises act to slow down price rise.* Second, technological progress in exploration, mining, and processing exerts a downward force, certainly not uniformly through time but always downward.

A third factor limiting the extent of price rise, although possibly increasing the *rate* in certain circumstances,† is the presence of what may be termed a *cost limit*. Several types can be distinguished. In some cases an essentially limitless source of the product may exist at a price above that now ruling but far below maximum price of the demand function. For some products, quantities available as it becomes feasible to go to lower grades are very large. In the case of energy, the breeder reactor will so increase the efficiency with which uranium and thorium are used as to provide a cost limit. If energy from fusion becomes practical, still another energy cost limit will be available. In the case of durable materials, a rising price will yield more and more recycling and there will be a

---

* Recall that $dp/dt = rp - (dC/dt)$.

† As Figure 4-11 showed, a cost limit increases the rapidity of exploitation and price rise of the cheaper source.

shift in demands away from those uses in which scrap recovery is costly to those in which recovery is cheap. The increasing stimulus to recycling could provide quite a firm limit in some cases, but even if not firm, it certainly operates to temper the rapidity of price rise.

4.8   ECONOMICS OF PETROLEUM PRODUCTION

Development Costs

Some of the economic aspects of petroleum production illustrate well a number of the theoretical ideas that have been presented. Here, as with any natural resource, economic analysis requires the integration of the physical or biological characteristics constraining the behavior of resource output over time with the alternative societal investment opportunities which are expressed through the discount process. Only certain selected aspects of the industry are considered here. The first topic is development and production costs.

Consider first the problem of optimizing production from a crude oil reservoir. The crude, which is under pressure (e.g., gas or water), can be extracted through wells. q_t, the rate of production per unit time at time t, can take on various courses through time. The crude can be extracted quickly or slowly, with more rapid extraction encountering higher costs. A larger number of wells will permit more rapid extraction, but there is some possibility of varying the shape of the production stream, given the number and configuration of the wells.

Thus the production profile, q_t, will depend on $q_t = g(n_t, Q_t, x_{i_t}, \ldots)$, where n_t represents the flow of services from N wells (some of which could be shut down), Q_t is cumulated production as of t, and x_i stands for other service inputs at t.

The P.V. of costs will be

$$C_0 = \frac{\sum(c_w N_t + c_{i_t} x_{i_t})}{(1 + r)^t}$$

with c as unit costs. Assuming the future course of the price of crude, p_t, is known, the object is to maximize P.V. of the opportunity:

$$\pi = \frac{\sum[p_t q_t - c_w N_t + c_{i_t} x_{i_t}]}{(1 + r)^t}$$

subject to $q_t = g(\ )$ and $Q_T \leq \bar{Q}$, the quantity of crude in the reservoir.

As it stands, it is clear that this is a complex problem calling for a formulation that will permit the use of the calculus of variations or some similar tool. The complexity arises mainly from the function $g(\ )$. Furthermore, it will be noted that there is no unit cost of crude which can be calculated apart from a solution of the whole problem. This results from the fact that C_0, the P.V. of all costs, is not related to a constant q_t or even a q_t with a specified path. Even Q_T, total production from the reservoir, is far from being a given quantity, the only restriction being that oil can't be produced which is not in the reservoir at the beginning. That is, oil will not be raised if it doesn't pay, and the usual situation is that it does not pay to raise a very large fraction of the crude originally in place.*

The problem can be greatly simplified, however, while still retaining important elements of actuality, thanks to the physical limitations on reservoir behavior and to the fact that discounting reduces the importance of outlays and revenues in years far into the future. This simplification will also permit the calculation of a historical per barrel cost of two of the important components of producing crude, development and operation costs.†

The basic fact about reservoir behavior for economic analysis is that pressure usually drops as production proceeds. Oil is generally produced, that is, raised to ground surface, by internal reservoir pressure. There are several types of internal drive or force, the two main categories being gas and water drives, but ordinarily there is pressure drop.‡

One type of situation which will serve to illustrate basic ideas can be schematized as follows:

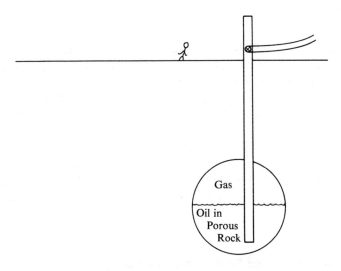

* Primary production utilizing internal pressure varies greatly among different deposits depending on their physical characteristics. In the United States it may range from as little as 5 up to as much as 80 percent of the crude originally in place, perhaps averaging around 20 percent. Secondary production taking place after internal pressure is exhausted has risen from around 18 to 30 percent over the last twenty-five years. Thus total recovery in this country averages around 50 percent. See *Energy Research Needs—A Report to the National Science Foundation* prepared by Resources for the Future, Inc. in cooperation with the MIT Environmental Laboratory, Contract NSF-C644 (October 1971), pp. II-44 and II-45.

† For nontechnical discussions of reservoir behavior, see Stephen L. McDonald, *Petroleum Conservation in the United States: An Economic Analysis* (Baltimore: Johns Hopkins Press, 1971); Paul Bradley, *The Economics of Crude Petroleum Production* (Amsterdam: North-Holland, 1967); and M. A. Adelman, *The World Petroleum Market, 1947–1969* (Baltimore: Johns Hopkins Press, 1971).

The following brief discussion of reservoir behavior and cost is based mainly on Bradley and Adelman.

‡ In some cases of water drive, pressure drop will be quite small, but there may be a decline in production of *crude* because of water intrusion.

Gas pressure forces oil up the tube to ground surface. Because of pressure differentials, oil migrates toward the bottom of the tube, but as oil is produced, gas pressure will go down as will the flow of oil.

Clearly the precise behavior of the reservoir will depend on a host of physical characteristics such as reservoir size, materials, structure, composition of fluids and gases present, etc. In addition, various practices will affect q_t and pressure drop, such as reinjection of gas produced with oil (commonly after stripping it of natural gas liquids such as propane and butane, or other liquids), fracturing rock, changing the number of wells that are producing, and so on. In any case, pressure drop is always present, although it can vary considerably among reservoirs.

For economic analysis, Bradley is of the view that pressure drop can be characterized adequately in a very simple way by specifying a linear relation between the production rate (proportional to pressure) and cumulated production:*

$$\text{(4-1)} \qquad\qquad \bar{q}_t = \bar{q}_0 - aQ_t$$

where $\bar{q}_t$ is the production rate of one well, Q_t is cumulated production from the reservoir, a is the decline rate in production if there is but one well, and $\bar{q}_0$ is initial rate of production when $Q_0 = 0$ at $t = 0$.

Alternatively, $\bar{q}_t$, $\bar{q}_0$, and a may be interpreted as averages per well, in which case N wells, each producing at the rate of $\bar{q}$, yield:

$$\text{(4-2)} \qquad\qquad q_t = N\bar{q}_t = N\bar{q}_0 - NaQ_t$$

Since $q = dQ/dt$, this is a simple first order differential equation, the solution to which is

$$\text{(4-3)} \qquad\qquad Q_t = \frac{\bar{q}_0}{a} (1 - e^{-(Na)t})$$

or, calling the decline rate for the whole reservoir $A = Na$,

$$Q_t = \frac{N\bar{q}_0}{A} (1 - e^{-At}) \dagger$$

---

* The hyperbolic function can be fitted to a wider range of cases, but the exponential used here is sufficiently accurate to be useful. The exponential is a special case of the hyperbolic.

† A particular solution to this with $dQ/dt = 0$ is $Q_t = \bar{q}_0/a$. The solution to the homogeneous form, $dQ/dt + NaQ_t = 0$, is $Q_t = Ke^{-(Na)t}$. Adding these two solutions yields

$$Q_t = Ke^{-Nat} + \frac{\bar{q}_0}{a} = -\frac{\bar{q}_0}{a} e^{-(Na)t} + \frac{\bar{q}_0}{a} = \frac{\bar{q}_0}{a} (1 - e^{-(Na)t})$$

which satisfies equation (1-2). $K = -(q_0/a)$ since $Q = 0$ at $t = 0$.

In the hyperbolic function (see previous footnote), $(1/q)(dq/dt) = -Aq^\alpha$. Thus the exponential is a hyperbolic with $\alpha = 0$. See Bradley, op. cit., p. 51, for further discussion and references.

Thus

$$q = \frac{dQ}{dt} = N\bar{q}_0 e^{-Nat} = N\bar{q}_0 e^{-At}$$

giving a constant relative rate of decline in output of

$$\frac{1}{q}\frac{dq}{dt} = -Na = -A^*$$

Looking *backward*, reservoir managers have reached certain solutions to the problem of deciding how many wells to drill. For the simple view of the problem taken here, that is equivalent to deciding on the decline rate for the reservoir, given a.†

Given the historical decisions that were made, the assumption of a constant relative rate of decline permits the calculation of a historical constant per barrel development cost, c. By definition, these costs over the life of the reservoir will have a P.V., C_0, equal to investment, I, assumed to be made at $t = 0$:

(4-4)
$$I_0 = C_0 = \int_0^T cq_t e^{-rt}\, dt$$

$$= \int_0^T cN\bar{q}_0 e^{-At} e^{-rt}\, dt$$

$$= \int_0^T cN\bar{q}_0 e^{-(A+r)t}\, dt$$

$$= cN\bar{q}_0 \frac{[1 - e^{-(A+r)T}]}{A + r}$$

As T increases, unit development cost approaches

(4-5)
$$c = \frac{I_0(A + r)}{N\bar{q}_0}‡$$

How can $N\bar{q}_0$ be estimated in a practical context? The difficulty is that any

---

* Just differentiate $\ln q = \ln N\bar{q}_0 - Nat = \ln N\bar{q}_0 - At$ to get $d\ln q/dt = (1/q)/(dq/dt)$.

† The reader may wish to formulate and solve this problem, say, with constant price of crude, given cost of a well, c_w, and with constant operating cost per year. The last element implies that $pq_T = c_0$ where c_0 is operating cost per year. The problem is to find N and T to maximize P.V. of the opportunity.

‡ Adelman (*op. cit.*) calls the expression $N\bar{q}_0[(1 - e^{-(A+r)T})/A + r]$, which approaches $N\bar{q}_0[1/(A + r)]$ for large T, the "present barrel equivalent" of the flow of output and the expression in square brackets the P.B.E. factor. That is, if the quantity of crude $[(N\bar{q}_0) \times$ (P.B.E. factor)] could be produced in one big glob at $t = 0$, its cost, reckoned at c, would be equivalent to the P.V. of the costs of the actual stream of output with cost of c ascribed to each barrel.

observed increase in productive capacity over a given period is a *net* increase
made up of two components: the gross increase minus the new capacity necessary
to replace the decline in capacity from that existing at the beginning of the
period. This is portrayed in continuous terms in Figure 4-13. If the rate of

COMPOSITION OF GROSS INCREMENT TO PRODUCTIVE CAPACITY

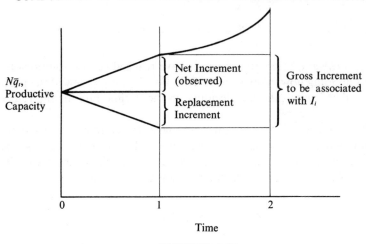

FIGURE 4-13

production at the beginning of the period and the applicable decline rate are
known, multiplication of these two quantities will yield replacement productive
capacity. This plus the net increase in productive capacity will yield the gross
increase, $N\bar{q}_0$, that is wanted but not observable. To complete the estimate of
c, all that is needed is the rate of discount and I, investment during the period
in question.

If decline rates are at all substantial, and they are for a good many areas, it is
clear that a considerable part of the gross development investment in any given
year takes place simply to replace capacity that is wasting away as a result of
production. Neglect of this factor would be a serious error.

So far the discussion has assumed that the progressive development of one
reservoir has been involved. This development will take place on both an intensive and extensive margin, of course, with the new information deriving from
past drilling and production operations playing a major role in guiding investment.

There is no need to confine the estimating procedure to a single reservoir.
Pooling of different reservoirs will yield an estimate of weighted average
development cost, however. If development investment is viewed over time,
allocation of investment among reservoirs will shift, with investment slowing
down where large enough cost increases are encountered in parts of the reservoir.

Adelman has used these concepts as a basis for estimating development costs
in various producing areas. The variation in cost among these areas is great.

In the United States, for example, crude production in 1960–63 was 10.18×10^9 barrels. The decline rate at full capacity was estimated at about 8 percent by the National Petroleum Council. But before multiplying production by this percentage to get capacity that had to be replaced, account must be taken of the fact that production was only at 65.1 percent of capacity, and the decline rate should be reduced. Thus:

Capacity to be replaced

$$= (.08 \times .651) \times (10.18 \times 10^9)$$

$$= .529 \times 10^9 \text{ barrels}$$

The *net* increment in producing capacity over 1960–63 was estimated by the National Petroleum Council to be $.367 \times 10^9$. Thus:

Capacity to be replaced	$.529 \times 10^9$ bbls.
+ Net increment in capacity	$.367 \times 10^9$ bbls.

$$\sum_{t='60}^{'63} N\bar{q}_{0_t} =$$ Gross increment in capacity, to be associated with development investment $.896 \times 10^9$ bbls.

In the work cited earlier, Adelman suggests that 9 percent is an appropriate discount rate for development investment in the United States.* The decline rate at capacity production was taken to be 8 percent.† Development investment for 1960–63 is estimated at 7.901×10^9. If life of the investment is taken to be 25 years, c, development cost per barrel, can be calculated according to equation (4-4), above.

$$c = \frac{\$7.901 \times 10^9}{.896 \times 10^9 \left[\dfrac{1 - e^{-(.157)25}}{.08 + .09} \right]}$$

$$= \$1.41 \text{ per barrel}\ddagger$$

---

* In a later letter of comment, he suggests that turbulence in capital markets subsequent to his writing would indicate a somewhat higher rate of discount.

† $A + r = .08 + .09 = .17$ is the nominal rate of effective discount. According to a frequently used convention, however, discounting of continuous flows is often done by using a continuously compounded rate (d_c) that gives the same growth as the nominal rate compounded annually (d_a):

$$e^{d_c t} = (1 + d_a)^t$$

or

$$d_c = 1n(1 + d_a)$$

In the present case,

$$1n(1 + .17) = .157$$

‡ For details of this and the other estimates to be discussed, see Adelman, *The World Petroleum Market, 1947–1969, op. cit.*

If a decline rate of 12.5 percent is used, the rate suggested by the Cabinet Task Force on Oil Import Control,* the cost per barrel declines to $1.30.

Similar estimates are possible for Venezuela. Using a decline rate of 16 percent and a discount rate of 20 percent, average development cost per barrel for 1966–68 was $.35,† but some fields were much cheaper. Average development cost for the Creole Petroleum Corp. is less than half the average for the country.‡

TABLE 4-1

DEVELOPMENT, OPERATING COSTS AND FREIGHT ADVANTAGE OVER PERSIAN GULF[a]

Area and data years	Cost per barrel			
	Develop-ment	Operating (including pipelines)	Develop-ment and operating	Freight advantage over Persian Gulf[b]
United States, 1960–63	$1.38	$0.17[c]	$1.55	
Venezuela, 1966–68	0.35	0.10	0.46	$0.42
Africa				
Libya, 1966–68	0.07	0.08	0.16	0.34
Algeria, 1966–68	0.18	0.10	0.28	0.37
Nigeria, 1965–66	0.09	0.07[c]	0.16	0.26
Persian Gulf				
Iran Consortium, 1963–69	0.05	0.05	0.10	
Iraq, 1966–68	0.02	0.05[c]	0.07	
Kuwait, 1966–68	0.06	0.04	0.10	
Saudi Arabia, 1966–68	0.04	0.05	0.09	

[a] From Adelman, *op cit.*, p. II-66. In a letter he points out that these estimates are based on Worldscale 40 (Worldscale is simply a way of characterizing the level of tanker rates) and represent the situation as of late 1969 and 1970. Tanker rates have gone up since then, say by 100 percent as of mid-1971. These will decline, but even a Worldscale 60 may be appropriate for some time.

[b] To Rotterdam, except for Venezuela, which is to United States. Persian Gulf crude assumed to move around Cape of Good Hope.

[c] Excludes pipelines.

* Cabinet Task Force on Oil Import Control, *The Oil Import Question: A Report on the Relationship of Oil Imports to National Security* (Washington: U.S. Government Printing Office, 1970), p. 223.

† Adelman, *op. cit.*, p. II-66.

‡ *Ibid.*, p. II-50.

Outside these two countries, Adelman used the expedient of assuming the decline rate to be equal to the ratio of production to reserves. This was about 1/75, which was rounded to 1 percent.

The resulting estimates of development cost, together with operating cost and freight advantage over Persian Gulf oil, will appear in Table 4-1. A discount rate of 20 percent was used for the African and Asian estimates, as it also was for Venezuela. Recall that finding cost, important for some areas, is not included in these estimates.

A part of the explanation for these large differences and their persistence is to be found in the earlier general discussion of minerals, but a full explanation requires a careful examination of the recent history and functioning of the petroleum industry, well provided by the study from which these estimates were drawn.

Petroleum and Efficiency in the United States

Crude petroleum production in the United States provides an excellent illustration of how inefficient governmental policies can produce, over the years, large-scale social costs.

The basic difficulty with petroleum production in the United States, but generally not in other countries, arises from the fact that the mineral rights to a single technological unit—a pool or a reservoir—are very often spread among different owners. Since petroleum can move underground across the property lines for mineral rights (petroleum is "fugacious"), absence of regulation permits the first producer(s) to extract not only the petroleum originally within their properties but also some or all of the neighbors', too. This is not a necessary result, for voluntary agreement on unified exploitation of the technological unit is possible, in principle, or the several properties could be united under one owner. In the years before 1930, however, agreements on unit operation were rare, if indeed there were any of consequence. The usual behavior was a rush to drill and produce as rapidly as possible.

As pointed out earlier, there is an optimum number of wells for a reservoir and an associated optimum production schedule which will maximize the P.V. of the opportunity. Fragmented ownership frequently resulted in too many wells and too rapid a rate of extraction, with a consequent increase in the cost of petroleum.

In the 1930s, a number of measures were adopted by the main producing states which had the effects of changing a rather chaotic situation into one of considerable order and also of subjecting the industry to a certain degree of price control. In spite of the great improvement, important sources of inefficiency remained, although their importance has diminished somewhat over the years because of improvements in the regulatory system.

The regulatory system is extremely complex and varies from state to state. The systems are similar, however, and two states, Texas and Louisiana, have dominated production for a long time. Consequently, the elements of the system can be described briefly in general terms.

First, many aspects of well drilling and oil production are subject to highly detailed regulation to prevent damage to other property owners or people These regulations cover such things as waste disposal, safety measures, protection of abandoned wells, and so on.

Over-drilling has been substantially reduced by the second type of regulation, limitation on well spacing. Minimum area per well has increased in the different states from, say, 20–40 acres around 1940 to 40–80 acres around 1962, and probably has risen substantially since then.*

Suppose you have a number of wells on a property drilled in conformity with spacing regulations. At what rate may you produce? In some states, the production rate is not regulated, but in the important producing states, production is subject to a "pro-rationing" system. Under it, each well is assigned an allowable rate of production. The general level of the allowables for different wells is somewhat arbitrary, but whatever level is chosen, the allowable for a particular well is associated with a *market demand factor* of 100 percent. That is, if the state regulatory authority determines that market conditions warrant production at a rate not to exceed 100 percent of the allowables, it will declare a market demand factor (MDF) of 100 percent for the period in question. A 50 percent MDF would mean that your production rate could not exceed 50 percent of the allowable for your well.

For many wells, the allowable will vary directly, but not necessarily proportionally, with spacing and depth. In some cases, as with unitized operations, a special allowable for the unit will be set.

As of 1945, twenty-one states had unitization laws that provide a procedure whereby property owners in a field can vote on whether they wish the field to be exploited as a unit or not.† If unitization is voted for by more than the percentage of mineral acres (i.e., owners weighted by mineral acres held) specified in the statute, usually somewhat more than 50 percent, all owners must participate. Unfortunately, Texas, California, and a few other less important producing states do not have unitization laws that are compulsory in this manner. Although a limited amount of regulation would still be desirable even if unitization were widespread, unitization is the answer to rational exploitation of petroleum deposits in the United States. Once the unit is established, no regulation of production rates, number of wells, and so on is necessary, for the effects of these and most other exploitation decisions are internalized.‡ McDonald estimates that in 1967, 24 percent of the U.S. crude was produced in unitization projects, which is different from unitized production.

Offshore oil is exploited in voluntary unit operations. Since the owners of the leases usually are oil companies, they perceive the advantages of unit operation with clarity.

---

* Cabinet Task Force on Oil Import Control, *The Oil Import Question, op. cit.*, pp. 243–44.
† McDonald, *op. cit.*, p. 217.
‡ For a definitive discussion, see Stephen McDonald, *op. cit.*

Stripper wells (in Texas, strippers are those pumping less than ten barrels per day) are exempt from production control, as are certain cases of secondary recovery and new discovery wells for a limited period.

Several sources of inefficiency exist in this regulatory system, although their cost has diminished over the years because of wider spacing, decreased discrimination against efficient wells in allowable schedules, and some increase in unitization. It is still true, however, that it is necessary to drill to get an allowable. Second, well spacing rules, although improved, still do not result in the well density that would be possible under unitization. Third, allowable schedules tend to favor inefficient wells. Fourth, production at a level that maintains a high price, say, as compared with world price, has resulted in production much below the optimum rates of low-cost wells while requiring no or only a small reduction in output of strippers and high-cost wells. In short, there are too many wells, and there is too much production from high-cost wells.

M. A. Adelman has estimated that in the early 1960s the unnecessary social costs associated with this set of policies, *given the output produced*, was $2.5 billion per year, a sizable sum equivalent to about $13 per capita.* The Cabinet Task Force on Oil Import Control believes that this cost has been reduced substantially in later years.

The quantitative significance of the above sources of inefficiency is increased the higher the price of crude, and price can be controlled by pro-rationing. In the absence of foreign competition, the combined result of inefficiency-producing policies plus pro-rationing with no restriction on capital entry tends to the result of competitive return on capital† but with excess capital investment.

Before World War II, foreign competition presented little obstacle to maintenance of price pro-rationing. Transport cost made it difficult for Middle Eastern crude to compete in the U.S. market, and Venezuelan production and exports did not develop, for whatever reason, to the point where it posed a threat to the U.S. price of crude.

The situation was different in the period after World War II. Tankers were bigger and more efficient, thus bringing Middle Eastern crude within easy reach of the U.S. market. The pressure of Middle Eastern crude was augmented by the development of many new sources of supply both there and in Africa which made "restraint" on exports to the United States more difficult. Venezuelan production grew and received special attention in the negotiation of a new reciprocal trade agreement (1952).

The steady growth of imports led to the formation of a Cabinet committee in 1954 to consider whether this development, which might have important effects on the U.S. crude industry—such as reducing the price of crude a great deal, with repercussions on coal and natural gas—constituted a threat to national

---

* M. A. Adelman, "Efficiency in Resource Use in Crude Petroleum," *Southern Economic Journal*, October 1964, p. 122.

† See Douglas Eldridge, *National Tax Journal*, Vol. XV, No. 2, June 1962, p. 209.

security.* The verdict was "yes," and a voluntary import control system was inaugurated, followed in 1959 by a compulsory system of import quotas limiting crude and product imports to about 12 percent of U.S. production.†

These quotas serve to insulate the United States from the world crude market, making it impossible for the U.S. consumer to purchase at world prices. How much is the consumer paying for this contribution, whatever it may be, to national security? What is this contribution costing the country as a whole in lost efficiency, that is, in foregone economic product?

The needed estimates could be made in various ways. For example, the present situation could be compared to one in which either or both import restrictions and the inefficiency-producing aspects of "conservation" regulations are eliminated. Data developed by the staff of the Cabinet Task Force on Oil Import Control permit a rough estimate of the cost of the present type of import controls in 1980. This estimate is based on the assumption that the sources of inefficiency in conservation regulation have pretty well been eliminated and that there has been full long-run adaptation to each of the situations compared. The situations are quotas yielding the present price per barrel of $3.30 and no quotas.

The situations are portrayed schematically in Figure 4-14.

Consumption in 1980 (crude plus residual fuel oil) is estimated to be 6.79×10^9 barrels at $3.30. With imports restricted sufficiently to maintain this price, U.S. production is estimated to be 4.93×10^9 barrels.‡

The Cabinet Task Force staff estimated that abolition of import restrictions would result in a weighted average saving in costs (weights are regional consumption) of $1.17 per barrel, or a nominal price of $2.13 per barrel without full adaptation of transport facilities to a greater volume of imports. The associated U.S. production estimate for 1980 is 3.47×10^9 barrels. If transport were fully adapted, however, about $.25 more would be saved per barrel.§

Now we are in a position to calculate the needed quantities. With respect to the $2.13 level, consumers are paying $6.79 \times 10^9 \times \$1.17 = \$7.94 \times 10^9$

---

* As is usual in cases like this, the mandate of the committee was a good deal broader, but the main focus of the committee's work was as described here, as is evident from its report, which is reproduced in Cabinet Task Force on Oil Import Control, *The Oil Import Question*, *op. cit.*, p. 163.

† There is a separate limitation on product imports which are "carved out" of the 12 percent quantity to determine the crude quota. These Presidential actions were possible because of "national security" provisions in the various trade agreement acts. For details of this astonishingly complex system, see *The Oil Import Question*, *op. cit.*, p. 163.

‡ This is an average of careful estimates of crude production submitted by various oil companies and the U.S. Department of the Interior with 1.6×10^6 barrels per day added for natural gas liquids. The estimates for the crude were rather closely grouped around an average of 11.9×10^6 barrels per day. The coefficient of variation was only 5.5 percent. See *ibid.*, p. 41 and Appendix D. Since production (6.79 in the figure) includes natural gas liquids, and since imports plus production equals consumption in *ibid.*, table on p. 41, it appears that U.S. consumption is defined to include natural gas liquids, too.

These estimates appear to be—and the one cited later for a price of $2.13 definitely is—based on a decline rate of $12\frac{1}{2}$ percent.

§ *Ibid.*, p. 262.

CRUDE PETROLEUM DEMAND AND SUPPLY, 1980

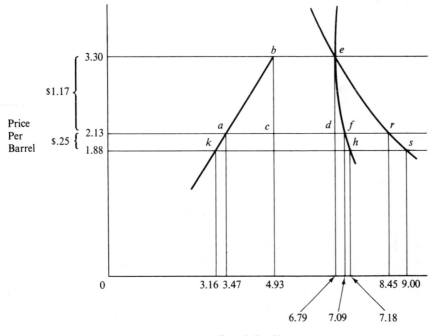

Barrels Per Year

FIGURE 4-14

more than the cost of the same quantity with no restrictions on imports. However, a portion of the saving on imports (quantity of imports is 1.86 = 6.79 − 4.93) goes to consumers in the form of lower prices. For example, residual fuel oil reaches the eastern states without restriction. If we follow the Cabinet Task Force staff estimate that 50 percent of these savings go to consumers,* the total consumer payment of $7.94 × 10^9 should be reduced by

$$.50 \times \$1.17 \times (6.79 - 4.93)10^9 = \$1.09 \times 10^9$$

The total extra consumer payment is thus $6.85 × 10^9.

Most of this is made up of transfers which do not use up productive services. That is, the ultimate consumers of crude are paying large sums to owners of mineral rights, state governments (royalties, taxes), and companies that have been given the privilege of importing oil bought at the low world price. These payments would be reduced if price were lower.

---

* *Ibid.*, p. 261. Cabinet Task Force staff calculations were based on per barrel savings weighted by present regional imports. We have simply assumed that regional imports would be distributed in the same way as production, thus leaving $1.17 as the appropriate weighted average.

If the same quantity, 6.79, were consumed, the real costs of import quotas to society as a whole would be represented by the triangle *abc*, which is

$$1/2 \times 1.17 \times \overbrace{(4.93 - 3.47)}^{1.46} = \$.85 \times 10^9$$

This assumes that the two points representing U.S. production at \$3.30 and \$2.13 are on a linear supply curve, every point of which is defined as are these two: They represent the quantity that could be produced in 1980 at the price specified. Thus transfer payments by consumers on the quantity actually consumed are $(\$6.85 - \$.85)10^9 = \$6.00 \times 10^9$.

If import restrictions were removed, consumers would gain by a redistribution of their budgets in favor of products "containing" crude and a substitution in industry processes of inputs containing crude for other inputs. This gain is represented by the triangle *def* if the elasticity of demand is $\eta = -.1$,* as suggested by Standard Oil (New Jersey), and we use the constant elasticity demand function $q = ap^\eta$ with *a* determined by price and quantity at *e*. In this case, *def* is only $\$.17 \times 10^9$. If η were $-.5$, the gain would be $\$.88 \times 10^9$, the area of *der*.

The total efficiency loss with respect to the \$2.13 level for effective cost of imports is the area of *abc* plus *def* or *der*:

$$(.85 + .17)10^9 = \$1.02 \times 10^9$$
or
$$(.85 + .88)10^9 = \$1.73 \times 10^9$$

Note that the sum of the two triangles in each case is the difference between the consumer plus producer surpluses in the two situations. That is, efficiency calculations assume, in effect, that we are all operating out of the same pocketbook, which, as was argued earlier, is not so silly as it may appear to be. Where the transfers are large, however, we certainly are interested in them as such.

If the calculation is made with allowance for full adjustment of transport facilities, the area of the trapezoid, *kafh*, or *kars*, must be added to the above numbers:

	$\eta = -.1$	$\eta = -.5$
Estimate of inefficiency cost for \$2.13 level	$\$1.02 \times 10^9$	$\$1.73 \times 10^9$
+ Trapezoid area	.96	1.34
= Estimate for \$1.88 level	$\$1.98 \times 10^9$	$\$3.07 \times 10^9$

These estimates are for 1980 and do not represent a constant annual cost of inefficiency. The supply estimates are based on the assumption of continued

---

* *Ibid.*, p. 38. Can this represent an estimate of truly long-run elasticity?

constant prices, but since the physical situation evolves, supply does not necessarily remain constant even with no change in price. Especially in the case of no restriction on imports, U.S. production would still be falling in 1980. Thus, a complete estimate of the cost of import restrictions would require a series of estimates for each year of the future. The P.V. of these would represent the total cost. This could then be converted to a per year basis.

Perhaps a very rough idea of a calculation for 1968 based on the same specifications is indicated by the ratio of consumption in the two years:

$$\text{1968 estimate for } \$1.88 \text{ level} = \frac{13.1}{18.6}^* \times \$1.98 \times 10^9 = \$1.4 \times 10^9 \quad (\eta = -.1)$$

$$\frac{13.1}{18.6} \times \$3.07 \times 10^9 = \$2.2 \times 10^9 \quad (\eta = -.5)$$

Whether the associated national security gain is worth the real costs and strains associated with the large transfers involved is not considered here. The Cabinet Task Force Report considers this problem in some detail.†

Petroleum and Federal Income Taxation

One important factor that has been assumed to remain unchanged in the two situations compared is the preferential tax treatment accorded investment in petroleum by the federal corporate and individual income tax laws. If there are no restrictions on investment in petroleum, equalization of the return to investment in petroleum with that in other industries can take place only by the influx of additional capital into petroleum and a lowering of price—all other pertinent factors (e.g., pro-rationing, allowable schedules, import restrictions) affecting return being held constant in whatever sense is relevant. A simple analysis of this situation has been provided by Arnold Harberger.‡

Capital Gains

First, consider the *hypothetical* possibilities open to a corporation that explores and then sells the deposits it finds, with a tax being imposed on the long-term capital gain. Costs are deducted from receipts from sale of the property to

---

* *Ibid.*, p. 41. Barrels × 10^6 per day.

† The Secretaries of the Interior and Commerce and the Chairman of the Federal Power Commission made a separate report disagreeing with much of the Cabinet Task Force Report (see p. 343). The dissent is a valuable supplemental dividend for the student because of the vigorous exercise it can provide for his logical and critical faculties.

‡ Joint Committee on the Economic Report, *Federal Tax Policy for Economic Growth and Stability*, 84th Congress, 1st sess. (Washington: U.S. Government Printing Office, 1955), p. 439. For an emendation of Harberger's analysis, see U.S. House of Representatives, Committee on Ways and Means, *Tax Revision Compendium*, Vol. 2, Peter O. Steiner, "Percentage Depletion and Resource Allocation" (Washington: U.S. Government Printing Office, 1959), p. 949.

compute the capital gain. We shall see in a moment why this case doesn't correspond closely to the true options that are open. The present situation still is approximately the same as it was when Harberger wrote, that is, the corporate income tax rate is about 50 percent and the effective tax rate on the capital gain is roughly 25 percent.

If the rate of return after tax on investment in other industries is 10 percent and competition brings the return in mineral exploration after tax to this level, the capital gains privilege results in investment in mineral exploration being carried to the point where its rate of return *before* tax is much lower than in other industries. In other industries, an investment of K will have to yield 20 percent before tax to give 10 percent after tax. In mineral exploration, however, an investment of the same sum, K, would have to yield only $13\frac{1}{3}$ percent before tax in mineral exploration to leave 10 percent after tax if the effective tax rate on the gain is 25 percent:

$$13\tfrac{1}{3}\% \ K(1 \ - \ .25) \ = \ \tfrac{40}{3}\% \ K(\tfrac{3}{4}) \ = \ 10\%K$$

Expensing plus Capital Gains

The actual possibilities result in an even greater encouragement of investment in exploration because most of the outlays on exploration may be expensed (that is, deducted against gross income) in one way or another.*

In other fields, investment will be carried to the point where K invested yields a capital good whose subsequent net revenue stream has a P.V. of K after tax, discounting at market rate of return on investment.

In contrast, if a mineral deposit worth K is "produced" instead of the capital good above, as much as $1.5K$ could be spent producing it while still reaping a competitive return on investment. If the $1.5K$ can be expensed against other income, there is a tax saving of $.50 \ (1.5K) = $.75K$. Capital gain must now be computed as ($K - 0$), on which the effective tax is $.25K$. The whole transaction results in a competitive return even though $1.5K$ was spent to produce an asset whose future revenue stream, reflecting the worth of the asset to society, has a P.V. of only K:

Outlay to produce deposit (including competitive return on investment)	$1.50K$
Tax on capital gain	.25K
Total outlay	$1.75K$
Receipt from sale of deposit	$1.00K$
Tax saving from expensing of $1.5K	.75K
Gross gain	$1.75K$

---

* See the Internal Revenue Code or any good tax service for details.

Percentage Depletion plus Expensing plus Capital Gains

Now suppose the privilege of expensing capital outlays is combined with the privilege of taking percentage depletion. Here we must pause to explain this device.

If income tax accounting for mineral deposits were handled in the same way as for other capital assets, the owner would be permitted to deduct as a current expense of production the annual depletion that the property suffered as a result of exploitation. The deduction probably would be related to production, but the total of such deductions taken over the life of the property could not exceed the amount paid for the property.

Under the present law, depletion may indeed be taken in this manner, but usually the owner of a mineral property will find it advantageous to take percentage depletion calculated as the *lesser* of (1) a statutorily stipulated percentage rate (as of 1971, 22 percent for petroleum) times gross sales from the output of the property or (2) 50 percent of the property's net income.

With this in mind, let us compare an ordinary capital asset, say a machine, with an assumed life equal to that of a petroleum property. If the corporate income tax rate is 50 percent, Y the P.V. of the income stream from the machine, and R its cost, the tax will be $.5(Y - dR)$; d is a discount factor such that dR is the present value of the stream of depreciation charges.

Under competition, production of the machine will be carried to the point where cost equals price, or

$$C = R = Y - \text{tax} = Y - .5(Y - dR) = \frac{.5Y}{1 - .5d}$$

In contrast, the owner of the mineral deposit will pay a tax of $.5Y(1 - p)$, where p is the ratio of the percentage depletion to *net* income and is not to be confused with the statutory rate applicable to gross income.

Thus, the P.V. of the deposit will be $R = Y - .5Y(1 - p) = .5Y(1 + p)$. To acquire this deposit with P.V. of R, an investor would be willing to spend the sum of C minus tax saving on the exploration expenditure,

or
$$C - .5C = R = .5Y(1 + p)$$

or
$$C = Y(1 + p)$$

Thus for the mineral deposit, the ratio of cost (to the economy), C_{MD} of the income stream Y, is

$$\frac{C_{MD}}{Y} = (1 + p)$$

whereas for an ordinary asset of the same life the same ratio is

$$\frac{C_{OA}}{Y} = \frac{.5}{1 - .5d} \quad *$$

$$\frac{C_{MD}}{C_{OA}} = (1 + p) \frac{(1 - .5d)}{.5} = (1 + p)(2 - d)$$

In 1960, p for oil and gas was 48 percent.† If, following Harberger, we take d as about .65, then at the margin we should expect that an investment in petroleum of $\$(1 + p) = \$1.48$ would be required to produce an income stream with a P.V. of $Y = \$1$ *before tax*, whereas in investment in general, only $[.5/(1 - .5d)] = \$.74$ is required. The ratio of the two costs is

$$\frac{1.48}{.74} = 2.00 = (1 + p)(2 - d)$$

as before.

4.9　STOCK GROWTH DEPENDENT ON SIZE

We have already considered two special cases of the general problem involving dependence of the natural rate of growth of the stock of an asset on the rate of exploitation. The minerals case just considered is a limiting case with natural growth rate of zero.‡ The tree case was cast initially in a simple manner known as "point input, point output" and then extended to continuous series of "point input, point output" cases. Here the problem was to choose the optimum time for harvest, which amounted to choosing the optimum rate of growth at harvest. Now we consider the general case in which a population of something (e.g., fish, trees, etc.) grows naturally in a given environment at a rate dependent only on the size of the population. The degree of abstraction involved here is extreme, for no such situation ever existed in nature although it has been represented in laboratory experiments. However, the simple function has been considered to be useful in application. More important, the approach to analysis of the simple situation can easily be extended, in principle, to match whatever degree of more sophisticated understanding of an actual situation is needed.

For our purpose we do not need to specify this simple function in any detail. The general idea is that a given type of bio-mass—fish in a fishery, trees in a forest, plants in a field, fruit flies in a certain environment, etc.—will grow at an absolute rate that depends on the density of the bio-mass in its environment.

---

* Derived from the first equation in this section, above.

† U.S. House of Representatives, Committee on Ways and Means, Hearings, *President's 1963 Tax Message*, Part I (rev. March 27, 1963), p. 298. The 1946–47 p, used by Harberger, was about 45 percent.

‡ Obviously this is not quite the case, but it is very nearly so. We don't yet plan economic activities over geologic eras.

Or, if we think of a bio-mass circumscribed in space, we may say that the absolute rate of growth depends on the size of the bio-mass. More concretely, growth may be thought of as the result of births, deaths, and average size of individuals in the mass. When the mass is small, each unit has great opportunity to extract nourishment from the environment, but the absolute growth is small because of the small mass. As the mass grows larger, the units begin to "compete" with each other. Relative growth may slow down, but absolute growth will increase to a point after which both rates of growth will decline until the maximum mass is reached and the now stable bio-mass is in equilibrium with its environment.

This relation may be expressed in various ways. First, the size of the bio-mass may be expressed as a function of time (Figure 4-15).

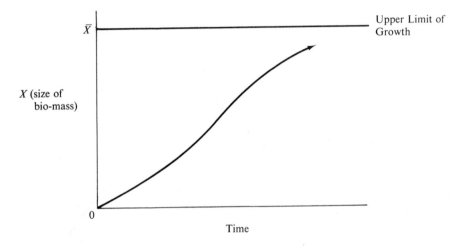

FIGURE 4-15

In some cases, a critical level of population is reached below which growth will be negative until population is zero. In this case the function intersects the abscissa at a positive level, say, X_E (E for extinction) (Figure 4-16).

The absolute rate of growth, $\dot{X} = dX/dt$, may be expressed as a function of X, say $F(X)$. It will have a maximum bounded by two zero values at maximum population, $\bar{X}$, and extinction level, X_E (Figure 4-17).

The relative rate of growth, $\dot{X}/X = (1/X)(dX/dt)$, on the usual view, will decline from the population level of $0a_1$ (Figure 4-17), reaching zero at population $\bar{X}$. The slope of $F(X)$, which is $d\dot{X}/dX$, is also shown in the figure.

These ideas have been expressed in a particular function sometimes called the Verhulst–Pearl logistic. The function has been used in a great deal of empirical work in various fields of biology and has even been applied (with dubious success) to mineral exploitation.

The function can be most simply described by saying that the relative rate of increase between X_E and $\bar{X}$ is a constant times the difference between maximum and actual population.

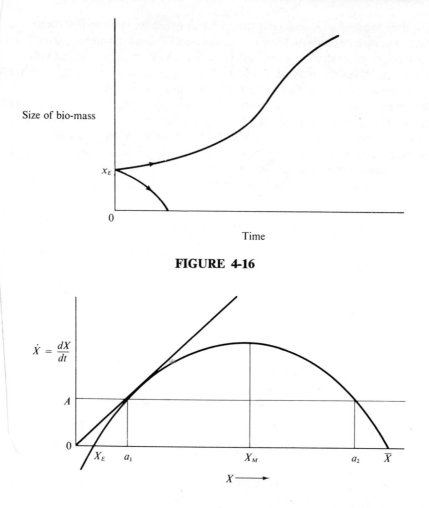

FIGURE 4-16

FIGURE 4-17

$$\frac{1}{X}\frac{dX}{dt} = \frac{\dot{X}}{X} = a(\overline{X} - X)$$

or even more conveniently

$$\frac{\dot{X}}{X} = r\left[1 - \frac{X}{\overline{X}}\right]$$

where $r = a\overline{X}$. Up to the maximum population, the relative rate of growth is simply r times the fraction of maximum population remaining to be filled.

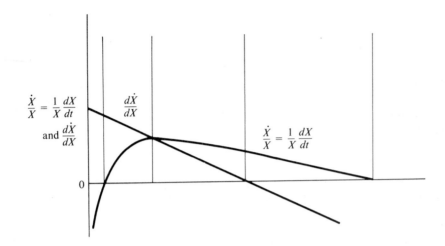

$$\dot{X} = \frac{1}{X}\frac{dX}{dt}$$

and $\dfrac{d\dot{X}}{dX}$

$\dfrac{d\dot{X}}{dX}$

$\dfrac{\dot{X}}{X} = \dfrac{1}{X}\dfrac{dX}{dt}$

0

FIGURE 4-18

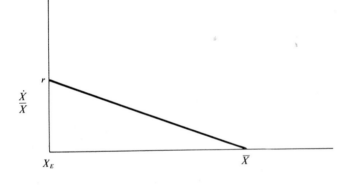

$\dfrac{\dot{X}}{X}$

r

X_E $\overline{X}$

FIGURE 4-19

The solution to this differential equation is

$$X_t = \frac{\overline{X}}{1 - [1 - (\overline{X}/X_0)]e^{-rt}}$$

(where X_0 is population at $t = 0$ with $X_0 \geq X_E$), the correctness of which can easily be verified by differentiation. $\dot{X} = F(X)$ will then be a parabola, $[rX - (r/\overline{X})X^2]$.*

---

* The logistic function has been applied to fisheries in, for example, Milner B. Schaefer, *Some Aspects of the Dynamics of Populations Important to the Management of the Commercial Marine Fisheries*, Bulletin, Vol. 1, No. 2, Inter-American Tropical Tuna Commission, La Jolla, California, 1954; and Michael Graham, editor, *Sea Fisheries: Their Investigation in the United Kingdom*, Chapter IX, "The Theory of Fishing," by R. J. H. Beverton and S. J. Holt (London: 1956).

The subsequent analysis will use the general growth function with single maximum $\dot{X}$.

A Simple View of Competitive Fishing

Suppose a new fishery is discovered and that it is open to competitive fishing without any payment required. What will happen? Will the fishery be exploited so intensively that it will be exhausted or will there be a stable equilibrium reached before that point?

The growth function, $\dot{X} = F(X)$, just discussed, has an essential role in these questions. Let us assume that this function has a positive extinction point, as in Figure 4-17. Assume also that the production function for fish caught has two inputs, the services of the stock of fish, measured by X, the size of the stock, and the services of capital, K, and that it is a constant returns Cobb–Douglas function. If the price of capital services is constant, these assumptions permit the derivation of a function giving average cost of capital services per fish caught as a function of catch, *given that catch is to be equal to the natural rate of growth of the stock*. The general form of the function will be as shown in Figure 4-20. It will have an upper and a lower branch divided by the maximum possible

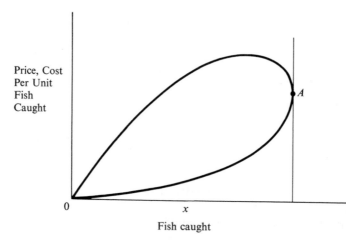

FIGURE 4-20

steady state catch, X_M, associated with point A, and by zero catch. That is, a given catch equal to $\dot{X}$ may be caught on either the right or left side of $\dot{X} = F(X)$. The maximum average cost per fish will be for a catch on the left side at that rate of growth and stock for which $\dot{X}/X$ is a maximum (see Figure 4-17).* Note that the catch rates for which average costs are equal may both be on the left side of the growth function, $F(X)$.

Now let us add a demand curve to Figure 4-20 (see Figure 4-20a). Next, what

---

* If the extinction point is zero, the steady state average cost function is different. The upper branch approaches infinity as catch and stock both approach zero.

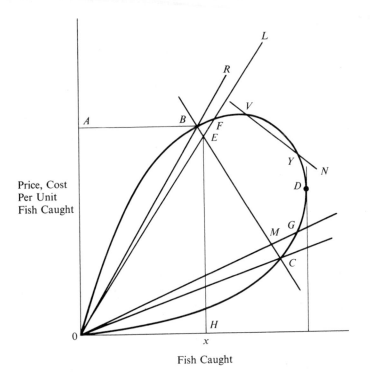

Price, Cost
Per Unit
Fish Caught

Fish Caught

FIGURE 4-20a

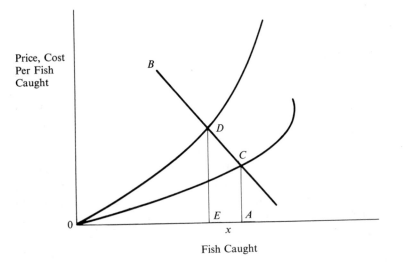

Price, Cost
Per Fish
Caught

Fish Caught

FIGURE 4-21

would be the long-run supply curve(s) for a competitive fishing industry? Suppose that the competitive price for fish is at OA. Point B surely must be on the competitive supply curve, for here average cost is equal to price. But what does a competitive supply curve mean in this case? One possibility, which is adopted here, is that entrants into this industry assume that the stock, X, associated with point B will continue at the same level regardless of the rate at which fishing takes place. On this assumption and those made earlier, we can trace out a supply curve, OBR, which passes through point B and which assumes no change in stock. Note that the closed curve already drawn involves a decrease in stock as we move to the left of B on the curve. In contrast, the competitive supply curve *assumes* (by hypothesis) no reduction in stock and hence requires that cost be lower for outputs to the left of B than for the closed curve.* Similarly, reduction in catch from point C on the closed curve involves an *increase* in stock, X, hence a lower cost than for the competitive supply curve going through C, which is based on an assumption of the same stock at all points as at point C. Thus if stock X_1 is associated with point B, the competitive industry, acting on the assumption that this stock is independent of the rate of fishing, will behave as if OBR is the long-run supply curve. The argument is similar for any other point on the closed curve, each of which has a competitive supply curve passing through it.

The next task is to locate stable equilibria, if any. Such a point requires that there be zero profits, that catch be equal to the natural rate of growth, *and* that a slight displacement from that point will set up forces that will result in a return to that point. There are two candidates, points B and C. At each of these points catch is equal to natural rate of growth and costs are equal to revenues (no profit). But will a small displacement from either of these points result in a return to it or in a still larger displacement?

Assume that the actual stock is that associated with point F and that the demand curve is BC. We know that size of stock increases as we move on the closed curve from the origin to B, to D, to C, and to the maximum stock as the origin is approached again. Therefore, if the competitive industry acts on the assumption that the stock associated with F will be unaffected by the rate of fishing, the rate of fishing, OH, indicated by its supply curve (OEL) will be *less* than that compatible with no change in stock. Therefore, stock increases and the new supply curve for the competitive industry is one going through a point on the closed curve to the right of F. Thus an initial displacement from B to F is followed by a still larger displacement. An analogous argument can be made for a displacement to the left of B; B is, therefore, a point of unstable equilibrium.

Now consider a displacement from point C. Suppose the actual stock is that associated with point G. The competitive supply curve results in a catch associated with point M, but since this is smaller than the catch that would permit stock to remain the same, stock increases and the competitive supply curve

---

* In fact, if the exponents in the Cobb–Douglas are .5, the competitive function will be a straight line ray from the origin.

moves down toward point C. That is, point C is a point of stable equilibrium with all three conditions met—zero profits, catch equal to natural growth, and return from displacement.

A competitive equilibrium on the left branch of $F(X)$ is possible. Suppose the demand curve is VN. Point Y then is a point of stable equilibrium. Point V, like point B, is unstable with a displacement from it resulting either in continuous decline of the stock to extinction or movement to the stable point Y.

If a stable equilibrium is reached, it clearly is inefficient since production decisions are based on the correct view that no price is charged for the services of the fishery but on the incorrect implication that the services of the fishery are not subject to diminishing returns.

How things might actually work out in reality depends on the size of the error that may be made in investment, on the rapidity with which capital enters and leaves the industry, and the size of stock in relation to catch. Suppose that there is great over-investment as compared with a stable long-run position. It is quite possible that stock would be so greatly reduced as to end up at a level associated with points to the left of the unstable point at the time when the capital wears out, leading to extinction of the fishery. Thus a diagram of this sort can serve only to indicate the general nature of the possibilities.

Steady-State Solution

It is not possible to discuss the full-blown problem of the optimum path of catch over time with simple graphics, but insight into a part of the economics involved can be had if the discussion is restricted to the steady state case in which catch—whatever it is—is required to be equal to natural growth. What would be the optimum rate of exploitation of the fishery if the manager were free to choose any steady state output?

The closed average cost curve of Figure 4-20 provides the essential tool for answering this question. Of course, the single manager of the fishery will be interested in only the lower branch of this curve, which is reproduced in Figure 4-21. If the demand curve is BC, he will not choose catch OA but rather that output for which marginal cost of fish is equal to price. Curve OD is marginal to OC. The output chosen is OE, as indicated by the intersection at D

A mathematical representation of this case—unitary operation of the fishery, freedom to choose any output and population but with a requirement that the solution be steady state—is easily possible. Admittedly, the case is unreal.*

The production function gives catch as a function of fish population and capital services, $x = G(X,K)$. It is assumed to be linearly homogeneous with the usual properties.

---

* What follows is an adaptation of a more complete model formulated by Gardner Brown of the University of Washington in an unpublished paper, "An Optimal Program for Managing Common Property Resources with Congestion Externalities." His more complete model will be presented later.

The relative rate of growth of fish population is assumed to have one maximum not at $X = 0$

$$\frac{\dot{X}}{X} = f(X), \quad f' \gtreqless 0, \quad f'' < 0$$

(contrary to a logistic function with $X_E = 0$. However, the analysis would apply without change to the more restricted logistic function.) $\dot{X} = Xf(X) = F(X)$. For completeness, we may think of $F(X)$ as having a solution $X = P(t)$.

Without fishing,

$$\dot{X} = Xf(X) = F(X)$$

but with fishing

$$\dot{X} = F(X) - x = F(X) - G$$

Since we are concerned, by assumption, with a steady state solution, it suffices to consider the optimum way to handle a single period since all others will be like it. Thus we seek to maximize $(PG - wK)$ subject to $\dot{X} = F(X) - G = 0$. P = constant price of product and w is the price of one unit of capital service.

As in preceding problems, a Lagrangian expression is appropriate, with the maximand being $Z = (PG - wK) + \lambda[F - G]$.

$$\frac{\partial Z}{\partial K} = PG_K - w - \lambda G_K = 0$$

$$\frac{\partial Z}{\partial X} = PG_X + \lambda[F' - G_X] = 0$$

and

$$\frac{\partial Z}{\partial \lambda} = F - G = 0$$

$$\lambda = P - \frac{w}{G_K} = \frac{PG_X}{-(F' - G_X)} = \frac{PG_X}{-(\partial \dot{X}/\partial X)}$$

We may interpret λ as the implicit price of a fish (assumed to be one unit) in stock and at the optimum value at the market price of a caught fish, P, minus the cost of catching it, w/G_K. That is, one more unit of capital service will cost $\$w$ and will increase catch by G_K, giving a marginal cost of w/G_K.

Suppose the stock is reduced by one unit and sold with net gain of $[P - (w/G_K)]$. What is sacrificed? This is indicated by the right side of the equation, but its interpretation may not be obvious. PG_X is the annual value of the marginal product of a unit of stock, but it would have been earned in this and in all subsequent periods. What is needed is to convert the right side to a present value of this flow of sacrificed product. The denominator may be thought of as equivalent to a rate of discount applied to the continued flow of value, PG_X.

To see that this is the case, consider $F' = d\dot{X}/dX$. Assuming no fishing for the moment, $\dot{X}$ is the annual natural flow of product of stock X, and $d\dot{X}/dX$ indicates the effect of a unit change in X on this flow. This derivative can be viewed as analogous to a rate of interest showing the productive power of the stock to increase the flow of product per unit time in relative terms:

$$F' = \frac{d\dot{X}}{dX} = \frac{d(dX/dt)}{dX} = \frac{d(dX/dt)}{dt} \cdot \frac{dt}{dX} = \frac{1}{\dot{X}}\frac{d\dot{X}}{dt}$$

The same line of thought is applicable to the whole denominator. The "rate of interest" must take account not only of the effect of a unit increase in X on natural growth $(-F')$ but also on the catch through the terms (G_X). If λ and G_X are positive, then any point on the right branch of $F(X)$ is possible so far as the requirement of positive λ is concerned, since F_X is negative. This requirement can also be met on the left branch if G_X is greater than $F'(X)$. However, unified administration of the fishery would always choose the right branch since any feasible output can be produced more cheaply on it than on the left since X is an input into the production function. This places output in the area of diminishing marginal returns of $P(t)$, shown in the top panel of Figure 4-22, which also shows schematically the relations among some of the other variables in this problem.

The dual production role of the stock of fish—the natural rate of growth of the stock depends on the size of the stock and the stock contributes a productive service to the catch activity—is clearly indicated by the expression for

$$\frac{\partial Z}{\partial X} = 0 = (P - \lambda)G_X + \lambda F'$$

The productivity of the stock in catching is valued, not at P, as would be the case with a piece of land used to produce wheat, but at $(P - \lambda)$, with the subtraction of λ indicating that a unit of caught fish had a value in bringing about growth of the stock of fish. In the static case, the stock is adjusted so that its marginal value productivity in catching fish is just balanced by value of the effect of stock on natural growth. The favorable effect on production of a unit increase in stock must be exactly offset by the unfavorable effect on natural increase; F' must be negative.*

Suppose now that there is a search for the proper value of λ. As stock decreases from $\bar{X}$, the ratio of X to catch decreases (see lowest panel of Figure 4-22). The only way to produce a larger catch is to increase the ratio of capital to catch, which implies that the ratio of capital to fish stock is increasing. Thus

---

* In the dynamic case, to be discussed later, these two terms sum to $r\lambda$ when a steady state is finally reached instead of to zero as above.

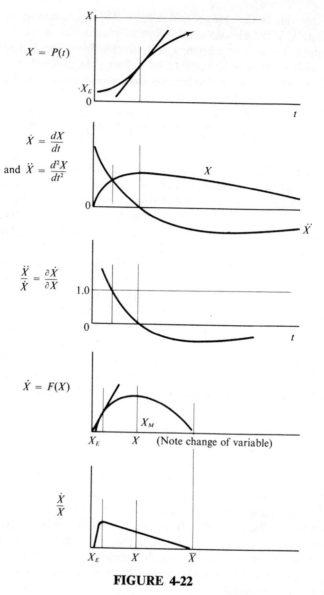

$$X = P(t)$$

$$\dot{X} = \frac{dX}{dt}$$

and $\ddot{X} = \frac{d^2X}{dt^2}$

$$\frac{\ddot{X}}{\dot{X}} = \frac{\partial \dot{X}}{\partial X}$$

$$\dot{X} = F(X)$$

$$\frac{\dot{X}}{X}$$

FIGURE 4-22

the marginal product of the stock, G_X, is increasing as X decreases, given the associated changes in capital. Thus $PG_X/[-(F' - G_X)]$ (from λ on page 162) increases as X decreases.* On the other hand $[P - (w/G_K)]$ decreases as X

---

* Differentiating λ with respect to X, we get

$$\frac{\partial \lambda}{\partial X} = \frac{P(F''G_X - F'G_{XX})}{[-(F' - G)]^2}$$

which is negative on the right branch of $F(X)$.

decreases.* Thus the two expressions for λ will come to equality at some point on the right branch if production is feasible.

How is it that the rate of interest does not appear in the solution of this static problem? If the perpetual flows are capitalized at r, it will be seen that r disappears in the maximizing expressions. The economic explanation lies in the odd nature of the static problem. We have said, in effect, that we will ignore all costs associated with getting to the position that will be maintained for all time. Obviously this is the position that maximizes annual net return to the resource, considering only cost of capital services. This position will yield the maximum P.V. of the perpetual flow of net returns no matter what the rate of interest is.

In the far more realistic case in which one cannot flout nature by jumping to any steady state position that may be desired and in which trees must be planted and grown to attain the steady state position or in which fish must be caught or allowed to increase, the rate of discount does have an essential role.†

The discussion so far has taken place from the point of view of a single manager of the fishery. Now suppose that manager is a government that wishes to induce competitive fishing firms to act so as to secure the benefits of unified management. Would a tax of λ suffice to induce the right output?‡ The answer is no, for the single firm will not take account of the effects of its efforts on the catch of other firms. From the social point of view, it is desirable that output be adjusted so that $(P - \lambda)G_K = w$ (see page 162). Each of the competitive firms, however, will take the average product per unit capital of the whole fishery as a constant, that is, that his additional capital will be able to reap this return. He will thus invest so that $(P - \lambda)(G/K) = w$. To restrict the volume of investment which would otherwise dissipate the rent on the fishery resource remaining after a tax of λ per unit of output, an additional tax on capital will have to be imposed that reflects the difference between average and marginal productivity of capital in the whole fishery. After this tax has been imposed, he will invest so that $(P - \lambda)(G/K) = w + t$. Substituting this in $(P - \lambda)G_K = w$, we have $t = (P - \lambda)[(G/K) - G_K]$.

---

* $\dfrac{\partial \lambda}{\partial X} = \dfrac{wG_{KX}}{(G_K)^2}$, which is positive.

† If there *is* a viable steady state solution, we have just said that the rate of interest has no essential role in determining the optimum state. However, the rate of interest must be taken into account in deciding whether a steady state solution other than $\dot{X} = 0$ is to be chosen. Its precise role cannot be indicated without specifying what non-steady state options are to be regarded as admissible. For example, if we admit the possibility of choosing any X_0 and immediately consuming all of it, then the condition for choosing a steady state solution rather than immediate consumption would be

$$\frac{\lambda x}{r} > (PX^* - wK^*)$$

where X^* is the immediately consumed stock yielding the largest surplus over cost of catching it and K^* is the volume of capital services required to catch it. All of this is unrealistic.

‡ Recall the assumption that $G(X,K)$ is linearly homogeneous. Thus we abstract from the problem of economies of scale to size of firm.

Non-Steady State Solution

A more realistic view of the problem must deal with optimizing the evolution of the system over time in contrast to the static formulation which, after the initial unrestricted choice, requires constancy in all variables over time. Whenever an action affecting the fishery is contemplated, any action taken at t_0 finds a certain stock in existence. If full management is contemplated, the problem is how to go from period to period so as to maximize the net returns to society or to the owner—in short, to find the optimum set of time paths for the variables of the problem.

Solution of this type of problem requires the use of one of the techniques for dealing with dynamic problems, the calculus of variations, optimal control, or dynamic programming, but it still is possible to make sense of the problem and its solutions in words. Retaining the simplifying features of the static problem— viz., a single maximum $F(X)$ and freedom to buy any quantity of capital services each period (i.e., no restrictions on capital entry or exit)—the essential characteristic of the dynamic case is that the actions taken in each of the periods are mutually dependent. The time dependent elements in the problem are in the growth of the stock, X, and the rate of discount. These must be properly balanced against the force of diminishing returns in production. The rate of discount is tending to encourage earlier consumption and to push outlays for capital services toward later dates. The value of the stock as a productive asset (i.e., as an aid in catching fish) must be balanced against its value if consumed. And proper account must be taken of the "natural productivity" of the stock, that is, that the natural time rate of increase in the stock is related to the size of the stock.

The solution possibilities are, of course, far richer in the dynamic than in the static case. If the initial position is at a small X_0, it may pay not to consume at all until the stock has increased to the point where the absolute time rate of growth is higher. If the initial stock is large (imagine $\overline{X}$ at the extreme), it will pay to consume and reduce stock to a point where annual growth is larger. If the value of the stock in production is not very great and the initial stock is on the right branch of $F(X)$, it seems possible that stock will be consumed and reduced to a point on the left branch. That is, the present value of the increased costs of production in future periods, because of lower stock, may be more than offset by the present value of the reductions in stock as consumption. Similarly, if the initial stock is small [on the left branch of $F(X)$] and the value of a larger stock in production is not very great, it may not pay to forego the consumption that would be necessary to increase the stock to the same rate of natural growth on the right branch. In the static case, in contrast, the right branch is always superior.

The fishery problem we have been discussing has been radically simplified so as to contain only the most important elements. There are various important ways by which the problem could be complicated—and would have to be in any attempt to apply these principles to a concrete case. One of the most important, especially if management is not unified but relies on the responses of competitive firms to prices, involves the rate at which capital can enter and leave the industry. We have assumed that capital services are instantly variable in quantity, but in any actual situation there will be a lagged response whose rapidity may vary. The lag involved in entry of capital probably would be much less than that involved in the exit of capital because of the long life of some of the capital instruments, thinking here of human skills as capital, too. The severity of the problems resulting from lagged response of capital flows is well illustrated by the problems of the cut-over areas of the Great Lakes states and the difficulties suffered by fishing communities in the northeast and eastern parts of the United States.

Another important respect in which the problem could be complicated is the production function, $G(K,X)$. One factor subject to regulation is net size, and this can be of great importance in the natural dynamics of the system since it can have a very important effect on the age distribution of the fish. If the assumption of a linearly homogeneous production is abandoned, the problem of economies of scale to the firm must be considered and conditions set up that will avoid diseconomies. In some cases outlays can be made (apart from those on catch activities) which will affect the natural dynamics of the system. Forests can be thinned, cleared of underbrush, and so on. In some cases, food or fertilizer can be provided for the fishery.

The final respect in which the model could be complicated is in the growth function, $\dot{X} = F(X)$, or $X = P(t)$. The preceding discussion serves as the merest introduction to the complexities of dynamic management of a biological system. While simple cases serve to reveal some of the important economic consider-ations and may be adequate for indicating valuable changes in grossly mismanaged situations,* a more complete analysis of many situations would be far more complex. In some cases, this greater complexity would be indispensable for capturing essential elements of the problem.

One type of complication is oscillation, arising either from inter-species relationships or changing values of exogenous variable such as rainfall or temperature.

To illustrate a simple form of oscillation, we move to a discrete formulation for a different system in which the change in number of females from one period to the next is given by $X_{(n+1)} = RX_n$, where R is average number of female offspring per adult female surviving to breed in the next period. If $R \gtrless 1$, X_t is increasing, stable, or decreasing.

Suppose that $X = \overline{X}$. Let us approximate the R function by a line tangent to it at this point. Let $X = \overline{X} + d$ where d is the deviation from $\overline{X}$. With $R = 1$ when $d = 0$, the tangent line has the equation $R = 1 - bd$ where $-b$ is the slope of the line.

---

* This certainly describes many actual fisheries. See Francis T. Christy and Anthony Scott, *The Common Wealth in Ocean Fisheries: Some Problems of Growth and Economic Allocation* (Baltimore: Johns Hopkins Press, 1969).

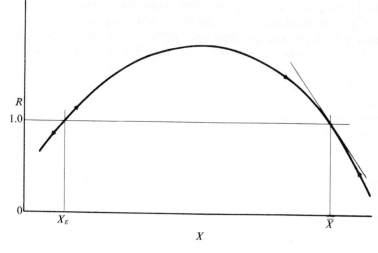

FIGURE 4-23

Substituting, $X_{(n+1)} = (1 - bd_n)X_n$. Hence

$$\overline{X} + d_{(n+1)} = (1 - bd_n)(\overline{X} + d_n) = \overline{X} + d_n - b\overline{X}d_n - bd_n^2$$

The last term is small in relation to the second. Hence approximately

$$d_{(n+1)} = d_n - b\overline{X}d_n$$

Substituting $C = b\overline{X}$,

$$d_{(n+1)} = (1 - C)d_n, \quad \text{or} \quad \Delta d_n = -Cd_n$$

    If $C < 0$,   any initial induced d increases without limit. (As in the neighborhood of X_E.)

    If $0 < C < 1$, initial d will decline steadily.

    If $1 < C < 2$, initial d will result in diminishing oscillations.

    If $C > 2$,   initial d will result in ever increasing oscillations.

    The above analysis could be applied to any point on the R function, say a steady state point sought by a fishery regulatory authority.

    Another source of fluctuation is a lagged relation between generations via food supply. A large population now, for example, may mean less food for the next generation, which in turn will have an effect on growth of food supply.

    In many cases the model of a single species growing in a simple relation with its "environment" is completely inappropriate. Two or more species may be involved in various types of relations. They may be related as competitors or the relationship may be complementary (symbiotic in biological terminology). It is obvious, both a priori and from a mountain of empirical evidence, that management practices that ignore, say, predator-prey relationships or host-parasite relations often bring unsuspected and highly undesirable results. Clearly any attempt to analyze such bio-economic systems must contain a biologic model a good deal more complex than the logistic function.

In short, biological systems are complex. It is difficult to know what character-istics are relevant for management, and even if these are known, the problem of estimating the parameters of the system is formidable. Natural populations, even when they can be estimated, are prone to vary for reasons not readily apparent, as a reflection of the complexity of the systems and our limited understanding of their behavior.

Our discussion indicated clearly that the external diseconomies associated with the exploitation of resources without owners can be overcome only by bringing these effects within the consideration of the decisions made by the exploiting economic units. This has proved to be a formidable task even for resources located within a single political jurisdiction such as the United States. The unfortunate fact is that a number of important resources exist where no political unit has jurisdiction, the most important being noncoastal fisheries. In the case of migratory fish, animals, and birds, several jurisdictions may be involved, or there may be movement between an unowned area, such as the open sea, and a political jurisdiction. In these cases the difficulties in securing any modification of competitive exploitation of the unowned resource are formidable.

Economic analysis of such situations is only a part of their "solution," but it is an essential part if only to prevent the adoption of proposals based on absurd implicit bio-economic models from making the situation even worse than it is.

Optimal Control Solution

Much can be learned about certain types of problems involving maximization of a function over time by putting them into the optimal control format. As said earlier, for certain problems, optimal control, the calculus of variations, and dynamic programming are equivalent in the sense that the one method can be transformed into the other, but it still will be true that certain problems can be more easily or more informatively cast in one of these modes. On the theoretical level, optimal control is an excellent medium for the fishery problem already discussed for the static case.

But what is optimal control? A number of references may be consulted for derivations and details of application. Here we confine ourselves to a few remarks to provide a general orientation.*

---

* If the reader possesses a reasonably high degree of mathematical sophistication, he would do well to consult L. S. Pontryagin, *et al.*, *The Mathematical Theory of Optimal Processes* (New York: Interscience Publishers [John Wiley], 1962). A compact and useful exposition is contained in Michael D. Intriligator, *Mathematical Optimization and Economic Theory* (Englewood Cliffs: Prentice-Hall, 1971). A summary statement is contained in Kelvin Lancaster, *Mathematical Economics* (New York: MacMillan & Co., 1968). An excellent introductory account for the economist has been provided by Robert Dorfman, "An Economic Interpretation of Optimal Control Theory," *American Economic Review*, December 1969, pp. 817–31. Unfortunately, the article contains a rather large number of typographical errors, most of which were corrected in a subsequent issue of the *AER* (June 1970, p. 524). A brief account well worth study is contained in the early pages of Kenneth Arrow and Mordecai Kurz, *Public Investment, The Rate of Return, and Optimal Fiscal Policy* (Baltimore: Johns Hopkins Press, 1970). A comprehensive explanation of variational methods (including optimal control) written for economists has been provided by G. Hadley and M. C. Kemp in *Variational Methods in Economics* (New York: American Elsevier, 1971).

Sketching Intriligator's development,* the control problem is one of maximizing an integral over time subject to certain conditions, and here is the source of kinship with problems in the calculus of variations. In addition to time, we have two classes of variables, state variables (which describe the state of the system at any time) and control variables. The control variables are indeed variables that can be controlled, thereby permitting the controller to cause the values of the state variables to change. His control is limited, however. His limitations, or restrictions, are expressed in the form of first order differential equations, each of them a function of the state and control variables and time, which describe the dependence of the state variables on the control variables. In addition, the control variables may be subject to restrictions, notably on the extreme values that they are permitted to take. For example, in a house hot air heating control system, the hot air chamber is not permitted to rise over a certain temperature. In addition, values may be specified for beginning and ending values of the state variables, or there must be something that confines the state variables if the system is to run indefinitely. The problem is to

$$\max_{(u(t))} J = \int_{t_0}^{t_1} I(x,u,t)\, dt + F(x_1,t_1)$$

(Note that I does not involve derivatives of the state variables.)

subject to the equations of motion to which the system must conform:

$$\dot{x} = f(x,u,t)$$

and

$$x(t_0) = x_0$$

$$x(t_1) = x_1$$

plus whatever restrictions there are on the control variables. [$u(t)$, the control trajectories are contained in U, the control set.]

Here x and u are to be understood as vectors of state and control variables, respectively, although they may contain only one member, as in our simple fishery problem.

Analogously with the static case, we now define a vector of *costate variables*, y, which may be thought of as similar to Lagrangian multipliers that change over time. The resulting Lagrangian expression is:

$$L = J + \int_{t_0}^{t_1} y[f(x,u,t) - \dot{x}]\, dt$$

$$= \int_{t_0}^{t_1} \{I(x,u,t) + y[f(x,u,t) - \dot{x}]\}\, dt + F(x_1,t_1)$$

---

* Intriligator, *op. cit.*, Chapter 14.

with the restrictions being under the integral since the y's are not constant. This can be converted (integration by parts) to:

$$L = \int_{t_0}^{t_1} \{I(x,u,t) + yf(x,u,t) + \dot{y}x\}\, dt$$
$$+ F(x_1,t_1) - [y(t_1)x(t_1) - y(t_0)x(t_0)]$$

The Hamiltonian function is defined as $H = I(x,u,t) + yf(x,u,t)$.* The expression for L must vanish as changes in the path of the control variable, if made from the optimum, become smaller and smaller—analogously with a static Lagrangian expression. The result is the necessary conditions that

$$\frac{\partial H}{\partial u} = 0$$

$$\dot{y} = -\frac{\partial H}{\partial x}$$

$$x(t_0) = x_0$$

$$y(t_1) = \frac{\partial F}{\partial x_1}$$

And, of course, the differential equations portraying the general behavior of the system can be expressed in terms of H as $\dot{x} = \partial H/\partial y$ (just look back at the formation of L).

In a practical application, the task of solving the system of differential equations remains. With fast computation, however, this can be avoided by assuming initial values where not given and passing from one (discrete) moment to the next, according to the equations. This procedure won't dispose of all difficulties, but the procedure would be a far cry from selecting control trajectories at random and calculating their worth.

All of this is simple so long as there are no restrictions on the values of u (or of x), and problems formulated in this way can be converted to the standard calculus of variation formulations. The great achievement of Pontryagin *et al.*, was to extend the Hamiltonian formulation to cases where $u(t)$ is restricted to a specified control set, U, and also to cases where x is restricted. This achievement is of great practical importance, for the values of control variables often are restricted in some way, and now there is available a highly practical method for solving such problems in a systematic way. Consider, for example, the number of control devices where the control may take on only two or a few values, since it is more expensive to design and manufacture systems with continuously

---

* Named for the Irish mathematician, William Hamilton. The number of languages he had mastered as a young man is almost unbelievable. In addition to his many other gifts, we are fortunate that he was a good swimmer, so good that an attempted suicide by drowning because of a rejected suit for marriage did not succeed.

variable controls. Systems using thermostats (defined in the everyday sense) and systems incorporating relays usually function in this way.

The calculus of variations says that optimal control values don't exist in these cases, or, if you know enough about the problem, you may be able to perceive that they do lie on the boundary, but there will be no general guidance on the switches that should be made in the values of the control variables. Writers of this calculus have established rigorously that if $\partial H/\partial u < 0$, then, one should choose the boundary values of u that will maximize H at that time. Thus H is to be maximized at each point in time by appropriate choice of the control variables. If $\partial H/\partial u = 0$, there is an interior (as opposed to boundary) solution. In the Dorfman exposition cited earlier, all solutions are interior. In the fishery problem, there are no restrictions on the values that may be taken by the control variable (K). If this feature of the problem is retained, as it will be, a dynamic analysis of the problem utilizing the Hamiltonian will also contain only interior solutions provided the other conditions of the problem are such that the system tends to a steady state with $X \neq 0$.

With this introduction to the maximum principle (or optimal control), we can proceed to discuss the fishery problem in dynamic terms.* Recall that we had:

$$\dot{X} = F(X) \qquad\qquad \text{biological system function}$$

$$x = G(X,K) \qquad\qquad \text{production (or catch) function,} \\ \text{linearly homogeneous}$$

$$P \qquad\qquad \text{price of product}$$

$$w \qquad\qquad \text{price of capital service per unit time}$$

$$\dot{X} = F(X) - G(X,K) \qquad \text{with fishing.}$$

We wish to maximize

$$J = \int_0^\infty \{(Px - wK)e^{-rt}\}\, dt$$

$$= \int_0^\infty \{(PG - wK)e^{-rt}\}\, dt$$

subject to $\dot{X} = F(X) - x = F(X) - G(X,K)$.

---

* This discussion borrows heavily from an unpublished paper by Gardner Brown, "An Optimal Program for Managing Common Property Resources with Congestion Externalities." His formulation utilized the ratio form of the production function ($k = K/X$), whereas we have chosen to leave X and K in their natural values. It seems to be difficult for some students to trace the changes in k as both X and K are varying, perhaps in opposite directions.

For a more extended analysis of the general fishery problem, see James P. Quirk and Vernon L. Smith, "Dynamic Economic Models of Fishing," in *Economics of Fisheries Management— A Symposium*, The Institute of Animal Resource Ecology (Vancouver: University of British Columbia, 1970). The person with a strong interest in fisheries will want to study the other essays in this volume, too.

A special case of the general problem that is labeled the fishery problem in this chapter is presented in C. G. Plourde, "A Simple Model of Replenishable Natural Resource Exploitation," *American Economic Review*, Vol. LX, June 1970, pp. 518–22.

From this we can form the Hamiltonian,

$$H = (PG - wK)e^{-rt} + y_2 e^{-rt}[F(X) - G(X,K)]$$

The standard formulation would call for, say, y_1 in place of $y_2 e^{-rt}$. Since we know (by analogy with the static case) that the "Lagrangian" multiplier, y, is going to turn out to be the implicit value of a unit of stock, X,* we have a choice between a y expressed in P.V. or a y in value as of t; y_1 would yield a y in P.V. as of $t = 0$, whereas $y_2 e^{-rt}$ will deliver y_2 in terms of its current value, which we prefer. Thus our "Lagrangian" multiplier *is* $(y_2 e^{-rt})$ and not just y_2.

Since this is not a problem with fixed end points, although X_0 is always given, transversality conditions must be met as one of the requirements for the existence of an optimum course. These are that $\lim_{t \to \infty} y_2 e^{-rt} = 0$ and that $\lim_{t \to \infty} Xy_2 e^{-rt} = 0$. These conditions and the concavity of H regarded as a function of X [$(P - y_2)$ assumed positive] ensure that the necessary conditions will yield a maximum course.†

Regarding K as the control variable, which it obviously is, we have

$$\frac{\partial H}{\partial K} = [PG_K - w - y_2 G_K]\, e^{-rt} \leq 0$$

or $(P - y_2)G_K \leq w$

and
$$\dot{y}_1 = \frac{d(y_2 e^{-rt})}{dt} = \dot{y}_2 e^{-rt} - re^{-rt}y_2$$

$$= -\frac{\partial H}{\partial X} = -(PG_X + y_2 F' - y_2 G_X)\, e^{-rt}$$

or, $-\dot{y}_2 = (P - y_2)G_X + y_2(F' - r)$

In a steady state interior solution, $(P - y_2)G_K = w$. That is, $(P - y_2) > 0$. If $\dot{y}_2$ is set at zero in the equation of the last paragraph, it then is clear that such a solution will require that $(r - F') > 0$. It of course will also be necessary that F' at some points be greater than the rate of interest. If this is not the case, either it will not pay to let the stock grow to a stationary level at which its product is exploited or it will pay to consume the stock without stopping at a stationary level.‡ That is to say, if the natural productivity of the bio-mass is too low, it will be more advantageous to consume it than to maintain it.

If $(F' > r)$ for some values, then $(r - F') > 0$ at all points on the right branch of $F(X)$ and over a part of the left branch to the left of the maximum.

---

* That is, the implicit value to be attached to the relaxation of a restriction.
† See Arrow and Kurz, *op. cit.*, pp. 45–51, for a clear discussion of these points, especially pp. 49 and 51.
‡ Minerals fall in the latter category, since F' is zero for all sizes of stock.

At the stationary position, $\dot{y}_2 = 0 = (P - y_2)G_X + y_2(F' - r)$. Note that this is the same as the expression for the static case (p. 160) *except* for the presence of $r : 0 = (P - \lambda)G_X - \lambda(-F')$.

How is the expression for $\dot{y}_2 = 0$ to be interpreted? y_2 is the current value of a unit stock in place; ry_2 is the annual interest on a unit of stock and, transferring this to the left side we have: $ry_2 = (P - y_2)G_X + y_2F'$. A unit of stock is productive in two ways, first in catching fish (it is one of the inputs of the catch production function) and also in "providing" the natural growth of the stock. Thus the real earnings per unit time of a unit of stock are $G_X + F'$. These are weighted by price of fish net of user cost (y_2) and by user cost to get a marginal value productivity which in a stationary position must be equal to the interest on the value of a unit of stock. If the stationary position is on the left side of $F(X)$, the productivities are both positive. If they are on the right side, however, the advantage in production gained by increasing the stock is offset by the adverse effect on natural productivity of the increased stock since $F' < 0$.

If the fishery is competitive and there are no restrictions on entry, y_2 indicates the tax that should be levied in order to have proper incentives at the margin. However, a tax of y_2 will not dissipate all of the rent on the fishery because each competitive firm will perceive the average product per unit of capital as the marginal product he can reap, thereby ignoring the effect that an additional unit of his capital has on the marginal product of capital enjoyed by the other fishing firms. With only a tax of y_2, entry will cease only at $(P - y_2)(G/K) = w$. What is needed, then, is a tax, t, on capital (which is the only input in this problem other than the services of the fishery) such that $(P - y_2)(G/K) - t = (P - y_2)G_K = w$. That is, $t = (P - y_2)[(G/K) - G_K]$. Both taxes change as time progresses since y_2, K, and X are all changing.

The nature of the unified management solution can be clarified by use of a phase diagram which will show, in general terms, the directions of the movements through time that are taken by y_2 and X for any combination of y_2 and X. What we need to establish the boundaries of the various "phases" of movement are two expressions:

$$\left. \frac{dy_2}{dX} \right|_{\dot{y}_2 = 0} \quad \text{and} \quad \left. \frac{dy_2}{dX} \right|_{\dot{X} = 0}$$

A convenient way to do this is to use a ratio of Jacobians. We have three equations:

$$A \quad (P - y_2)G_K - w = 0$$

$$B \quad (P - y_2)G_X + y_2(F' - r) + \dot{y}_2 = 0$$

$$C \quad F(X) - G(X,K) - \dot{X} = 0$$

Our variables are y_2, K, X, $\dot{X}$, and $\dot{y}_2$.

Then

$$\left.\frac{dy_2}{dX}\right|_{\dot{y}_2=0} = -\frac{J\begin{pmatrix} A & B & C \\ X & K & \dot{X} \end{pmatrix}}{J\begin{pmatrix} A & B & C \\ y_2 & K & \dot{X} \end{pmatrix}}$$

$$= -\frac{\begin{vmatrix} (P-y_2)G_{KX} & (P-y_2)G_{KK} & 0 \\ [(P-y_2)G_{XX}+y_2F''] & (P-y_2)G_{XK} & 0 \\ F'-G_X & -G_K & -1 \end{vmatrix}}{\begin{vmatrix} -G_K & (P-y_2)G_{KK} & 0 \\ -G_X+F'-r & (P-y_2)G_{XK} & 0 \\ 0 & -G_K & -1 \end{vmatrix}}$$

$$= \frac{-[(P-y_2)^2G_{XK}^2 - (P-y_2)^2G_{KK}G_{XX} - (P-y_2)y_2G_{KK}F'']}{-(P-y_2)G_{KX}G_K - (P-y_2)G_{KK}(F'-G_X-r)}$$

$$= \frac{(P-y_2)(G_{KX}^2 - G_{KK}G_{XX}) - y_2G_{KK}F''}{G_{KX}G_K + G_{KK}(F'-G_X-r)}$$

Now we take advantage of our assumption that $G(X,K)$ is linearly homogeneous. Because of this, $(G_{KX}^2 - G_{KK}G_{XX}) = 0$.*

Hence
$$\left.\frac{dy_2}{dX}\right|_{\dot{y}_2=0} = \frac{-y_2G_{KK}F''}{G_{KX}G_K + G_{KK}(F'-G_X-r)}$$

If $P > y_2 > 0$, the numerator of this expression is less than zero. Since $F' < r$, the second term of the denominator is positive and the first term is, too. Hence

$$\left.\frac{dy_2}{dX}\right|_{\dot{y}_2=0} < 0$$

when there is production.

---

* We have $x = G(X,K)$. Euler's theorem says $x = (\partial x/\partial X)X + (\partial x/\partial K)K$ for *all* values of X and K. Hence

$$\frac{\partial[X(\partial x/\partial X) + K(\partial x/\partial K)]}{\partial X} = \frac{\partial x}{\partial X}$$

That is,
$$\frac{\partial x}{\partial X} + X\frac{\partial^2 x}{\partial X^2} + K\frac{\partial^2 x}{\partial X\partial K} = \frac{\partial x}{\partial X}$$

or
$$\frac{\partial^2 x}{\partial X\partial K} = -\frac{X}{K}\frac{\partial^2 x}{\partial X^2} = -\frac{K}{X}\frac{\partial^2 x}{\partial K^2}$$

Hence
$$\left(\frac{\partial^2 x}{\partial X\partial K}\right)^2 = \frac{\partial^2 x}{\partial X^2}\cdot\frac{\partial^2 x}{\partial K^2} \quad \text{or} \quad G_{KX}^2 = G_{XX}\cdot G_{KK}$$

Next,

$$\frac{dy_2}{dX}\bigg|_{\dot{X}=0} = \frac{-J\begin{pmatrix} A & B & C \\ X & K & \dot{y}_2 \end{pmatrix}}{J\begin{pmatrix} A & B & C \\ y_2 & K & \dot{y}_2 \end{pmatrix}}$$

$$= -\frac{\begin{vmatrix} (P-y_2)G_{KX} & (P-y_2)G_{KK} & 0 \\ (P-y_2)G_{XX}+y_2F'' & (P-y_2)G_{XK} & 1 \\ F'-G_X & -G_K & 0 \end{vmatrix}}{\begin{vmatrix} -G_K & (P-y_2)G_{KK} & 0 \\ -G_X+F'-r & (P-y_2)G_{XK} & 1 \\ 0 & -G_K & 0 \end{vmatrix}}$$

$$= \frac{(P-y_2)[G_{KX}G_K + G_{KK}(F'-G_X)]}{G_K^2}$$

This is necessarily positive if $G_X > F'$, assuming $(P-y_2) > 0$, and will be positive over a part of the range for which $G_X < F'$. Thus a portion of the phase diagram will be as the solid portions of the functions in panel (a) in Figure 4-24, but the reasons for the dotted portions for low values of X require explanation.
The function,

$$\frac{dy_2}{dX}\bigg|_{\dot{X}=0}$$

is an answer to the question, given X, what level of y_2 would induce (assuming the rules of equations A, B, and C are followed) a catch equal to natural growth, $F(X)$?* Panel (b), derived from $F(X)$, shows that natural growth per unit stock rises as X decreases from $\overline{X}$. Now suppose we are at X_0 and then move to X_1 on the production function panel (b'). The associated natural yields are F_0 and F_1, but F_1 cannot be produced with the same ratio of capital service to stock service (the tangent of ray R_0). That is, we cannot stay on ray R_0 (with decreases in capital and stock services proportionate to the change in product as per the linear-homogeneity of the production function) but must move to R_1 at a point on F_1 above X_1. Panels (c), (d), and (e) show what happens to the other quantities involved here. The only way to induce the increased shift of stock to catch and thereby reduce the ratio of stock to capital services in production is to increase the reward to marginal product of stock, that is, to increase $(P-y_2)$.†

---

* Note that the $\dot{X}$ being held constant at zero refers to $F(X) - G(X,K)$ and not just $F(X)$.
† Refer to equation B.

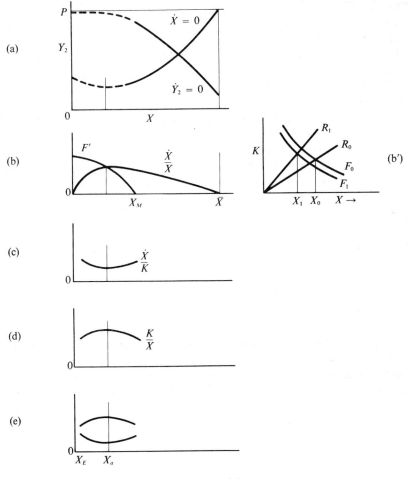

FIGURE 4-24

Thus, y_2 as a function of X with $\dot{X} = 0$ decreases from $\bar{X}$ to X_a. By a similar argument, it increases from X_a to 0.

Now what about the upper left of

$$\left.\frac{dy_2}{dX}\right|_{\dot{y}_2=0}$$

Here the question to be asked is, what value of y_2 will ensure that catch is zero, that is, that no part of the stock is converted to product? Let us try $y_2 = P$ in equation B. This yields $r = F'$. We had observed before that production requires that $r > F'$. Will production occur all the way to $r = F'$ as stock is reduced? With a linearly homogeneous production function, yes, since if there is any reward at all from the conversion of stock to product, capital stock (under our assumptions) can be adjusted so as to attain the appropriate value of G_K to satisfy equation A.

The value of X at which y_2 reaches P depends on the relation of the function, F', to r. For an $F(X)$ without an extinction point, as F' is drawn here, this point could be at any output between zero and X_a, depending on how far r is below the y intercept of $F'(X)$.*

At $\overline{X}$, the maximum stock with zero natural growth, it seems clear that the function for y_2 with $\dot{X} = 0$ must reach P if the catch is to be held at the level of natural growth, which is zero. However, inspection of equation B with $\dot{y}_2 = 0$ permits y_2 to be positive, with the immediate reduction of stock to optimum level being prevented by diminishing returns to capital if too much is introduced.

Next we investigate the movement from one moment of time to the next from a given point, y_2^0, X^0, on a path satisfying the three equations, A, B, and C. This movement can be viewed as the result of two vectors, one in the vertical direction and the other in the horizontal. To determine the vertical component imagine a series of curves similar to

$$\left.\frac{dy_2}{dX}\right|_{\dot{y}_2=0}$$

but with $\dot{y}_2$ held at different levels. As we move down this series of curves at a given value of X, on crossing the curve for $\dot{y}_2 = 0$ we probably shall pass from positive values of $\dot{y}_2$ to negative or vice versa. To determine this, we investigate the behavior of $\dot{y}_2$ as y_2 changes to see if this continuity of movement exists (that is, is the sign of

$$\left.\frac{d\dot{y}_2}{dy_2}\right|_{X^0}$$

always the same?), and, if so, to see in which direction $\dot{y}_2$ increases (up or down) as $\dot{y}_2 = 0$ is passed.

The quantity to be investigated is:

$$\left.\frac{d\dot{y}_2}{dy_2}\right|_{X^0} = -\frac{J\begin{pmatrix} A & B & C \\ y_2 & K & \dot{X} \end{pmatrix}}{J\begin{pmatrix} A & B & C \\ \dot{y}_2 & K & \dot{X} \end{pmatrix}} = \frac{G_K G_{XK} - G_{KK}G_X + G_{KK}(F' - r)}{-G_{KK}} > 0$$

Thus $\dot{y}_2$ increases as we move up, decreases as we move down, and must be negative below the curve for $\dot{y}_2 = 0$ and positive above it. (The vertical vector points up above this curve and down below it.)

---

* What difference would be made by the presence of an extinction point?

The direction of the horizontal vectors can be determined similarly:

$$\frac{d\dot{X}}{dy_2}\bigg|_{x^o} = -\frac{J\begin{pmatrix} A & B & C \\ y_2 & K & \dot{y}_2 \end{pmatrix}}{J\begin{pmatrix} A & B & C \\ \dot{X} & K & \dot{y}_2 \end{pmatrix}} = -\frac{G_K^2}{(P - y_2)G_{KK}} > 0$$

Thus $\dot{X}$ increases as we move up and is positive above the curve for $\dot{X} = 0$ and negative below it.

A schematic indication of these vectors is shown in Figure 4-25.* The main

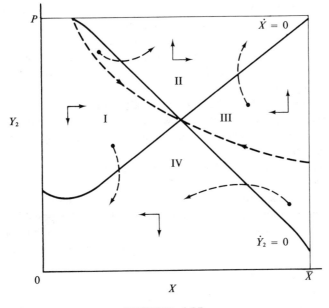

FIGURE 4-25

points to be noted are these. First, the heavy curve indicates the optimum path for any given X; it has a higher P.V. than any other. If the initial X is low, the value of a unit in stock is high and declines and vice versa. Natural growth is correspondingly above or below the catch. The stationary position at $\dot{y}_2 = 0$ and $\dot{X} = 0$ will be approached as $t \to \infty$.

The optimal control schema is a determinate system. Consequently there is only one optimum path for y_2 and X, and there is an associated stationary position, X^*, that will be reached ultimately. If there is an error in the initial y_2 and equations A, B, and C are used to generate the path of y_2 and X, this stationary point, X^*, will not be reached except in special cases. If the erroneous

---

* Schematic is certainly the word to be used here! Little attention has been paid to the details of the approaches to boundaries or to the curvature of the functions.

y_2 is in phase II or IV, the path prescribed by A, B, and C will reach either the boundary $y_2 = 0$ or $y_2 = P$. If the initial y_2 is in phase I or III, the path will remain there for a time, depending on the error in the initial y_2, but finally will cross into one of the explosive phases, II or IV, without reaching the stationary point, (X^*, y_2^*). Note that one vector approaches zero as the path for the initial point in question approaches one or the other of the two functions defining the phases. Penalties for error in choice of the initial y_2 probably increase more than in proportion to the size of the error.

In any practical application of a model like this, one would first either solve the equation system or simulate the behavior of the system through time, using a number of different initial values of y_2 for the known initial X. In equations A, B, and C, for example, an assumed initial value of y_2 permits determination of K (X being known), and $\dot{y}_2$ and $\dot{X}$, thereby permitting movement to the values of X and y_2 for the next period. The calculations can then be repeated over and over again, finally permitting a calculation of the P.V. of the path. Of course errors are all too possible. An indication that something may be wrong would be provided by a change in the sign of the *actually* unfolding dy_2/dX—by a movement from a "stable" phase to an unstable one. Such a change would not point clearly to any one type of error, which might be in calculation, estimation of parameters, or—very likely—in incomplete or erroneous specification of the biological system.

The curves defining the different phases might not intersect within the rectangle defined by the axes, P, and $\overline{X}$. The economic significance of many of the logical possibilities simply seems to be that there is no path to viable production, either with or without a period of no production. One of the possibilities is more interesting—production with stock decreasing to zero, as in Figure 4-26.

Models of this general type could be complicated in a number of ways, for

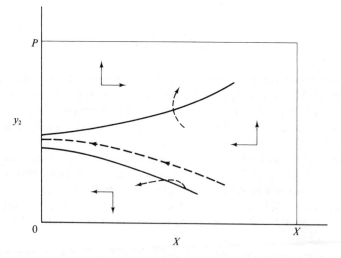

FIGURE 4-26

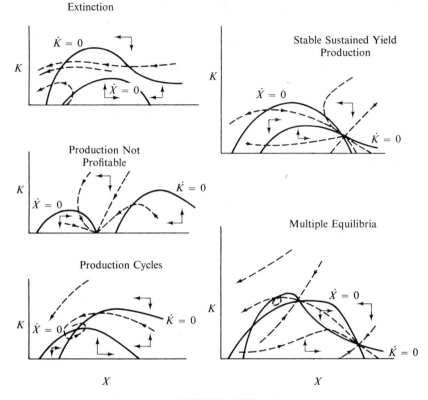

FIGURE 4-27

example, by using more elaborate and complete functions for describing the biological system and production. The equations for the biological system might include a number of species instead of one. The production function might include certain types of gear (the quantity of which could be controlled) which affect catch and natural rate of growth. Another type of complication pertinent for some problems would be to introduce an investment behavior function. A system with such a function is called a behavioral system by Quirk and Smith in contrast to normative systems.* However, this basis for distinction is obscured somewhat by the fact that even the investment decisions of controllers are subject to restrictions of various kinds which play a role entirely analogous to the equations describing the decisions of private investors. For systems that contain no normative element, the inclusion of an investment behavior function permits a number of possible outcomes of practical significance. These are illustrated in Figure 4-27 using phase diagrams based on quantity of capital, K, and the stock, X. The phases are separated by $\dot{K} = 0$ and $\dot{X} = 0$.†

---

* *Op. cit.*, p 28.
† *Ibid.*, p. 31.

4.10   MINERALS AGAIN

Calculus of Variations Formulation

Let us return to the problem of finding the optimum path for the exploitation of minerals in the simple situation where cost rises linearly with cumulated production and possibly with time. Using the notation of p. 138,

$$u_t = \int_0^q [a - bq - c - \beta x]dq = kq - \frac{bq^2}{2} - \beta xq \qquad \text{where} \qquad k = a - c$$

Note that the problem would be no different mathematically if we had

$$P = a - b_1 q \qquad \text{and} \qquad L = c + b_2 q + \beta x$$

We would still have $p = a - bq - c - \beta x$ with $b = b_1 + b_2$. Note that $dx/dt = q$.
    We want to maximize

$$V = \int_0^T F \, dt = \int_0^T ue^{-rt} \, dt$$

As above,

$$F = e^{-rt}\left[kq - \frac{bq^2}{2} - \beta xq \right]$$

$$\frac{\partial F}{\partial x} = -e^{-rt}\beta q$$

$$\frac{\partial F}{\partial q} = e^{-rt}[k - bq - \beta x] = pe^{-rt}$$

In the general case where p is a function of x, $\dot{x}$, and t

$$\frac{d(\partial F/\partial q)}{dt} = -rpe^{-rt} + e^{-rt}\frac{dp}{dt} = -rpe^{-rt} + \left(\frac{\partial p}{\partial t} + \frac{\partial p}{\partial x}\frac{dx}{dt} + \frac{\partial p}{\partial q}\frac{dq}{dt} \right)e^{-rt}$$

In this particular case, $\partial p/\partial t$ does not exist. Thus we have

$$\frac{d(\partial F/\partial q)}{dt} = -re^{-rt}(k - bq - \beta x) + \left(-\beta\frac{dx}{dt} - b\frac{dq}{dt} \right)e^{-rt}$$

Hence from $\partial F/\partial x - d(\partial F/\partial q)/dt = 0$,

$$-e^{-rt}\beta\frac{dx}{dt} - \left\{ -re^{-rt}\left(k - b\frac{dx}{dt} - \beta x \right) + \left(-\beta\frac{dx}{dt} - b\frac{d^2x}{dt^2} \right)e^{-rt} \right\} = 0$$

or

$$\frac{d^2x}{dt^2} - r\frac{dx}{dt} - \frac{r\beta x}{b} = -\frac{rk}{b}$$

$$\left(q = \frac{dx}{dt} \qquad \text{and} \qquad \frac{dq}{dt} = \frac{d^2x}{dt^2} \right)$$

Following standard procedures, our search for roots must satisfy

$$m^2 - mr - \frac{r\beta}{b} = 0 \quad \text{or} \quad m = \frac{r \pm \sqrt{r^2 + (4r/b)}}{2}$$

The solution of the complementary function is $x_t = C_1 e^{m_1 t} + C_2 e^{m_2 t}$. A particular solution is $x_t = k/\beta$. Hence

$$x_t = C_1 e^{m_1 t} + C_2 e^{m_2 t} + \frac{k}{\beta}$$

At $t = 0$, $x = 0$, so

(1) $$0 = C_1 + C_2 + \frac{k}{\beta}$$

At $t = T$, cost is $L = a = c + \beta x_T$, so $x_T = [(a - c)/\beta] = k/\beta$, giving

(2) $$0 = C_1 e^{m_1 T} + C_2 e^{m_2 T}$$

Also at $t = T$,

(3) $$q_T = 0 = m_1 C_1 e^{m_1 T} + m_2 C_2 e^{m_2 T}$$

m_1 can equal m_2 only if $r = 0$, contrary to assumption.

With $r > 0$, m_1 and m_2 are of opposite sign. Take m_1 as positive. From (2) it is clear that C_1 and C_2 cannot be of the same sign if T is finite. But if they are of opposite sign, then (3) cannot be satisfied if T is finite (either both terms are positive or both are negative).

If T is infinite, however, the three equations can be satisfied by $C_1 = 0$ and $C_2 = (-k/\beta)$.

Thus $$x_t = \frac{k}{\beta}(1 - e^{m_2 t})$$

$$\frac{dx_t}{dt} = q_t = -m_2 \frac{k}{\beta} e^{m_2 t}$$

$$P_t = a + bm_2 \frac{k}{\beta} e^{m_2 t}$$

dP/dt approaches zero ($m_2 < 0$) as $t \to \infty$.

$$\frac{1}{P}\frac{dP}{dt} = \frac{m_2(P_t - a)}{P_t}$$

That is, the relative rate at which market price rises approaches zero as the price approaches its limit.

Optimal Control Formulation

The same minerals problem can be formulated simply for optimal control. Indeed, the salient aspects of the problem arise directly and simply out of this formulation.

The flow of net social utility at a given moment is as before:

$$V = \int_0^u [a - bu - c - \beta x - \gamma t] \, du = au - \frac{bu^2}{2} - cu - \beta xu - \gamma tu$$

We have used u here instead of q simply to remind the reader of the preceding optimal control formulation; $dx/dt = u$, and u, the quantity produced and put on the market per unit time at time t, is our control variable.

Referring to pp. 170 and 172, we seek to maximize

$$J = \int_0^t Ve^{-rt} \, dt + (y_2 e^{-rt})u$$

Thus
$$H = Ve^{-rt} + (y_2 e^{-rt})u$$

$$\frac{d(y_2 e^{-rt})}{dt} = -ry_2 e^{-rt} + \dot{y}_2 e^{-rt}$$

$$= -\frac{\partial H}{\partial x} = \beta u e^{-rt}$$

or,
$$\dot{y}_2 = ry_2 + \beta u$$

$$\frac{\partial H}{\partial u} = (a - bu - c - \beta x - \gamma t)e^{-rt} + y_2 e^{-rt} = 0$$

or
$$y_2 = -(P - MC)$$

And, as assumed,

$$\frac{dx}{dt} = u$$

Note that y_2, the variable "multiplier" which is a function of t, is negative. How is this to be interpreted? The economic sense of it seems to be that in this formulation x does not refer to stock in ground but rather to a unit of separated stock. If we change the sign of y_2 and $\dot{y}_2$, thereby changing the interpretation, then as before on p. 130 we have $\dot{y}_2 = ry_2 - \beta u$. If γ is positive, then the terminal condition with $u = 0$ and $y_2 = 0$ will be reached at a finite time, but if $\gamma = 0$, then the problem is as before. A cost function with a negative linear time term could not represent reality if the horizon is indefinitely long, as here, for the implication would be that cost could be reduced to zero simply by waiting.

PART III

Government Investment in
Natural Resources Production

All modern governments have found it necessary or desirable to make direct investments in certain productive activities. In some western countries, such as France, the nationalization of industry has penetrated deeply into the basic economy. In the United States this process has not gone so far. With the exception of wartime activities and the post office, direct investment and operation of productive facilities has been limited. Even management of the vast public lands in the West has been only under the general control of federal authorities. Prospecting, mining, ranching, and timbering have largely been carried out by private enterprises within the rules set by government.

One of the most important direct government investments in the natural resources area has been in water resources—especially reservoirs, hydroelectric and irrigation facilities, and navigation installations. Local governments and to some extent states have also invested heavily in water resources facilities. Local water and sewage systems and the water system of California are major examples. From our point of view, however, federal investments are of more direct interest because of the relatively systematic, if not necessarily satisfactory, way in which they have been subjected to economic analysis.

Federal activities in water resources are partly a product of history, having grown to some extent out of the federal government's interest in navigation investments to open up the young country. To a large extent, too, they are the rational result of economic circumstances. They are usually characterized by indivisibilities which lead to decreasing cost types of situations, and by outputs which to a substantial extent embody public good characteristics (flood control is an outstanding example). Finally, they often involve externalities to an unusual degree. A simple but important example of the last is the effect of an upstream flow-regulating reservoir on the quantity and pattern of downstream power generation. Our objective in this part of the book is to discuss the issues of economic theory pertaining to government investment and to illustrate them with some brief analyses of actual problems in the water resource field.

While we emphasize the water resources field (for the reasons given above) and the specific character of time streams of costs and returns characteristically found in that sector, it would be a mistake to infer that the subsequent analysis applies only to such situations. While not large relative to investments in heavy structures, federal (and state and local) investments are made in projects which have very little investment in the early period but do involve long-time streams of operation, maintenance, and replacement costs in the future. Other types of public operations involve virtually no direct investment or other outlays but imply an "implicit" investment. The archetype of such an investment would be a wilderness area in which virtually no direct investment has been made but whose preservation requires foregoing a stream of explicit returns (say from lumbering activity). In each case, returns and costs (even if implicit) must be compared if a rational decision is to be made.

The general objective of benefit-cost analysis is to provide a useful picture of the cost and gains from investment. Such analysis should be sufficiently precise and meaningful so that it will lead to higher-level performance (greater goal fulfillment) than more intuitive methods of decision-making. The intellectual "father" of benefit-cost analysis is often said to be the nineteenth century Frenchman Jules Dupuit who in 1844 wrote a frequently cited study, "On the Measurements of the Utility of Public Works." In this remarkable article he recognized the concept of consumer surplus and saw that consequently the benefits of public works are not necessarily the same thing as the direct revenues that the public projects will generate. We might add that the error he spotted so early continues to be made in the most diverse circumstances.

In the United States, early contributions to development of benefit-cost analysis generally did not come from the academic or research communities but rather from government agencies. The agencies responsible for water resources development have for a long time been aware of the need for economic evaluation of projects. In 1808, when Albert Gallatin produced a report on transportation programs for the new nation, he stressed the need for comparing the benefits with the costs of proposed improvements. The Federal Reclamation Act of 1902, which created the Bureau of Reclamation and was aimed at opening western lands to irrigation, required economic analysis of projects. The Flood Control Act of 1936 proposed a feasibility test based on classical welfare economics which required that the benefits to whomsoever they accrue must exceed costs. In 1946 a federal interagency river basin committee appointed a subcommittee on benefits and costs to reconcile the practices of federal agencies, in making benefit-cost analyses. In 1950 this subcommittee issued a landmark report entitled *Proposed Practices for Economic Analysis of River Basin Projects*.

While never fully accepted either by the parent committee or the federal agencies, this report was remarkably sophisticated in its use of economic analysis and laid an intellectual foundation for research and debate in the water area which sets it apart from other major reports in the realm of public expenditure.

Following this report came outstanding publications from the research and academic communities. Several books appearing over the past two decades have gone much further than ever before in clarifying the welfare economics concepts applicable to water resources development and use, and exploring the fundamental rationale for government activity in the area. Otto Eckstein's *Water Resource Development: The Economics of Project Evaluation* (Harvard University Press), which appeared in 1958, is particularly outstanding for its careful review and critique of federal agency practice with respect to benefit-cost analysis. A clear exposition of principle, together with application to several important cases, was provided by Jack Hirshleifer, James C. DeHaven, and Jerome W. Milliman in *Water Supply: Economics, Technology and Policy* (University of Chicago Press, 1960). Another pair of books, one by John V. Krutilla and Otto Eckstein, *Multiple Purpose River Development: Studies in Applied Economic Analysis* (Johns Hopkins University Press, 1958) and one by Roland N. McKean, *Efficiency in Government Through Systems Analysis, With Emphasis on Water Resource Development* (New York: John Wiley & Sons, 1958) are notable for having helped lay the foundation for economic systems analysis by emphasizing the external effects of water development and the impossibility of arriving at optimum development and use unless these are taken explicitly into account. Another report which is especially notable for its deep probing into applications of systems analysis and computer technology to water resources planning was produced by a group of economists, engineers, and hydrologists at Harvard and published in the important, interdisciplinary book called *The Design of Water Resource Systems* in 1962 (Harvard University Press).

In the same year, a new federal document providing guidance to field-level planners for the evaluation of water resources projects and systems was issued. The official name is *Policy Standards and Procedures in the Formulation, Evaluation, and Review of Plans for Use and Development of Water and Related Land Resources.* The report is popularly referred to as Senate Document No. 97. In part it reflected the broader systems approaches growing out of contemporary research, and in part it resulted from the Kennedy administration's desire to ease up on evaluation standards so that more projects would qualify. The new report was approved by the President for application by the water resource agencies and by the Bureau of the Budget. It was still at the time of this writing the basic federal guidelines document.

Another current in the economics of water resources planning and research is a new analytical interest in aspects of water development and use previously termed intangible and regarded as not subject to quantitative analysis. We particularly mean water quality and water-based recreation. In this connection, two large federal studies which appeared in the 1960s have had a profound effect on water policy and water research. In 1958 the U.S. Senate established a special select committee under the chairmanship of the late Senator Robert S. Kerr to assess the national water resources situation. The resulting study was by far the most intensive and extensive study of the national water situation and of prospects ever conducted. Among its major results was a much greater emphasis on problems of water quality. Further extensions of this work have been carried on by Professor Nathaniel Wollman of the University of New Mexico, and his study of future water supply and demand in the United States has been published under the title, *The Outlook for Water*.* The study emphasizes even more strongly than the Senate report the important role of water quality in future water resource planning. The other large federal study is that of the Outdoor Recreation Resources Review Commission. Their massive and detailed reports strongly stressed the recreational values of water. At the present time, federal agencies routinely claim benefits to recreation and water quality from their investment programs. Our discussion of benefit and cost evaluation pays particular attention to these two aspects of water resources project evaluation. This reflects the current importance of these aspects, the interesting problems of methodology which they present, and the fact that they are not so well covered in the literature as other benefit evaluation problems.

Before proceeding to the discussion of the economics of benefit-cost analysis, we should mention that a revised set of federal guidelines was under consideration as this text was being prepared. Recent decisions to increase the discount rate on public projects (discussed further below), with the implication that fewer federal projects could be justified, generated pressures by and on the federal water agencies to account for benefits more comprehensively than had been done before and also to include benefits for objectives other than economic efficiency. In consequence, the Water Resources Council (the top interagency water resources body at the national level) established an interagency task force which drafted proposed new planning and evaluation standards. The most important change was that in the proposed standards emphasis would be given to the effect of projects on regional income, environmental quality, and something called "human well-being" in addition to economic efficiency.

In the immediately following chapter, we turn to a discussion of some basic concepts of benefit-cost analysis. In subsequent ones we treat a number of important applied theory problems in evaluating benefits and costs, designing systems, and pricing outputs.

---

* Nathaniel Wollman and Gilbert W. Bonem, *The Outlook for Water: Quality, Quantity, and National Growth* (Baltimore: The Johns Hopkins Press, 1971).

CHAPTER 5

Investment Criteria and Time

5.1 BENEFIT-COST ANALYSIS—BASIC CONCEPTS

Benefit-cost analysis usually has focused on the objective of economic efficiency, giving only secondary attention to other possible objectives such as income distribution. However, even pursuit of the efficiency objective raises a severe conceptual problem. Since the costs of government investment and operating costs for federal water resources projects are usually not fully reimbursed by beneficiaries, they generate an inherent income redistribution effect. Thus it is really not possible to pursue the economic efficiency objective without making some kind of an assumption about income distribution or the utility of income to different individuals or without developing some general view on the desirability of the ad hoc transfers of income resulting from public investment in these projects. The views developed on this question in turn will have their impact on the design of the finance and reimbursement aspects of projects and indirectly on the practical possibility of attaining efficiency in the decisions. For the moment we will follow Eckstein* in assuming that the marginal utility of money is equal, between individuals, and constant over the range of effects we are considering. This simple but unrealistic assumption permits us to discuss efficiency analysis questions separately from distribution. Later we will discuss the matter of income distribution and multiple planning objectives in some detail.

---

* See Chapter 2.

Given the above assumption, we can take the efficiency objective to mean that we wish to maximize the positive difference between benefits (measured by the willingness of beneficiaries to pay for outputs) and costs (the willingness of persons to pay to keep resources in alternative employments).* If we assume that resource inputs all are obtained from competitive sellers (an assumption we will question in certain instances), and that full employment of resources prevails, the market price of these inputs measures the marginal willingness to pay to keep them in alternative employments (why?).† The willingness of consumers to pay for the output of the project must often be simulated, and this presents very difficult problems which will occupy us considerably in later sections.

For the moment we will assume that we know how to measure benefits (the sum of individual demand curves added vertically or horizontally, depending on whether the good is public or private) and costs so that we may discuss a few matters of concept with respect to efficiency. These are elementary but nevertheless capable of causing endless confusion unless clearly understood.

5.2   THE DEMAND FUNCTION AS A MARGINAL BENEFITS FUNCTION

If we could think of the output from a public project as having a totally elastic demand or being such a small increment to output that the consumers' marginal willingness to pay is unaffected by its level, the government would be in the same position as a competitive firm. It would simply accept a single price for the output and adjust to it. For the most part this is unrealistic, however. In general, the rationale for public output is to deal with situations where competitive markets cannot function or function efficiently. In many cases, for example, the market for the product of a project is of limited geographical size. So, normally, output will be large relative to the market and the demand function will be downward sloping like an industry demand function in private markets. Now we say that if the government wishes to maximize net benefits, it must carry output to the point where marginal cost equals marginal benefit. It is important to understand that this is not the same as a monopolistic private producer maximizing profits. When a monopolist faces a downward sloping demand (average revenue) curve, this means that his marginal revenue must lie below it. Since maximizing his profit requires that he equate marginal cost and marginal revenue, price (as indicated on his demand curve) must lie above marginal cost, a result which cannot be Pareto optimal.

The gross benefit from a public project is measured by the total willingness to pay (consumers surplus if a zero price is charged) for any given level of output.

---

* The willingness-to-pay measure is, strictly speaking, correct only when the income effects of actual payments, if they were made, is zero. Then the area under a "Marshallian" demand curve can be taken to measure benefit.

† If this is not clear to you, go back and review Chapter 2. The reader would do well to think carefully about the general theoretical statements made in this section, and if he feels uncertain about any of them he should review Chapter 2.

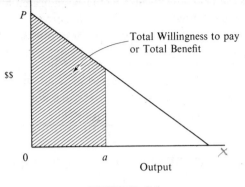

FIGURE 5-1

See Figure 5-1. Let us define a general demand function for a publicly provided output to be $P = f(x)$ where x represents the level of output. Now $B = g(x)$, the total benefit function, for some level of output a is given by $\int_0^a f(x)\,dx$. Thus the function g is the primitive of the function f. By the same token, the function f is the first derivative of the function g. But since g is the total benefit function, it is logical to refer to f as the marginal benefit function. Thus when the government acts to equate marginal benefits and marginal costs, which, as we know, is a necessary condition for maximizing net benefits under our assumptions, the result is the same as would be automatically obtained in a competitive market.

5.3 BENEFIT-COST RATIOS

Planners and government officials often discuss benefit-cost (B-C) analysis in terms of benefit to cost *ratios*. Sometimes they say the objective of the benefit-cost analysis is to maximize the benefit-cost ratio. *Clearly this is nonsense.* In Figure 5-2 we show a pair of marginal cost and marginal benefit functions. For

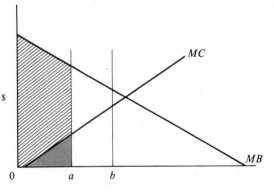

FIGURE 5-2

any given output, the benefit-cost ratio would be indicated by the ratio of the sum of the hatched and dotted areas to the dotted area. It can be seen that this ratio increases as output is reduced from (say) $0a$ to practically zero, since each reduction in output of one unit results in a smaller percentage reduction in benefits than in costs. Thus the maximization of the benefit-cost ratio for a project is a ridiculous objective. The criterion would be useful in ranking objectives only if they have to be built to a fixed scale. But, as we will see shortly, the concept of a *marginal* benefit-cost ratio is useful.

5.4   THE BENEFIT-COST CRITERION

We now proceed toward a more formal discussion of the benefit-cost criterion which will permit us to be more precise in regard to its meaning and to relate to our discussion of basic theory in Chapter 2. Also, it will permit us to introduce time explicitly into the analysis. In the following several paragraphs we follow a particularly good exposition presented by Marglin.*

Let $E(A)$ be the gross benefits (willingness to pay as defined above) for a particular project design A. The gross costs $C(A)$ are the money value of goods foregone throughout the economy to construct and operate A. Net benefits then are $E(A) - C(A)$, the difference between willingness to pay and the value of goods and services displaced by the project.

Let $\mathbf{Y} = (y_1, y_2, \ldots, y_m)$ be a vector of outputs from the project and $\mathbf{X} = (x_1, x_2, \ldots, x_n)$ be a vector of inputs to the project. We designate a *ranking function* for the project

$$W(A) = E(\mathbf{Y}) - C(\mathbf{X})$$

where $W(A)$ are the net benefits of the project, and outputs and inputs are related to each other by a general production function $f(\mathbf{X}, \mathbf{Y}) = 0.$† $C(\mathbf{X})$ is then the cost of inputs used efficiently, and $E(\mathbf{Y})$ is benefit measured as the area under the demand curve, i.e., for any particular output y_j,

$$E(y_j) = \int_0^y D(\eta)\, d\eta$$

where η is rate of output per unit time.

The efficiency ranking function reduces in effect to a balancing of individual preferences (indicated by willingness to pay) for the final goods of a water-resource system against individual preferences (indicated by marginal costs) for the goods displaced by the project.

---

* See Arthur Maass *et al.*, *Design of Water Resource Systems* (Harvard University Press, Cambridge, Mass., 1962), Chapters II and IV.
† Recall the discussion of production functions in Chapter 2.

Here we are using the analysis with respect to a particular *project*. However, the same principles apply to a *system* of interrelated projects although then the production function (and the benefits function) may become complicated. (See Chapter 7.)

The development so far has been for a single-period, single-purpose project. Multiple outputs are easily introduced so long as the willingness of beneficiaries to pay for them are independent of each other. $C(\mathbf{X})$ remains the same as before and aggregate benefits are the sum of the benefits of the individual outputs.

$$E(\mathbf{Y}) = \sum_{j=1}^{m} \int_{0}^{y_j} D_j(\eta_j) \, d\eta_j$$

where $\mathbf{Y}$ is the vector of outputs $y_1, \ldots, y_m$.

We will not treat the interdependent demands case which is more complex.*

The multi-period aspect is a considerably more difficult matter, and we will introduce it first in a simple fashion and then explore it more thoroughly later. It is really, as we have already hinted, one of the central problems in the evaluation of government projects. Let us assume, at least initially, that we are given a market rate of interest which can appropriately be used to discount future streams of costs and benefits.

First, define a multi-period, multi-output benefit function.

$$E_t(\mathbf{Y}_t) = \sum_{j=1}^{m} \int_{0}^{y_{tj}} D_{tj}(\eta_{tj}) \, d\eta_{tj}$$

where $D_{tj}(y_{tj})$ represents the demand for the jth output in year t.

The ranking or net benefit function for a multi-purpose, multi-period project can then be expressed as

$$\sum_{t=1}^{T} \frac{E_t(\mathbf{Y}_t) - M_t(\mathbf{X})}{(1 + r)^t} - K(\mathbf{X})$$

where $M_t(\mathbf{X})$ is the operation, maintenance, and replacement (OMR) cost associated with the vector of inputs $(\mathbf{X})$ in the year t and $K(\mathbf{X})$ are the capital investment costs associated with the input vector $(\mathbf{X})$. In this formulation the latter are assumed to occur only in the initial year.

We can calculate a discount factor θ, where $\theta = [1/(1 + r)^t]$ for each year $1, \ldots, T$, and write the ranking function

$$\sum_{t=1}^{T} \theta_t [E_t(\mathbf{Y}_t) - M_t(\mathbf{X})] - K(\mathbf{X})$$

---

* See Marglin in Maass *et al.*, *op. cit.*

where t indicates the number of years in the life of the project. As an example of the discount factor, which can readily be looked up in a book of mathematical tables, for 5 percent interest rate and $T = 40$, θ is about .14, i.e., the present value of a dollar is about 14¢.

$E_t(\mathbf{Y}_t)$ denotes the annual benefits in period t as a function of the outputs in period t, i.e.,

$$E_t(\mathbf{Y}_t) = \sum_{j=1}^{m} \int_0^{y_{tj}} D_{tj}(\eta_{tj})\, d\eta_{tj}$$

We can now state the criterion as maximizing the ranking function (present value of net benefits) where the production function is

$$f(\mathbf{X},\mathbf{Y}_t) = 0 \qquad t = 1, \ldots, T$$

This is done by differentiating the objective constrained by the production function and setting first derivatives equal to zero. We assume that the second order conditions hold for a maximum.

When we follow these procedures,* we obtain the following marginal conditions for a maximum:

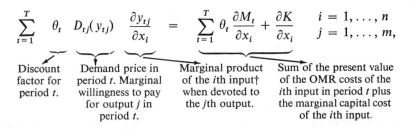

$$\sum_{t=1}^{T} \theta_t\, D_{tj}(y_{tj})\, \frac{\partial y_{tj}}{\partial x_i} = \sum_{t=1}^{T} \theta_t \frac{\partial M_t}{\partial x_i} + \frac{\partial K}{\partial x_i} \qquad \begin{array}{l} i = 1, \ldots, n \\ j = 1, \ldots, m, \end{array}$$

| Discount factor for period t. | Demand price in period t. Marginal willingness to pay for output j in period t. | Marginal product of the ith input† when devoted to the jth output. | Sum of the present value of the OMR costs of the ith input in period t plus the marginal capital cost of the ith input. |

Simply summarized, what the equation says is that for maximum net benefits the present value of the marginal benefit derived from an extra unit of each input must equal the present value of its marginal cost. Another way of putting this (which relates back to our earlier discussion of benefit-cost ratios) is that the *marginal benefit-cost ratio*, for optimum combinations of inputs and outputs, when expressed in terms of present values, must be equal to unity for maximum net benefit.

5.5   BUDGET CONSTRAINT

Our development so far has assumed no restriction on the funds available for the construction or operation of the project. This means that the budget passively adjusts to the availability of efficient projects. However, Congress may not

---

* See Marglin, *ibid.*

† Input is regarded as physical structure.

in fact make budgets this way. For example, Congress may decide that a certain budget total for a particular program area or for the federal budget as a whole is the right one. Thus using other criteria, it may decide to allocate either more or fewer funds than could be absorbed by the roster of projects designed to a scale such that their *marginal* benefit-cost ratios have just been reduced to unity. The impact of this on optimal design could be quite complicated since budget restrictions might very well change over time, affecting not only availability of funds for present construction but operations possibilities in the future as well.

Here a particularly simple case is examined in which the budget constraint pertains to construction costs only. Also we assume that the budget will be less than that needed to implement the full complement of efficient projects, although it should be recalled that in principle it could go either way.

Assume the budget available for water resource projects is $\bar{K}$ and this is to be allocated among P projects. The subbudget allocated to the pth project is $\bar{K}_p$. The design criterion for the pth project is to choose the most efficient design among all designs which cost less than or equal to $\bar{K}_p$ dollars, or maximize

$$\sum_{t=1}^{T} \theta_t [E_{tp}(\mathbf{Y}_{tp}) - \mathcal{M}_{tp}(\mathbf{X}_p)] - K_p(\mathbf{X}_p)$$

subject to the budget constraint

$$K_p(\mathbf{X}_p) \leq \bar{K}_p$$

as well as to the production function for P.

Going through the usual Lagrangian analysis yields

$$\sum_{t=1}^{T} \sum_{j=1}^{m} \theta_t D_{tj}(y_{tj}) \frac{\partial y_{tj}}{\partial x_{pi}} = \sum_{t=1}^{T} \theta_t \frac{\partial \mathcal{M}_{pt}}{\partial x_{pi}} + (1 + \lambda_p) \frac{\partial K_p}{\partial x_{pi}} \qquad \begin{matrix} i = 1, \ldots, n \\ j = 1, \ldots, m \end{matrix}$$

By rearranging terms and simplifying notation, we can rewrite this as

$$\frac{\sum_{t=1}^{T} \theta_t [MVP_{tp}(x_{pi}) - M\mathcal{M}_{tp}(x_{pi})]}{MK_p(x_{pi})} = 1 + \lambda_p$$

where the M's stand for marginals. The left-hand side is the marginal benefit-cost ratio. The numerator is the present value of the difference between the marginal benefit derived from an extra unit of each input minus the OMR costs associated with it. The denominator is the marginal capital cost associated with the input. The whole expression says that the marginal benefit-cost ratio (for each input and each output) must be equal to unity plus some constant (the Lagrange multiplier). If λ_p is 1, for example, this means that the marginal benefit-cost ratio must be 2 for project p. This can be referred to as the "cutoff" benefit-cost ratio.

The problem then becomes that of determining the appropriate subbudget for system or project p. We will not go through this analysis because what is required is immediately clear. A single lambda (yielding a uniform marginal cutoff B/C ratio of $1 + \lambda$) must apply to all projects; for if it did not, it would be possible to trade inputs and outputs among projects in such a way as to increase the present value of net benefits.

We may note that λ once again has its usual interpretation. It is the marginal value of the constraint. In other words, it indicates how much the present value of net benefits would rise if the constraint were relieved by one unit.

If the entire government budget is constrained and if the central objective of government policy is to maximize the present value of net benefits, then of course all agencies should use the same λ in scaling their projects, and budgets should be readjusted to permit this. Clearly, things are unlikely to work this way in practice. For one thing, many government projects are not readily amenable to explicit benefit measurement, so that the maximum economic analysis to be hoped for in those cases is some sort of cost effectiveness analysis, which would make it quite difficult to equate margins in the prescribed way. In addition, as already mentioned, Congress may set budgets on the basis of other criteria. Nevertheless, the concept of equating marginal benefit-cost ratios at the margins of programs is a valid one and should provide useful general orientation.

Within the water resources sector itself, there are substantial difficulties in implementing the criterion explained above. In principle, what should happen is that field level planners should provide a central budgeting office, say, the Office of Management and Budget, with tentative plans on the basis of which the central office would make a preliminary estimate of λ. By a series of successive approximations, convergence toward a final λ and a consistent set of projects would be achieved.

Such a process is beset by several important institutional obstacles. First, numerous federal agencies engage in water resources development projects, and to achieve disinterested communications among them would be difficult, to say the least.

More important are the problems resulting from the Congressional process of authorizing and appropriating funds. Without lingering over details, we may characterize this process briefly as follows: Congress first authorizes study of the area for the purpose in question; if it deems the results desirable, it may authorize some projects; at some uncertain time in the future (sometimes a decade or more later) it *may* appropriate funds for some of the projects. In all likelihood, designs will be revised to some degree as they are brought to the stage required for use in actual construction. It hardly seems necessary to point to the severe problems this presents for implementing a program of maximizing net benefits under budgetary constraints.

In view of these circumstances, our *judgment* is that the best policy for field-level planners to follow is to scale their projects to the point where the *marginal* benefit-cost ratios are reduced to unity. Sluggishly and imperfectly, to be sure, we feel that budgets would respond to a roster of efficient projects.

5.6   CONCEPTS OF TIME DISCOUNT

In Chapter 3 the concept of present value and its rationale, based on neo-classical capital theory and Pareto welfare economics, was explained. Here we wish to review with the reader some of the formulas involved and how they are applied.

Present value is defined by the formula

$$V_0 = \frac{S_1}{1 + r} + \frac{S_2}{(1 + r)^2} + \cdots + \frac{S_n}{(1 + r)^n}$$

where V_0 represents present value, $S_t = (b_t - c_t)$ the net benefit (which may be negative) in year t, and n is the termination period for the investment. It is also possible to separately discount streams of costs and returns and get the same results. Interest and depreciation are implicitly allowed for in the formula and *require no separate accounting*. While t is often taken to be a year, the compounding can be applied to as short an interval as desired. In the limit for continuous discounting, the formula for the present value of a single sum paid or received at time t becomes

$$V_0 = \frac{S_t}{e^{rt}} = S_t e^{-rt}$$

As we have already seen in Chapter 3, continuous discounting functions are easy to use in theoretical problems because of the simplicity of their derivatives and integrals. In public investment problems, however, discrete discounting is used since the time unit of account for benefits and costs is normally one year and probably because of the correspondence of discrete compounding to the usual interest payment practices.

Where an initial outlay occurs contemporaneously with V_0 (the time for which present value is being calculated), the discrete discounting formula above can be written

$$V_0 = -c_0 + \frac{S_1}{1 + r} + \frac{S_2}{(1 + r)^2} + \cdots + \frac{S_n}{(1 + r)^n}$$

where c_0 indicates the immediate outlay.

A special case of present value calculation is that in which the net benefits stream is infinite and constant. The present value formula then reduces to $V_0 = s/r$, where s is the constant annual benefit with the first payment received at $t = 1$. We will need this formula in our later discussion of social rates of discount.

While of no particular theoretical interest, we also present the procedure for finding the *annual* equivalent of a stream of values (which could be net benefits, gross benefits, or costs). Government officials and others often prefer to see information presented in this form. If the calculations are correctly made, the rule, "Adopt any project for which the annual net benefits are greater than zero when computed at the appropriate rate of interest," is the same as saying adopt any project with a positive present value of net benefits. The equivalent annual net benefits are calculated by finding the level stream of net benefits over the life of the project which has the same present value as the actual stream of costs and benefits arising from the project.

The level annual net flows in the equation corresponding to V_0 as above are:

$$\frac{s}{1+r} + \frac{s}{(1+r)^2} + \cdots + \frac{s}{(1+r)^n}$$

$$= c_0 + \frac{s_1}{1+r} + \frac{s_2}{(1+r)^2} + \cdots + \frac{s_n}{(1+r)^n} = V_0$$

or $$V_0 = s \cdot \frac{1 - (1+r)^{-n}}{r}$$

i.e., the formula for the present value of an ordinary annuity of n payments. Given r, n, and V_0, there is a unique s. As n approaches infinity, the formula approaches: $V_0 = s \cdot (1/r)$, which is the expression for the present value of an infinite stream of annual payments of s dollars beginning at $t = 1$, a perpetual ordinary annuity.

5.7 INTERNAL RATES OF RETURN

The internal rate of return on a project is that rate of discount which makes the present value of the stream of *net* benefits equal to zero:

$$\sum_{t=0}^{n} \frac{b_t - c_t}{(1+i)^t} = 0*$$

In other words, knowing the streams of benefits and costs, we can find one or more rates of discount which make the present value of net benefits zero.

The internal rate of return has had great appeal as a criterion for choice in public and private investment theory and in economic theory generally. The reason is that it *appears* to permit a ranking of investments without prespecifying an interest rate. Because of this it has been advocated for use in instances where it is uncertain which rate should be used in project evaluation (which is most of the time—see below). It has also been used in certain formulations concerning how interest rates are determined by the supply of saving and the demand for investible funds. For instance, in the Keynesian system investments are ranked on the basis of their internal rate of return to form an aggregate investment demand schedule.

Since we do not use the internal rate of return in this book, we merely mention some of the pitfalls of using it and give an intuitive feeling for why they occur.

---

* The case of an initial outlay occurring contemporaneously with V_0, as above, is covered by this formula for

$$\frac{-c_0}{(1+i)^0} = c_0$$

as above.

First, there is not necessarily a unique solving rate. Compare two types of net benefit streams which are sometimes referred to as *conventional* and *nonconventional*. The former is depicted in Figure 5-3a and the second in Figure 5-3b.

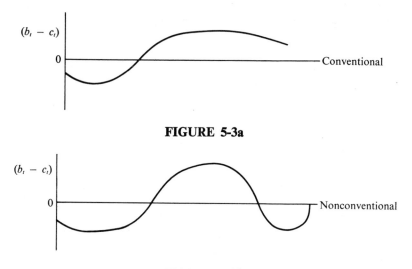

FIGURE 5-3a

FIGURE 5-3b

All cases of the type in Figure 5-3a will yield a unique internal rate of return while all of the type in Figure 5-3b may yield multiple solving rates. The latter type of stream may seem a bit strange, but important cases of it can occur in the natural resources industries. For example, an open pit mine might have first to be opened, then operated with positive net returns, and then closed and the area landscaped, thus giving rise to a net return stream which is first negative, then positive, and finally negative again. Intuitively, it is easy to see why this situation gives rise to multiple solving rates. At very low rates of interest the negative returns at the end of the time stream are weighted comparatively heavily and thus will have a zero present value at some relatively low rate. At intermediate rates the negative returns at the end weigh less heavily and we have positive V_0. But at very high rates the losses in the early period dominate and we once again have a negative value.*

---

* The mathematical explanation is also quite simple. The equation at the bottom of p. 198 is equivalent to

$$f(x) = a_1 x^t + a_2 x^{(t-1)} + \cdots + a_n x^{(t-t)} = 0$$

This equation will have t roots, all of which may be real and identical as in the case of the conventional stream of net benefits. Recall that Descartes' rule of signs says that the number of positive roots of $f(x)$ will not exceed the number of changes in sign of the sequence $a_1, a_2, \ldots, a_n$ and that the number of negative real roots will not exceed the number of changes in sign of the successive terms of $f(-x)$. Thus the conventional stream in Figure 5-3a has but one change in sign whereas the particular nonconventional stream in 5-3b contains two changes in sign, and hence will have two real roots.

Perhaps the most significant general objection to the internal rate of return is that it does not rank mutually exclusive projects properly, in the sense that the rankings may not correctly reflect the investment alternatives open to the firm as revealed by a present value calculation based on the market rate of discount. Consider, for example, the two "conventional" cases with net benefit streams as indicated on Figure 5-4.* In Case I, the net benefit stream is -1, 0, and 4 in

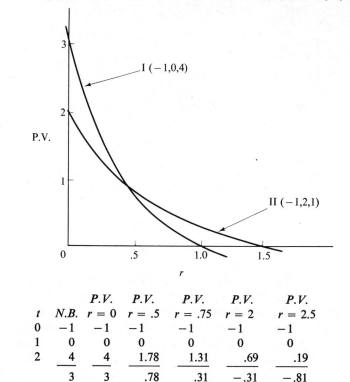

Case I

	t	N.B.	P.V. $r = 0$	P.V. $r = .5$	P.V. $r = .75$	P.V. $r = 2$	P.V. $r = 2.5$
	0	-1	-1	-1	-1	-1	-1
	1	0	0	0	0	0	0
	2	4	4	1.78	1.31	.69	.19
		3	3	.78	.31	$-.31$	$-.81$

Case II

		t	N.B.	P.V. $r = 0$	P.V. $r = .5$	P.V. $r = .75$	P.V. $r = 2$	P.V. $r = 2.5$	
1		0	-1	-1	-1	-1	-1	-1	-1
3		1	2	2	1.33	1.14	1	.829	1.60
9		2	1	1	.44	.33	.25	.171	.64
			2	2	.77	.47	.25	0	1.24

FIGURE 5-4

successive years. The graph shows the present value of this case for different market rates of interest. The present value is zero for an interest rate of 100 percent (the internal rate of return). Case II has a net benefit stream of -1, 2, and 1. Its internal rate of return is equal to the square root of 2. The present values

---

* For general discussion of this and related points and these particular numerical examples, see Jack Hirshleifer, James C. DeHaven, and Jerome W. Milliman, *Water Supply: Economics, Technology, and Policy* (Chicago: University of Chicago Press, 1960), p. 348.

of both options are equal at a discount rate of about .5 At market rates of discount less than .5, Case I has the higher present value whereas the internal rate of return ranks the projects in reverse order, as indeed will any market rate of discount higher than .5. Obviously the relative superiority of different investment options, given their net benefit streams, may be changed depending on the level of market rate of discount. It follows that the internal rate of return can yield a correct ranking of the projects only for a certain range of market rates of discount.

Because the internal rate of return cannot rank mutually exclusive projects in an unambiguous way, it also can provide no guidance as to the optimum scale of a project for which scale can be varied.

The problem here is analogous to the "maximizing the benefit-cost ratio" problem, although in our development of that matter time was not explicitly taken into account. Assume that a certain scale of project has an internal rate of return of 20 percent and that a next increment in scale has a return of 15 percent. If the rate of interest were 10 percent, the increment would be profitable but it would reduce the internal rate of return. If we then say that all increments should be undertaken until the internal rate of return on the last increment is equal to the rate of discount, we are right back to the present value criterion.

The only circumstances under which the internal rate of return procedure can result in an unambiguous ranking of projects is when the projects have conventional streams of returns, are mutually exclusive, and every individual project has a fixed scale. These conditions are sufficiently restrictive to make internal rates of return, at least when used by themselves, virtually useless. We can also see now why the internal rate of return cannot be used to specify a demand schedule for investible funds independent of the supply schedule and then an intersection of the two used to determine a rate of interest. Just as an example, the optimum scales of the projects cannot be determined unless the interest rate is known. Thus a demand for capital schedule must contain all projects which have a positive present value of net returns at alternative interest rates *and* must reflect their optimum scales. These cannot be determined without specifying a rate of discount.

A final objection which has seemed important to some* is that the internal rate of return is a single rate and cannot reflect changes in the scarcity of funds in different periods in the future. The present value calculation, on the other hand, is flexible in this regard. In its most general form the discrete formula can be written as follows:

$$V_0 = -c_0 + \frac{S_1}{1 + r_1} + \frac{S_2}{(1 + r_1)(1 + r_2)} + \cdots$$

$$+ \frac{S_n}{(1 + r_1)(1 + r_2) \cdots (1 + r_{n-1})(1 + r_n)}$$

---

* See A. C. Harberger, "Survey of Literature on Cost-Benefit Analysis for Industrial Project Evaluations," in United Nations Industrial Development Organization, Project Formulation and Evaluation Series, Vol. I, *Evaluation of Industrial Projects*, United Nations, New York, 1968.

or more compactly

$$-c_0 + \sum_{i=1}^{n} \frac{S_i}{\prod_{t=1}^{i} (1 + r_t)}$$

Thus a different rate of interest reflecting capital scarcity in each period can be inserted if such differential rates are known or can be estimated.

It has sometimes been claimed, probably with validity, that the calculation of internal rates of return for projects and project increments is useful in the presence of uncertainty concerning future costs or returns. The idea is that since the present value calculation focuses only on net benefits, it will not distinguish between a project (or project increment) that has small costs and relatively large benefits and one that has large costs and relatively small benefits if the present value of the net benefits is the same. Compare, for example, these two projects:

	Project 1	Project 2
P.V. of benefits	$20	$200
P.V. of costs	10	190
P.V. of net benefits	$10	$ 10

Under no-risk conditions this lack of distinction between the two cases is appropriate, but where risk must be taken into account, the former may be preferred. Consequently, in risky situations both present value and internal rate of return calculations may yield useful information. Note, however, that the present value criterion can be generalized to take specific account of risk, as will be shown later.

5.8   TIMING OF INVESTMENT

We have not yet addressed the question of the optimum timing of investment. The implication has been that undertaking immediately all investments with a positive present value of net benefits will produce maximum present value of net benefit. But this proves not to be correct once the dynamic aspect of invest- ment is considered. This point has been developed by Marglin, and we shall present one of his examples here.*

Assume that a project has a projected construction cost of $1,000. Assume also a simple form of growth in demand such that the project will yield benefits (net of OMR costs) of $10 per year in the years from 1971 through 1990 and that the same outputs will yield $100 per year after that. We assume that net benefits are realized at the end of the year and that all present values are calculated as of January 1, 1971.

---

* See Maass et al., op. cit., p. 179.

Assume further that the construction outlay remains the same regardless of the year of construction and is incurred on the first day of the year. Assume also that project age has no influence on the benefit rates that are scheduled. That is, the pattern of potential yields is the same regardless of the year of construction. Finally, assume that the project yields benefits of $100 indefinitely into the future *once this level has been reached*, and that all the benefits accrue on the last day of the year, with the benefits stream starting at the end of the year of construction. Thus the stream of benefits could be:

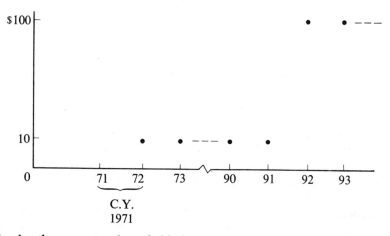

Clearly, the present value of this investment opportunity is going to vary according to the date of construction. If the project is constructed at the beginning of 1971, the present value of the construction cost will be higher than if it is constructed later.

At a 5 percent rate of discount, it turns out that the present value (as of January 1, 1971) of the benefit stream is $878.40. This is made up of two components: first, $124.62 which is the present value of the initial benefit stream of $10 per year running from the end of 1971 to the end of 1990, and second, the present value of the perpetual stream of net benefits beginning at the end of 1991 which is $2,000 as of the end of 1990 which, when discounted back to January 1, 1971, has a present value as of then of $753.78. Costs exceed benefits by $121.60 and it is clear that the project is not economically efficient.

If similar calculations are made for later dates of construction, there will be a saving in construction costs in terms of present value $= 1000 \times (1 + r)^{-(t_0 - 1971)}$ as of January 1, 1971, because the construction outlays are made at a later time. On the other hand, the present value, again as of January 1, 1971, of the initial benefit stream of 10 per year will be less because it starts later.

The results of a series of these calculations are shown in Figure 5-5. Until 1991 the gain in net present value from delaying construction is positive, but in 1991 it changes sign. Therefore, 1991 is the year in which net present value as of 1971 is at a maximum and equals $376.89. The ratio of present value of gross benefits to present value of costs is 2/1. Figure 5-5 shows the path of net present

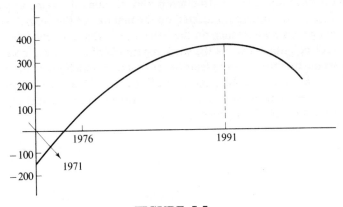

FIGURE 5-5

value of benefits for the project as a function of time.

The case described is a simple one because of the various assumptions made above (especially that benefits are independent of the age of the project) and because it takes no account of the possibility of staging. Nevertheless, it communicates the essential idea that if demand is changing over time there is an optimum date of construction. The mere fact that a project has a positive present value if constructed as of "now" does not mean that it should be constructed at that time, for the present value as of the same date may be greater if constructed at another point in time. The techniques for making analyses like the above have been elaborated for much more complex cases,* but analysis of optimal timing of public investment projects has by no means become routine practice.

5.9　WHICH RATE OF DISCOUNT?

We now must look at one of the current controversial questions with respect to the evaluation of public investment. Granted that the present value criterion is the appropriate one for comparing future streams of benefits and cost, which discount rate should be used? Argument concerning this issue is complex and multi-faceted. We hope here to sketch some of the major positions that have been taken and the rationales supporting them, and to state a *judgmental* position of our own.† We start with some general background on the question.

For many years the federal water resources agencies have used rates of discount which many economists have regarded as being excessively low. For a

---

* See Stephen A. Marglin, *Approaches to Dynamic Investment Planning* (Amsterdam: North-Holland Publishing Co., 1963).

† A rather complete discussion is found in *The Discount Rate in Public Investment Evaluation* Conference Proceedings, Committee on the Economics of Water Resource Development of the Western Agricultural Economics Research Council, Denver, Colorado, Dec. 17–18, 1968.

long time (through the 1950s and into the 1960s) the rate stood at $2\frac{5}{8}$ percent. For much of the period, this was below even the rate on long-term government securities. This low rate resulted from a combination of the "pegging" of interest rates at a low level by the Federal Reserve through the early post-war years and the way the discount rate was calculated.

The same rule for calculating the rate was stated in the "Greenbook" and in "S-97" (the two federal guideline documents mentioned in the introduction to this chapter). The rate was to be based on the coupon rate of interest on U.S. government securities outstanding which, upon original issue, had terms to maturity of 15 years or more. In recent years, as interest rates rose far above their post-war average, the computed discount rate has crept up, until in late 1968 it was at $3\frac{1}{4}$ percent.

Largely due to continued pressures from economists and the interest shown by several members of Congress, the discount rate policy was changed near the end of 1968. The new policy is that discount rates are to be based on " . . . the *yield* during the preceding fiscal year on interest-bearing marketable securities of the United States which at the time the computation is made have terms of 15 years or more remaining to maturity."* This change in policy brought the discount rate to $4\frac{5}{8}$ percent in the fiscal year 1969. Some economists believe that this rate is still much too low and that the rate for public projects should reflect opportunity costs of capital in the private sector which they estimate to be 8–10 percent.

Nevertheless, this change caused consternation in the federal agencies and their clientele groups, and much pressure has developed to revise project evaluation procedures with a view to increasing calculated benefits, thereby maintaining positive net benefits in spite of the higher rate of discount.

It is easy to understand the concern of the federal agencies. Most water resource projects produce a stream of costs and returns such that there are heavy net outlays in the early period, and net benefits start to accrue only after some lapse of time. Thus the present value of net benefits is very sensitive to increases in the rate of discount. A pertinent empirical study was made several years ago by Fox and Herfindahl.† They reevaluated federal projects authorized by Congress in 1962, which had generally been evaluated at $2\frac{5}{8}$ percent, at successively higher rates of 4, 6, and 8 percent. The following percentages of the initial gross investments in these projects would have had benefit-cost ratios of less than unity: 9 percent at the 4 percent rate of discount, 64 percent at the 6 percent rate of discount, and 80 percent at the 8 percent rate of discount. These calculations exaggerate the actual effects somewhat because they do not provide for rescaling the projects to reflect the higher rates. Nevertheless, the point is clear—with discount rates of 8–10 percent and present evaluation procedures very few projects would have a present value of benefits n excess of costs.

---

* *Federal Register*, December 24, 1968, p. 19170.
† Irving K. Fox and O. C. Herfindahl, "Attainment of Efficiency in Satisfying Demands for Water Resources," *American Economic Review*, Vol. 54, No. 2, May 1964, p. 198.

A countercurrent to the pressure for higher discount rates has also been running with increasing velocity since the 1950s. Eckstein, in his excellent study mentioned in the introduction to this chapter, was concerned that high rates of discount would prevent distribution of income to future generations which the present generation might deem desirable.* He saw dams as almost uniquely durable items of capital which could be bequeathed to future generations. He also saw, however, that if rates of discount used on public projects are substantially below rates of return in the private sector, private projects which would be more productive might be displaced and therefore the heritage of capital available to future generations might actually be reduced. He therefore resorted to the device of evaluating both public projects and private alternatives at the "social rate of discount" and accepting only those public projects for which as a whole, and for each separable increment, the present value of net benefit equalled or exceeded the revalued private alternatives. This put extremely long-lived projects in a more favorable relative position but still did not accept a project whose "social rate of return" was below that of projects in the private sector—when discounted at the social rate of return. This line of thought was greatly elaborated by Marglin, and we shall sketch at least his basic model shortly. Before we begin, however, we should point out that the proposed devices lead us inevitably into the world of the "second best" where analytically satisfying results are notoriously hard to derive.

One response to Eckstein's argument was that if there is such a thing as a social rate of discount, then surely the optimal solution would be to use monetary and fiscal tools to bring the private and social rates into conjunction. All participants in the debate seem to agree that this would be the optimal procedure. But the proponents of devising investment criteria to reflect divergencies between social and private costs argue that political and institutional obstacles may make this impossible. (We will return to this point shortly).

Marglin believes that divergencies between private and social discount rates are possible even if there are no barriers to free exchange.† He uses an example to show how a collective saving decision might differ from the individual decisions of private parties due to differences between the social and individual time preference of each individual. Assume that $1.00 of consumption available to future individuals satisfies individual i equivalently to $.10 of his own consumption today. If investment of $1.00 will at the margin provide $2.00 for a future member of the community (investment is productive), individual i would not undertake investment *specifically* for the benefit of a future individual because the psychic cost would be $1.00 for psychic gain of $.20 (2 × $.10).

In public investment decisions, however, the outcome may change. Here, individual i knows that his sacrifice will be accompanied by sacrifices imposed on all other members of the community. Thus the pyschic gain to individual i

---

* Recall the discussion in Chapter 3.
† Recall that in Chapter 3 we said this was obvious—if the social rate of discount is determined by some means other than transactions in the capital markets, say by voting.

from the increased future consumption is no longer $2 \times .10 = .20$ but $n(2 \times .10) = n(.20)$.

Individual i also incurs a psychic cost because of the consumption sacrificed by his contemporaries, each of whom provides a dollar for investment. Suppose that $1.00 of a contemporary's consumption is viewed as worth $.15 of i's own consumption.

Then, assuming that all are required to undertake an equal amount of extra investment to provide for future generations and that all members of the present generation have similar preferences with respect to their own, their contemporaries', and future individuals' consumption, the marginal time preference for each person is the ratio of psychic gain to him from future consumption to psychic loss from contemporary consumption sacrificed, *as valued by him*:

$$\frac{2n(.10)}{1 + (n - 1)(.15)}$$

With each dollar of investment returning $2 of future consumption, this ratio is greater than 1 for $n > 17$, in which case the investment would be regarded as desirable by each person if it were financed so that the burden fell equally on himself and his fellow contemporary consumers, say through a uniform tax. The reader will, of course, recognize this as a species of externality argument based on interdependence of utility functions of different individuals.

Clearly, what the argument purports to demonstrate is that if this type of interdependence exists, and if it is assumed that we can sum and compare the utility functions of different individuals in the same and in different generations, market interest rates may not generate a socially optimal rate of investment. Of course, it does not demonstrate that individuals must value the consumption of future generations resulting from a dollar's worth of present investment more highly than the foregone consumption of the present generation. Given the fact that income has tended to rise over time, and if there exists diminishing marginal utility of income, it would seem reasonable to assume that a rational and informed person would value other people's future consumption *less* at the margin than his contemporaries'. Nevertheless, many proponents of the social rate of discount have tended to assume that if a collective choice were made, it would come out as in the above example. They then proceed to spell out the implications for public investment criteria.

As previously noted, everyone seems to agree that the overall optimal response to a divergence between private and social rates is to use monetary and fiscal policies to bring them into conjunction so that all investment decisions (public and private) would be discounted at the same rate. Again, proponents of devising public investment criteria to reflect social rates of discount cite institutional and political obstacles. Of course, once different rates are used in the public than in the private sector, no matter how elaborate the criteria devised to compensate, we are inevitably in the world of second best where analytically firm conclusions are difficult to obtain.

Another counterargument to using social discounting in the evaluation of public projects is that maximum future consumption can be achieved by using the rate of return in the private sector and accepting no public projects which display a non-positive present value of net benefits when discounted at this rate. This conclusion would follow if public investment displaced private investment dollar for dollar and all "throwoff" (monetary return) from public investment could be reinvested. The government could then engage in direct redistribution of consumption to meet the time pattern implied by the social rate of discount. Two arguments are brought against this proposition. First, public investment does not necessarily displace private investment dollar for dollar but may also displace current consumption. Secondly, it is asserted that the government cannot necessarily rearrange consumption separately from its investment activities. Two reasons are brought forward for the latter. First, much of the output of government activities is consumed without any flow of funds, which could be reinvested, back to the government. This results from little or no reimbursement being required for many outputs. Second, there is no institutional mechanism whereby the government can, like a private decision maker, "borrow" consumption against the security of future benefits. Thus, the argument runs, there is no escape from giving attention to the time stream of consumption directly when evaluating the benefits of a public investment.

An example of proposals to deal with this situation is provided by the simplest of the investment criteria models devised by Marglin. He argues that the discount rates used for private consumption and investment activities are relevant to the formulation of intertemporal public investment criteria even though the social rate of discount is different. This results from the fact that public investment displaces private investment to some extent.

The device used to incorporate the higher return on private investment into the criterion is to discount the private sector rate of return with the social rate of discount to get a "shadow price" representing the opportunity cost of public investment. The simplest case is where every dollar used for public investment displaces private investment. Assume that the rate of return in the private sector is ρ. It is assumed that all returns from private investment are consumed as they become available to avoid having to take into account reinvestment of "throwoff" in the private sector. If we designate the social rate of discount as r, the present value of the opportunity cost of capital is ρ/r.* In other words, the "cutoff" benefit-cost ratio would have to be ρ/r when marginal net benefits (or benefits and OMR costs) are discounted at the social rate.

This model can be elaborated slightly to allow variable fractions of private investment to be displaced per dollar of public investment. Let that proportion be designated by α where $0 \leq \alpha \leq 1$. With this additional variable, the opportunity cost of water resource development accounting for private invest-

---

* Recall the formula for the discounting of perpetual benefit streams from our earlier discussion in this chapter: ρ is to be regarded as a perpetual stream of income which is capitalized at the rate r to obtain the social value of a dollar of capital taken from the private sector.

ment foregone for each dollar of capital outlay in the current period is

$$\frac{[\alpha\rho + (1 - \alpha)r]}{r}$$

The opportunity cost of systems construction then becomes

$$\frac{[\alpha\rho + (1 - \alpha)r][K(\mathbf{X})]}{r}$$

where $K(\mathbf{X})$ represents the normal or money cost of the vector of capital inputs. As the reader can readily calculate for himself, if the private rate is 10 percent and the social rate 5 percent and investment is drawn half and half from private investment and consumption, the "cutoff" benefit-cost ratio must be 1.5. In other words, at the margin, a dollar's worth of investment must return at least $1.50 in present value of net benefits evaluated at the social rate of discount.

The above analysis has assumed that "throwoff" from both the private and public investments is immediately consumed.

This intertemporal criterion can be greatly extended and complicated by taking into account reinvestment of throwoff from both sectors. We shall not do so here, but the interested reader can consult the work of Marglin.*

In our *judgment* (previously explained) no very strong case has been made for the application of social rates of time discount to public projects. But, even if this judgment is accepted, we are still far from being on firm ground on the discount rate question. In order to reveal more clearly the considerations involved, let us examine the discount rate problem in abstraction from the question of altering the market-determined overall rate of saving for the benefit (or loss) of future generations.

Four positions are considered here: those of Hirshleifer–Shapiro, Arrow–Lind, Baumol, and Steiner. We shall try to explain the differences between these writers and the extent to which their recommendations for practice are in accord.

The State-Preference Approach

Both Hirshleifer and Arrow approach the problem of the discount rate by use of state-preference theory.† This theory has the merit of isolating what seem to be the important elements in this problem, including the role of risk in the discount

---

* Stephen A. Marglin, "The Social Rate of Discount and the Optimal Rate of Investment," *Quarterly Journal of Economics*, Vol. 77, No. 1 (Feb. 1963), pp. 95–111.

† See J. Hirshleifer and D. L. Shapiro, "The Treatment of Risk and Uncertainty," in *ibid.*, pp. 505–30; and K. J. Arrow and R. C. Lind, "Uncertainty and the Evaluation of Public Investment Decisions," *American Economic Review*, June 1970, Vol. 60, No. 3, pp. 364–78, and articles cited therein.

process. In addition, it will provide a basis for understanding how Baumol's position differs from those of these two writers.

We begin with the notion of a *basic claim*.* This is a claim to one dollar to be received at a specified future time. If it is not a certain claim (i.e., to be received with certainty), it will be contingent on the existence of a certain state of the world (prosperity, depression, war, peace, drought, etc.). There are many possible states, of course, and they are multi-dimensional, although for many types of investments many of the dimensions will be of no importance. Thus a claim has a date tag and a state tag. Each claim has a present value price, P_{1a} being the present price of a claim to \$1 at $t = 1$ which is to be paid if state a happens to exist at that time. Thus, we may have P_{2b}, P_{3e}, P_{1b}, etc. In the case of certainty (the claim is to be paid no matter what the state of the world), the present price of a claim to \$1 in period 1 is defined as $P_1 = [1/(1 + r_1)]$, where r_1 is the rate of interest.

Now suppose an additional increment of investment, Δi, is under consideration. It will result in an addition to net receipts of ΔS_1 in period 1 and there will be an associated increment in present value, ΔV_0. Note that ΔS_1 is a sum of money. It may be thought of as a quantity of some physical product sold in period 1 multiplied by the period 1 price of that product minus production outlays made in period 1.

The criterion for deciding whether or not to undertake the investment is the sign of the increment in present value. If the increment is positive, invest. If negative, do not. The increment in present value, ΔV_0, is found by multiplying Δi_0 and ΔS_1 by the prices that express the values of these dated claims as of now; that is, by prices that convert current values to present values. Thus $V_0 = -P_0 \Delta i_0 + P_1 \Delta S_1$. Since P_0 is the present price of a dollar received or paid in period o, it is equal to 1. P_1 is the price at $t = 0$ of a certain dollar received at $t = 1$.

This formulation can be extended to the uncertain case, and a V_0 can be formed which reflects all the possible states and which may be called the *present certainty-equivalent value*, so that $\Delta V_0 = -P_0 \Delta i_0 + P_{1a} \Delta S_{1a} + P_{1b} \Delta S_{1b} + \cdots$ if the P's have been determined in perfect markets. This V_0 pertains to a particular type of investment. The net returns in period 1 (or any other period in the general formulation) depend on the state of the world that actually exists. S_{1a} and S_{1b} may differ, for example, because of different physical yields (e.g., crop yields in drought and non-drought years) and/or because of different current prices for product. The P's in the equation, which pertain to contingent claims for a dollar in each of the possible states, are viewed as objective market prices. Thus V_0 does not depend on the individual decision maker's time preference nor on his estimates of the probabilities of the different states of the world at time $t = 1$. The market has arbitrated among the time preferences and estimates of state probabilities of all participants and produced a set of equilibrium prices for claims. Thus the P's reflect the time preferences and wishes for income-cum-

---

* This section is essentially a recapitulation of the Hirshleifer–Shapiro exposition.

state of everybody in the economy plus demands for goods in the different states and investment opportunities.

To illustrate, assume an investment of \$1 with a return of \$3 if state a but with \$0 if state b (there are only two states). If $P_{1a} = .3$ and $P_{1b} = .5$ then $\Delta V_0 = -1 + .3(3) + .5(0) = -.1$. Do not invest! On the other hand, a riskless investment opportunity with a return of \$2 regardless of state (symbolized by $(-1\frac{2}{2})$) would have a P.V. of $[-1 + .3(2) + .5(2)] = .6$. Invest!

Analogously with the certainty case, where $P_1 = [1/(1 + r_1)]$, the riskless rate of interest associated with a certain claim can be expressed as

$$P_1 = P_{1a} + P_{1b} = \frac{1}{(1 + r_1)}$$

In the preceding cases, for example, $P_1 = .3 + .5 = [1/(1 + r_1)]$, or $r_1 = .25$.

We are now in a position to see what is involved in discounting the mathematically expected return by the riskless rate of interest. Since the criterion for undertaking an investment is that the present certainty-equivalent value (see above) be positive, what conditions are required for this value to be equal to that obtained by discounting expected returns by the riskless rate of interest?

The key condition here is that state probabilities be proportional to basic claims prices. If they are, discounting expected returns by the riskless rate of interest, r_1, will give the correct *present certainty-equivalent value*. If they are not, this will not be true, and the derivation of the correct certainty-equivalent value will require the use of the appropriate *risky rate of interest*, r_1^*.

To see why this is so, first let us define the risky rate of interest as that rate which will yield the correct present certainty-equivalent value when used to discount expected returns. That is, with state probabilities designated as π_{1a}, π_{1b}, etc.,

$$\Delta V_0 = -P_0 \Delta i_0 + \frac{\pi_{1a} \Delta S_{1a} + \pi_{1b} \Delta S_{1b}}{1 + r_1^*}$$

$$= -P_0 \Delta i_0 + P_{1a} \Delta S_{1a} + P_{1b} \Delta S_{1b}$$

That is, r_1^* will depend on the ratio of two weighted sums of the net returns, the weights being state probabilities for one sum and basic claims prices for the other:

$$1 + r_1^* = \frac{\pi_{1a} \Delta S_{1a} + \pi_{1b} \Delta S_{1b}}{P_{1a} \Delta S_{1a} + P_{1b} \Delta S_{1b}}$$

Under what conditions would discounting by the *riskless* rate give the correct ΔV_0? That is, what would be required for $1 + r_1^*$ to be equal to $1 + r_1 = 1/(P_{1a} + P_{1b})$? The required condition is that state probabilities be proportional to basic claims prices (i.e., that $\pi_{1a} = kP_{1a}$, etc.), for then

$$1 + r_1 = \frac{1}{P_{1a} + P_{1b}} = \frac{kP_{1a}\,\Delta S_{1a} + kP_{1b}\,\Delta S_{1b}}{P_{1a}\,\Delta S_{1a} + P_{1b}\,\Delta S_{1b}}$$

or $$\frac{1}{k(P_{1a} + P_{1b})} = 1$$

which is true since

$$\pi_{1a} + \pi_{1b} = kP_{1a} + kP_{1b} = 1$$

(state probabilities add to one).

If investors were indifferent among the different states with respect to receipt of income, then the P's would be proportional to state probabilities and the riskless rate applied to expected returns would give the correct present certainty-equivalent value. If this is not the case, the appropriate risky rate differs from the riskless rate, depending on the differences between the expected pattern of returns and the preferred pattern of returns. If a certain type of investment has low expected returns for states for which investors would like to have higher returns, the risky rate will be higher than the riskless rate, and vice versa.*

It is clear from this expression that the appropriate discount rate, r_1^*, given the probabilities of the various states and the market determined P's, will vary among investments except for those investments that have similar relative patterns of ΔS's among the different states. The patterns are similar for the ith and jth investments if $\Delta_i S_{1s} = k\,\Delta_j S_{1s}$ where k is a constant. Such groups of investments may be said to form a *risk class*. One such class is the class of riskless investments, that is, those with the same return in all states.

Let us consider in more detail how it may happen that the P's are not proportional to the probabilities of occurrence of the various states. Remember that the P's are prices for contingent dollars and do not refer to prices of products resulting from a particular investment.

Suppose there is a society in which food is produced by agriculture and there is no fluctuation in yield. Now imagine that some observant fellow sees that in some years fish come up the nearby river in large numbers but that in some years there are no fish. There seems to be no pattern in their arrivals. It is not possible

---

* To illustrate the possibility that the risky rate, r_1^*, can be lower than the riskless rate, r_1, consider an investment, $(-1\frac{2}{3})$, with $P_{1a} = .3$ and $P_{1b} = .5$. Here P_1, the price of a certain claim, is .8 and $1 + r_1 = 1/P_1 = 1.25$, and $r_1 = .25$. The risky rate, assuming state probabilities are each .5, is given by

$$1 + r_1^* = \frac{.5(1) + .5(3)}{.3(1) + .5(3)} = \frac{2}{1.8} = \frac{10}{9} \qquad \text{with} \qquad r_1^* = \tfrac{1}{9} = .111$$

This happens because preferences, as reflected in the market determined P's, are not distributed as are the state probabilities. This investment opportunity generates returns that are relatively larger in the favored state.

to store fish for more than a year. If there is investment in fishing equipment, however, fish can be caught in the years in which they come. The investment is subject to diminishing returns. How is this new investment possibility to be evaluated? Each increment of investment in fishing equipment gives rise to contingent claims for two states—with fish, without fish. To simplify matters further, assume that fish are a perfect substitute for the agricultural product. First, consider the special case in which the social totals of income are the same in different states. Here, the P's clearly will be proportional to the π's whether there is risk aversion or risk neutrality. Everyone would be willing to pay the same price for a \$1 contingent claim to any state, scaled down, of course, by multiplying by its probability of occurrence. If returns for some types of investment vary among states, however, there is a possibility that the P's for the claims will not be proportional to the π's.

In the case of agricultural investment, the S's for the two states will be the same. In the case of fishing investment, the pattern will be a positive real return for one state and zero for the other. With agricultural investment alone, the P's clearly would have been proportional to the π's, for the state actually realized would not affect return. With investment in fishing, however, expected income for the one state will differ from that for the other, and the P's must be adjusted by the market so that the participants are willing to hold all of the contingent claims generated.

What happens to the P's depends on how the participants in the market view fluctuations in income. If there are enough persons to whom fluctuation in income is a matter of indifference (i.e., the utility loss from a \$1,000 fall from average income is fully compensated by a \$1,000 surplus over average next year), there will be hardly any change in the P's, for such persons can be induced to hold the contingent claims generated by investment in fishing by a negligible "premium," the only requirement being that at the margin the investment of a dollar in fishing will yield the same expected annual return in fish as would investment of a dollar in agriculture yield in equivalent agricultural product.

Suppose, however, that there are not enough such people—indeed, there may not be any. Then the only way to induce the holding of contingent claims that open the possibility of a societal fluctuating income will be to pay to induce somebody to do so. That is, in those states whose claims form a larger percentage of claims for all states than their π's, the price of a contingent claim will go down and vice versa for the price of a unit claim for those states which find themselves "short" of claims. If incomes were uniform and utility functions the same for all persons, including attitudes toward fluctuating incomes, each person would end up with a package of claims. The social risk of fluctuating income—which is inescapable if there is any investment in fishing—would be spread as widely as possible in order to minimize the utility cost of fluctuating income. Note that nothing has been said so far about private risk premia that may be required because of inability to disperse risk of fluctuating income.

A numerical example may help to clarify some of the above points. Suppose that the probability of state a with fish is .5 and that of state b without fish is .5.

The market has established P_{1a} at .4 and P_{1b} at .5. At the margin, we have

$$0 = V_0 = -1 + P_{1a}\,\Delta S_{1a} + P_{1b}\,\Delta S_{1b}$$

or for agriculture

$$0 = -1 + .4(\tfrac{10}{9}) + .5(\tfrac{10}{9})$$

and for a \$1 investment in fishing

$$0 = -1 + .4(\tfrac{5}{2}) + .5(0)$$

For agriculture the rate to be used for discounting expected return is

$$1 + r^* = \frac{.5(\tfrac{10}{9}) + .5(\tfrac{10}{9})}{.4(\tfrac{10}{9}) + .5(\tfrac{10}{9})} = \frac{\tfrac{10}{9}}{1} = 1\tfrac{1}{9} \quad \text{or} \quad r^* = \tfrac{1}{9}$$

This is the same as the riskless or certainty rate given by $1/(1 + r_1) = P_{1a} + P_{1b}$ since agriculture is a certain investment (return the same in all states). For fishing, however, the proper discount rate is higher:

$$1 + r^* = \frac{.5(\tfrac{5}{2}) + .5(0)}{.4(\tfrac{5}{2}) + .5(0)} = \frac{\tfrac{5}{4}}{1} = 1\tfrac{1}{4} \quad \text{or} \quad r^* = \tfrac{1}{4}$$

In the foregoing example there is only one type of risky investment and variability in its outcome necessarily causes variation in the income of the society. Suppose, however, that the keen observer discovered not one river with random arrival of fish, but several such rivers. In this case the return from a particular type of investment will vary with the state of the world actually realized, but societal income will be approximately stable if the number of different types of investment is large enough. By combining claims from different types of investment, a constant annual income could be secured. The result would be that the prices of the basic claims would be equal, adjusted of course by the probability of occurrence of the state. That is, the P's would be proportional to the probabilities of state occurrence.* However, if society is not indifferent to

---

* The two rates of discount indicate that this society is averse to risk (fluctuation in income). Suppose that the P's as they are, a new investment prospect is conceived whose returns complement those of investment in fishing. Initially, the risky rate for this investment based on the old P's will be very low. Suppose that the returns are just the reverse of those for fishing investment. Then the risky rate for the new type of investment will be:

$$1 + r_1^* = \frac{.5(0) + .5(\tfrac{5}{2})}{.4(0) + .5(\tfrac{5}{2})} = \frac{\tfrac{5}{4}}{\tfrac{5}{4}} = 1 \quad \text{or} \quad r_1^* = 0$$

The increase in the volume of this type of investment will change the composition of the claims available, and if the offsetting of social income fluctuations is complete, claims prices for the two states will be equal, say at .45 (or, in the more general case, proportional to state probabilities). In this case, the risky rate is the same for all three types of investment even though the distribution of net returns among states is different. For the new type of investment,

$$1 + r^* = \frac{.5(0) + .5(\tfrac{5}{2})}{.45(0) + .45(\tfrac{5}{2})} = \frac{10}{9} \quad \text{or} \quad r^* = \tfrac{1}{9}$$

For fishing investment,

$$1 + r^* = \frac{.5(\tfrac{5}{2}) + .5(0)}{.45(\tfrac{5}{2}) + .45(0)} + \frac{10}{9} \quad \text{or} \quad r^* = \tfrac{1}{9}$$

as it does also for agricultural investment.

changes in the composition of returns from different types of investment (recall that in this case fish were perfect substitutes for agricultural product), then variability in investment outcome may be associated with variation in societal income and P's will no longer be proportional to probabilities of state occurrence.

The basic Arrow–Lind analysis is the same as that of Hirshleifer–Shapiro, although the formulation of the former in the publication cited is more general than that of the latter in the Joint Committee version. Thus if there were perfect markets for the basic claims, each pair of writers would be in agreement that the risky rate for each investment should be used if returns to a type of investment vary with societal income. They would also agree that the riskless rate should be used for investments, private and governmental, where this is not the case, for then free trading of claims would result in the same price of claim per expected dollar of return in each state. There is no social risk in this case.*

The disagreement, if that is the proper word, between the two pairs of writers has its roots in differing views with respect to two basic elements in this problem: (1) How great is the departure of actual markets from perfect markets for the P's? and (2) Are returns correlated with changes in societal income? If they are, is it appropriate to proceed on the assumption that they are not?

Arrow–Lind put considerable stress on imperfections in the markets for claims. In general terms, the imperfections are two, moral hazard and the cost of operating markets. Moral hazard refers to the situation in which a person, supposedly obligated to maximize expected return in the interests of his principal (or insurer), may not do so for reasons of his own that may be legal or illegal. Burning an over-insured house is a case of moral hazard being realized for an illegal reason. Moral hazard—for reasons ordinarily regarded as legal—is also exemplified by the corporate or governmental bureaucrat who, in order to avoid occasional spectacular losses that may arouse questions about his competence, makes decisions so conservative that the long-run interests of his principal are damaged. Other costs of operating markets for claims are clearly far from negligible, a fact well demonstrated by the existence of brokers' fees.

Arrow–Lind recognize that returns are not always independent of changes in societal income but conduct their analysis on the assumption of independence, justifying this procedure by observing that evaluations of investment opportunities usually do not attempt to take this association into account, either because anti-cyclical policy is expected to be successful or because market prices may be used for valuations if maintenance of full employment is assumed.

Now we come to the question of private risk as distinguished from the social risk we have just been considering. If markets for basic claims are imperfect in substantial degree, claims prices will then reflect differing degrees of private risk (in the sense of dispersion of return from investments of a given size and type). The utility flow of some individuals will be less (assuming risk aversion) because of this than it would be if they could trade claims in markets without imperfections.

---

* Remember that we still are assuming no corporation income tax.

From this it follows—almost immediately on the basis of "intuition" but not quite so readily in a mathematical formulation—that if a particular investment is shifted from the private to the public sector, if returns are not correlated with fluctuations in societal income, if there is no moral hazard in the public sector, *and if returns are shared by all*, that the adverse effect of private risk on utility is reduced by the fact that it is now shared by all "owners" of the government. An improvement is possible in the sense that it would be possible to finance from the same sources, and offer a certain return with no diminution in social product. Indeed, there would be an improvement even if the government investment displaced a private investment with a higher return calculated with the riskless rate, provided only that the private return calculated with the risky rate is lower than that of the government alternative. *The main point to be noted here is that moving funds from the private to the government investment brings about a different and more advantageous distribution of risks, assuming risk aversion.*

Suppose, for example, that a given increment in a government investment of a particular type yields \$4 and that $P_1 = [1/(1 + r_1)] = .7$, or $r_1 = \frac{3}{7}$. This is superior to a private investment of the same size yielding \$5 but with P_1 reduced by a private risk premium of .2 because of imperfections in the market for basic claims. That is, $4(.7) = 2.8$ is greater than $5(.7 - .2) = 2.5$. Of course if it were possible to eliminate the .2 risk premium by insurance (ruled out by assumption) then the private investment would be superior with $5(.7) = 3.5$.

Arrow–Lind do not consider the possibility of moral hazard in the public sector (at least as defined above), but do make one important qualification to the basic argument. If benefits and/or costs do accrue to particular individuals in such a way that they bear the risk of uncertainty of income, allowance for risk would be appropriate. For example, if income from irrigation investment is uncertain and is not correlated with the other components of the income of the farmers affected, a deduction from the riskless P_1 would be in order. However, if the investment served to stabilize income, a higher P would be applied to irrigation investment than had been applied to the farmer's investment made previously.

Hirshleifer–Shapiro probably would agree with this analysis—given the assumptions.* It appears, however, that they attach considerably less importance to imperfections in the market for claims than do Arrow–Lind, although neither pair has attempted to quantify their view of the imperfection in the articles cited.† Hirshleifer–Shapiro also feel that the assumption of independence between returns and social income is an inappropriate basis from which to derive prescriptions applicable to the evaluation of public investments. If there is correlation, they point out that even with perfect claims markets the P's per dollar of expected income would not be uniform because of the diminishing utility of income. Claims for states with relatively lower returns would

---

* See *op. cit.*, p. 527.

† There is a great deal of evidence that bears somewhat indirectly on this question although, as Hirshleifer points out (*op. cit.*, p. 511), a complete resolution does not seem to be possible.

have higher prices. Thus with P's not proportional to state probabilities, the riskless rate of discount would not be appropriate. Another point they have emphasized, which is important for prescription, is that the government does not distribute time-state claims in accord with consumers' marginal preferences, this difficulty casting some doubt on the ability of the government to bring about a "real" improvement rather than only bring about its possibility.

Recall that the assumption thus far has been that there is a basic claim, with its corresponding price, for each state in each period. Clearly this does not describe the real world, in which there are innumerable states (each of them multidimensional, too). Ordinary securities represent combinations of basic P's, being claims covering many periods and many states. If the basic P's are not observable, how can the appropriate r_1^*'s (risky rates) be determined? Hirshleifer suggests that the concept of *risk class* provides the key here. That is, a certain type of investment undertaken by government will be a member of some risk class. If there also are private investments that are thought to be in the same risk class, then claims prices (for actual securities and not P's for basic claims) as determined on the private market can be used to determine the appropriate r_1^*. This would be an average of yields on stocks and bonds weighted by the finance provided by each. This would be equivalent to return on capital in firms corresponding to this class of investment.

To summarize, Arrow–Lind suggest using the riskless rate as the criterion for evaluating government investment; Hirshleifer–Shapiro suggest using a rate that reflects market valuations for the *risk class* in which the government investment opportunity falls. One final reminder. The decision on whether a particular investment should be undertaken by government or the private sphere does not depend only on choosing the appropriate rate of discount. It depends on the benefits and costs for *each* case, and they are not necessarily the same in each sphere. This is merely to say that government is more efficient at doing some things—some even being impossible for either the private or governmental sphere—and private enterprise is more efficient at others.

Baumol's Analysis*

Baumol begins by suggesting that if consumers are willing to purchase long-term government bonds at an interest rate of r percent, this constitutes a reasonably acceptable estimate of their time preference. Use of the long-term rate of government bonds has been advocated as an appropriate rate of discount for public projects on this ground. The reader will realize that this basically is present government policy. The problem is, however, that even if r is accepted as an estimate of marginal time preference, it is not an adequate estimate of the marginal return to private investment. There are three reasons for this. The first is the distorting effect of the corporate income tax, the second the matter of how

---

* See W. J. Baumol, "On the Discount Rate for Public Projects," in Joint Economic Committee, *The Analysis and Evaluation of Public Expenditures: The PPB System, A Compendium of Papers*, pp. 489–503, and Baumol, "On the Social Rate of Discount," *American Economic Review*, Vol. 58, No. 4, September 1968.

risk is to be accommodated in the two sectors, and the third is externalities (not discussed here).

The effect of the corporate income tax can be analyzed with a simple model that assumes (1) full employment, (2) no risk, (3) corporations are financed entirely by equities, (4) corporate income is taxed uniformly at 50 percent, (6) there is a single rate of interest, r, at which the government borrows money, and (7) no taxes are paid by noncorporate producers or individuals.

In this model inputs which the government uses for construction of a project have their only alternative use in production by corporations. Thus the opportunity cost of using these resources is the return they would have earned if used in the private sector. Since riskless investments must earn the same marginal return in the public and private sectors, the 50 percent corporate income tax dictates that the rate of return in the private sector be $2r$. In other words, the resources, if left in the private sector, would have produced a real rate of return evaluated by the market at $2r$. It is notable that regarding the matter in this way avoids the need for the elaborate calculations which have sometimes been made to determine sources of finance for government projects and the rates pertaining to these sources.* The focus here is rate of return on the real resources if they were left in the private sector. If the rate on government securities is 5 percent, this means that the rate of return in the private sector would have to be 10 percent.

Thus, with $(1 - t)$ the fraction of before tax income which remains after paying the tax, before tax income must be $1/(1 - t)$ times the after tax income, r_0, or in this case two times. Now suppose the government investment displaces private investment from several sectors, each paying a tax at a different rate, t_i. The ratio of before to after tax income will be $1/(1 - t_i)$ in each case. The appropriate rate for the government investment will be a weighted average of the before tax rates of return, with the weights being the relative amount of investment displaced in each industry. That is, the government rate

$$r_g = r_0 \sum_i w_i \frac{1}{(1 - t_i)}$$

---

* See John V. Krutilla and Otto Eckstein, *Multiple Purpose River Development* (Baltimore: The Johns Hopkins Press, 1958). Because it represents such a great simplification over earlier approaches, Baumol's explanation is worth quoting:

> The form of the argument can easily lead to some sort of misunderstanding. It would seem to suggest that all government projects must draw their resources from private investment and that none of them can be taken from private consumption. But nothing of this sort is implied or intended. It is obviously possible that the steel used in some governmental undertaking is all taken from consumers and so results in no reduction in the output of producers' goods. The consequent decrease in manufacture of automobiles, refrigerators, and bird cages then represents the real cost of the government project. But this in no way conflicts with my way of regarding the matter which states only that this transfer of resources must take place *through the agency of the corporation.* The automobile factory will have fewer tons of steel to process, as will the producer of refrigerators and other steel product consumers goods. And I am arguing only that the outlays of these firms on the steel which they would otherwise have used would have brought them a rate of return of *2r as a result of the consumers' marginal valuation of these commodities.* Baumol, *ibid.,* pp. 791–92.

In Baumol's schema, premiums for risk are regarded as completely analogous to the taxes just discussed. Thus in a system with the displaced investment subject to different tax rates and different premiums for risk, the appropriate rate of discount for the government project is a weighted average of the observed before tax rates of return.

The preceding discussion along state-preference lines enables us to see more clearly what is involved in the Baumol position. First, let us abstract from the corporation income tax and also from what we have termed social risk, a risk that produces P's not proportional to the probabilities of state occurrence even with perfect markets for the P's. Now suppose these markets are *not* perfect, with the result that premia are required to induce investment in the face of private risk that cannot be insured away. Baumol's position asserts that this higher required rate of return is the relevant opportunity cost and *also* that the elimination of the private risk that occurs if the government undertakes the investment is *not* to be regarded as a social gain. That is to say, a change in the amount or risk to which some individuals are exposed is not regarded as producing a change in the flow of anyone's utility. Thus Baumol is squarely at odds with the Arrow–Lind (and Hirshleifer–Shapiro, too) position so far as private risk is concerned.

Now assume that there is fluctuation in societal income, that the market for claims is perfect, with the result that the P's for claims are not proportional to probabilities of state occurrence. Certainly we want to use the concept of opportunity cost in evaluating a potential government investment, but the question is whether the rates of return in those industries whose investment goes down as a result of undertaking the governmental investment are the relevant measure of opportunity cost. Recall that the discussion of evaluation of investment along state preference lines said nothing about the need to refer to rates of return in industries affected by the potential investment.

These industries—and all others—have an effect on the appropriate discount rate, of course, but only through their influence on the current market prices of the products of the potential investment (thus affecting the S's) and by their joint influence on the set of P's determined on the market for basic claims. In general, the reason why the rates of return in the affected industries are not directly relevant is that their patterns of returns as among the different states differ from those of the challenger investment. As noted, however, if the relative pattern of S's is the same in some industry as for the challenger investment, its rate of return is indeed the one that has to be met, but investment in that industry is not necessarily adversely affected by undertaking the new governmental investment unless they happen to be competitive.

The Corporation Income Tax

Many students seem to feel that the corporate income tax results in a much larger discrepancy between private discount rates (before tax) and the riskless government rate than do the imperfections in the markets for claims and the correlations between returns and states. It seems clear that both Baumol and Hirshleifer–Shapiro are of this view.

Recall that the Arrow–Lind argument on private risk premia called attention to the fact that if the government undertakes the investment, the reduction or elimination of this private risk purely by spreading it over many more people is to be counted a social gain. The same argument does not apply, of course, to the corporation income tax. It is not likely that knowledge that your corporation has to pay an income tax is productive of ulcers to anywhere near the same extent as the knowledge that some quirk of nature may wipe you out financially.

In the face of this giant size impediment to proper allocation of investment, what policy should be followed? Again, there seems to be quite general agreement that the best solution—at least so far as efficient allocation is concerned—would be to repeal the corporation income tax, thus permitting return on corporate investment to come more nearly into line with the time preference rate of individuals as reflected by the rate on government bonds. But if this can't be done, then what? Clearly investment in general ought to be increased, but how? Should the increase be in private or governmental investment? How should it be brought about?

Hirshleifer suggests a subsidy to private investment, but it might be as easy to repeal the corporate income tax. An attempt to devise a subsidy scheme acceptable to the Congress might raise some serious dangers. If the tax is not abolished and a subsidy scheme not adopted, some concession to time preference as expressed in the riskless government bond rate seems in order. The private rates or the risk rates (Hirshleifer) or for the displaced investments (Baumol) would accordingly be adjusted downward to derive the rate of discount appropriate for government investments. This is necessary, assuming nothing can be done to favor risky private investment, "to strike a balance between the desired expansion of risky investment in general but the undesired preempting of more productive private investment."[*]

A rather general solution for this second best compromise has been derived by Usher for a two good (private and public) two period model.[†] Among the important simplifying assumptions are that all persons have the same tastes and assets (to ensure a meaningful social welfare function) and that the marginal rates of transformation in production between private and public goods are unity within each period of time, thus implying a production function

$$T(C_{0p} + C_{0g}, C_{1p} + C_{1g}) = 0$$

where the double subscript refers to time period and sector. The solution values for these four items of consumption differ from the first best values because of the wedge introduced between consumption and production rates of substitution by the tax. In general, the rate of substitution between public consumption

    [*] Hirshleifer–Shapiro, op. cit., p. 514.
    [†] Dan Usher, "On the Social Rate of Discount: Comment," American Economic Review, Vol. 59, No. 5, December 1969, pp. 925–29.

now and public consumption in the future (the rate of discount on public investment) will lie between the rates of interest on private goods consumption in production and in use.

Steiner

An entirely different view of the discounting process is presented by Steiner.* He argues that there is not a close substitution relationship between private and public investment, but rather that when a public program is proposed, Congress will look at it in general terms and decide whether or not it is a good thing. If it is deemed so to be, a percentage will be added to last year's appropriation to add to the program in question. Since the determination of the budget, in this view, is partially or totally independent of the economic evaluation of the project, the substitution between the public and private projects need not enter decisions concerning discounting. The argument goes that the only relevant consideration is then to allocate the fixed budget optimally and that this may require quite different relative evaluations of future costs and returns as between different programs and projects. How one evaluates this argument depends on the accuracy of Steiner's version of the budgetary process.

5.10 CONCLUDING COMMENTS ON DISCOUNTING

If repeal of the corporate income tax is not to take place, we find ourselves in the realm of the second best where usable welfare theorems are difficult to come by. If credit markets are imperfect, if public and private rates of return differ, if private marginal time preference is not equated with private rates of return, and if collective decisions about the future depart from individual ones, there does not appear to be a partial equilibrium criterion which can take us into the world of the first best—no matter how sophisticated it is. The solution, if any, has to be found in general equilibrium analysis.

Our judgmental position is that we should follow Hirshleifer's advice that we look at return on private investment that appears to be in the same risk class as the proposed governmental investment with some concession to the all too evident fact that time preference rates are below private returns. A simple average of the governmental bond rate (not exactly a precise concept in itself!) and the relevant private rate would be too low in view of the magnitude of private investment, but in the absence of a clearly better approach may be justifiable. At least it has the virtue of simplicity.

---

* Peter O. Steiner, *Public Expenditure and Budgeting* (October 1968), draft manuscript.

CHAPTER 6

Theoretical Problems in the Estimation of Benefits and Costs

6.1 INTRODUCTION

The operational meaning of benefits and costs is not obvious. Both terms can be defined precisely only with reference to a particular objective. As we have pointed out before, the objective with respect to which these terms have usually been defined is maximization of national income—the positive difference between willingness to pay for output and the cost of providing it. This is usually called the "efficiency" objective. We also found that a definition which is at all simple and empirically manageable, even for this objective, requires further simplifying assumptions concerning how the willingness to pay and costs borne by particular individuals are to be weighted. And if social welfare, the ultimate maximand, is to include other objectives, some way must be found to incorporate them into the maximization process. Discontent with the efficiency objective, and especially with the weighting schemes or other devices that must be adopted to make it operational, has led to discussion in recent years of what has come to be called "multiple objective planning."

Many objectives of public investment have been suggested. One could write a general function $U = U(Z_1, Z_2, \ldots, Z_i)$ where the Z's are different aspects of the public interest, such as economic efficiency, the pattern of income distribution, criteria of environmental quality, national security, etc. But, as Steiner has remarked, this sort of formulation identifies possible conflicts between objectives without resolving them.*

The incorporation of multiple objectives into the investment decision-making process can be approached in several ways. One is to restrict the objective functions for one objective (say, economic efficiency) in such a way that it is maximized subject to other stated objectives. Another (and analytically a closely related one) is to apply weights to different arguments in the objective function so as to come up with a single-valued (scalar) measure of benefits. In connection with the latter, one can identify two points of view. One is that weights can be established prior to evaluation, by consulting legislators or by considering previous government decisions. The second is that weights can only be established by an iterative process.

A final approach is that of viewing the various possible objectives of public policy as being substantially incommensurable on any simple scale and therefore necessitating the generation of various kinds of information, not summable into a single number, as a basis for political decision. (Our own view, which we will argue later, is a version of this last one.)

Before proceeding, however, we wish to note a possible source of confusion. Restrictions on an objective function are often used in analytical models when they are not regarded as representing conflicting objectives. In these cases they are used to represent values which are thought to be in principle measurable in a commensurable way but for which, due to empirical difficulties or other reasons, measurements have not been made. In later sections we will discuss efficiency models of a constrained optimization type related to water quality management—instances where the restrictions do not, in principle, represent incommensurable objectives. In these situations, it is usually desirable to perform economic sensitivity analysis on the constraints. As we will see, it is important, for analytical reasons, to distinguish clearly the situations in which constraints represent alternative objectives from the ones where they do not. Since virtually all the systematic discussion of multiple objectives has related to efficiency and income distribution objectives, we will confine our own presentation to these.

6.2 EFFICIENCY AND DISTRIBUTION MODELS

Let us look first at the method of maximizing efficiency subject to a redistribution constraint, say, subject to the decision that the income of a region† must be increased by a predetermined amount. Using the notation of the previous

---

* Peter O. Steiner, "The Public Sector and the Public Interest," in the *Analysis and Evaluation of Public Expenditures: The PPB System*, a Compendium of Papers submitted to the Subcommittee on Economy in Government of the Joint Economic Committee, U.S. Congress (Washington, D.C.: GPO, 1969).

† From the point of view of national welfare, redistribution of income toward particular regions is, at best, irrelevant, and, at most, perverse. Maximizing the national income may require reducing income in a particular region. Still, Congress may wish to redistribute income to chronically depressed regions. Also, although less nobly, Congressmen have a strong interest in the impact of projects on income in their districts.

chapter, and again following Marglin's exposition, we assume first that the multi-period objective function is to maximize efficiency

$$\sum_{t=1}^{T} \theta_t [E_t(\mathbf{y}_t) - M_t(\mathbf{x})] - K(\mathbf{x})$$

subject to

$$E_1(\mathbf{y}_1) - \sum_{j=1}^{m} \bar{P}_{y1j} Y_{1j} \geq \bar{I}_1$$

$$\vdots \qquad\qquad \vdots \qquad \vdots$$

$$E_T(\mathbf{y}_T) - \sum_{j=1}^{m} \bar{P}_{yTj} Y_{Tj} \geq \bar{I}_T$$

and to the production function

$$f(\mathbf{x},\mathbf{y}_t) = 0 \qquad t = 1, \ldots, T$$

In the above formulation, the restrictions upon project or system design imposed by the income distribution objective are embodied in a set of constraints $\bar{I}_1, \ldots, \bar{I}_T$, representing the annual increases in income to be achieved in the region within each demand period; $\bar{P}_y$ is the choice of price at which the beneficiaries are willing to take just enough of the output to yield a net income to the region of I.

Through the usual Lagrangian analysis the following marginal conditions for optimization are obtained:

$$\sum_{t=1}^{T} \theta_t \left[D_{tj}(y_{tj}) \frac{\partial y_{tj}}{\partial x_i} - \frac{\partial M_t}{\partial x_i} \right] - \frac{\partial K}{\partial x_i} = \sum_{t=j}^{T} \lambda_t [D_{tj}(y_{tj}) - \bar{P}_{xtj}] \frac{\partial y_{tj}}{\partial x_i}$$

$$i = 1, \ldots, n$$
$$j = 1, \ldots, m$$

Rewriting the equation using marginal expressions, the left-hand side becomes

$$\sum_{t=1}^{T} \theta_t [MVP_t(x_i) - M\mathcal{M}_t(x_i)] - MK(x_i)$$

The interpretation of this is clear from our discussion in Chapter 5.
In similar notation, the right-hand side becomes

$$\sum_{t=j}^{T} \lambda_t MI_t(x_i) \qquad i = 1, \ldots, n$$

The right-hand side is thus the sum of the multiplicative products of the λ_t's (Lagrange multipliers), and the marginal net increases in annual income to the region in period t from a unit increase in the size of the ith input or project denoted by $MI_t(x_i)$.

The λ's represent the loss in efficiency (in terms of the present value of marginal net efficiency benefits) caused by the last dollar of annual net income redistribution in period t. The most desired (by Congress) values of these would be extremely difficult to determine. This is because, for example, some initial, and necessarily arbitrary, set of λ's might turn out to require an unacceptable efficiency sacrifice after a set of projects is designed using them as restrictions. Then the whole project or system design would have to be reconsidered. Some sort of an iteration process would in principle be needed.

The second method at first seems more promising. It combines the two objectives into a single objective function. Rather than maximizing one subject to the constraint of the other, it merely adds the efficiency function to a weighted redistribution function. Psychologically, if not mathematically, it seems to be a more satisfying approach.

When the opportunity cost is preassigned u_t (the negative of the marginal opportunity cost λ_t) it can be introduced directly into the objective function. Given values of $u_1^0, \ldots, u_T^0$, the objective function becomes a weighted sum of redistribution and efficiency net benefits,

$$\sum_{t=1}^{T} \mu_t^0 \left[E_t(\mathbf{y}_t) - \sum_{j=1}^{m} \bar{P}_{yti} y_{tj} \right] + \sum_{t=1}^{T} \theta_t [E_t(\mathbf{y}_t) - \mathcal{M}_t(\mathbf{x})] - K(\mathbf{x})$$

where the weights are the efficiency value of redistribution benefits.

In application, this technique presents basically the same problems as the first method. If the values of the weights μ_t^0 can be selected ahead of time, the second method can be treated simply as an unconstrained maximization problem. If they cannot, then the desired balance between efficiency and redistribution can be found only by a process of iteration, and finding it can be regarded as determining either the proper level of the constraint or of an income distribution weight which will produce the desired combination.

Marglin suggests a third method which is to maximize redistribution given an efficiency constraint. Since this method is formally equivalent to the previous two and provides no new insights, we will not discuss it here.*

---

* None of these methods is likely to lead to fully optimum results given the decision makers' preferences for different objectives. Ralph d'Arge has made this point in an interesting unpublished paper from which we quote:

Finally, we may ask where this brief journey into the realm of conjecture has led us. If the establishment of a particular goal leads to the application of a specific decision criterion (including value weights in objective functions), and alternative decision criteria lead to different problem solutions, it appears to me that there are two alternatives for analyzing multiple-goal water resource problems. A first approach would be to develop our models with reference to all relevant goals simultaneously. The second approach is to develop models with reference to only one specific criterion and then attempt to learn the physical and (or) technological tradeoffs between other goals through sensitivity analyses. But, if a specific criterion leads to a particular structuring of the physical and technological components of the model, the second approach is bound to err. It is caught in a circular argument . . . a goal determines a model structure that determines the potential for other goals which in turn determines the appropriate level of the single goal. Obviously, the first approach does not contain this problem but presents a whole catalog of new problems in structuring models of water resource systems.

Marglin observes that while the policy maker should know explicitly the characteristics and values of the multi-objective function, he should also know what is being sacrificed in terms of pure efficiency. Therefore, in combination with the multi-objective analysis, the project or system should simultaneously be designed solely to maximize economic efficiency. Then the policy maker may compare the two solutions so that he knows what the nation will lose in national efficiency by promoting regional income redistribution.

The above analysis has been developed in connection with regional income redistribution, although an exactly parallel one could be built with respect to redistribution by income class. Many economists might regard the latter as being the more fundamental of the two since in the final analysis we are presumably more interested in the welfare of individual human beings than in the welfare of regions.

Some empirical work on personal income distribution has been done using a distribution weighted efficiency function with assumed weights or weights calculated from past governmental decisions.* We will review briefly the particular model used in one of these efforts and state the main results.

Freeman† starts with a social welfare function

$$W = W(Y_1, Y_2, \ldots, Y_n) = \sum_{i=1}^{n} W(Y_i)$$

W is aggregate social welfare, and Y_i is the net income of the ith individual. For convenience, a constant elasticity social marginal utility function of the form

$$\frac{\partial W}{\partial Y_i} = Y_i^{-a}$$

is specified.

A value of zero for a is equivalent to the constant and uniform marginal utility of income assumptions we have used earlier. Income distribution does not matter when this is the case. In his empirical work Freeman (arbitrarily) chose $a = \frac{1}{2}$ and performed some sensitivity tests. Persons affected by a policy can be divided into two groups—gainers $(i = 1, 2, \ldots, n)$ and losers $(j = 1, 2, \ldots, m)$. The welfare criterion can then be written

$$\Delta W = \sum_{i=1}^{n} \int_{Y_{i1}}^{Y_{i2}} Y_i^{-a} \, dY_i + \sum_{j=1}^{m} \int_{Y_{j1}}^{Y_{j2}} Y_j^{-a} \, dY_j$$

For actual calculation, the terms in the above expression were altered by certain linearity assumptions which greatly ease computation, but the general

---

* For an example of the latter, see Robert Haveman, *Water Resource Investment and the Public Interest* (Vanderbilt University Press, 1965). Haveman used information on the progression of the tax system to calculate his weights.

† A. Myrick Freeman III, "Six Federal Reclamation Projects and the Distribution of Income," *Water Resources Research*, Second Quarter (1967).

conclusion of the study was that given the choice of *a* above, all six federal projects studied had favorable effects on income distribution (by the criterion that reducing income inequality is a good thing). However, these effects were insufficient to justify the projects, given the deficiencies of the latter on efficiency grounds. In arriving at this result, a number of adjustments were made to the benefit-cost calculations performed by the federal agency to bring it into closer alignment with the efficiency concept. Regional distribution effects of the project were not evaluated.

The routine application of income distribution criteria to public projects implies a generally unsatisfactory income distribution and this presents deeper problems for benefit cost analysis than most of the authors favoring the introduction of such criteria have recognized explicitly. We make some further comments on this in connection with the section on cost estimation.

6.3 ESTABLISHING THE "OBJECTIVE FUNCTION" THROUGH POLITICAL CHOICE

Interesting discussions of the *theoretical* models relating to the establishment of an objective function through collective choice have taken place. One line of theoretical development views the government as being a quasi-market in the sense that it simply registers and transmits individual preferences given the distribution of votes. The prototype model of this sort would be based on the assumption that each public issue is resolved by a referendum universally participated in by fully informed voters. The "market type" formulation of the political process has frequently been criticized by those who note that most political decisions are and must be made through representatives. The market type of model has, however, given rise to a result which has been discussed almost endlessly since it was published in 1951. This is the famous "Arrow Paradox." The essential ideas of this paradox of collective choice can be simply illustrated.*

TABLE 6-1

Individual	Individual's Preference Ordering
1	$A \to C \to B$
2	$C \to B \to A$
3	$B \to A \to C$

As can be readily shown, sets of individual preferences may lead to no unambiguous collective preference. In the situation shown in Table 6-1, two-thirds prefer *A* to *C* and two-thirds prefer *C* to *B*. Thus, if the choice is between *B* and *C* and then between *A* and *C*, *A* will have a majority. But two-thirds

---

* See Kenneth J. Arrow, *Social Choice and Individual Values*, Introduction to Second Edition (New York: John Wiley & Sons, 1963). Arrow makes no claim that he was the discoverer of the paradox. Indeed, he traces the idea back to the Marquis de Condorcet in the eighteenth century. His rigorous methodology and attention to formal proof was, however, unique.

prefer B to A, and a different order of choice can produce any one of the choices. To the aficionados, this phenomenon is known as "cycling" or "intransitivity." It may be noted that the result is a consequence of the ordering of choices by one of the participants which leads to the preference for either extreme rather than a middle position. Thus, say the order ABC proceeds along a spectrum politically. For concreteness, say A is complete equality of income distribution, B is some redistribution, and C is no redistribution at all. In this case, Individual 1 prefers complete equality but would rather have no redistribution at all than a moderate amount. The paradox has sometimes been cited as a demonstration that democratic choice cannot lead to an unambiguous selection of objectives. The paradox, however, has been developed with mutually exclusive alternatives (either A or B or C but not A and B, etc.) and democratic choice operates this way only in elections. Legislative bodies, which are the usual selectors of objectives, normally have many independent issues under review at one time.

The result of a formal proof that intransitivity may arise given certain conditions which Arrow regarded as reasonable is known as "Arrow's Impossibility Theorem."* The three most important conditions specified are:

(1) "Independence of Irrelevant Alternatives" (pairwise comparisons). This condition says that the choice-making procedure should make choices between the alternatives x and y taken pairwise, and in the choice between x and y the only circumstances taken into account shall be the relative positions of x and y on the preference schedules of the members of the group. In other words, the introduction of a third alternative z should not affect the relative preference for x and y. This condition has been critical in recent discussions and should be noted carefully by the reader.

(2) "Monotonicity." The essence of this condition can be stated as follows: If for a given group of preference schedules the social choice-making procedure chooses x in preference to y and if then x is displaced upward relative to y on some of the schedules in the original set, the procedure shall still choose x in preference to y.

(3) "Unanimity." If, in any set of schedules, x stands higher than y in the preference schedule of every member, the procedure shall choose x rather than y.

Duncan Black, in the article previously cited, has proven that if the condition of unanimity is imposed as a decision criterion (rather than, say, majority rule), intransitivity will arise very rarely, under the specified conditions, if the membership of the group is at all large. Of course, if vote trading is not allowed [and it is precluded by condition (1)], very few people would seriously propose the unanimity rule since it would virtually foreclose anything but negative

---

* For a self-contained and relatively clear exposition of the theorem and its formal proof, the student should refer to Duncan Black, "On Arrow's Impossibility Theorem," *The Journal of Law and Economics*, Vol. 12, No. 2, October 1969.

decisions. It is reminiscent of the liberum veto which historians say wrought havoc in the Polish Diet from the mid-17th to the end of the 18th century. Under this system, any motion to change the status quo was defeated if one member of the diet shouted, "I disapprove."

Haefele has recently completed an analysis of the problem of collective choice in a more political context, first with mutually exclusive alternatives (elections) and then with independent issues (legislatures)*. In brief, he has shown that, with independent issues, intransitivity does not arise given vote-trading and majority rule. With mutually exclusive alternatives, he has shown that intransitivity does not occur under rules that approximate the two-party system. (The latter conclusion follows Arrow's possibility theorem for two alternatives). Finally, he has shown that, for given issues, both elections, following two-party rules, and legislatures, using vote-trading, produce the same outcome. Thus he concludes that representative legislatures, using vote-trading, can arrive at the same conclusions on issues as their constituents would have, had vote-trading been possible for the latter. The analysis implies that, even if it were possible, recourse to referendum-type decision-making would be *undesirable* because it makes no provision for vote-trading.†

The basic building block of the Haefele model is a vector of preferences related to a given set of independent issues, e.g.,

$$\begin{bmatrix} Y_2 \\ N_1 \\ Y_3 \end{bmatrix}$$

which combines yes-no voting stances with an ordinal ranking of the importance of the issues to any individual. Thus, above, the individual is for the first issue, against the second, and for the third. The second is most important to him, the first next important, and the third issue least important. A display of three such vectors (a three-man legislature) might give us:

Issue	I	II	III	
A	Y_2	N_1	Y_1	—Pass
B	N_1	Y_3	Y_3	—Pass
C	Y_3	Y_2	Y_2	—Pass

---

* See Edwin T. Haefele, "A Utility Theory of Representative Government," *American Economic Review*, June 1971.

† Madison, in Federalist Paper No. 55, expresses the point most succinctly, "Had every Athenian citizen been a Socrates, every Athenian assembly would still have been a mob." Need it be added that Madison's words relate to information costs, revealed preferences, and the lack of a vote-trading mechanism, or that modern proposals that everyone vote on all issues by electronic processes suffer the same defect as the Athenian assembly? (Haefele, *op. cit.*).

If votes are summed across rows, all three issues would be passed by the legislature (assuming majority rule) in this case. However, note that the first two men can trade votes on issues A and B.

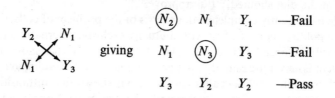

making both better off. The outcome on the three issues now is that the first two fail and the third passes. The two men have improved their positions (both are better off) at the expense of the third, who is now worse off. (In larger matrices, some non-traders gain and others lose.)

Let us look again at the vectors:

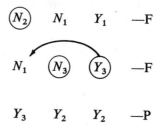

The third man will find it to his advantage to offer to change his vote on the middle issue if the first man will agree *not* to trade off his vote on the first issue. Then the vote will go

$$
\begin{array}{cccl}
Y_2 & N_1 & Y_1 & -P \\
N_1 & Y_3 & N_3 & -F \\
Y_3 & Y_2 & Y_2 & -P
\end{array}
$$

If we take the three original vectors:

$$
\begin{array}{ccc}
Y_2 & N_1 & Y_1 \\
N_1 & Y_3 & Y_3 \\
Y_3 & Y_2 & Y_2
\end{array}
$$

in the context of election strategy, we could imagine a candidate taking one of eight possible positions regarding the three issues.

Issue *A*   P P P F F F P F

B   P P F P F P F F

C   P F P P P F F F

The implications of each position for each of the three voters is shown in the following table which shows for each voter the importance to him of the issues that would pass for each of the possible candidates' positions.

Issue *A*	P	P	P	F	F	F	P	F
B	P	P	F	P	F	P	F	F
C	P	F	P	P	P	F	F	F

Levels of importance

1st voter later wins* on issues of:	2nd 3rd	2nd	1st 2nd 3rd	3rd	1st 3rd	none	1st 2nd	1st
2nd voter later wins* on issues of:	2nd 3rd	3rd	2nd	1st 2nd 3rd	1st 2nd	1st 3rd	none	1st
3rd voter later wins* on issues of:	1st 2nd 3rd	1st 3rd	1st 2nd	2nd 3rd	2nd	3rd	1st	none

Opinion polls would reveal to the candidates that a majority favors passage of all three issues $\begin{bmatrix} P \\ P \\ P \end{bmatrix}$, yet inspection of the display above shows one vector $\begin{bmatrix} F \\ F \\ P \end{bmatrix}$ that can defeat $\begin{bmatrix} P \\ P \\ P \end{bmatrix}$ in majority voting. Should one candidate choose $\begin{bmatrix} F \\ F \\ P \end{bmatrix}$ then the second candidate can defeat him by running on a platform $\begin{bmatrix} P \\ F \\ P \end{bmatrix}$, i.e., the same outcome as the vote-trading outcome. Haefele demonstrates this con-

---

* For example, with candidates favoring the first position, $\begin{bmatrix} P \\ P \\ P \end{bmatrix}$, the first man would later win on the issues that are of second and third degrees of importance to him—if candidates of this persuasion won the election.

vergence holds for considerably more complicated cases, including the cyclical cases to which we referred earlier.

What has been demonstrated here is that, in principle, a democratic legislature can make unambiguous choices which maximize the fulfillment of preferences given a set of issues and vote trading. But this is far from saying that a legislature could pre-specify a social welfare function or even a moderately complicated objective function for the planning and design of public projects. What can be done is for the legislature to give the planner some general indications of what the important considerations are and to rely on him to elaborate alternatives and options and to supply the necessary information to make informed choices.

Of course the degree to which such aberrations as seniority and regional representation disturb the normative value of the legislature decision is not yet rigorously understood but is. no doubt, quite important.

6.4   CONCLUSIONS ON OBJECTIVES

Three basic approaches to the problem of multiple planning objectives have been explored in the literature. One is to set trial constraints on the efficiency objective, do sensitivity analysis on them, and let the final outcome arise from a political process. However, this approach fails to make full use of the contribution that economic analysis can make to decisions, thus imposing an unnecessary burden on an already overloaded political process.

The second is to try to infer weights from previous political decisions, but we are particularly skeptical of trying to build "preexisting" weights into the objective function. For one thing, if public interest decisions are truly multidimensional, the decisions of public officials must reflect non-economic as well as economic considerations and cannot be expected to yield a consistent preference pattern with respect to income distribution or any other single objective. Second, experience indicates that the question of income distribution is often deliberately used for politically strategic reasons, and true preferences are hidden beneath pious statements.*

The third is to regard the public interest as genuinely multidimensional, and thus to expect the planning process to generate information useful for the political analysis of conflicts among objectives.† We incline toward this view although the possible implication that all objectives can be treated as coequal is unrealistic and unnecessary in view of the possibilities for reducing conflicts between straightforward application of efficiency calculations and other objectives. The efficiency objective has been accorded high priority throughout the history of the use of formal evaluation techniques. There is a body of well-

---

* For further discussion, the reader can consult the papers by Nelson, Weisbrod, and Haveman in Samuel B. Chase, Jr., Ed., *Problems in Public Expenditure Analysis* (Washington, D.C.: Brookings Institution, 1968).

† We suggest that readers interested in further discussion of these positions consult the excellent article by Steiner, *op. cit.*

developed technique with respect to it, and it has an attractive conceptual clarity. Consequently, it will continue to be an important item in the evaluation of public investment.

Efficiency Calculations in Choices Involving Multiple Objectives

In explaining our view on the role of efficiency-oriented calculations of benefits and costs in decisions on public economic projects, it will be helpful to remember a few fundamental features of our economic system.

First, society must agree on ground rules under which the pursuit of maximum social welfare is to be conducted. The major feature of these ground rules for our society (and for our problem) is reliance on a market system based on consumer sovereignty and encouragement of competition to stimulate efficiency and to contain and minimize monopolistic exploitation. Private ownership of capital assets and the institution of inheritance are integral parts of the system. In the first instance, rewards are to be those resulting from the operation of market forces, with rewards related to marginal productivity.

Society has chosen to alter this distribution of rewards for two different types of reasons, however. First, it is desirable and necessary to provide some goods and services directly by government, either because they are public goods which cannot very well be provided privately or because there are other difficulties in providing them privately.

Although use of the market system has great advantages in stimulating efficiency in production and in directing production to satisfy the demands of consumers, other general features characterizing the operation of the system as a whole are also important. One of these, the rate of capital accumulation, has already been discussed in connection with capital theory and the choice of the discount rate. A second, the distribution of income, is important for the problem at hand. Actions taken by society to modify the distribution of income indicate dissatisfaction with initial market results. Modification is undertaken for three basic reasons. First, it is desired to relieve the situation of those with low incomes, whether chronically or temporarily low.* Second, modification is undertaken to prevent in some measure the growth of concentration of wealth and the concentration of political power that might be associated therewith. Third, the burden of covering the costs of publicly provided goods and services must be divided up in some equitable way.

These three factors have resulted in a redistributive system involving the use of taxes, publicly provided goods and services, and "welfare" programs which have changed initial earned real incomes toward equality, but with substantial inequality in disposable real income remaining.

Alteration of the results ground out by the market system requires the use of the political process, but it cannot be too strongly emphasized that the frequency

---

* Needless to say this is a statement of a rationale and not an evaluation of the present redistributive system.

with which it is used and the manner in which it is used depends on the particular procedures adopted for handling the problems that arise. In particular, if the designing of a public investment project is posed only in a formal way as one of maximizing its contribution to social welfare (expressed as a sum of project net benefits and its contribution to benefits other than calculated economic benefits), the result can be misleading. A merely formal analysis of the problem tends to obscure the possibilities for reducing the necessity for resort to the political process and for increasing the significance of efficiency oriented calculations of benefits and costs for decisions in public investment and related matters.

Attainment of certain objectives to which public investment projects may be related can be handled in such a way as to eliminate or reduce the need to consider them in the planning and decision process. These possibilities are discussed here for three different problems:

(1) Hard-to-measure variables.
(2) Equity problems arising in the provision of services by government.
(3) Attaining the desired overall income distribution.

1. *Hard-to-Measure Variables*

As suggested earlier, the problem here is not that values attachable to hard-to-measure variables are in principle incommensurable with the value of other benefits and costs. In view of the difficulty of measuring them, however, perhaps the political decision process can be aided best by including analysis of the sensitivity of project net benefits to various possible values for these variables, leaving the decision makers free to develop such other evidence as can be mustered to give some clues to the best values to use.

2. *Two Types of Equity Problems in Distribution*

The provision of goods and services by government results in equity problems of distribution which should be carefully distinguished from the problem of the overall distribution of income. The point is not that the provision of services by government has no effect on the overall distribution of income. Rather, a government investment project, say, may create distributional equity problems which are peculiar to it, which are different from the grand problem of the overall distribution of income, and which are of far more limited scope. In the overall distributional problem the question is, what distribution of income (described, say, in terms of inequality) is wanted? There is no interest in particular transactions, for the object of interest involves the outcome of the whole system.

In contrast, a public investment project may have redistributional effects on a few people which are of considerable or even overwhelming importance to them, but whose effect on the whole distribution is negligible. That these are two different matters is easily demonstrated by an example in which a transaction changes incomes with no effect on the whole distribution:

Person	Present income	Change because of project	Final income
A	5,000	−1,000	4,000
B	4,000	+1,000	5,000
C	8,000	+2,000	10,000
D	10,000	−2,000	8 000

3. Overall Distribution of Income; Decisions on Public Provision of Goods and Services

Public projects—for example, investment projects—may alter the overall distribution in some small degree. To what extent, if any, should this effect be taken into account when deciding on a particular investment project? There is a societal consensus that the initial distribution of incomes resulting from the market system needs modification. This consensus is reflected in several instruments, mainly the income tax and the "welfare" system, that do exactly this. Furthermore, they do this by taking into account (imperfectly, to be sure) the total economic circumstances of the individual, including income received from whatever source. In the light of this characteristic, there would seem to be little need to inquire what further contribution a particular transaction can make to achieving the desired overall distribution of income. It does not seem feasible to examine the total income position of the persons affected by, say, a particular investment project. In addition, it would be quite difficult to make such decisions consistent with other similar ones. The likelihood of attaining a satisfactory distribution of income would be much higher by relying on the comprehensive measures already available for modifying the whole distribution.

One can argue, however, that society cannot attain the distribution it really wants. The significant question here would be the nature of the obstacles that stand in the way of achieving its distributional desires. It is hard to imagine what they might be, as it appears to us that considerable practical scope remains for modification of the tax or welfare system to achieve the desired distribution if it differs from the present one.

The special case of an unattainable but desired *equal* distribution of income is said by some to warrant consideration of effects on the overall distribution in the evaluation of public investment projects. Any redistributive effect of a project in the direction of equality would be regarded as desirable; projects with such effects would be viewed as valuable over and beyond their calculated net benefits. This view is sometimes explicitly stated, but more often is implicit.

An individual can certainly hold this position. Obviously some do, but clearly it is not the consensus of this society. This is not to say that the society will never choose to alter the distribution toward equality. Indeed, the possibility of doing this by means of a negative income tax is under consideration at the time this is being written, but the final decision surely will be to retain a substantial amount of inequality, with incentives being the principal justification in the minds of most people.*

Problems of Equity other than Overall Distribution of Income

To see how problems of equity in distribution relate to benefit-cost analysis, recall first how they arise. In voluntary market transactions, inequities in distribution do not arise provided the initial distribution of endowments (incomes) is accepted as equitable. That is to say, because of this and the voluntary nature of the transactions, a maximum welfare position in the Pareto sense is attainable.

Involuntary transactions, such as may be involved in the provision of public services, change this situation radically. If the assumption of the addibility of the (assumed) equal marginal utility of income of different people implied by the summing of benefits and costs is carried over to the case of involuntary transactions, we may encounter cases where my loss is presumably cancelled by your gain, or, perhaps even more serious, cases in which the large loss of one person is more than offset by the trivial gains of a number of persons.

Clearly, it would be desirable to avoid such situations so far as possible. The first and most effective way of achieving this for public investment projects is by having beneficiaries pay for the costs of providing the service. If this is done by the use of prices, the situation is close to that of voluntary transactions in the private market. There are conceptual difficulties in doing this for cases of joint cost and in cases where marginal cost pricing yields more or less revenue than needed to cover costs. These difficulties do not arise from the fact of public production, of course, but are inherent in the production functions for these cases.

Where pricing is not possible, it is still feasible to have beneficiaries cover costs by requiring the governmental units in which beneficiaries are located to pay the costs. These governmental units, in turn, may be able to identify beneficiaries and assess costs on them in an agreed manner.

Collection of costs from beneficiaries has another important effect in addition

---

* In some of the discussion in the literature there seems to be an implicit assumption that public projects always lead in the direction of greater income equality. This is not necessarily the case. George Tolley calculated that about one southern farm worker in every twenty has been displaced by the Federal Reclamation Program. [George S. Tolley, "Reclamation Influence on the Rest of Agriculture," *Land Economics* (May 1959).] Krutilla and Eckstein traced the distribution of costs and benefits from a power project in the Pacific Northwest. Assuming that the project had been financed through a tax reduction favoring consumption, over 75 percent of the redistribution was found to have occurred at the expense of income classes of $7,500 and under. (Krutilla and Eckstein, *Multiple Purpose River Development, op. cit.*) See the discussion of the results in Robert H. Haveman, "Benefit-Cost Analysis: Its Relevance to Public Investment Decisions—Comment," *Quarterly Journal of Economics* (November 1967) and the reply by Arthur Maass in the same issue. Maass points out that these investments might have been designed differently had redistribution been an explicit objective.

to eliminating or reducing equity problems of redistribution. This additional advantage arises from the fact that the process of estimating benefits and costs is very sensitive to a lack of correspondence in the incidence of benefits and costs. Suppose, for example, that group A has an effect on the decision to undertake a project. If group A knows that it can benefit at the expense of group B, the incentive to make sure that benefits exceed costs, let alone to make sure that marginal net benefits are zero, is greatly reduced for group A. That is, if the beneficiaries in a locality know they can benefit from a project with costs covered out of the general treasury, there is no pressure from the potential beneficiaries to make sure that benefits and costs are accurately estimated. Such pressures are badly needed to offset the inevitable tendency of governmental construction agencies to overestimate the net benefits of potential projects. Indeed when full repayment is not required, local interests may well encourage this tendency.

Even if efforts to have beneficiaries pay costs are successful, in many cases a project will create redistributive problems. The two types of cases that pose an equity problem are of the same general nature: the decision on whether to proceed with a project or not involves redress of a change in income that has been (or will be) experienced for which society "feels" the individual should not be held responsible.

The first type of case is that in which income has been reduced (e.g., regional unemployment arising from a fall in demand for its products), and a public investment project under consideration would increase these incomes—probably temporarily. However, this fact is not sufficient to warrant giving an additional plus mark to the project beyond its net benefits, for there are competing measures for redressing the situation, which include movement of mobile resources (especially labor) to other occupations and/or locations in response to better income prospects, subsidized mobility, and temporary transfer payments. The investment project should get an additional plus only if it is superior to these other options.*

In the second type of situation, proceeding with an investment will redistribute real income in an undesirable way by arbitrarily reducing some incomes or wealth with inadequate compensation.

One type of inadequate compensation raises no difficult questions of principle. A typical example is the compensation for 1 percent of the area of a house lot taken for a highway at 1 percent of the going price for the lot when in fact the value of house and lot declines by a much larger percentage of the market price of house and lot together. Many persons would regard such a compensation standard as inequitable. The remedy would be simple—compensate for market values destroyed by the condemnatory act and not just for an inappropriate measure of property taken.

---

* Even if it has been decided that a project is the best means for achieving a desired redistribution (e.g., irrigation water to Indians), the best means for achieving the redistribution should be considered. As a somewhat nonconventional example, where marginal costs of water use are high (operating costs, congestion costs, or opportunity cost of water use), one should price at marginal cost (so water will be treated as the scarce input it is) but pay a per-acre subsidy for land irrigated.

The other type of inadequate compensation—exemplified by the Kinzua Dam case involving the displacement of Indians in New York from ancestral tribal grounds and by the pathetic cases of old people ousted from a locale and associations that constitute the whole web of their lives—does raise serious questions of principle. In these cases, a payment much larger than the market value of the condemned property may be required to leave the person as well off as before. It may even be much larger than the present value of all the person's resources.

In a system in which there are no forced sales, this creates no problem. Indeed, the fact that most properties are not for sale at the going price suggests that forced sale would require compensation at greater than market value if the person's estimated welfare position were to remain unchanged. With forced sales, however, it seems clear in principle that thoroughgoing utility maximization would require compensation at more than market value in such cases. It would appear, then, that efficiency calculations based on assignment of market values to inputs will necessarily result in a utility position inferior to that ideally attainable.

No possibility exists for a thoroughgoing, practical solution to this problem, for there is no way to find out reliably how much compensation over market value is needed to leave utility positions unchanged. No doubt, alleged psychic pain would increase enormously at the mere prospect of compensation. In some cases of this type, lifetime tenancy has provided a reasonably satisfactory solution, and other accommodating actions may be possible. If not, a project with such features deserves a deduction from the calculated net benefits.

Summary Statement of Position

In our view, the calculation of benefits and costs on the basis of the usual economic efficiency rationale has an important and probably dominant role to play in the decision process for public investments and related matters, provided that:

(1) It is agreed that societally desired overall distribution objectives are to be attained by general measures not requiring examination of the overall distributional effects of particular transactions. The case for this is very strong, in our opinion.

(2) Beneficiaries are made to pay for costs, thus eliminating or reducing the importance of the redistribution effects of projects.

Even if a serious effort is made to adhere to these conditions, residual distributional effects (other than effects on the whole distribution) are likely to occur in practical situations. There are several reasons for this. First, as we have just discussed, compensation of real costs is likely to be incomplete under forced sale conditions. Second, it may be difficult to collect full payment from beneficiaries when benefits are widespread and diffuse. Third, the allocation of joint costs is, as we will see later, necessarily somewhat arbitrary, giving rise to arbitrariness in the distribution of burden if prices are based on allocated costs. It is important, therefore, that project analyses include not only estimates of total benefits and costs, but that the distribution or incidence of benefits and costs be analyzed. The display of such information would be of great help to those involved in the decision process.

In the following sections we turn to problems in the estimation of efficiency benefits and costs. Types of evaluation problems are selected because they illustrate salient theoretical issues, although the particular problems chosen are also of great practical importance to current evaluation.* For concreteness, two actual cases of benefit evaluations are examined in some detail and empirical results are presented with respect to them. They are a recreation evaluation study in Texas and a water quality evaluation study in the Potomac Estuary. They illustrate two different techniques of benefit evaluation. Also, they involve types of outputs which are of great current importance in water resources planning.

6.5   PROBLEMS IN COST ESTIMATION

Estimation of the costs of a project or a system is often regarded as being considerably simpler than the determination of benefits. While this is often true, the estimation of costs does present its share of difficulties. We will discuss four of these briefly: (1) cost estimation involves forecasting and therefore uncertainty; (2) when capital assets, such as land, are acquired, cost estimates based on assessed valuations may present difficulties; (3) frequently opportunity costs internal to the project or system itself must be considered, which means that cost estimation *becomes* benefit estimation; and (4) unemployment or under-employment of resources presents a problem in the estimation of opportunity cost.

Before proceeding to these relatively specific matters, we wish to explore briefly a point which has, we think, not received adequate attention in the literature on benefit-cost analysis, especially in the literature on multiple objectives. There is an "adding-up" problem in connection with the estimation of costs as well as with the estimation of benefits. Ordinarily, the assumption is made that resources used in a project are drawn from the margins of use elsewhere so that the project demand for them does not alter their price. When this condition prevails, the cost of the resources reflects the value of their marginal product in alternative uses. However, this VMP is only a measure of the welfare loss elsewhere if we can assume that either the distribution of income does not matter (constant and uniform marginal utility of income) or that the overall distribution of income is acceptable from a social welfare function point of view.

---

* The reader interested in a more complete discussion should consult Otto Eckstein, *Water Resource Development: The Economics of Project Evaluation* (Cambridge: Harvard University Press, 1961).

Thus, in terms of applying welfare economics principles the cost side is symmetrical with the benefit side with one exception. Since most resources used are purchased at market value, their owners are compensated for releasing them. Thus the problem of *changes* in the distribution is largely concentrated on the benefit side. Nevertheless, if the distribution of income matters and is not optimal, market costs have as little claim to being a measure of welfare loss as calculated "willingness to pay" has to being a measure of welfare gain. When this situation prevails, we are reduced to weak criteria for welfare improvement— basically we can say only that welfare is improved if someone is made better off and no one else is made worse off as would tend to be the case if those providing resources for the project or the system were in fact fully compensated by the beneficiaries. This point is another strong argument for approaching income distributional questions directly through the general tax and welfare systems rather than by trying to build distributional criteria into every decision.

Uncertainty and Cost Estimation

Of course all estimates of future economic magnitudes are beset by uncertainty and cost is no exception. A lengthy period often elapses between the time cost estimates are made and the time construction is actually undertaken. OMR costs can be estimated for even longer periods into the future. Our previous discussions of how risk and uncertainty should be taken into account have generally assumed that overall there is no systematic bias in the estimates of costs and benefits by public agencies. The small amount of empirical work on cost estimation suggests that this has not been true of costs but that it is more nearly true now than it was in earlier years. We will review the results of the pertinent studies quickly.

Altouney estimated the actual as contrasted with the estimated costs of one hundred and three Bureau of Reclamation projects planned prior to 1955. He found that cost estimates were undervalued to the extent of average cost estimates running 75 percent below actual cost and median cost estimates running 30 per- cent below actual costs. This was after adjustment of actual costs for construction price trends, changes in project planning, and structural and engineering modifications.*

Hufschmidt has reported the results of a study of 68 Corps of Engineers projects for which the original estimates had been made in 1954 or later. After price level adjustments, actual costs for the projects were 23 percent *below* original estimated costs. A study of more recent Bureau of Reclamation projects also shows small cost *underruns* on the average. It appears from the studies that have been made that the major construction agencies have greatly improved the quality of their cost estimates in recent years. TVA cost estimation has

---

* Edward Gregory Altouney, *The Role of Uncertainties in the Economic Evaluation of Water Resource Projects* (Institute in Engineering-Economic Systems; Stanford University, August 1963).

apparently been relatively close to the mark throughout the history of that organization.*

Costs and Capitalized Values

Conceptual and empirical problems of considerable difficulty occur in connection with the acquisition of durable assets—particularly land, homes, etc.—for reservoir sites, rights of way and other space-consuming purposes. For example, as we have already implied above, the destruction of an entire community (as may occur when a large reservoir is built) infringes upon social relationships and institutions that a piece-by-piece consideration of assessed property values based on actual sales does not encompass (assessed value is the usual basis for figuring costs). Attachments to churches, schools, cemeteries, cultural opportunities, and access to the homes of friends (all those qualities that the term "community" conveys) assume a value not completely registered by market prices when individual properties are sold. Many residents (whose properties are not for sale at the going price) receive a surplus return from their property that cannot be compensated for by paying the going market price. This is probably the major factor in the frequent strong resistance to property condemnation, especially in densely occupied areas. Furthermore, there are disadvantages (costs) imposed upon an individual or business when condemnation causes forced sale. In expositions of the welfare economics of public investments, this important point is usually neglected.

We have explored just part of a wide range of problems associated with the condemnation of land for public purposes (parks which displace residents from sites of aesthetic or historical value to them, nominal payments for power line rights of way which destroy landscapes, etc.). These problems appear to have obtained little or no theoretical or empirical attention. They may be responsible for serious cost underestimation when land and durable facilities are acquired, thus leading to inefficiencies and, we think, serious inequities.†

Another point leading to the conclusion that value placed on property by real estate appraisals understates the real cost of property is explored by Eckstein.‡ A privately held asset is evaluated by capitalizing the future income stream at the rate of time preference of the owner. Since cost is usually measured by private asset values obtained by application of a rate of discount containing risk factors and possibly the corporate tax factors explored earlier, an understatement of cost at the low public discount rate usually used, occurs. Con-

---

* See Maynard M. Hufschmidt and Jacques Gerin, "Systematic Errors in Cost Estimates for Public Investment Projects," Conference on Economics of Public Output, April 26–27, 1968, National Bureau of Economic Research.

† Inefficiencies and inequities of this kind have sometimes received attention in the actual execution of property acquisitions. These are the cases in which property is acquired subject to the condition that the person presently occupying it be permitted to remain there for some stipulated period, which might be the rest of his life.

‡ Eckstein, *op. cit.*

sistency could be achieved by determining an asset value through discounting estimated private returns with the public rate. This would, of course, result in an imputed cost rather than the actual outlay that would have to be made. An illustrative calculation for a major federal project raised annualized land costs by about 40 percent.* A more appropriate response, it seems to us, would be to raise the public discount rate more nearly into conformity with private rates.

It appears that the use of assessed values of property for cost evaluation can lead to substantial downward bias of the actual cost of devoting land to public purposes. Of course, neither of the sources of bias discussed here would show up in the empirical studies cited earlier since those related to actual outlays.

Benefits as Costs

When purposes within a single project are competitive rather than complementary or when projects in a system are mutually exclusive, the incremental evaluation of a purpose or a project involves internal opportunity costs. Thus, if providing recreation involves maintaining a pool of stored water during the summer, thus foreclosing uses dependent on flow regulation releases, the marginal cost of the recreation purpose must include these foregone benefits and vice versa. In these instances, cost estimation involves all the problems of benefit evaluation, some of which we shall review below. We return to this matter when we consider pricing of outputs from public projects.

Unemployment and Underemployment

Public works projects have long been viewed as weapons in the arsenal for combatting unemployment. In the decade preceding and following World War II, discussion of projects in these terms was very common. In recent times, however, much less attention has been accorded this aspect of public investment. There are probably two main reasons: (1) recognition of the fact that, due to great lags between planning and construction, public works projects at best might perform poorly as anti-cyclical devices and at worst might aggravate the cycle;† (2) due to improved conduct of monetary and fiscal policy, the post-war period has not seen depression-style levels of unemployment. Accordingly, benefit-cost analysts have generally assumed that the employment level is unaffected by the construction of a public works project. With the exception of considerations such as those discussed in the sections immediately above, this meant that actually incurred costs could be taken as measures of social opportunity cost.

It has, however, been recognized that there are pockets of unemployment and

---

* Eckstein, *op. cit.*, p. 148.

† See Julius Margolis, "Public Works and Economic Stability," *Journal of Political Economy*, Vol. LVII, No. 4 (August 1949).

underemployment, both regionally and by occupation, and that these may be directly and indirectly drawn on selectively by different investments. Until recently, because of the magnitude of the empirical task of tracing sectoral demands through several layers of transactions, no operational techniques for tracing employment impacts and adjusting opportunity costs have been available. In the past few years, however, empirical information has come to hand and an analytical model has been devised to use it which makes approximate adjustments possible.* In other words the model makes possible an estimate of a "shadow price" for inputs, used directly and indirectly in projects which reflects the degree to which they would otherwise be unemployed.

The model is of theoretical and methodological interest, and we will trace through at least its simpler version in some detail. In accordance with the objectives of this book, we will merely report representative or illustrative empirical results.

The model can best be explained by following through the system of matrix equations of which it is composed. For our purposes we need not concern ourselves with the dimensions of the matrices and vectors involved.

In the model there are z occupation categories and n industries each of which produces a homogeneous output by combining factor inputs with purchased inputs from other sectors. All exchanged commodities and services are measured in physical units and evaluated at base year prices.

The first equation divides expenditures for project construction into (a) on-site employee compensation, (b) final expenditures for materials, equipment and supplies, and (c) contractors' profit, overhead, and other project costs not included in (a) and (b). So the first equation is

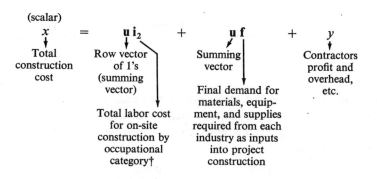

The gross output of each industry generated by the final demand for its products is given by pre-multiplying the final demand vector for materials

---

* Robert H. Haveman and John V. Krutilla, *Unemployment, Idle Capacity, and the Evaluation of Public Expenditures: National and Regional Analyses* (Baltimore: The Johns Hopkins Press, 1968).

† The subscripts are used to distinguish on-site labor cost from labor cost in induced sectors. For the latter see below.

equipment and supplies by industry and the inverse of the interindustry technical coefficient matrix

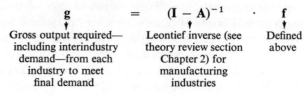

$$\mathbf{g} \qquad = \qquad (\mathbf{I} - \mathbf{A})^{-1} \qquad \cdot \qquad \mathbf{f}$$

g	$(\mathbf{I} - \mathbf{A})^{-1}$	f
Gross output required—including interindustry demand—from each industry to meet final demand	Leontief inverse (see theory review section Chapter 2) for manufacturing industries	Defined above

Man-year labor requirements classified by industry are the product of **g** and a matrix with man-year to output ratios (defining total man-year labor requirements per dollar's worth of gross output in each industry) along the principle diagonal. The industries are in the same order as in **f** and **g**.

$$\mathbf{d} \qquad = \qquad \mathbf{E} \qquad \cdot \qquad \mathbf{g}$$

d	E	g
Man-year labor requirements classified by industry	Matrix with man-year to output ratios along the principal diagonal	Defined above

An occupational breakdown of man-year labor requirements (stemming from final demands) by all industries taken together is obtained by premultiplying **d** by a matrix of industry occupational coefficients. The coefficients define the volume of occupational requirements in each industry per unit of man-year labor requirements in that industry.

$$\mathbf{m} \qquad = \qquad \mathbf{B} \qquad \cdot \qquad \mathbf{d}$$

m	B	d
Man-year labor requirements by occupation stemming from final demand	Industry occupational coefficients	Defined above

A breakdown of generated labor income by occupational category is obtained by pre-multiplying **m** by a matrix which has average annual occupation wage and salary income payments down its principal diagonal with occupations in the same order as **m**.

$$\mathbf{i}_1 \qquad = \qquad \mathbf{W} \qquad \cdot \qquad \mathbf{m}$$

$\mathbf{i}_1$	W	m
Labor cost generated by final demand of occupational category	Diagonal matrix of annual occupational wage and salary income payments	Defined above

Value-added components generated by final demand for materials, equipment and supplies by industry are obtained by multiplying a matrix with the gross output level of each industry required by the final demand entered on the principal diagonal in the same order as the industries in **f** and **g** and a matrix of value-added component to gross output ratios. The columns of this matrix are composed of six ratios of value-added components (respectively, employee compensation, net interest, capital consumption allowance, indirect business taxes, corporate profits and proprietor and rental income) to gross output by industry;

$$\mathbf{D} \quad = \quad \mathbf{G} \quad \cdot \quad \mathbf{C}$$

D	G	C
Six column vectors of value-added components stemming from final demand classified by industry. Dimension $n \times 6$	Diagonal matrix with industry gross output stemming from final demand down main diagonal (components of g)	Value-added-component-to-gross-output ratios. Dimension $n \times 6$

For actual empirical applications, a few further adjustments had to be made, but for our purposes we can stop here and observe how the outputs of the calculation were used. Of central interest are i_1 (the vector of wage cost by occupational category stemming from final demands) and **D** (the matrix of generated value-added components by industry).

Labor cost for on-site project construction by occupational category (i_1 plus i_2) equals total labor cost by occupational category generated by the project (i). For a particular type of project (several were analyzed) **i** and **D** give the occupational patterns of labor costs and other value-added components stemming directly and indirectly from project construction. The next step in adjusting costs for resources that would otherwise be unemployed is to examine levels of occupational unemployment and excess capacity. In general, the more unemployment of labor and capital exists the more likely it would appear that unemployed resources would be brought into employment by an increment of expenditure. In the absence of knowledge of such response functions, a set of synthetic response functions was used which related the probability that a given increment in the demand for labor and capital will be drawn from otherwise unemployed resources to the level of occupational unemployment and industrial excess capacity. In general, it was assumed that at unemployment levels comparable to those in the Great Depression all new labor and capital inputs would be drawn from the unemployed stock whereas at high levels of employment very few would be.

An analysis was made of adjustments to contract costs under 1960 conditions to account for unemployment, assuming zero opportunity cost for unemployed resources drawn into employment by water projects. This analysis indicated that under 1960 conditions, the opportunity cost for project construction was between 65 and 85 percent of nominal money costs (disregarding other possible biases such as those discussed above).

The basic model we have described has been refined to account for differences in regional levels of unemployment and differences in regional adjustments implied by the analysis.

The type of analysis presented and the operational models provided appear to be a substantial forward step in the analytical tools available for the evaluation of public projects. We must register two cautions, however. The first is that unemployment under recent conditions is in large measure a result of the inability of labor supply—both with respect to its location and its skills—to adapt rapidly enough to a changing structure of demand. Accordingly, education and training programs as well as assistance to mobility should always be considered as at least partial alternatives to public works programs to employ existing skills. Secondly, if such analyses are to be applied to public projects, there seems little reason in principle not to apply them to private projects as well. Indeed, subsidization of private projects might in some instances be preferable to public works.

Concluding Comment on Cost Estimation

While the estimation of cost is generally more straightforward than benefit estimation, we feel that this point has sometimes been overdrawn in the literature. Our discussion above suggests considerable complications and a number of theoretically interesting questions which probably have not received the research attention they deserve. Theoretical and empirical considerations suggest that there are significant sources of bias in cost estimation as conducted by public agencies, but their net effect is uncertain.

6.6   BENEFIT EVALUATION—WILLINGNESS-TO-PAY MEASURES

As mentioned previously, two methods for estimating benefits for the efficiency objective are in current use. The first is to make actual estimates of willingness to pay for the output in the sense of estimating an actual demand function, and the second is to calculate the alternative cost of achieving some projected output by an alternative means and counting that as the benefit of providing it via the project (this necessarily involves at least an implicit estimate of the demand curve over a certain range). The second is always regarded as limiting the first,* but in some instances is used as the actual measure of benefit. The most important instances of project outputs for which willingness-to-pay measures are made are irrigation, flood control, and recreation. In addition to being the most important outputs evaluated in this way, they illustrate a variety of theoretical and methodological matters.

The reader interested in a fuller review of federal agency benefit evaluation practice should read Otto Eckstein's excellent book, *Water-Resource Development: The Economics of Project Evaluation,*† in connection with this chapter.

---

* The reader should think through why the cost of a genuine alternative limits the willingness to pay or surplus associated with an output.
† *Op. cit.*

The book is by now somewhat dated but still very useful. Its least satisfactory aspect from the point of view of current issues is the virtually complete absence of any discussion of recreation or water quality. At the time the book was written, these project outputs were still thought of as "intangibles" and subject only to qualitative description, but in a number of recent project evaluations the claimed benefits from these outputs have exceeded all others. In view of this, we present a somewhat fuller description of policies and techniques in these areas than in the others.

Irrigation

Together with navigation, power, and flood control, irrigation is one of the historically important outputs of water resources projects. In recent years, the amount of new land brought under irrigation through federal programs has been quite small and a very small proportion of the total land newly irrigated has been federally watered. This results because most of the land with readily accessible water sources in the arid west has been brought under irrigation and most of the new irrigation has either been from wells (the Texas high plains being the prime example) or in the humid east where supplemental irrigation is provided privately from surface and ground water. However, irrigation evaluation is once more coming into the spotlight in a different context from the historical development one. Vast interbasin diversion projects are in "scheme" or early planning stages which would have to be justified primarily for "rescuing" already irrigated areas. These rescue operations pertain to either or both of the following situations: (1) a non- or slowly replenishing groundwater stock is being drawn down or (2) water is being diverted from water-intensive irrigation use to higher productivity municipal and industrial (M & I) use. The Texas high plains is the archetype of the first sort of situation and a multi-billion dollar diversion scheme from the Mississippi has been planned. Analogous situations exist elsewhere on a smaller scale, especially in various arid areas of the Southwest. Accordingly, we will devote only a small amount of space to discussion of the traditional developmental evaluation procedures but bear down heavily on the theoretical and methodological issues associated with rescue operations. An additional reason for doing this is that excellent detailed discussion of the former are more readily available.*

The Reclamation Act was passed in 1902, establishing the Bureau of Reclamation, and a reclamation fund was created to support its activities. Money for the fund was obtained from the sale of public lands. In more recent times, the Bureau has operated from Congressional appropriations in a manner similar to the Corps of Engineers, the other major federal construction agency. The law requires that irrigators repay the cost of irrigation, but through a variety of devices this obligation has been greatly reduced (these include no payment of interest, transfer of funds for repayment from project to project, and repayment

---

* See especially Eckstein, *op. cit.*

from power revenues after power features are reimbursed). As little as 7 percent of the estimated real project cost of irrigation has been repaid on some projects. The Reclamation Act and the activities of the Bureau can be regarded historically as part of a pattern of policies to settle and develop the West, also embodied in such other legislation as the Desert Land Act and the Homestead Act.

Benefit-cost analysis has been used in connection with Bureau irrigation projects from the beginning, but the procedures used have come in for much criticism from professional economists. Since, with the exception of the "secondary benefits" controversy, most of the criticisms has been with respect to applications rather than fundamental principles, we will not review these criticisms in detail here.* They relate to such matters as whether all opportunity costs are properly considered and how crop surpluses should be treated.

The general procedure the Bureau uses with respect to so-called "primary" benefits is conceptually correct although it does not capture all of the efficiency benefits of projects under every circumstance. Through farm budget studies, an effort is made to ascertain the increase in net farm income resulting from the project. In principle, this measures the maximum willingness to pay for project water of the direct beneficiaries and the contribution to national income.

The main matter of concept which has stirred criticism of the Bureau's methods is in response to its routine calculation of "secondary benefits." These are obtained by the application of standard factors to the projected value of project outputs and costs and are supposed to estimate the benefits accruing from sales by suppliers and from transportation and processing activities. There is no disagreement with the idea that, under some circumstances, national income benefits can accrue from such activities (see the "rescue operation" discussion below), but the complaint is that they cannot be taken to occur routinely or be adequately represented by the kind of standard factors that are used.

Under conditions of full employment of resources, secondary benefits should not be counted at all as a national efficiency benefit since the resources used in secondary activities would be employed elsewhere in equivalently productive activities.† Thus, the occurrence of national income benefits in secondary activities must be an artifact of general or structural unemployment or factor immobilities.

Sometimes secondary benefits are purported to be justified on income distribution grounds. But this position cannot really be sustained because the calculations made have nothing to do with either regional or personal income distribution.

Actually, from a theoretical point of view the terminology and techniques which have come to be employed are unfortunate. Where unemployment and

---

* Probably the best discussion is found in A. Myrick Freeman III, "Adjusted Benefit-Cost Ratios for Six Recent Reclamation Projects," *Journal of Political Economy*, Vol. 74, No. 6 (November 1966).

† Assuming marginal productivities are equivalent in alternative employments. Economies of scale or agglomeration economies may make this condition not strictly valid.

immobilities exist, primary benefits (as presently conceived) do not fully comprehend the contribution to national production, and secondary benefits (as presently conceived and calculated) do not, as far as we can see, measure anything of interest whatever. We believe a change in terminology would be helpful. A category called something like "Contribution to National Production Benefit" would be useful. This would pertain to the net increase in national income accruing from the project whether in primary or interrelated activities and taking account of unemployment, immobilities, etc. On the other hand, regional and personal distribution impacts could also be calculated. This should be much more useful to rational decision-making than calculations based on the concepts now used.

*National Income Benefits from Rescue Operations**

In areas of contracting production (say, where groundwater exhaustion has occurred), especially if they are large, mobility from agricultural and related activities may be limited. Thus, the productivity of some factors of production will be eliminated or reduced for a time after contraction occurs. Accordingly, part of the national income benefits from a project which would prevent such contraction is the maintained productivity of these resources. We will call this a "rescue operation benefit."

In order to analyze these benefits, it is necessary to have a usable model of interindustry linkages which must account for both forward "supply push" and backward "demand pull" effects. An example of the former would be a sugar-processing plant based on the irrigation of beets. The sugar is delivered to final demand and the processing plant in turn exerts "demand pull" through its linkages with supplying industries. The latter is the type of problem traditionally treated through conventional input-output analysis, i.e., a change in "final demand" affecting the supplying industry and the supplying industries for the supplying industries, etc.

The best tool for analyzing both these project impacts together would be a multi-regional closed input-output model which would permit tracing impacts not only in the region where the project is located, but in all other affected regions.† This would permit tracing not only the expansionary effects of the project, but also losses of output in regions which may be adversely affected. Presently available models are of an "open" state or regional type but they are nevertheless useful for the analysis of certain aspects of the impact problem.

---

* This discussion relies heavily on *Interbasin Transfers of Water: Economic Issues and Impacts*, by Charles W. Howe and K. William Easter (Baltimore: The Johns Hopkins Press, 1971).

† The "closed" version of the input-output model is a (still highly simplified) general equilibrium model in which final demands are determined endogenously. The reader will recall that the model we reviewed in Chapter 2 was an "open" model for which demands are externally given. Closed models are not as yet empirically operational.

State input-output tables have been used in connection with illustrative case studies of importation projects.* Basically, the technique involves determining which type of crops are likely to be affected, to what extent, and calculating the direct and indirect (forward and backward linkages) on value added†—the latter with the aid of the input-output analysis. A number of difficult empirical problems arise in doing this, among them, determining demand elasticities for the affected commodities, but we will not review these here.

The final result of this phase of the analysis is an estimate of regional value added with and without the rescue operation project. This is a measure of the impact on the size of the regional economy but not of a net impact on the national economy since it takes no account of reemployment of factors outside the region. Under the most extreme mobility assumptions, all movable factors would be immediately reemployed and the only loss to the nation would be any unusual profits and rental returns otherwise earned in the region. At the other extreme, with all factors completely immobile, the entire loss in regional value added would be a net loss to the nation and could be counted as a benefit of avoiding the decline.

In the rescue operation problem the result lies somewhere in between— resources will be reemployed, but not immediately. Consequently, it is necessary to estimate what part of the value-added would accrue to immobile factors of production and what their periods of immobility would be in the absence of the rescue project. The process of adjusting should assume something like the following pattern. In the long term, displaced labor and capital will be reemployed or the latter will become useless. The only *permanent* loss of income will be the rent to land and its permanent improvements.

Thus, some estimates of the mobility of resources sector-by-sector must be made. So far all efforts of this type have been based on plausible assumptions rather than empirical information.‡ To lend some concreteness to the discussion, we will review assumptions made in one case study.§ An exponential decrease in the lost incomes attributable to immobile labor in the absence of the rescue operation was assumed over a period of 10 years. Alternative assumptions as to the amount of labor still unemployed at the end of 10 years were explored.

---

* See Howe and Easter, *op. cit.*

† Value added in the case of a business firm is the gross value of its output minus purchased materials and services from other firms. One way to calculate gross national product is to sum value added for all firms and governments in the economy. Regional value added is the value of gross production in the region minus the value of materials and services imported from other regions. The reader unfamiliar with aggregate income and product accounting may wish to read Chapter 10 in Paul A. Samuelson, *Economics*, 8th edition (McGraw-Hill Book Co., New York, 1970).

‡ This was done in connection with the Texas Water Plan (*The Texas Water Plan*, Texas Water Development Board, Austin Texas, No. 5, 1968), which as far as we know was the first and only instance in which an actual planning effort made the above type estimates. Similarly, Howe and Easter assumed rates of reemployment as explained below.

§ Howe and Easter, *op. cit.*

The total present value of the income loss avoided by the rescue operation is given by

$$PV_L = \int_0^{10} [B_0 e^{-rt}] e^{-\rho t} \, dt = B_0 \left[\frac{1 - e^{-10(\rho + r)}}{\rho + r} \right]$$

where r is the rate of decrease implied by the terminal unemployment rate, and ρ is the discount rate. B_0 is, of course, the loss in the initial period.

An analogous formulation was prepared with respect to land and capital. An exponential decay pattern was again assumed, starting at a level of full payments to capital and land just before contraction, and decreasing to the level of returns to land and its permanent improvements—the latter being the permanent income loss.

Each pattern is determined by *two* parameters: α, percentage of total returns to capital and land represented by returns to land and its permanent improvements; and T_m, the time after contraction by which 50 percent of the stock of capital goods (excluding permanent land improvements) has either been sold to other users or has deteriorated beyond economic usefulness. T_α is the time at which all potentially mobile capital has been moved or completely deteriorated. Each agricultural sector has its own values of α and T_m.

The present value of returns to capital and land for a particular sector is given by

$$PV_k = \int_0^{T_\alpha} [B_0 e^{-rt}] e^{-\rho t} \, dt + \left[\int_{T_\alpha}^{\infty} \alpha B_0 e^{-\rho t} \, dt \right]$$

$$= B_0 \left[\frac{1 - e^{-T_\alpha(\rho + r)}}{\rho + r} \right] + B_0 \frac{\alpha}{\rho} e^{-\rho T_\alpha}$$

By using these formulas and various assumed parameters, it was possible to compute sector by sector present value multipliers for labor and capital. By application to case area data it was possible to compute present value of income foregone as a result of acreage contraction as a function of (1) the different degrees of forward linkages, (2) the characterization of labor immobility by percent remaining unemployed at the end of 10 years, and (3) the degree of capital mobility as characterized by T_m. It was found that in the cases studied the degree of forward linkages from agriculture to other sectors is the most critical factor in determining the amount of national benefits from a rescue operation.

Progress has been made in the theory and methodology of dealing with rescue operation problems. However, empirical information bearing on appropriate parameters is practically non-existent and regional economic models need improvement. Also deep questions of policy still are by no means resolved. How far should a government go in executing rescue operations in view of the incentives which such a program may induce? For example, there may be an excessive propensity to take risks or a less than optimal incentive to organize for conservation purposes if it is felt that rescue operations will be conducted. It is clear that the rescue operation type of models could have application far beyond the water resources field.

Flood Damage Control

The first large flood control efforts by the federal government came with the founding of the Mississippi River Commission in 1879 for construction of levees and for their maintenance on the lower Mississippi. This commission is still in operation. Through the First World War, however, federal activity mostly took the form of relief payments. The 1928 Flood Control Act inaugurated the Corps of Engineers' famous "308" planning reports in which flood control played a major part. Other early acts, such as the TVA Act and the Boulder Canyon Act, could be mentioned as containing flood control features but the act which set the stage for contemporary federal flood control activities was the Flood Control Act of 1936. The Act was passed during a time of heavy flooding and was in fact quickly amended in 1938 because the Congress felt that progress on the flood control program was not proceeding rapidly enough. The 1936 and 1938 Acts put the federal construction agencies, particularly the U.S. Army Corps of Engineers, full-scale into the flood control business and virtually eliminated any local or state reimbursement for the structures provided. The 1936 Act also contained the often quoted passage which says that the benefits "... to whomsoever they accrue" must outweigh the costs. This was perhaps the highest status ever accorded to benefit-cost analysis in public law.

Development of large-scale flood control in the United States moved roughly through the following stages: levees, channel improvement, and reservoirs. Until very recent times, the emphasis has been almost entirely on structural measures rather than management of land in the flood plain. The last area began to get consideration with Gilbert White's pioneering work, *Human Adjustment to Floods* (1942).*

So far, about one quarter of all federal funds spent on water resources projects have been allocated to flood control. Something between 2.5 and 5 percent of the U.S. land area is in flood plains, and the magnitude of the flood control effort continues at a high level—and so does flood damage. The current rate of expenditure for control is about $500 million per year, and flood losses exceed $1 billion annually. The annual losses appear to have risen over time and the inference is often drawn that the program has been unsuccessful (economically not optimal) and therefore is in need of major reorientation. Of course, these gross figures cannot by themselves sustain such an argument.†

Methods of flood damage control can be characterized in various ways. The following terms and categories are often encountered in the literature. The term

---

* Chicago, University of Chicago, Department of Geography Research Paper No. 29.

† The reader should pause and explain to himself why the increasing damages are not prima facie evidence of an economically unsuccessful program.

structural is usually applied to control over the watercourse itself and includes levees, flood-walls, channel improvements, dams, and reservoirs. Watershed treatment to control runoff is the basic *non-structural* method associated with the watercourse itself. Flood proofing and building code requirements are *structural* means associated with land use. Flood forecasting, evacuation, zoning ordinances, development policies, open spaces, subdivision regulations, tax policy, warning signs, and similar regulation of flood plain occupancy are the *non-structural* means. Insurance neither prevents nor controls either the flood or its associated damages, but covers losses by spreading risk. But, as we discuss below, insurance may affect damages indirectly by altering the behavior of the flood plain occupant. From the point of view of economic theory and methodology, the evaluation of flood control benefits involves several matters.

(1) For the first time we explicitly include a probabilistic element in the evaluation of a benefit.

(2) A public good (in a rather strict sense) is evaluated by making certain assumptions about rational behavior on the part of the beneficiaries.

(3) The matter of public information and how it is obtained becomes a central issue in developing evaluation methodology.

Standard Benefit Evaluation Technique for Flood Control Projects

Evaluation of benefits from reducing water discharge through flow regulation proceeds by the construction of a set of interrelated curves. Figure 6-1 shows a

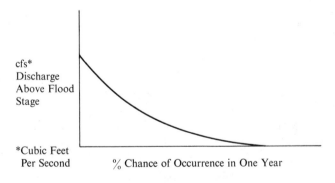

FIGURE 6-1

discharge probability curve which is self-explanatory. Figure 6-2 shows a so-called index station rating curve. This relates flood stage in feet to the rate of discharge. Figure 6-3 shows a stage damage curve. This relates damage to the stage in feet. The assumption is made that at the moment when the damage occurs, the longer-term level of activities in the flood plain is the same, assuming that an equilibrium has been established between flooding and the level of economic

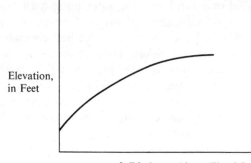

FIGURE 6-2

activity in the flood plain. Enhancement of flood plain land use through protection is also considered in the benefit evaluation and often looms quite large.
Its calculation is not included in the present exposition.*

The final curve in this sequence is obtained by combining the others into one

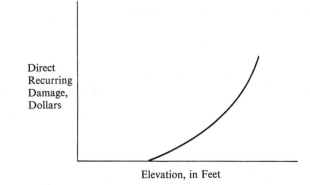

FIGURE 6-3[a]

---

[a] Of course the shape of this curve (given the others) depends on the distribution of activities
in the flood plain.

* Land value enhancement benefits have come under fire from some members of the economics profession (see Eckstein). S-97 suggests that these benefits can be measured as the increase
in net income of property in the flood plain or failing that, the increase in rental value of flood
plan lands. It has been argued that this is an overestimate since there will be "almost as good"
locations off the flood plain. Robert C. Lind in *The Nature of Flood Control Benefits and the
Economics of Flood Protection* (Stanford University: Engineering Economic Systems Program,
1966), has demonstrated that the latter view is basically incorrect and that the federal
procedures have merit even though they may over- or underestimate in particular instances.
Unfortunately, his proof is too long and complex for us to reproduce it here. In crude outline,
however, it proceeds by tracing the full sequence of "next best" choices set in motion by a forced
move by the flood plain user. He preempts an alternative site that would have been the first
choice of some other user. He, in turn, displaces a third, and so on, a net loss of efficiency
occurring each time. It is the sum of these losses rather than just the first one which is the
relevant measure of efficiency loss or gain.

which relates damage to percentage chance of occurrence. Such a curve is illustrated in Figure 6-4. That is, functions 2 and 3 are combined to give direct

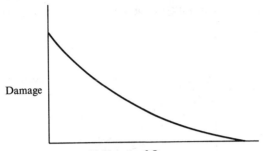

Damage

% Chance of Occurrence

FIGURE 6-4

recurring damage as a function of discharge. This function is then combined with function No. 1 to yield the function depicted in Figure 6-4. In accordance with usual statistical concepts, the area under this curve is the expected value of damage or the mathematical expectation of damage. More formally, if f is the probability function* and x is a random variable representing damage, the expected value of damage is

$$\mu = \int_{-\infty}^{\infty} xf(x) \, dx$$

Now to obtain a benefit function (or expected value of damages avoided function), the calculation proceeds as follows: The effect of an increment of

---

* The probability function associates the probability of occurrence of some value of a random variable x with that value. The probability density function of a continuous variate is defined so that for any given pair of values a and b, such that $a < b$

$$p(a \le x \le b) = \int_{a}^{b} f(x) \, dx$$

Also the condition must hold that

$$\int_{-\infty}^{\infty} f(x) \, dx = 1$$

$f(x)$ is defined to be zero throughout those ranges where x cannot take values so that x can always be treated as having the theoretical interval of possible values $(-\infty,\infty)$ although its range may be $(-\infty,k)$ or (k,∞) or (k_1,k_2) where k, k_1, k_2 are any finite constant with $k_1 < k_2$.

The *arithmetic mean or expected value* of a continuous variate x is defined by

$$\mu = \int_{-\infty}^{\infty} x f(x) \, dx$$

Roughly speaking we can regard this as all possible values of x multiplied by their probability of occurrence. In many actual repetitions of the random event this would be the actual average outcome. The variance of the continuous variate x is defined by

$$\delta^2 = \int_{\infty^-}^{\infty} (x - \mu)^2 f(x) \, dx$$

A useful and reasonably accessible reference on probability is J. R. Gray, *Probability*, University Mathematical Texts, 1st edition (New York: Interscience Publishers, Inc., 1967).

storage (with an assumed operating rule) on the probability of various peak discharges is determined. Then this effect is traced through the other curves to the probability damage curve. The effect on this curve is to shift it leftward as shown in Figure 6-5.* The integral of the new curve is determined and the

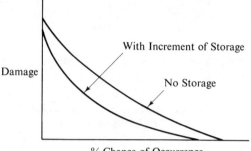

Damage

With Increment of Storage

No Storage

% Chance of Occurrence

FIGURE 6-5

difference between the two integrals is taken to be the expected value of the benefit associated with the increment of storage. A succession of such calculations will yield points on a curve relating the expected value of benefits to increments of storage.†

---

* The damage frequency functions have been drawn so as to intersect the axes, which surely portrays reality correctly since infinite discharges are out of the question, as is also infinite damage. In a practical case, however, estimation of the maximum discharge presents a very difficult problem.

† We can construct a similar curve relating total costs to increments of storage. Both these curves can be taken to represent annual values or present values. We depict a pair of such curves in Figure A. Of course, we assume that costs have been optimized in accordance with principles developed earlier. If we can take these relations as being continuous bounded functions that behave in what we regard as a normal manner, maximum net benefit is found where $C'(x) = B'(x)$ or, to use the marginal terminology, where $MC = MB$.

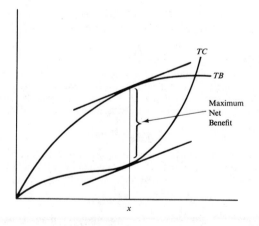

TC

TB

Maximum
Net
Benefit

x

FIGURE A

Now we must examine in what sense the benefits thus derived can be considered a measure of the "willingness to pay" for flood protection.* The basic idea is that a rational, fully informed flood plain occupant would be willing to pay up to the expected value of his losses in order to avoid them. Since protection of one flood plain resident through reservoir storage automatically provides a degree of protection for all others, the demand or willingness to pay functions for all affected flood plain occupants must be added vertically in classic public good style.

Now the main problem about this is the assumption that people make decisions based on expected values. There are three potential problems—all of which turn out to be real ones.

One is that for various reasons people may not find it reasonable to act on the basis of expected values of damage (for example, in decisions to occupy flood plain lands).

A second is that even if people are willing to act on this basis, they almost never understand the concept or have the necessary information to do so.

And a third follows from the other two, i.e., since other decisions, occupance, flood proofing, etc., are not based on expected values, designing flow control structures on the basis of the above criterion will not lead to an optimal combination of measures for flood damage reduction.†

Mathematical expectation is a good decision rule when it is in fact true that risk can be pooled in some fashion. It represents the realized average value of outcomes if there are many repetitions of the event. But this situation frequently is not characteristic of the individual household or even firm which is subject to flood hazard. In the presence of limitations of credit, a single extreme event can spell financial disaster so that the individual decision maker may well be a risk averter. Or possibly some individuals may have a propensity to gamble and therefore conduct short-term activities in the flood plain in the hopes of getting in and out before the flood occurs. Such persons presumably would not be willing to pay up to the expected value of their loss to obtain protection.

But the above discussion assumes that the decision maker has full knowledge of the probability distribution of flood elevations and the damaging effects on his property. Even where good and pertinent information on such matters exists in the hands of the U.S. Geological Survey or the Corps of Engineers, the flood

---

* We will not go into the empirical difficulties of estimating damages although these are considerable. See Eckstein, *op. cit.*

† In fact, the scale of flood control reservoirs is usually not determined on the basis outlined by the text although the calculations described there are made. Usually the scale of projects is increased beyond the point where marginal costs and benefits are equal, ordinarily to a point where the reservoir will control the "maximum" probable flood. (This is a specialized hydrological concept explained in Eckstein). Scaling the structure in this way is ordinarily justified on the grounds that lives are saved by the extra capacity. This view would seem difficult to support. In the first instance, only a comparatively small number of lives are actually lost in floods (about 50 per year on the average) and of these only a small part could potentially be saved by reservoir storage; secondly, heavy construction is one of the most dangerous occupations and it is rare that a major project is completed without deaths or serious injuries; and finally the implied value per life must be astronomically high (in the millions probably) compared with that in other government programs to reduce death from other causes.

plain occupant seldon goes to the trouble to get it (probably because he would have only the vaguest idea about how to use it). Also, the construction of flood control works which provide partial protection (all that can be provided in most instances) frequently leads to the conclusion that the flood threat has been eliminated. It appears in fact that most people do not think in probability terms at all when viewing natural phenomena. It is frequent, for example, that persons will feel just after a large flood that it will now be "a long time" before such a flood occurs again.*

In view of these difficulties, one may seriously doubt that the use of expected value in benefit calculation is appropriate. For example, if occupancy decisions and decisions to use highly localized protection measures like flood "proofing" of buildings are decentralized, flow control and other alternatives are most unlikely to stand in an optimal relationship to one another.

For these reasons, among others, a strong body of opinion has developed, most recently embodied in the report of the President's Task Force on Federal Flood Control Policy† that a deemphasis of structural measures is needed and much more emphasis should be put on other measures, particularly land use control. These arguments have as often as not been devoid of economic analysis and more effective in calling attention to problems than in devising methods for analyzing alternatives. Nevertheless, they have been useful in illuminating the failings of the expectational model on which evaluation of flood control has been based.

Another recent line of discussion, and accompanying initial steps toward action, is interesting from an economic theory point of view. This is flood insurance, especially compulsory flood insurance. Public management and subsidy of an insurance program has been widely advocated and was abortively tried in 1956. The effort failed, at least in part, because it was designed more as a relief measure than as a true insurance program. A 1966 report from the Department of Housing and Urban Development advocates a program of flood insurance.‡ Subsequently, in August 1968, the "National Flood Insurance Act of 1968" was passed. The purpose of the Act is to establish a nationwide system of federally backed flood insurance. Implementation is made contingent on localities providing land use controls, however.

It was not the kind of act (because it did not provide for compulsory flood insurance) which some economists felt could cope most effectively with a variety of problems in the flood damage control field.§ We will discuss some of the

---

* Floods probably are not completely random through time, but they are random enough to make adherence to the "longt-ime" rule highly inadvisable.

† U.S. Congress, House Committee on Public Works, *A Unified National Program for Managing Flood Losses*, House Document 89–465, August 10, 1966 (Washington, D.C.: U.S. Government Printing Office).

‡ U.S. Congress, Senate Committee on Banking and Currency, *Insurance and Other Programs for Financial Assistance to Flood Victims*, 89th Congress, 2nd. Sess., 1966 (Washington, D.C.: U.S. Government Printing Office).

§ See John V. Krutilla, "An Economic Approach to Coping with Flood Damage," *Water Resources Research*, Vol. 2, No. 2 (1966).

desirable attributes of compulsory insurance programs shortly, but first let us consider the question whether flood risk is insurable at all in the actuarial sense of the terms. This question has been investigated by Lind* and we rely heavily on his discussion.

The simplest kind of risk-pooling problems occurs when each person's losses are independent random variables which are identically distributed. The random variable X, with mean μ and variance σ^2, then represents the losses of any individual. When this situation prevails, the amount of risk borne by any individual can be made very small by arranging for the pooling of risks.

When this happens, the risk of loss to any individual in a given year equals the total losses in that year divided by n, where n is the number of individuals in the pool. With pooling, the average loss per individual is still μ, but the variance of this average loss is now σ^2/n instead of σ^2 because the average loss to the individual as a member of a pooling group will vary only as the group mean loss varies.

In reality, of course, losses for all individuals are not identically distributed and each individual's contribution to the pool would be proportioned to his expected losses. This is the situation confronted by mutual insurance companies and does not present any great complications, especially when the number of individuals involved is large.

A much greater complication arises when the losses of different individuals are not statistically independent. Indeed, for obvious reasons, there tends to be a high positive correlation between the losses of different individuals in a particular flood plain or a river basin or perhaps even a larger region. This presents the possibility that it might not be possible to significantly reduce the risk of each individual through a mutual insurance scheme. Thus, straight-forward cross-sectional pooling may not be very promising with respect to flood damage problems. So it is important to inquire whether insurance schemes could be worked out which would be applicable when losses are highly corre-lated. What is required is that the underwriter(s) be in a position to consolidate the experience of regions whose flood experience is not correlated and also to consolidate the experience of a number of different years.

Lind investigates this matter in an ingenious manner. A situation is envisaged in which full coverage is provided flood plain residents at a premium equal to the expected value of damages. This eliminates risk for the flood plain occupant and transfers it to the underwriter—taken in this analysis to be the entire population of the country. Lind shows that under some reasonable assumptions, if the number of people with assets subject to the hazards of flooding is a small percentage of the total population, then by spreading the risk among all in-dividuals the total cost of risk-bearing will be very small. He shows further that under these conditions it is possible to design an insurance scheme where the insurance can be underwritten for a premium which includes a small loading

---

* See Robert C. Lind, *op. cit.*

charge, and yet to have the underwriters fully compensated for the risk they bear.*

If the premium is slightly higher than the expected value of flood losses, each individual whose income is not subject to fluctuations because of flooding will accept a share in the insurance arrangement. If the number of these individuals is large, then the sum of a's will be greater than 1. In this case, the loading charge paid by each policy holder can be very small and the shareholders in the insurance company are at least as well off as before. This arrangement is possible if the number of individuals affected by flooding is relatively small and the total of incomes subject to the hazards of flooding are small relative to the total population and the total of all incomes. Since about $1 billion of flood losses occur in the U.S. annually and the gross national product is about a trillion dollars these assumptions would seem to be reasonably met.

The small loading charges possible under a compulsory scheme are in its favor as is the fact that no selling costs would be involved and that there are probably scale economies in the estimation of flood losses. Now let us relate flood insurance to our earlier discussion of evaluation.

Flood Insurance and Flood Damage Evaluation

A program of compulsory flood insurance with premiums closely linked to the expected value of damages to the flood plain occupant would have several desirable features from an economic efficiency point of view.

First, and certainly among the most important, the occupant would for the first time have a succinct summary statement of the expected value of the cost of flooding to him. This would go far toward removing the informational perceptual problems we discussed earlier in connection with benefit evaluation.

---

* Assume each individual's utility is a function of his income. Further, let U be a bounded increasing function of income so that $U'(Y) > 0$. Assume that among risky alternatives the individual selects the action for which the expected value of his utility $E[U(Y)]$ is a maximum. Since he is assumed to be a risk averter, $U''(Y) < 0$.

Let his income be a random variable A and define a second random variable X which represents the profits of an insurance company (positive and negative). Each individual is given the option of becoming a stockholder free of charge. The individual's income then can be written $Y = A + aX$, where a is the percentage of the stock of the insurance company he chooses to hold. Then the circumstances under which a will be positive must be examined.

Define $W(a) = E[U(Y)] - E[U(A + aX)]$. The individual will attempt to choose a so that $W(a)$ is maximized. $W'(a) = E[U'(Y)X]$ and $W''(a) = E[U''(Y)X^2]$ and since from an earlier result $U''(Y) < 0$, it must follow that $W''(a) < 0$. If $W(a)$ has a maximum at $a = 0$ this implies that $W'(0) \leq 0$. However, if $a = 0$, then $Y = A$ and $U'(Y) = U'(A)$, and $W'(0) = E[U'(A)X]$. Since A and X are independent random variables, $W'(0) = E[U'(A)]E[X]$, so $a = 0 \leftrightarrow E[X] \leq 0$. (Since $U'(A)$ is positive and $W'(0) \leq 0$.) Thus, unless the insurance premium is equal to the expected value of the losses, plus a positive loading charge, no individual will voluntarily choose to accept a share in the company. However, if $E(X) > 0$, then $a > 0$, which means that if the expected value of receipts exceeds the expected value of claims by an amount, however small, each individual will choose to hold a share in the arrangement. The exact value of a for any given individual will in general depend both on his utility function and on the distribution of the A component of his income.

Secondly, since the insurance would eliminate risk the occupant would have every reason to base his decisions (about occupancy, flood proofing, etc.) on the expected value of his damage. This would greatly improve the justification for using this parameter in the design and evaluation of flood protection works.

Since the expected value of damages would be the basis both for the insurance premium and the evaluation of flood control benefits, the benefit for an increment of protection would be measured by the reduction in the premium which could be charged for flood insurance. Some portion of this difference could be used to reimburse the cost of the flood works which, as we noted previously, are presently non-reimbursable.* Many students of flood problems have observed that this fact is most likely to give rise to pressures for uneconomic protection works—however, some countervailing inefficiencies might result from this in the short run because of the "public good" nature of flood protection. Moreover, the collection of insurance premiums would provide an administrative base for the collection of "externality" charges on occupants. While there is little empirical information concerning its magnitude, the effect of development in the flood plain causing channel constriction and higher flood elevations is well known. Finally, if such a strategy were accompanied by more careful planning of other public works, such as streets and sewer and waterlines, which affect the comparative advantage of locations, a rational pattern of flood damage control could emerge. In the absence of such approaches, evaluation of structural measures will continue to be on shaky ground and our use of flood plains beset by ad hoc and strictly sub-optimal management programs.

Recreation Benefits

The use of federal reservoirs for recreation activities has been heavy for many years and is increasing at a rapid rate. However, it is only since authorization to do so was given by Senate Document 97 that recreation benefits have been considered "tangible" and evaluated in quantitative terms. In recent times, some federal projects have been "justified" very heavily on the basis of calculated recreation benefits. The attempt to include recreation benefits certainly is a great advance over the previous practice of not counting recreation benefits at all in the B-C analysis. In some cases, the benefits of reservoirs were no doubt substantially undervalued as a result of failure to include these benefits. For example, Lake Texoma on the Red River between Texas and Oklahoma has had up to 11 million visitor-days of use per year—more than any of our national parks—and no recreation benefits were attributed to it in the project evaluation. While this defect has in principle been remedied, the techniques used for evaluation leave much to be desired from a conceptual point of view. Moreover, the value of recreation is still given little or no attention in design decisions (scale and location of reservoirs).

---

* Land enhancement benefits present some complications in this connection which we will not go into,

Federal Agency Procedures

Senate Document 97 specifically states that recreation benefits should be evaluated and included in the project cost allocation. The technique for making the evaluations is set out formally in a supplement to that document.*

The Department of the Interior (with the Bureau of Reclamation as the construction agency) uses its own Bureau of Outdoor Recreation (BOR) to do the evaluation. The U.S. Army Corps of Engineers generally does its own, and other agencies that require such information usually rely on BOR estimates. In 1965, the Federal Water Project Recreation Act was passed† and its intention is to create uniform policies with respect to recreation, fish and wildlife benefits, and costs of federal multiple-purpose water resource projects. We will outline the type of analysis normally done by BOR as being reasonably typical of the procedures generally followed.

The usual steps, leaving out those which are not essential for our purposes, are as follows:

(i)   Estimate the zone of influence of the project.

(ii) Determine the present and future populations that would probably be served by the recreation area.

(iii) Estimate visitor-days or activity occasions for each activity within the study area during the life of the project. A visitor-day is one visit during a day for any length of time to a recreation facility. Recently, the trend has been toward activity occasion analysis—an activity on one day. For example, a person who fishes and boats during a day will represent one activity occasion of fishing and one of boating.

(iv) Standard values are then attached to participation by activity and the resulting number represents an unweighted benefit of those activities. Supplement No. 1 specifies values per day ranging from $.50 to $6.00 depending on whether the activity is strictly routine or of a highly specialized type.

(v)   The values so obtained are then weighted up or down depending on such factors as water quality, scenic beauty, etc., which vary from site to site.

(vi) The weighted value represents the benefits which will accrue to the facility and which are used in the benefit-cost analysis.

Of course, in specific instances other factors may be considered and (as will already be clear) judgment enters into the procedure in various ways. If the

---

* Senate Document 97, *Policies, Standards, and Procedures in the Formulation, Evaluation, and Review of Plans for Use and Development of Water and Related Land Resources: Supplement No. 1, Evaluation Standards for Primary Outdoor Recreation Benefits*, ad hoc Water Resources Council, Washington, D.C., June 4, 1964.
† Public Law 89–72 (1965).

benefits calculated for the project exceed the separable costs (amount by which total costs would fall if the purpose were excluded) of the project, recreation is considered justified as a project purpose. Under current law, one half of the separable costs and all of the joint costs allocated to the project are non-reimbursable. Local interests must bear half of the separable costs and administer the recreational aspects of the project.

The weaknesses of the evaluation technique now used are fairly obvious. There is no systematic method for forecasting visitations or activity rates; standard values per day for highly diverse situations are unlikely to be accurate (moreover, it is not clear where these values came from to begin with); and, in general, the methodology probably leaves an unwarranted scope for judgment by the individual planner.

In view of these shortcomings, it is worthwhile to explore other possible methodologies. We will discuss one which might be called the Hotelling–Clawson–Knetsch (H-C-K) procedure and which was used as a planning tool for the first time in connection with the Texas Water Plan.*

A Recreation Demand Model

The basic idea underlying the H-C-K recreation demand estimating procedure is that increased access cost associated with distance will tend to affect recreation visits in the same manner as an increase in access cost resulting from a rise in admission fee. If it were feasible to experiment with the latter, it would of course be possible to define a relationship between demand and price (a demand function). The basic principle of the H-C-K procedure can be clarified by a simple numerical example.

Assume that we have divided the "market area" for a recreation facility into three zones and we have the information shown in Table 6-2 about them.

TABLE 6-2

Zone	Population	Access cost per visit	Number of visitors	Visits per 1000 population
1	1,000	$1	500	500
2	4,000	$3	1,200	300
3	10,000	$5	1,000	100

If we assume there is no entrance fee to the recreation area, there will be 2,700 visits and this will be one point on the demand curve.

Now let us simulate the effect of a $1.00 admission charge on the assumption that its effect on visitation rates will be similar to the effect of a $1.00 difference in access cost related to distance.

---

* The Texas Water Plan, *op. cit.*

The people in zone 1 will now be paying \$2 a visit, those in zone 2 \$4 a visit, and those in zone 3 \$6 a visit. By interpolating in columns 3 and 5 of Table 6-2 we can infer that the rate of visits would be 400 per thousand of population at \$2.00. Thus, visits from zone 1 would drop from 500 to 400. We can go through a similar analysis for the other zones, add up the results, and establish a point on the demand curve corresponding to a \$1 admission fee. These calculations can be repeated for successively higher admission fees until a complete demand curve is obtained. The area under this demand curve is the consumers surplus yielded by the recreation facility or the total willingness to pay for it.

Of course, we have assumed extremely simplified conditions, and an actual application must utilize a more complex model, as was the model used in the Texas planning study.* This model uses a multiple variable equation, the parameters of which are estimated from sample survey data by least squares analysis.† With the aid of this equation, H-C-K's demand curves were estimated for particular time periods (in this case one year) for each of 50 reservoirs in the plan. The equation was also used to shift the demand curve as a result of population growth and rising income. By using the demand function for future time periods, a rising stream of annual benefits could be calculated for incorporation in the benefit-cost analyses for the projects. We now proceed to more detailed discussion of the model.

As a first step, a recreation visitation relationship was obtained by relating sample survey visitation data for 1965 to recreation visitation associated factors (income, population, travel cost, reservoir size, and population proximity to available reservoirs).

The general form of the equation used was

$$(Y + .8)\ddagger = A X_1^{b_1} X_2^{b_2} X_3^{b_3} X_4^{b_4} X_5^{b_5}$$

Y is the number of visitor-days from a particular county of origin per unit time (one visitor per day is considered one visitor-day).

X_1 is the population of the county of origin of visitors.

X_2 is round-trip cost of travel from the county of origin of visitors.

X_3 is per capita income in the county of origin of the visitors.

X_4 is a "gravity" variable constructed to reflect the competitive effect of other reservoirs available to visitors of the county of origin upon visitation to the reservoirs being studied.

X_5 is the surface acreage of the conservation pool of the reservoir visited.

---

* The following exposition relies heavily on Herbert W. Grubb and James T. Goodwin, Texas Water Development Board, Report 84, *Economic Evaluation of Water-Oriented Recreation in the Preliminary Texas Water Plan*, September 1968.

† Chapter 2 of Almon (*op. cit.*), has a brief but reasonably complete discussion of the method of least squares for those readers not familiar with it.

‡ The small constant was introduced to deal with a technical problem in the use of log transforms.

The gravity variable $X_4{}^*$ was constructed for each county and included competing lakes within 100 miles of the center of each county.† It was assumed that the larger the number of reservoirs near a county, the less likely residents of that county are to visit a particular reservoir, and that reservoir size is an important factor attracting recreationists.

The specific form of the gravity variable for a county j is as follows:

$$X_{ij} = \sum_{i=1}^{n} \frac{\log_{10} S_i}{d_i}$$

where S_i is surface acre size of the conservation pool in reservoir i, and d_i is the distance from reservoir i to the center of county j; n equals the number of reservoirs within 100 miles of the center of county j. Use of the gravity variable requires that actual or assumed patterns of reservoirs be available. It reflects the competition of reservoirs with each other—a factor which is usually not explicitly taken into account in the analysis of recreation demand.

For statistical reasons, logarithmic transforms of the raw data were used. Among other benefits of this is the fact that it permits standard linear regression to estimate the parameters of the non-linear equation. Also, as we noted in Chapter 2, in this form the β coefficients of the regression equation are elasticities. The demand function estimated from this particular equation will be forced to have a constant elasticity.

The actual statistical equation obtained was as follows:

$$\log_e (Y + .8) = -8.60308 + .57373 \log_e X_1 - 1.18626 \log_e X_2$$
$$(2.08063) \quad (.04404) \qquad\qquad (.07502)$$

$$+ 0.75292 \log_e X_3 - .32666 \log_e X_4 + .20955 \log_e X_5$$
$$(.26744) \qquad\qquad (.04806) \qquad\qquad (.06377)$$

$$R^2 = .41$$

For visitation projection purposes, projection of county income and population were used. For the gravity variable, new reservoirs were entered in accordance with the assumed pattern of development for the plan as a whole.

The first step in obtaining a demand curve for a particular period and a particular reservoir is to solve the equation partially for each county in the zone of the reservoir by inserting values for the appropriate variables. This yields visitation from each county and these can be summed for all relevant counties to yield an estimate of visitations at zero user fee. Estimates for positive user

---

* Gravity models are adaptations of a concept of Newtonian physics. One of the earliest formal models of this type was produced by Stewart. He called it "demographic potential"; it corresponds to gravitational potential in physics. For a detailed discussion of gravity models, see Walter Isard, *Methods of Regional Analysis: An Introduction to Regional Science* (New York: John Wiley & Sons, 1960).

† The survey data used in the analysis indicated that more than 90 percent of visitors originated within 100 miles of each reservoir in the sample.

fees are then made by adding appropriate increments to the value of X_2. Solutions for as many levels of user fees as desired can be obtained by continuing this process. Time-related variables can have appropriate increments added to them by using projected values for the variables which shift the demand function. By means of this process, a stream of benefits can be generated. As already mentioned, these procedures were used to estimate recreation values for reservoirs included in the Texas Water Plan. A sampling of these is shown in Table 6-3.

Shortcomings and Possibilities

Two general problems besetting the H-C-K technique were fortunately not too important in applying it as described in the preceding sections, but they could be very destructive for other applications. One is the "single-purpose" trip assumption. The method as presently constituted requires that no utility has been obtained from visits along the way to the site being evaluated and that the trip itself has not yielded utility. In the Texas situation where almost all visits were from what in the "age of interstates" is a short distance (less than 100 miles) and where (with our apologies to Texas sensibilities!) there tend to be few intervening points of major interest, this is probably not a serious difficulty. The other potentially limiting assumption is that the cost of travel is equivalent to entrance fees in its propensity to limit use. Again with relatively short travel times, as in the Texas case, this problem is likely to be minor. However, if there are substantial travel times involved, the assumption becomes dubious indeed. Should the trip be single-purpose and lengthy, time itself becomes a scarce resource (recreation time budget constraint) and the method as presently constituted cannot deal adequately with this problem. Quite possibly future research will show how to cope with these problems.

Other problems, which are not so much deficiencies of method as of data, did beset the Texas study. These could be lumped as "quality of the recreation experience." Variables such as shore characteristics, investment facilities, water quality, reservoir drawdown, congestion, etc., were not included, although with large samples there is no reason why they could not be. If they are important variables (explain significant amounts of variance in visitation rates), then the explanatory value of the distance variable may well have been exaggerated in the actual results. However, in our *judgment* the method is promising and deserves additional development and use in planning.

Concluding Comment

We have discussed the major outputs of water resources projects for which benefit functions are directly estimated. We have found reasons to be critical of certain aspects of these procedures but in general they are well developed and sophisticated—especially when compared with the primitive or non-existent methods used in connection with other areas of public expenditure.

Certainly, we feel there is every reason to continue the development of improved techniques for the estimation of demand.

We turn now to an evaluation technique which often rests on much shakier foundations, the so-called alternative cost method. It is typically used in connection with navigation, power, municipal and industrial water supply, and at least until recently, water quality. First we will discuss the technique in theoretical and conceptual terms and then we will present two examples—water quality and navigation. We treat the former by studying a particular case. Our discussion of water quality and navigation well illustrates the difficulties involved in applying the technique properly.

6.7   BENEFIT EVALUATION—ALTERNATIVE COST

Steiner* has examined rigorously the situations in which alternative cost can be taken as a measure of benefit (willingness to pay) for a publicly produced output. We will state his main results (augmented with our own comments) without presenting the mathematical derivations since all of them are intuitively reasonable. Most of his discussion relates to private alternatives but we will also comment on public alternatives. Some care has to be taken in defining what an alternative is in the latter instance since it would always be possible to design a public project which would cost just 1¢ more than the project under consideration and thereby inevitably generate net benefits. Unfortunately, such misuse of the technique has happened, as we shall see later.

The term "alternative" must, in connection with this evaluation technique, refer to a way of doing the same or a similar thing in a manner that is in some sense substantially different. While public alternatives to public projects have often been used in estimating benefits, the reader must be forewarned that the comparison of public projects can in no way relieve the decision maker from estimating the "absolute merit" of the project.

The first instance we discuss is the case in which no alternative project exists. This is the case we have been implicitly assuming in our previous discussion of benefit estimation. In this instance, a demand function for the public project must be estimated if total willingness to pay is to be determined.

Other cases where there are private alternatives to public output can be explained with the help of a simple diagram, shown in Figure 6-6.

Take first the instance where both the private and the public projects produce the same output, D. We assume throughout that the private alternative *would be provided* if the public alternative would not be. This could result from one of two possibilities: either demand becomes perfectly inelastic at that output or the scale of the project is fixed at that level for some physical or technological reason. If output is fixed at D, for example if demand became completely

---

* Steiner, "The Roles of Alternate Cost in Project Design and Selection," in Allen V. Kneese and Stephen C. Smith, eds., *Water Research* (Baltimore: The Johns Hopkins Press, 1966).

TABLE 6-3

ESTIMATED RECREATIONAL BENEFITS OF PROPOSED RESERVOIRS, 1970–2020 (IN THOUSANDS OF DOLLARS)

River basin and reservoir	1970	1975	1980	1985	1990	1995	2000	2005	2010	2015	2020	Total un-discounted benefits 1970–2070	Present worth in 1970 of future benefits[a]	Equivalent annual benefits[b]
Red River basin														
Sweetwater Creek	130	146	161	175	189	205	221	242	262	317	371	28,295	c	c
Bois d'Arc	0	108	121	134	146	161	175	192	209	273	336	24,350	4,960	158
Big Pine	0	0	0	0	0	0	0	400	440	561	682	41,105	5,140	174
Pecan Bayou	0	0	0	0	0	0	0	376	421	568	714	42,525	5,250	177
Timber Creek	13	16	18	20	22	24	26	29	31	41	50	3,700	c	c
Sulphur River basin														
Sulphur Bluff 1	0	0	0	209	233	261	288	315	341	464	586	39,855	6,490	219
Naples 1 and 2	0	0	0	0	0	0	0	270	286	424	562	33,005	4,010	135
Cooper	165	191	216	244	272	305	337	368	398	543	685	49,445	9,780	331
Cypress River basin														
Franklin County	0	491	552	636	719	719	720	870	1,020	1,257	1,494	109,620	21,310	723
Titus County	0	223	240	288	335	373	412	457	503	621	740	54,260	9,780	331
Marshall	0	0	0	0	0	0	0	383	401	579	756	44,615	5,450	184
Black Cypress	0	0	0	0	0	0	0	397	448	623	797	47,190	5,780	195
Sabine River basin														
Mineola	0	0	0	461	512	564	616	680	745	973	1,201	82,805	13,710	464
Lake Fork	0	0	0	458	510	559	608	707	806	972	1,137	79,950	13,470	456
Kilgore 2	143	163	184	210	236	259	282	314	345	445	544	40,105	c	c

TABLE 6-3 (Cont.)

Neches River basin													
Blackburn Crossing													
Enlargement	280	319	359	410	461	499	536	596	655	866	1,076	78,705	15,900	538
Rockland	0	0	0	0	0	0	0	771	857	1,299	1,740	101,635	12,260	415
Ponta	0	0	0	0	0	0	0	475	520	739	958	56,570	6,910	234
Trinity River basin													
Lakeview	0	428	480	590	699	709	719	798	878	1,096	1,315	97,835	19,310	654
Aubrey	0	144	161	178	194	214	234	256	279	364	449	32,570	6,250	212
Richland Creek	0	0	0	590	650	720	789	853	917	1,337	1,757	117,130	18,650	632
Tehuacana Creek	0	0	0	415	460	503	545	626	706	1,244	1,782	111,595	16,250	551
Tennessee Colony	382	446	510	567	626	695	767	798	830	1,188	1,546	111,345	22,180	751
Bedias	0	0	0	0	0	0	0	537	537	745	954	56,795	6,980	236
Wallisville	248	295	342	393	444	481	517	579	641	845	1,049	76,375	15,240	516
San Jacinto River basin													
Cleveland	343	407	471	552	633	681	729	797	865	1,145	1,425	104,365	c	c
Humble	566	667	768	876	985	1,052	1,119	1,257	1,394	1,691	1,988	151,275	c	c
Lower East Fork	410	474	538	661	783	792	801	927	1,053	1,341	1,630	120,400	c	c
Lake Creek	280	320	360	384	408	434	460	490	521	761	1,001	72,140	c	c

a Present worth in 1970 of the estimate benefits stream. Benefits begin in the year of anticipated project completion and continue at estimated levels to the year 2070. Present worth of benefits is calculated at 3.25 percent annual discount rate.

b Equivalent annual benefits are the undiscounted level annual benefits for the period 1970 to 2070, which when discounted at 3.25 percent would produce the corresponding 1970 present worth estimates.

c Construction staging has not been suggested; therefore, present worth has not been calculated.

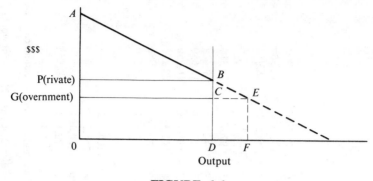

FIGURE 6-6

inelastic at that point, and average and marginal costs of the private and government alternatives are at *P* and *G* respectively, the gross benefit of the government project is *OPBD* and the net benefit is *GPBC*.

Another category of cases occurs when there is a higher-cost private alternative which would be implemented in the absence of the project, but neither project need be built to a fixed scale and demand is not totally inelastic. In this case, referring again to Figure 6-6 and assuming constant costs, the optimum output under public provision would be at *F*. In this case, the demand function would have to be estimated at least from *B* to *E*. For outputs up to *D*, the benefit from public provision is limited (and measured) by the private cost. For outputs up to that point, beneficiaries would be willing to pay *OPBD* for provision of the output from the public project. Added to this must be the area *BCE*.

Now let us assume *P* and *G* are both public projects. In general, if one considers the government as a single entity, alternative cost estimation cannot substitute for estimating a demand function in this instance, although in practice the alternative cost technique has been used with respect to public alternatives. The only way this could conceivably be sensible is if one agency is evaluating a project the output of which would otherwise be supplied by another public agency. Sometimes the technique has also been used when some sort of a physical target had been set externally (politically) and alternate public projects for achieving it were under consideration. The case study we discuss briefly below contains elements of both these situations and shows clearly the possible pitfalls. We feel it is much more conducive to clear thought on the matter if the type of situation involving public alternative and fixed output targets is viewed as a cost minimizing rather than a net benefit maximizing one.*

Water Quality Benefits in the Potomac Basin

With the passage of the Water Pollution Control Act in 1948, the federal government took its first step into what had been an exclusive area of state

---

* Since cost allocation is required, it is sometimes argued that benefits must be calculated to permit application of the separable costs remaining benefits procedure.

sovereignty. The Act was amended in 1956 and again in 1961 and several times later. The feature of the 1961 Act which is salient to our purposes is that it provided for the inclusion of storage in federal multi-purpose reservoirs to augment low flows for water quality improvement. In general, the costs of such storage were to be considered nonreimbursable—that is, no cost assessments or prices for the service were to be levied on the beneficiaries. The relation between levels of river flow and water quality is a complicated one and all we need note here is that the probability of high concentrations, of undesirable substances occurring in rivers, and estuaries, can sometimes be reduced by storing water in reservoirs and releasing it during low-flow periods. The procedure used to evaluate the benefits from such water quality improvement has been taken to be the cost of achieving a similar improvement by alternative means, usually a single-purpose project, although this has now apparently been amended somewhat.

Pursuant to a resolution of Congress in 1963, the U.S. Army Corps of Engineers submitted the *Potomac River Basin Report*. This report was the first one in which a federal water resource agency submitted a "comprehensive" plan in which water quality management was a major consideration. The plan took a quality objective stated in physical terms (parts per million of Dissolved Oxygen)* as given and recommended a program of waste treatment and low-flow regulation to meet this objective in the future. While it was a pioneering effort, the benefit evaluation based on alternative cost was grossly deficient; and for various reasons pertinent to our consideration of the alternative cost technique, the range of alternatives considered for water quality improvement was narrow. Basically, the Corps of Engineers limited its planning to consideration of those quality improvement facilities which could clearly be implemented through existing government institutions. As we shall see, this limited range of choice greatly and led to the recommendation of a set of facilities which was far from the least costly which could have been devised to achieve the objective.

A later Resources for the Future study† which forms the basis for our discussion used the Corps of Engineers data plus considerable additional information to further define the range of alternatives for water quality management in the Potomac estuary in the neighborhood of Washington, D.C., the locus of most of the water quality problem.

The Basin and Its Problems

The watershed of the Potomac, an area of about 14,000 square miles, lies in portions of four states and District of Columbia. About three-fourths of the population in the basin is found in the Washington metropolitan area. This area, which extends beyond the District of Columbia into Maryland and Virginia,

---

* Factors bearing upon oxygen levels in streams are discussed in some detail in Chapter 8.
† A full report on this study is found in Robert K. Davis, *The Range of Choice in Water Management* (Baltimore: The Johns Hopkins Press, 1968).

already has a population of over 2 million persons and is one of the most rapidly growing metropolitan areas in the nation. The Washington area lies near the head of the Potomac Estuary which is heavily used for recreation. Water supply for the area is taken from the Potomac River above the estuary. The estuary periodically experiences low dissolved oxygen—a condition which could get much worse as waste loads from the metropolitan area and upstream sources mount. The Corps of Engineers as part of its planning effort projected water demands and waste loads to the year 2010. One of the central objectives of the plan was to control the effects of waste loads expected to prevail then. Among the planning assumptions was that the maximum feasible control of waste loads would result from conventional secondary sewage treatment (about 90 percent Biochemical Oxygen Demand (BOD) removal).*

MAJOR RESERVOIRS IN RECOMMENDED PLAN
FOR POTOMAC BASIN

FIGURE 6-7

The plan made public in 1963 recommended the construction by the year 2010 of sixteen major reservoirs in the Potomac basin and more than 400 headwater structures. These were meant to meet projected supply, quality, and flood control objectives. Of the sixteen major reservoirs, ten were planned to meet projected upstream objectives for the low-flow regulation for water supply and

---

* For our purposes we can define BOD as measuring the demand for dissolved oxygen (DO) placed upon a receiving water by a waste discharged to it. Low levels of DO are destructive to life in a stream and oxygen exhaustion causes aesthetic problems also.

quality control. At the same time, this group of reservoirs would provide a sufficiently higher sustained flow at Washington to meet the projected municipal water diversions there. The remaining group of six reservoirs (providing 60 percent of the proposed yield—2340 cfs out of 3931 cfs) was designed to augment flows into the estuary sufficient to maintain 4 ppm of dissolved oxygen (24-hour monthly mean for the minimum month). The projected storage was based on counteracting residual 2010 waste loads and an assumed replication of the historical record of flows into the estuary (i.e., the so-called mass curve approach was used to determine required storage to sustain flows calculated to be needed to offset residual waste loads to the extent of maintaining 4 ppm DO). From a statistical point of view, the mass curve approach has great deficiencies (which are explored in the next chapter).

A benefit-cost analysis was presented which indicated that the benefits from flow regulation would outweigh its costs. But this analysis did not do what benefit-cost analysis is intended to accomplish—assist in deciding whether a proposed investment is socially worthwhile. The pre-set physical quality objective of 4 ppm of DO was taken as given in the planning. It was assumed that treatment of the sewage from the Washington metropolitan area could not succeed in removing more than 90 percent of the waste load. This is insufficient to meet the objective. The only alternative seriously investigated was low-flow regulation to improve the waste assimilative capacity of the estuary. Benefits from low-flow regulation were taken to be the cost of a single-purpose reservoir designed to meet low-flow requirements at each point of projected need without regard to the complementary effects of meeting upstream needs. Moreover, costs of the alternative reservoirs were calculated at a higher rate of interest—presumably because it was assumed they would be implemented by state or local governments which have to pay higher rates of interest than the federal agencies use in their own calculations.

This string of planning assumptions was bound to produce positive net benefits for flow regulation. But this result was obtained without even addressing the real question—is the 4 ppm objective justified by the willingness of beneficiaries to pay at least as much as it costs to maintain it? Clearly, the benefit-cost analysis as it was performed is not helpful in deciding whether the plan is justified.

Furthermore, for various reasons having to do with limitations on the authority of water resources agencies and their perception of problems and appropriate solutions, the planners made no concerted or systematic effort to search for and evaluate alternative ways (in addition to flow regulation) of achieving the specified water quality objective. The measures recommended for quality control were limited to basic conventional treatment and low-flow augmentation—measures which could clearly be implemented by the federal and local government agencies which are the traditional purveyors of water services in the U.S. To have implemented a program embodying less conventional measures would probably have required institutional change. The possibility of such change was not contemplated in the planning process.

Searching for Additional Alternatives

The RFF study showed that including certain collective measures, which no existing agency had a clear authority or incentive to finance, construct and operate, would very likely have entered into a least cost system for meeting the oxygen objective. Had such a system served as the alternative for benefit analysis, net benefits for flow regulation, at least for the larger-scale reservoir systems, would have been grossly negative.

In going through the analysis, the Corps assumption that 90 percent treatment would be given wastes in the Washington metropolitan area was (somewhat arbitrarily) used as a baseline. The costs of other alternatives were then weighed off against the incremental cost of flow regulation for counteracting the residual oxygen deficit.

Costs were obtained for various levels of low-flow regulation by scaling down by various amounts the Corp's proposed low-flow regulation system. The scaled-down systems were roughly optimized by using a computer simulation program which permitted the historical trace of hydrology to be regulated by the various systems. In the initial instance, historical hydrology was used to maintain close comparability with the Corps results. In computing costs for the successively smaller reservoir systems, account was taken of the difference in flood damage reduction and recreation services realized by any scaled-down system in comparison to the full proposed Corps of Engineers system.

With the assistance of consultants, costs of several alternate ways of equivalently offsetting the waste load were developed. These included processes for further treatment of the waste load (microstraining, step aeration, chemical polymers, powdered carbon, and granular carbon). Costs for effluent distribution via pipeline along the estuary to better use its naturally occurring assimilative capacity, and reoxygenation of the estuary (which, like low-flow regulation, improves assimilative capacity) were also obtained with the help of outside consultants.

Computer simulation of the effects of these processes in view of variations of river flow (using the historical hydrologic trace) into the estuary show that they need to be operated on the average only 3.5 months per year in order to meet the DO objective. Because the alternative systems are high in operating cost and low in capital cost relative to low-flow regulation they can be comparatively efficient if operated only as needed but would not be competitive if operated continuously, thereby overshooting quality goals most of the time. Accordingly, they could enter efficiently into the quality management system only if institutional means existed for carefully articulated design and operation in conjunction with other elements of the system.

Establishing combinations which would meet the standard required that if one process was reduced another had to be equivalently increased. It was possible to use computer simulation to exhaust all possible combinations of the feasible and sufficient processes given the relatively large increments defined for them.

TABLE 6-4

SYSTEM COSTS BY GENERAL CLASS OF PROCESS COMBINATIONS
3.5 MONTHS OPERATION

(Present worth, 50 year period, 4% discount)

$000,000's

Alternative Systems

1. Reoxygenation	$20
2. Chemical Polymers and reoxygenation	22
3. Step Aeration and reoxygenation	25
4. Microstrainers and reoxygenation	28
5. Diversion and reoxygenation	33
6. Diversion, waste treatment, and reoxygenation	45
7. Low-flow augmentation and reoxygenation	60
8. Low-flow augmentation, reoxygenation, and waste treatment	60
9. Low-flow regulation	140

The computer program gave a complete listing and cost ranking of all systems—some 300 in all.

A sampling of alternate feasible and sufficient systems is shown in Table 6-4.

This analysis shows that many combinations of processes could achieve the objective at less cost than the proposed system based upon conventional treatment and flow regulation. It is notable that all of them except the flow regulation alternative would require the construction and closely articulated operation of facilities which have not traditionally been in the purview of either the federal or local government (particularly reoxygenation and regional effluent distribution works). Another salient point is that while low-flow regulation is vastly more costly than reoxygenation or some of the other alternatives, from the point of view of the people in the basin it costs much less. Low-flow regulation for water quality improvement has been, as previously mentioned, a fully nonreimbursable purpose of federal water development in the United States, while no subsidy at all is available for measures like reoxygenation and waste diversion. Thus, the fact that federal water development policy is such that certain measures for development confer large subsidies on a region while others do not can also contribute to choices among alternatives which are distorted from a broader economic point of view. We will consider this matter a bit further in the next chapter.

Both of these factors were undoubtedly implicit considerations in the plan recommended. By means of economic-systems analysis which does not operate only within the existing institutional and policy restraints, it is possible to examine them and thus provide information on the desirability of institutional change. In the case of the Potomac it appears that much could be gained by institutional arrangements permitting the planning, design and operation of quality management systems embodying a wide range of alternatives.

Concluding Comments

The above discussion has indicated that alternative cost as a measure of benefit can obscure rather than illuminate the economic choices that have to be made when a physical target is chosen for design and institutional factors circumscribe the search for alternatives. Furthermore, when a target is stated in physical terms and benefit measures are not available to aid in the decision as to whether it is at an appropriate level, it is better to view the problem as one of cost minimization, although as we will see in the next chapter this presents problems of joint cost allocation for multiple-purpose projects under current procedures. A natural economic extension of the cost minimization view is to conduct an analysis of the sensitivity of costs to different levels of target. This was done in the RFF Potomac study but we will not report the results here.* Discussion of cost sensitivity analysis is found in later chapters.

Navigation

Background

Inland waterways played an important role in the early development of the U.S. and their extension was the main type of public works in the new country. In his report on a transportation program for the new nation, Albert Gallatin pointed to the need for comparing reduced transportation costs afforded by them with the cost of new or extended ground transportation systems. By the end of the 1820s, a canal boom of major proportions had developed which was heavily financed by the states and by private investors. However, starting about the mid-nineteenth century, the waterways began to face heavy competition from the railroads, often accompanied by the use of monopolistic economic power to force the waterway operators to the wall. The construction of the new railway system was stimulated by heavy public subsidies to railway construction. Revival of the waterways started with the Transportation Act of 1920 which asserted a national interest in further waterway development. In the postwar period several large projects have been completed on the Missouri, the Delaware, the St. Lawrence, and the Ohio, among others. The percentage of freight moving on inland waterways has increased in the postwar period and a number of other large projects are underway or in advanced planning. Among these are projects on the Arkansas, the Trinity, and the Muskingum, all of which are in the $1 billion-plus category. The benefit evaluations which served to "justify" these

---

* See Davis, *op. cit.*

projects have come under severe fire from economists. Probably there are two main reasons for this: (1) the procedures used are dubious and (2) political pressure for favorable economic evaluations has been so patently obvious. We will return to both of these shortly.

Technique Used

The usual procedure in navigation evaluation studies is for the Corps of Engineers staff of transportation specialists to make studies of the traffic that can be expected to develop on a new waterway. Then a determination is made as to what costs would be incurred if a *similar volume* of traffic were to move by waterway. The alternative cost considered is usually the cost of shipment by railway. The cost estimate for the railway alternative is the published railway rate. We will discuss the procedure used with the aid of a simple equation and a diagram.

$$B = C_a - C_w - C_p + \Delta D$$

where

B is the net benefit of the waterway.

C_a is the cost of the alternative mode for that amount of freight *which would actually* move on the alternative route.

C_w is the waterway cost for that amount of freight.

C_p is the premium which shippers who use the waterway would have paid to use the alternative rather than the waterway.

ΔD is the net increase in willingness to pay for waterway transport for freight which would not have moved on the alternative but will move on the waterway.

The same variables can be depicted graphically; see Figure 6–8.

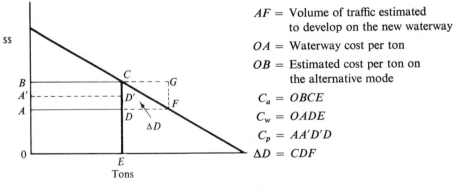

$AF =$ Volume of traffic estimated to develop on the new waterway

$OA =$ Waterway cost per ton

$OB =$ Estimated cost per ton on the alternative mode

$C_a = OBCE$

$C_w = OADE$

$C_p = AA'D'D$

$\Delta D = CDF$

FIGURE 6-8

The first criticism which has been made of the evaluation procedure used relates to the estimation of C_a. As already mentioned, railroad *rates* are usually used as estimates of B. Railroads are good examples of decreasing cost industries. Fixed investments are large relative to out-of-pocket operating costs.* For diverted traffic, clearly the only saving in opportunity costs for the economy is the reduction in operating costs since the fixed costs are sunk. Even for future traffic which would have moved by rail in the absence of a waterway what is important is the increment of railway cost in terms of actual outlay on resource inputs. This is unlikely to be measured by the average historical cost upon which rates are set. Studies of railway costs and of rate reductions when competitive routes develop suggest that using rates overstates social opportunity costs by 20–40 percent.†

A second problem in the benefit evaluation procedures as applied is that instead of an area ΔD (which requires estimation of at least part of the waterway transportation demand curve) normally the entire area $CDFG$ is counted as a benefit for the traffic induced by the lower cost of the waterway. This results from applying the alternative cost estimate to the entire projected shipment on the waterway.

An additional difficulty and one that has not been very much discussed in the literature results from the fact that moving freight from point x to point y by alternative means is not necessarily equivalent in economic terms. Handling costs may differ and transit times certainly do. The latter reflects itself in differences in inventory costs and flexibility of delivery schedules. Thus, even though traffic moves by waterway the shipper might have been willing to pay a premium to ship by the alternative means. As long as this premium does not cancel the difference in cost, the goods will continue to move by water, but the measured difference in cost will not accurately reflect the willingness to pay for the water route. In principle, of course, this variable could take on either a positive or a negative value. In the diagram an amount equal to $AA'D'D$ should be subtracted from the usual measure of benefit to get an approximate estimate of willingness to pay. In other words, whereas the usual measure of benefit is $ABGF$, the approximate one is $A'BCFDD'$.

Finally, since estimates of *future* traffic on the waterway are based on *current* railroad rates, these estimates are likely to exaggerate the shift of traffic. It is well documented that railway rates adjust to competition on particular routes and a railroad can be expected to cut rates close to out-of-pocket cost rather than lose the traffic.

Thus, there are several possible sources of overestimation of benefits from development of inland navigation. In the above discussion we have assumed that a new waterway is under consideration. It is not difficult to translate the analysis to a situation where improvement of an existing waterway is at issue. In both

---

* For simplicity in the diagram we have depicted constant average costs for both the waterway and its alternative.

† See Eckstein, *op. cit.*

cases there are significant design problems involving benefit estimation which we have not treated explicitly.*

Of course, all the problems above could be solved if a reasonably good estimate of an actual demand relationship for shipment on a particular waterway were available. Some interesting work on the estimation of demand functions has been done.† But improvement of the alternative cost technique could be very helpful too in improving benefit estimates. The professional economists in the Corps have pressed hard for improvement, especially for the use of social opportunity cost, rather than railroad rates, in the evaluation of waterways. These efforts have been nullified by pressure from Congress.‡

Concluding Comments about Alternative Cost Techniques

The advantage of the alternative cost technique is that sometimes it permits benefit (willingness to pay) evaluation without the actual estimation of demand curves. Also, however, we have seen that the circumstances under which this is actually possible are severely limited and that in applications the method has led to serious mistakes. Nevertheless, where demands are rather inelastic and where the effect of the public project is primarily to reduce the cost of producing an output which would otherwise be provided privately, or by an independent public agency, the technique can be useful.

In addition to water quality and navigation, alternative cost-benefit evaluation is regularly applied to power and municipal and industrial water supply. In the former instance the alternative considered has usually been utility steam generation of power and in the latter self-provision of water by municipalities and industries.

---

* For example, expansion of the cross-section of a canal reduces viscous drag but, of course, is costly. Hence, this cost must be weighed off against the reduction in tow-operating cost (benefit) in order to optimize design. Improvement in a particular lock must be viewed in terms of system performance rather than as an individual item, since the improved flow of traffic through the lock (benefit) must be weighed off against the increase in congestion elsewhere in the system. Economists have made notable contributions to the study of these questions. See Charles W. Howe *et al.*, *Inland Waterway Transportation: Studies in Public and Private Management and Investment Decisions* (Washington, D.C.: Resources for the Future, Inc., 1969).

† See E. Silberberg, "The Demand for Inland Waterway Transportation," *Water Resources Research*, Vol. 2, No. 1 (First Quarter 1966).

‡ See Robert H. Haveman, "The Domestic Program Congress Won't Cut," *The Reporter* (February 22, 1968), pp. 36–37. In 1960, the Corps, in principle, adopted the use of alternative cost rather than rates, although rates could be used if cost estimates were unavailable. However, estimates of traffic expected to move on the waterway remained primarily based on a comparison of current rail rates and barge rates expected to prevail when the waterway is completed. In 1964, this latter procedure was changed so that traffic estimates were to be based on rates *after* they had been adjusted for likely changes resulting from the waterway competition. Because of these changes, fewer projects were able to demonstrate positive net benefits. Powerful members of Congress strongly objected to the new procedure, especially those from states with strong waterway interests. Through Section 7 of the Transportation Act of 1966, Congress forced the Corps to revert to the pre-1960 practice of estimating both waterway traffic and unit savings on the current railroad rate basis.

In practice, the technique has frequently proved useful and defensible in connection with these outputs, but serious complications arise in its applications. Most dubious perhaps have been certain applications to industrial water supply. Over a considerable range, the demand for industrial water intake is highly elastic (since internal reuse is usually cheap). This factor has sometimes been overlooked in applying the alternative cost technique to project output.

CHAPTER 7

Production Function, Cost Allocation, and Problems in Pricing

7.1 THE PRODUCTION FUNCTION REVISITED

In the discussion of investment criteria in Chapter 5, it was highly useful to assume the existence of a production function summarizing technological relationships between inputs and outputs for a project or a system. As the reader will recall, the production surface defined by this function is conceived of as containing only those points which are technically efficient. Assuming the existence of a known production function greatly simplified our discussion. In principle, this function could be used to restrict an objective function and standard calculus methods used to derive a maximum solution. The conditions for an optimum so obtained are valid and useful, but we must now recognize that in something as complicated as many natural resource management systems, the engineer cannot be expected to supply the economic analyst with a production function.*

At least two main reasons account for this: (1) Even a simple problem involves a huge number of alternatives and some of these are interrelated in complicated ways. For example, the Harvard Water Program studied a moderate size river basin problem in which there were 52 design variables. If each of these is assigned only three values, there exist a total of 3^{52} or about six million

---

* For much simpler problems, the use of an explicit production function is sometimes possible. See P. H. Cootner and G. O. G. Löf, *Water Demand for Steam Electric Generation: An Economic Projection Model* (The Johns Hopkins Press for RFF, 1966). See also Vernon L. Smith, *Investment and Production* (Cambridge: Harvard University Press, 1961).

billion billion different designs—far too many to be exhaustively examined!
Of course, many billions of these can be eliminated very quickly if the problem
can be analyzed to any significant degree, but the fact remains that the number
of possibly viable designs is still extremely large in practical problems of any
size. A related and perhaps even more disturbing factor is that in many cases
we cannot be sure that all of the design variables have been identified. Also,
relations between inputs and outputs would be greatly different depending on
whether reservoirs are in series or in parallel and whether water uses are
competitive or complementary, for example.* (2) Inputs from the natural
environment (hydrological and meteorological primarily) are time dependent
and stochastic. Frequently, demands are stochastic too (supplementary irrigation
is a readily grasped example). Analytical procedures (the calculus and mathematical programming) for solving production problems are basically deterministic.

Thus, water resource planning presents a complex and difficult problem of
design which in practice does not allow the neat separation of technological
and economic factors implied by the production function analysis. The practical
solution to this problem has for the most part been to analyze a few alternative
systems under highly restrictive assumptions concerning stochastic elements
interspersed with liberal doses of "engineering judgment."

In recent years much progress has been made in applying more systematic
and conceptually satisfying procedures to this problem—to a large extent
under the auspices of the Harvard Water Program. Two main approaches have
been examined. One is an analytical models approach and the other is a system
simulation approach. The analytical models have been primarily of the linear
programming type. Both types involve numerical experiments with candidate
systems. We have already seen one application of the simulation approach with
the Potomac study reported in the previous chapter.

Analytical models can deal only with highly simplified characterizations of
the actual system. This simplification permits the equations characterizing the
interrelations of the system to be manageable enough so that they can be solved
for an optimum value of the objective. In the process of simplification to the
point where the outputs of the system can be expressed as explicit functions of
the design variables, the temporal relationships that the system must obey
frequently are destroyed. The problem is basically treated as a static (although
possibly comparative static) and deterministic one. What is bought in return is
the possibility of an analytical solution in a finite number of steps.

Linear Programming

Before proceeding to a discussion of simulation, we will review a mathematical
programming formulation of a highly simplified river basin planning problem

---

* For a good discussion of technological relations in a river basin system, see Blair T.
Bower, "Some Physical, Technological, and Economic Characteristics of Water and Water
Resource Systems: Implications for Administration," *Natural Resources Journal*, Vol. III,
No. 2 (October 1963).

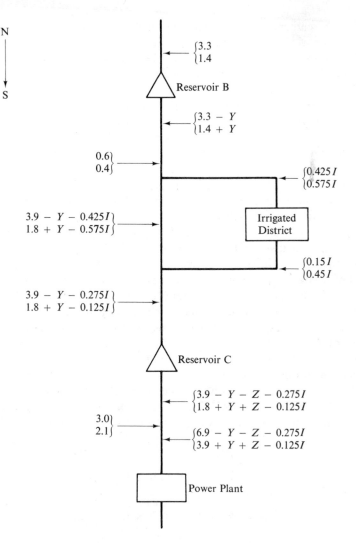

SIMPLIFIED RIVER VALLEY SYSTEM

FIGURE 7-1

just to give a suggestion of the approach. The configuration to which the formulation applies is shown in Figure 7-1.

The example we use was developed by Dorfman.* The main complication of Dorfman's solution to the example results from a non-linear objective function. We will not introduce this complication even though it adds some realism to the

---

* Robert Dorfman, "Mathematical Models: The Multistructure Approach," in Maass *et al., op. cit.* Readers may need to review Chapter 2 at this point.

problem. A mathematical programming problem with a non-linear objective function is considered in Chapter 11.

Only two seasons are used in this example. The top figure in each brace is the wet-season flow and the bottom one the dry-season flow. Y is capacity of reservoir B, Z is capacity of reservoir C, and I is annual irrigation supply. For realism, all figures can be taken to be in 10^6 acre-feet. There are only two reservoir sites, an irrigation project, and a run-of-the-river power plant in this system.

In developing the example, data will be taken from the figure. In its flow from north to south, the river first encounters reservoir B. The capacity Y of this reservoir is one of the unknowns in the problem. Since $Y \times 10^6$ acre-feet will be retained in the wet season and released in the dry, the flows below the reservoir are $3.3 - Y$ in the wet season and $1.4 + Y$ in the dry, as seen in the figure. Other flow figures are obtained similarly. Below the confluence of the first tributary, water is diverted to an irrigated area. The amount of water diverted, I, is another unknown of the problem. For assumed technical reasons, 42.5 percent of whatever diversion occurs must be in the wet season and 57.5 percent in the dry. Return flows in percentages of I are shown just below the irrigated area. The next unknown in the problem is the capacity of reservoir C, represented by Z. The fourth and final variable is the energy output of the power plant, denoted by E. The objective of the design problem is to obtain the maximum possible net benefits from the given system.*

To put this problem into a programming format, the constraint sets must be specified. As always in such problems, one set requires that none of the decision variables be negative. The second set requires that flows in all reaches of the stream must be nonnegative. Taking data from the map, these constraints are:†

$$3.3 - Y \qquad\qquad\quad \geq 0 \qquad \text{(F1)}$$

$$3.9 - Y - .425I \qquad \geq 0 \qquad \text{(F2)}$$

$$1.8 + Y - .575I \qquad \geq 0 \qquad \text{(F3)}$$

$$3.9 - Y - Z - .275I \geq 0 \qquad \text{(F4)}$$

Only four of the ten constraints involving decision variables are listed because if they are met, the others are too; hence, they are redundant. For example, $1.4 + Y \geq 0$ is satisfied for all nonnegative values of Y and, of course, we have already constrained Y to be nonnegative.

The third group of constraints requires that flow at the power plant must, in both seasons, be greater or equal to the amount needed to meet the power

---

* If we do not restrict the number of values these can take, the number of possible combinations will be infinite although most will not be consistent with the constraints we are about to impose. If we let each decision variable take on 10 values, there are 10,000 possible combinations.

† For practice the reader could, after reviewing this section, write the constraint set looking just at the map.

target established. Assume $E = .144F$, where E is power generated in a period and F is water flow through the turbines in the period. It is assumed that half the output of energy must be generated in the wet season and half in the dry. Thus the power constraints are

$$F_W = 6.9 - Y - Z - .275I \geq .5E/1.144 = 3.47E$$

$$F_D = 3.9 + Y + Z - .125I \geq .5E/1.144 = 3.47E$$

or rewriting:

$$Y + Z + .275I + 3.47E \leq 6.9$$
$$-Y - Z + .125I + 3.47E \leq 3.9$$

In general form, the objective function to maximize is

$$\Pi = B_1(E) + B_2(I) - K_1(Y) - K_2(Z) - K_3(E) - K_4(I)$$

where Π is the present value of net benefit.

If the objective function is linear so that the B's and K's are simply co-efficients, the problem is mathematically complete and can be solved by the standard techniques of linear programming.*

For future reference we may note that had one of the outputs been regarded as a physical "requirement" instead of an economic variable, it could have been entered as a restriction and the objective function maximized subject to that additional restraint. We will find this sort of formulation useful in later discussion.

Much more complex linear programming models of river systems have been built,† but they all share generally the same deficiencies—a severely limited ability to accommodate non-linearities, submergence of time-dependent variables, and the ability to handle stochastic variables in only the most elementary sense. (The last deficiency may require an additional word of explanation. We can regard the benefit and cost coefficients as representing expected values based on some known probability distribution but this is more of a terminological than a substantive difference.) Nevertheless programming offers a powerful solution technique which, when imaginatively used and results carefully interpreted, has proved very useful.

Simulation

In simulation approaches many of these difficulties can be overcome, but not without cost. The time structure of inputs and outputs can be maintained although calculation with respect to them does not proceed in real time but is

---

* The reader might find it useful practice to write it, and its dual, out in standard form and to reflect on the economic meaning of the dual solution. Notice that if the objective function is linear, the two coefficients relating to each of E and I can be combined into single coefficients.

† For example, Ralph C. d'Arge, *Quantitative Water Resource Basin Planning: An Analysis of the Pecos River Basin, New Mexico*, Department of Economics, University of New Mexico, June 1968, preliminary draft.

of course greatly accelerated. Also, by letting inputs and outputs (or demands) be the result of stochastic processes, probability elements can be handled much more adequately. The simulation models themselves consist of sets of difference or differential equations which express the relationships between various magnitudes describing the state and operation of the system during the time segments of its history. Unfortunately, these relations tend to be unique from system to system so that it is hard to generalize further about such models.* Of course, if the system is at all complex, the simulation requires a computer. In water systems the simulation usually accepts hydrologic data and cost and demand functions as inputs and permits experimentation with design variables (alternative scales and types of facilities and alternative target levels of output) and operating rules (storage and release rules for reservoirs, for example). Since the equations in a simulation model do not have to be solved for all the variables, some of which they determine implicitly, they can be a good deal more complicated than those of an analytical model and thus can represent the complexities of a real system with greater fidelity—including its non-linear aspects. What is involved is working out the consequences of a large sequence of models linked together by the condition that the terminal state for one model provides the initial conditions for the next one.

Of course, the penalty (relative to an analytical model) is that each simulation spells out the consequences (say in terms of the present value of net benefits) of only one choice of design parameters and does not incorporate any inherent technique for seeking an optimum. If the system is at all complicated, there may easily be billions of possible choices of these parameters. Thus, seeking an optimum by this means must either involve considerable "judgment" in selecting a limited set of design parameters which are "probably" close to the optimum one or systematic sampling techniques. The former is more nearly characteristic of the way simulation is now used in design and evaluation, although there has been considerable experimentation with the latter. It has also been suggested that programming and simulation models might well be in tandem—the former to find a set of design parameters "near" the optimum and the latter for sweetening.†

Benefits and Simulation

To make good use of the time sequence preserving characteristic of simulation, we must introduce additional complexity into the estimation of benefits. Since

---

* The most comprehensive discussion of the application of simulation techniques to water resource system design is Maynard M. Hufschmidt and Myron B. Fiering, *Simulation Techniques for Design of Water Resource Systems* (Cambridge: Harvard University Press, 1966). See also Robert Dorfman, "Formal Models in the Design of Water Resource Systems," *Water Resources Research*, Vol. 1, No. 3 (Third Quarter, 1965), p. 329. Some of our discussion leans heavily on this article.

† There have also been applications of "transportation problems" to water resources—especially to diversion schemes. The advantage of this formulation (which is a variety of linear programming) is its relatively simple computation algorithm.

output (of water) will be time variable rather than constant or uniformly increasing, account must be taken of the effect on benefits of failures to meet target outputs and of exceeding them. This is done by dividing actual benefit each year into a normal benefit (obtained when the quantity of water for which the project was designed is available) and a loss (resulting from under- or over-supply). If there is an oversupply, the loss might be negative; however, overage water is not likely to be as valuable per acre-foot as design water. The relationship between loss and departures from the design amount of water in a given year has been termed a "loss function."*

Generally we can write:

$$B(Y_n, Y_t) = N(Y_n) - L(Y_n - Y_t)$$

which says that benefits are a function of the design amount of water Y_n and the actual amount Y_t of water delivered in year t. The first term on the right-hand side is the normal benefit and the second term is the loss. The normal benefits N depend on Y_n alone, the loss L depends on the difference between Y_n and Y_t and the actual benefits B depend on both Y_n and Y_t. Generally speaking, the expected loss will be an increasing function of two factors: the excess of Y_n over the expected value of Y_t and the standard deviation of Y_t.

We can also depict the loss function graphically as in Figure 7-2. The curve A shows the relationship between planned or target output (say $\bar{x}$) and total benefit

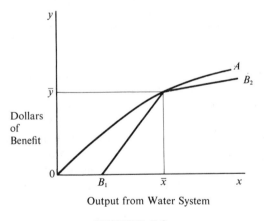

Output from Water System

FIGURE 7-2

for a specified year. B_1 and B_2 show how benefits vary as the specified target output $\bar{x}$ is missed in a particular period. $L(Y_n - Y_t)$ is the vertical difference between OA and $B_1 B_2$. For an irrigation system, for example, the relationship indicates that a planned reduction in water supplies is less costly than an unanticipated one. The reasoning behind this is obvious. Similarly, an

---

* See Dorfman, *op. cit.*, p. 157.

unplanned increase in water supply, although worth something, is less valuable than a planned one.

The loss function has the effect of diminishing estimated benefits in response to variability and consequently makes some allowance for this aspect of uncertainty. Of course, the uncertainty accounted for is that resulting from variability of water yield and not that resulting from uncertainties in the projection of economic functions, which may be much greater. Nevertheless, the loss function is a useful concept and has been used in research simulations of water resource systems.*

The loss function and simulation are especially illuminating when combined with an analysis of hydrological (or other) inputs which takes better account of their stochastic characteristics than the conventional design procedures have done.

Stochastic Hydrology

The traditional method of determining the needed minimum storage in a reservoir to sustain a target yield is the so-called mass curve analysis. This assumes that inflows and outflows from a reservoir are given functions of time. The system simulation analogue of this is to use the historical record of flows as input to the simulation program. The flaw of this procedure is that it assumes the future pattern of flows will be an exact replication of the past.† An alternative is to assume that the historical record is a sample from a much larger population and that what will remain invariant in the future are certain moments of the distribution of observed flows, say the mean, standard deviation, and skewness. Based on the latter assumption, stochastic hydrology generators have been devised which can generate long hydrologic sequences incorporating extreme values and patterns of events not in the historic record but which maintain these moments of the frequency distribution of that record. There are difficult problems associated with such generators, many of which have been overcome. The problems involve such things as serial correlation in the record of flows and maintaining cross and serial correlations for separate gauging stations in the same system. We will not treat these since our intent is just to acquaint the reader with the basic recursive relationships used in the generation.

The use of Markovian models for generating synthetic hydrological records has been extensively discussed in the literature.‡ The basic recursive relation used can be represented by the following equation:

$$x_{i+1} = \mu + \beta(x_i - \mu) + t_{i+1}\sigma(1 - \rho^2)^{1/2}$$

---

* See Dorfman, *op. cit.*, and Fiering, *op. cit.*
† Or at least that it will change only in known ways.
‡ See Myron B. Fiering, *Streamflow Synthesis* (Cambridge: Harvard University Press, 1967).

In this model, x_{i+1}, the flow in the $(i + 1)$st interval, is a linear function of x_i, the flow in the ith interval; of a standardized random deviate t_{i+1}; and of the population parameters μ (the population mean flow), σ (the population standard deviation), β (the regression coefficient of flows in the $(i + 1)$st interval on values in the ith interval), and ρ (the correlation coefficient between flows in successive time periods). The standardized random deviate t_{i+1} has zero mean and unit variance.

If the distribution of flows is normal and the regression functions of x_i on x_{i-1} is linear and homoscedastic (of constant variance), the conditional expectation of x_i given x_{i-1} is given by

$$E(x_i | x_{i-1}) = \mu + \beta(x_{i-1} - \mu)$$

and the expected variance of x_i given x_{i-1} is

$$\text{Var } (x_i | x_{i-1}) = \sigma^2(1 - \rho^2)$$

Thus, we can see in the recursive equation that the first two terms on the right-hand side are the expected value of x_{i+1}, given x_i has occurred (February's flow, January having occurred), and the last term is the random component consisting of a randomly selected normal deviate which, when multiplied by the expected variance of x_{i+1} given x_i, brings the result back into the proper dimension comparable with the first two terms of the right side. It can also be shown that to treat non-normal distributions it is sufficient to alter the distribution of the random additive component and thus maintain higher moments of observed data.*

A recursive model of this type could be used to generate indefinitely long sequences of hydrological record to be used as inputs to the simulation model.†
Several thousand years of simulated sequence may be used in the analysis of the performance and benefits and costs of a system. We will sketch only one of the variety of ways this could be done.

The simulation program discounts capital costs, OMR costs, and benefits from the year of occurrence back to the present. The period of economic analysis corresponds to the simulation period, say, 50 years. Simulations are then run repeatedly for intervals of this length. The outcomes (say, in terms of the present

---

* For discussion and justification of these assertions, see Hufschmidt, *op. cit.*, Chapter 2, and Fiering, *op. cit.*, Chapter 2.

† Usually stochastic hydrology programs will also generate flood events for the analysis of flood damage reduction. In simplest outline this works about as follows: the stochastic hydrology program performs a linear regression of daily peak flow on monthly discharge to estimate the daily peak corresponding to a (generated) monthly discharge. By using a multiplicative factor, the daily peak flow is increased to a value corresponding to the 3-hour peak. Finally, the duration is estimated as a linear function of peak and volume. The program can be arranged to automatically shift into flood mode when a certain (generated) daily peak flow is surpassed. It will then generate 3-hour flows for the designated duration.

value of net benefits) then can themselves be thought of as forming a distribution, the mean of which might be taken as the expected value of outcomes.

Full-scale simulation of systems has up to now been done solely in research studies, but partial simulations are becoming more common in planning and design of water resource systems.

7.2   COST ALLOCATION AND PRICING

We enter somewhat reluctantly into the discussion of cost allocation and pricing of outputs because it is a "messy" area. In the case of cost allocation where products are jointly produced by the same facilities, no conclusive results appear to be possible, even in principle. In regard to pricing, while rigorous conclusions are possible at a theoretical level, the economics profession is by no means agreed on implications for policy. As elsewhere we will try to distinguish between our own opinions and what appear to be rigorous theoretical results or matters of consensus of the profession.

Cost Allocation

A private profit-maximizing competitive firm has no need to allocate joint costs to multiple outputs. It must simply check to see that marginal costs and marginal benefits (for a competitive firm this, of course, means prices) are equal in all directions. If this is true, profit will be at a maximum in either the short-run or long-run sense, depending on which situation is in question, and the allocation of joint costs is redundant. If two products are produced in strictly fixed proportions, the sum of their prices must equal marginal cost. For long-run equilibrium, total benefits must exceed total costs at least by a "normal" return on capital if the firm is to stay in business. In fact, basing any output decision on allocated joint costs almost certainly will lead the firm away from the optimum position unless the allocative system is accidentally equivalent to equation of marginal costs and benefits.

The same principles would hold for government projects except for some complicating factors. Assume first we have a government project which has constant long-run and short-run marginal costs and produces only private outputs to which the exclusion principle can be applied at low cost.* In this case, equating marginal costs and marginal benefits in all directions and pricing at marginal cost would produce maximum net benefit, no income redistribution, and no need for any sort of allocation of joint costs. Now if either some of the outputs are public goods (zero marginal cost in the short run) or there are decreasing costs, a marginal cost-pricing policy will produce income redistribution. Possibly average cost-pricing would be advocated to prevent these income redistributions (or more vaguely on "equity" grounds). A more

---

* Did you ask why it should be a government project?

sophisticated procedure to achieve the same result but avoiding the inefficiencies of average cost-pricing would be a two-part tariff or a lump-sum payment reflecting joint costs, combined with marginal cost-pricing. In either case, some system for sharing joint costs among beneficiaries is needed.

In actual practice, power and municipal and industrial water supply are considered fully reimbursable outputs, including allocated costs, of federal multi-purpose projects. Irrigation is considered fully reimbursable (without interest), but water prices are based on a "payment capacity" calculation with deficits made up from other sources (excess power revenues primarily).* For recreation, one-half of the separable costs are reimbursable by local interests. Water quality benefits are basically non-reimbursable. Flood control and navigation are non-reimbursable purposes. Thus, clearly, under current procedures allocation of joint costs is required but enters into pricing decisions only for power and municipal and industrial water supply. In general, the decisions on reimbursement have turned on equity issues, the diffuseness or concentrations of benefits, and the ease of identifying specific beneficiaries. Considerations of efficiency have been absent.

The history of cost allocation is characterized by a long, and unsuccessful, search for a rigorous or theoretically sound method. The one now in use, the so-called "separable costs remaining benefits" method is justified primarily on the basis that it will not produce an adverse benefit-cost relationship for a project purpose which is economically efficient. We will return to this method later, but first we will take a quick look at two other methods which have been proposed.

Proportionate Use of Capacity

The method favored by the Engineers' Joint Council, an association of professional engineering societies, is the "proportionate use of capacity method." The engineers' sanction is the only reason for discussing it since it makes no economic sense. It proceeds by determining how much of the capacity of an installation is needed for each purpose and then allocates joint costs in proportion to the required capacity. There are some purely technical problems in assigning capacity, such as the situation where the same storage space in a reservoir is assigned to different purposes in different seasons, but more important is its deficiency from an economic point of view.

This difficulty can be shown by the example in Table 7-1, which was developed by Gertel.† The table gives hypothetical benefit-cost relationships for flood control and irrigation. If the dam were built for flood control alone, the ratio

---

* Recall our discussion in Chapter 6 where we pointed out that users of irrigation water from Bureau of Reclamation projects, in fact, often pay only a small percentage of total cost attributable to irrigation.

† Karl Gertel, "Recent Suggestions for Cost Allocation of Multiple-Purpose Projects in the Light of Public Interest," *Journal of Farm Economics*, Vol. 33, No. 2 (Second Quarter, 1951).

TABLE 7-1

Hypothetical Example Showing Allocation of Costs
of a Multiple-Purpose Project by Proportionate
Use of Capacity[a]

	Costs	Benefits	Benefit/cost ratio	Percentage of capacity required	Allocation by proportionate use of capacity
Flood control alone	$100,000	$160,000	1.60:1.00	50%	$65,000
Additional reservoir capacity for irrigation	30,000	60,000	2.00:1.00	50	65,000
Total	130,000	220,000	1.69:1.00	100	130,000

[a] For purposes of clarity, separable costs such as those for floodways and irrigation ditches are not shown; the same relationships are obtained if separable costs are included.

of benefits to costs would be 1.6 to 1.0, while a multiple-purpose structure yields a ratio of almost 1.7 to 1.0. The incremental capacity for irrigation has a benefit/cost ratio of 2 to 1 and creates an additional $30,000 of net benefit. However, under the proportionate use of capacity method of cost allocation, irrigation would appear uneconomic since it could not meet its $65,000 allocation, even though it enters into a project which maximizes net benefits.*

Lagrange Multipliers

A recent and much more sophisticated proposal for allocating joint costs is due to Weil.† Weil uses Lagrange multipliers to find what he calls a "persuasive" allocation. He illustrates his technique by the classical example of allocating the cost of a cow to beef and hides which are taken to be joint products. He assumes that one cow costs $10 and that the demand curve for beef and hides is

$$P_b = 30 - 2Q_b$$

$$P_h = 20 - Q_h$$

* A much more sophisticated version of what is basically a proportionate use of capacity method using dynamic programming concepts is found in Warren A. Hall, "A Method for Allocating Costs of Water Supply Canal," *Journal of Farm Economics*, Vol. 45, No. 4 (November 1963). But sophistication cannot overcome defects of principle.
† R. L. Weil, Jr., "Allocating Joint Costs," *American Economic Review* (December 1968).

He then argues that a correct allocation can be found by using constrained optimization. The problem is formulated as

$$\text{Max } P_bQ_b + P_hQ_h - 10C, \text{ s.t.} \qquad Q_b \leq C \quad \text{and} \quad Q_h \leq C$$

where C is the number of cattle bought.

If we substitute the demand equation into the objective function, we get

$$\text{Max } (30 - 2Q_b)Q_b + (20 - Q_h)Q_h - 10C, \text{ s.t.} \qquad Q_b \leq C \quad \text{and} \quad Q_h \leq C$$

Form the Lagrangian:

$$\text{Max } \Pi(Q_b, Q_h, C, \lambda_1, \lambda_2)$$

$$= 30Q_b - 2Q_b^2 + 20Q_h - Q_h^2 - 10C - \lambda_1(Q_b - C) - \lambda_2(Q_h - C)*$$

Setting the first partial derivatives of Π with respect to its arguments equal to zero and solving yields the solutions

$$Q_b = Q_h = C = 6\tfrac{2}{3}$$

$$\lambda_1 = 3\tfrac{1}{3}$$

$$\lambda_2 = 6\tfrac{2}{3}$$

Weil claims the multipliers λ_1 and λ_2, which sum to 10, the price of a cow, are the cost allocation we seek. The constraints to which they apply require that only as much beef can be sold as cattle are bought and only as many hides can be sold as cattle are bought. The conditions of demand help to determine λ_1 and λ_2, and they are in fact the marginal revenues. In a case of fixed proportions, maximization of net revenue will require that these two marginal revenues sum to marginal cost of the joint output, which is 10 in this example. Alternatively, they can be interpreted as the return that would occur if proportions of beefs and hides could be changed by a small amount. Or as Weil puts it, "... the maximum prices the cattle buyer should be willing to pay for extra beef and extra hides will always be exactly equal to the price of one cow,"† and that price is indicated by the multipliers. Undeniably the method, for which Weil displays

---

* This is a somewhat different formulation of the Lagrangian analysis than we have seen before (it involves inequality constraints) and is really an application of the more general Kuhn–Tucker theorems. The steps needed for a solution are given as follows:

a. Determine the optimum by using Lagrange multipliers for each inequality, assuming each holds as a strict equality.

b. If all the multipliers are non-negative, the optimum so obtained is also the optimum subject to the inequality constraint.

c. If any multiplier is negative, resolve the problem without regard to that constraint. The resulting optimum will usually satisfy the disregarded constraints and will be a solution to the problem.

† Weil, *op. cit.*, p. 1343.

a considerably more complicated application, could be useful if in fact a producer were faced with buying from an outside source a product which he can also produce jointly with another output, but even here it would seem to be only the equivalent of comparing marginal revenue with the purchase price.

The examples to which the technique is applied involve zero fixed costs and constant marginal costs (for the joint outputs) which therefore equal average cost. Should this not be the case, difficulties arise because the multiplier technique will only divide up marginal cost. In this technique, marginal cost comes to be handled in a way symmetrical with marginal revenue, and hence it is marginal cost that gets divided up into the two marginal revenues and not average cost if this is different from marginal cost. Since in water investments we are frequently dealing with decreasing cost situations, the technique would at best be of limited usefulness.

Separable Cost—Remaining Benefit

The most widely accepted method of cost allocation at the present time is based on the separable costs-remaining benefits principle. First, separable costs for each purpose are determined (i.e., costs incurred specifically for that purpose and which would be avoided if the purpose were not included). These are charged against the purpose. Next, the separable costs of the purpose are subtracted from the benefits of the purpose. The benefits for cost allocation are taken to be limited by what it would cost to furnish the output by the best single-purpose alternative. If there is no feasible alternative, the benefits of the purpose are used. Joint costs are allocated in proportion to the benefits remaining after the separable costs have been deducted. The appeal of this method is to a certain sense of equity and that it, unlike proportionate use of capacity, will never make a purpose appear inefficient when in fact it is not. There is really not much more to be said about its justification.

The only way its use might disturb the efficiency of an investment is if the price of the output is based on it, and this causes a significant departure from marginal cost pricing. As we have seen, power and M & I rates are based upon separable plus allocated costs. We have also noted that pricing decisions have in the past have been little influenced by considerations of efficiency. Let us look afresh at the economic issues surrounding pricing of the various outputs and then reconsider the actually existing policies.

Pricing Issues

Economists usually advise that the outputs of government projects should be priced at their short-run marginal cost of production. They further state that capacity should be increased when the discounted value of these costs exceeds the investment plus present value of OMR costs of investing in a new or augmented facility minus the increase in net benefit which may be associated with it. The rationale is that once a facility is in place, marginal opportunity cost of serving additional users may be very low, and to restrict use by causing the user to pay an allocated "sunk" cost would lead to a misallocation of resources.* Several questions have been raised about this in recent times.† We will review these briefly before going on to explore in some detail the peculiar nature of the short-run marginal costs of many water-related outputs.

One set of issues, already mentioned previously, surrounds the income redistribution which accompanies marginal cost pricing, unless the output is produced at constant average cost. Some argue on ethical or equity grounds that "each project should sit on its own bottom" and that the way to achieve this is through average cost pricing. Of course, two-part pricing has also been advocated in this connection as making it possible to price efficiently while at the same time recovering the cost of the project. Another approach would be to try to make an explicit judgment concerning the desirability of the income redistribution resulting from marginal cost pricing and adjust accordingly.

A broader argument and one possibly quite important, but difficult to assess quantitatively, is that the income redistribution resulting from non-reimbursable features of projects will set in motion political forces to implement inefficient projects. It is true, for example, that the Trinity navigation project, which will cost $1 billion-plus, will constitute a huge boost to the regional economy of the Dallas-Fort Worth area, even though it is almost certainly unjustifiable from an economic efficiency standpoint. It does not necessarily follow, however, that the best way to deal with this situation is to pursue a a policy of average cost pricing. It might be preferable to require reimbursement but not necessarily fully via pricing. Local units of government and special districts with taxing power might be required to undertake reimbursement. This seems especially appropriate in instances like navigation where the income distribution effects are likely to be capitalized into property values to a high degree—especially industrial and commerical properties. In this way the adverse income redistribution effects could be mitigated without the undesirable effects on short-run use decisions which a policy of pricing well above marginal cost might have.

Another argument asserts that where intermediate goods (in contrast to final consumption goods) are priced marginally, perhaps even at zero in a pure joint supply case, secondary types of inefficiencies may arise because investment in industries using the output of the project as an input may be distorted. The

---

* The reader should make sure he understands clearly why this result would follow. The situation of short-run marginal cost differing from long-run marginal cost also may arise if demand was misestimated in designing capacity so that there is excess capacity.

† The reader interested in reviewing extensive discussion of these matters should consult the following papers: Jack Wiseman, "The Theory of Public Utility Price: An Empty Box," *Oxford Economic Papers*, Vol. 9, No. 1 (January 1957), and "The Theory of Public Utility Price: A Further Comment," *Oxford Economic Papers*, Vol. II, No. 1 (January 1959); and the papers by J. V. Krutilla and J. Milliman in *The Analysis and Evaluation of Public Expenditures: The PPB System*, a Compendium of Papers submitted to the Subcommittee on Economy in Government of the Joint Economic Committee, U.S. Congress, 91st Cong., 1st Sess. (Washington, D.C., 1969).

technology chosen for combining this input (say, industrial water) with capital investment should be based on the long-run costs of producing water—including all capital costs. A less drastic form of the argument asserts that at least the long-run marginal costs of producing the water is the datum on which the investment decision should be based. The first would not occur in decreasing cost situations even if the price were based on long-run marginal costs. The second might not occur if pricing were based on short-run marginal cost. In the latter case presumably prices would be low or zero when the project is first implemented but would rise as demand increased and short-run marginal costs rose. The user of the input (water, power, whatever) might regard the low price early in the history of the project as the long-term price and make his investment plans accordingly. In principle, this could be prevented by supplying the user not only with the current price but also with estimates of probable future prices.

Another line of argument relates to the definition of marginal cost itself. The argument is that the meaning and results of an instruction to equate marginal cost and price is determined by the length of the planning period to which the marginal cost is intended to refer. Wiseman has commented on this in connection with public utility pricing as follows: "At one extreme the period chosen may be as long as the lowest common multiple of the life periods of the assets required to produce the public utility product. At the other extreme, the consideration of 'current' opportunity costs only, if interpreted rigorously, would seem to require that products should be given away—between these two extremes, there is a range of possible marginal cost rules, differing from each other in the planning time period chosen as appropriate and hence in the 'durable' assets they ignore and in the opportunity costs they treat as relevant to decisions about price and output."*

The marginal cost function depends on the number of inputs whose quantities are open to variation for the planning period in question. As was pointed out in Chapter 2, the function is steeper the smaller the scope for variation is. However, in the simple case of constant expected demand, marginal cost pricing principles require a price below the marginal cost used in planning (which would be long-run marginal cost if variation in all inputs is possible) only if demand turns out to be less than expected.†

Much of the discussion of pricing based on short-run marginal cost has missed the essential point—the relevant short-run marginal cost is not largely the OMR cost of the project itself. In the case of almost every output of a water resources project, the greatest influences on short-run marginal cost, properly conceived, are *congestion* and *internal opportunity cost*. Congestion results in users imposing external diseconomies on each other, and internal opportunity costs

---

* Wiseman, *op. cit.*, 1957, p. 61.

† Any usable set of marginal cost pricing principles ought to yield the same result for both short- and long-run if expectations are realized (again for the case of constant demand). In the simple and unreal situation of constant short-run marginal cost up to a rigidly limited plant capacity, consistency would require that price equal minimum long-run marginal cost. From a "graphic" point of view, the short-run marginal cost function would have to be regarded as being vertical at capacity.

result from operating a project to benefit one set of beneficiaries at the expense of another purpose. An example of the latter is drawing down a reservoir during the recreation season to raise low flows to improve navigation. In the case of a public good, strictly characterized by jointness in supply when use is not congested, congestion is the sole cause for rising short-run marginal costs of serving users. We will develop this point in regard to navigation in a little detail.

Locking operations aside,* a navigation channel once installed is an almost pure case of a public good as long as there is excess capacity. Servicing an additional user has literally no opportunity cost except for those relatively small costs that are unique to the individual user even when there is excess capacity. With increased use of a locking facility, at some stage of use locking costs become primarily congestion costs.

In developing the navigation example we follow an analysis presented by Lave and De Salvo.†

Locks are the bottlenecks in waterways which require them, and the physical capacity of a waterway might be measured in terms of the number of barges that could be locked through in the course of a year (C). The barges are grouped together in tows (*pushed* by a towboat), and the rate at which tows can be served $[\mu(b)]$ is inversely related to the number of barges in the tow (b). The number of tows that could be served in a year is designated by (K). If all tows are of the same size, K can be calculated as follows:

$$K = \frac{8{,}760}{1/\mu(b)} = 8{,}760\mu(b)$$

where 8,760 is the number of hours in a year and $1/\mu(b)$ is the service time (hours) for a tow of b barges. If all tows have b barges, the number of barges that could be served in a year is $C = Kb$. This capacity could be attained, however, only if there is always a tow ready for servicing when the previous tow has gone through. In fact, the arrival of tows is more like the arrival of customers at a checkout counter which involves a somewhat random process—sometimes there are queues and other times there is idle capacity. It is very costly to keep tows waiting. The capital and labor cost of keeping a 3,000 hp towboat and 15 barges waiting is perhaps $200 per hour.

Physical measures of capacity like C are not too useful in *economic* analysis, especially when a random process is involved, so further analysis must proceed in terms of queuing theory.‡

DeSalvo and Lave assume that the number of tows arriving at a lock in a

---

* Many inland waterways are improved by introducing dams in the channel to improve draft and introduce "slack" water. These dams are traversed by means of a "lock," in effect a hydraulic elevator.

† Lester B. Lave and Joseph S. De Salvo, "Congestion, Tolls, and the Economic Capacity of a Waterway," *The Journal of Political Economy*, Vol. 76, No. 3 (May/June 1968).

‡ Introductory expositions of queuing theory may be found in any operations research text.

given time interval t is given by a Poisson* distribution with parameter λt, where λ is the arrival rate. The number of tows serviced in t is also assumed to be Poisson distributed μt where μ is the service rate. Given these assumptions, a simple application of queuing theory will show that waiting time T_{Lq} and total locking time T_L for a tow are given by

$$T_{Lq} = \frac{\lambda}{\mu(\mu - \lambda)} \qquad \text{and} \qquad T_L = \frac{1}{\mu} + T_{Lq} = \frac{1}{\mu - \lambda}$$

The second equation indicates that total locking time is the sum of waiting time and service time.

The individual tow arriving at a lock will have no incentive to consider congestion costs imposed on others by its use of the lock. Hence, most congestion costs are external costs. Thus a substantial portion of the short-run marginal cost of locking is the external cost imposed by one tow operation on others. This can be calculated as follows:

Suppose total tonnage P per year, with average tow load A, moves over a particular waterway. Accordingly, P/A full tows must traverse the waterway and locks. If p is the proportion of full tows that have an empty back-haul, the total number of tows per year is $K = (1 + p)P/A$, or on a per-hour basis

$$\lambda^* = \frac{K}{8{,}760} = \frac{(1 + p)P/A}{8{,}760}$$

Table 7-2 shows the relationship between λ^* (arrival rate), ρ (percentage utilization of the lock assuming a service time of $1/\mu$ of one hour), and T_L (total locking time).

For a given K adding another tow to the waterway would result in greater waiting time spread across existing tows. For each individual tow the increase in waiting time may be quite small, that is, the average locking time, T_L, may not rise very much.

Total locking time for all tows during the year, $\tau = KT_L$, rises much faster, however. Increased locking time resulting from an extra tow is given by the following equation and shown in the table:

$$\frac{\partial \tau}{\partial K} = \frac{\partial[8{,}760K/(8{,}760\mu - K)]}{\partial K} = \left(\frac{8{,}760}{8{,}760\mu - K}\right)^2 \mu$$

As percentage utilization rises $\partial \tau/\partial K$ rises quickly. For efficiency in the short run, no additional tow should be admitted unless it earns at least $(\partial \tau/\partial K)V$ profit (per hour) where V is the hourly cost of keeping a tow waiting. One way

---

* The Poisson distribution of a variable, x, is given by $f(x) = e^{-\lambda}(\lambda^x/x!)$, where λ is the mean of the distribution, and $\sum_x f(x) = 1$. Number of arrivals—of customers, tows, autos at toll booths—in fixed time units are often Poisson-distributed.

TABLE 7-2

RELATIONSHIP BETWEEN ARRIVAL RATE, PERCENTAGE UTILIZATION OF THE LOCK, AND TOTAL LOCKING TIME

K	$\rho = \dfrac{100\lambda^*}{\mu}$	T_L	τ	$\dfrac{\partial \tau}{\partial K}$	Θ	$-\dfrac{\partial \tau}{\partial \mu}$
1	.01	1.00	1	1.00	.00	1
100	1.14	1.01	101	1.02	.01	102
1,000	11.40	1.13	1,129	1.28	.15	1,280
2,000	22.90	1.30	2,592	1.69	.39	3,380
2,190	25.00	1.33	2,920	1.77	.44	3,876
3,000	34.30	1.52	4,563	2.31	.79	6,930
4,000	46.70	1.84	7,361	3.39	1.55	13,560
5,000	57.10	2.33	11,648	5.43	3.10	27,150
6,000	68.50	3.18	19,043	10.11	6.93	60,660
7,000	80.00	4.98	34,841	24.80	19.82	173,600
8,000	91.40	11.52	92,210	132.71	121.19	1,061,680
8,750	99.90	876.00	766,500	767,376	766,500	6,714,548,000

NOTES.—μ: average number of tows serviced per hour by the lock (to illustrate the calculation, μ is assumed equal to unity).

K: number of tows serviced per year; λ^* is the number of tows serviced per hour.

ρ: utilization rate of lock (the lock is operating ρ percent of the time); $\rho/100 = K/(8,760\mu) = \lambda^*/\mu$.

T_L: average locking time (including waiting time) in hours. $T_L = 8,760/(8,760\mu - K) = 1/(\mu - \lambda^*)$.

τ: total locking time per year for all tows in hours. $\tau = KT_L = 8,760K/(8,760\mu - K) = 8,760\lambda^*/(\mu - \lambda^*) = K/(\mu - \lambda^*)$.

$\partial\tau/\partial K$: marginal locking time; the change in total locking time due to the addition of a tow, $\partial\tau/\partial K = [8,760/(8,760\mu - K)]^2\mu = T_L^2\mu$.

$\partial\tau/\partial\mu$: marginal locking time; the change in total locking time due to an increase in the service rate of the lock. $\partial\tau/\partial\mu: -[8,760/(8,760\mu - K)]^2K = -T_L^2K$.

Θ: $(\partial\tau/\partial K) - T_L^2$, ΘV is the optimal toll (where V is the hourly cost of keeping a tow waiting); this toll equates private cost and social cost.

to achieve this result is to levy a charge, θV, per hour of locking time equal to the difference between social and private cost where

$$\theta V = \left(\frac{\partial \tau}{\partial K} - T_L\right) V^*$$

The short-run marginal cost of the waterway operation is θV plus the lock operating cost of taking a tow through the lock. Neglecting this for the moment, let us follow Lave and De Salvo's development of how short-run congestion costs are related to long-run optimization.

---

* The reader will recall that T_L is total locking time per tow.

The change in total waiting time as the service rate is changed is given by

$$\frac{\partial \tau}{\partial \mu} = -\left(\frac{8,760}{8,760\mu - K}\right)^2 K$$

In the long run, lock capacity should be augmented until V, the cost of keeping a tow waiting one hour, equals the cost of expanding the lock to save the hour. Hence, the lock should be expanded (μ increased by a small quantity, say ε) if $(-\partial \tau / \partial \mu)V$ exceeds the cost per unit of increasing the service rate (μ)—that is, if marginal benefit exceeds marginal cost.

DeSalvo and Lave illustrate this analysis with data from Illinois waterway operations.* This example shows that the short-run congestion cost function (in the pure congestion case) is related to the long-run cost of capacity expansion in precisely the same way as is the short-run cost function for conventional production processes.† We will return to this question below in our discussion of water quality.

Note that if the cost of expanding capacity is constant, then an optimum congestion toll (in a pure congestion case) will just cover the cost of capacity expansion. If the average cost of capacity expansion is decreasing or increasing, the tolls will fall short of or exceed total cost exactly in the manner of conventional cost relationships.

Conclusions on Pricing

Where marginal cost pricing does not yield sufficient revenue to cover costs, two-part pricing or some similar device should be considered. In cases where imposition of a price is costly or not feasible, there is often an identifiable

---

* Strictly speaking, this calculation is valid only for infinitesimal changes in lock size. Lave and DeSalvo adapt it for finite changes as follows: The benefit of increasing lock capacity is taken to be the reduction in total locking time assuming K is fixed. $T_L(K)$ is average locking time before expansion and $T_L^*(K)$ is average locking time after expansion. If V is the hourly cost of keeping a tow waiting, the benefit of expansion is

$$B = [T_L(K) - T_L^*(K)]KV$$

As long as B exceeds the annual cost of expansion, the lock should be expanded. This, however, assumes that the number of trips to be serviced is fixed. Since a finite expansion would reduce costs, it is necessary to account for benefits of the induced increase in tonnage. Take K_0 to be the number of trips before expansion and K_1 the number of trips after expansion. Then $T_L^*(K_0)$ is the new average locking time per tow for K_0 trips and $T_L^*(K_1)$ is the average locking time for K_1 trips. The additional benefit from this increase in trips could be estimated by B^*,

$$B^* = [T_L(K_0) - T_L^*(K_1)]\tfrac{1}{2}(K_1 - K_0)V$$

A question for the reader—under what circumstances would this approximation be precise?
† This question has been examined by several scholars in the transportation field. Perhaps the most complete discussion is found in Robert H. Strotz, "Urban Transportation Parables," *The Public Economy of Urban Committees*, Julius Margolis, ed. (Washington, D.C.: Resources for the Future, Inc., 1965).

group of beneficiaries—perhaps the property owners of a local jurisdiction—who should be made to share the costs.

In addition to these major guides, attainment of efficiency would be much aided by better estimates of costs arising from congestion phenomena and competition among uses. In the case of water, its opportunity cost is often neglected in formulating pricing policy. Once allocated to a particular purpose, the water itself (in contrast to conveyance facilities, for example) often is treated as a free good despite conflicting uses for it. This practice is bound to lead to inefficiencies.

PART IV

Residuals from Natural Resource Inputs to the Economy

So far we have concentrated on the social economics of production from natural resources including production under government entrepreneurship. We have discussed the rules society must devise as parameters for private production decisions if it wishes to obtain efficiency in the broader social sense. We have also discussed extensively the criteria government must use in its own decision-making to achieve the same result and also some pertinent problems in the measurement of benefits and costs. So far, except incidentally, we have neglected the fact that production of natural resources commodities is not the end of the story. The simplest laws of physics tell us that mass is essentially conserved and that the amount of material extracted from the natural environment must be returned to the natural environment—except for the amount that accumulates in the economic system, if for the moment we regard the latter as being separate from the natural system. From the point of view of a market economy, the serious thing about this is that the residuals are almost always returned to environmental media which are common property resources—primarily the water and the air. Because of this, market exchange processes cannot perform their normal functions, and inefficiencies are likely to occur unless collective compensating action is taken. Of course, this is not true if these environmental media are "free goods" in the economist's sense, and in the past they were often cited as such. It must be abundantly clear, however, even to the most casual observer, that these resources can no longer be regarded as free goods.

Currently, there are two major economics approaches to the question of residuals in the environment. The first, and certainly the one which has received most attention, is a partial equilibrium one heavily based on conventional externalities theory. The second is based on general equilibrium theory and tries to incorporate materials and energy flows into the corpus of general interdependency models for the economy. Both have advantages and disadvantages and we will review both approaches.

The first permits one to get into the details of managing a particular type of residual (like waterborne) in a particular situation. This is important, for it is easy to gloss over the complexities of efficient residuals management. The second, on the other hand, emphasizes the broader interdependencies in the residuals management question which must be accounted for lest the detailed management be like efforts at fine tuning a system which is grossly out of focus. We will develop the latter point in more detail in Chapter 11. In the next three chapters we turn to a detailed analysis of the economic theory relevant to the management of waterborne residuals in a particular river basin. We could as well have used gaseous residuals as an example. However, waterborne wastes suffice to illustrate the basic economic concepts applicable to partial equilibrium analysis of environmental pollution. Furthermore, analytical and empirical results are more developed with respect to water than in regard to other environmental media, and we present some case material based on them.

CHAPTER 8

Partial Equilibrium Approach to a Specific Residuals Problem: Water Quality Management

8.1 THE CONCEPT OF EXTERNAL COSTS

The theory of external effects, which we reviewed briefly in Chapter 2, has been enormously helpful in understanding the nature and origin of pollution problems in market-type economic systems. In one form or another, the idea of external effects has been present in economic reasoning for at least three-quarters of a century. It is only in the last decade or so, however, that economists have been willing to "bite the bullet" and bring it to bear analytically and empirically on the pollution problem.*

An external effect occurs when the activities of one economic entity—producer, consumer, unit of government—have a *direct* impact on the production or preference functions of a fiscally independent entity. By "direct" is meant that the effect occurs without any intermediary economic transaction. The discharge of waste water by an upstream entity which has adverse effects on downstream producers and consumers serves as an excellent illustration.

Mathematically, the presence of an external effect can be shown by the following notation:

$$U^1 = F^1(x_1^1, x_2^1, \ldots, x_m^1; x_n^2)$$

---

* A review of some of the more recent literature on externalities is found in E. J. Mishan, "The Postwar Literature on Externalities: An Interpretative Essay," *Journal of Economic Literature* (March 1971). The next few paragraphs of our exposition build heavily on it.

Another excellent discussion is W. J. Baumol, "On Taxation and the Control of Externalities," *American Economic Review*, June 1972, Vol. LXII, No. 3, pp. 307–22.

Here, an external effect by some entity 2 on some entity 1 is depicted. If F^1 is taken to stand for the preference function of a consumer, the x's are the amounts of goods $X_1, X_2, \ldots, X_m$, used by him and X_n^2 is the amount of some good used or produced by a second entity. The above function shows that the consumption or production activities of the second entity enter directly into the utility function of the consumer. The reader should go through the analogous reasoning where F is taken to be the production function of a firm.

In both cases the activities of entity 2 produce incidental and unintended side effects directly on entity 1. These effects can be either favorable or unfavorable. But since we are here concerned with unfavorable effects, or external costs, we will develop only this type.

An externality experienced by entity 1 as a result of the marginal unit of entity 2's equilibrium level activity is indicated by $\partial F^1/\partial x_n^2 \neq 0$. Assume that entity 2 is a productive enterprise and let p_n^2 and c_n^2 stand for price and marginal cost of any output of the good X_n chosen by entity 2. If entity 2 ignores the external effect, and if it is a competitive enterprise, it will, as internal efficiency requires, choose to equate c_n^2 to p_n^2. But then, $(p_n^2 - c_n^2) + (\partial F^1/\partial x_n^2) \neq 0$. The presence of this inequality has allocative significance. If an external cost is being imposed, the inequality means that the marginal cost to the broader society exceeds the marginal cost to the producer. Because he equates his *internal* marginal cost to price, the social marginal cost exceeds the price consumers are willing to pay for the commodity. The result thus cannot be Pareto optimal. In view of this, economists have usually concluded that the external cost-producing activity should be taxed in such a way as to "internalize" the externality. For reasons we explain in detail later, we feel this is still, in general, the correct conclusion for pollution-type externalities.

In the recent literature on externalities, the concept and its significance have been considerably clarified by analyzing it in terms of the possibilities of bargaining and monetary exchanges between the parties involved in the externality. This discussion has revolved around the concept of property rights and what has come to be known as "transactions costs." Several authors have pointed out that external effects can in some instances be brought under optimal control by defining property rights to what was previously common property or by merging activities having external effects on each other. As an example of the latter, if a firm discharges waste water to a stream and imposes an external cost on another firm downstream but then the two are merged, the external effect is made internal to the enterprise. The upstream unit would now find it worthwhile to take account of any effects on the downstream unit in making its production decision. The practical value of this conclusion is, however, limited. Typical pollution situations involve numerous affected entities. Often the effects on each of them are small, but in the aggregate they may be substantial. One can hardly take seriously the possibility of merging all (or even many) of the multitudinous activities in a river basin for the sake of internalizing pollution problems.

But it might be possible to define a property right to the "commons" such that exchange between independent entities could take place. For example, again in the case of the upstream and the downstream firms, if (say) the upstream firm were accorded a clear right to discharge its waste waters, then the downstream firm could purchase part of this right to protect itself against damage. Moreover, it would pay the damaged party to continue to purchase units of the right until his marginal gain is equal to the marginal cost of the waste discharger for reducing the discharge. This result can be demonstrated with the aid of Figure 8-1.

Curve AY indicates the incremental damage cost imposed by the waste discharger. Curve CZ'' can be interpreted as the marginal gain open to the waste discharger as he increases his discharge, or the cost he avoids by not having to control his waste discharge. Curve CZ' is explained and used in the next footnote. If the waste discharger holds the property right and the two parties can negotiate, it will pay the damaged party to offer payment to the discharger to reduce his discharge. From discharge level Z'' to level Z', the damaged party's incremental damages are higher than the waste discharger's marginal gain due to his avoided waste reduction cost. If this level of discharge reduction is passed, the marginal damage cost becomes less than the cost of control, and it will not pay the damaged party to bid enough to induce the waste discharger to cut back further. Thus, the equilibrium will be at the point where the marginal cost of damages equals the marginal cost of discharge control. This point will be Pareto optimal and will minimize the sum of internal and external costs.* An important result to note is that at the optimal point the external cost is not eliminated, but is merely reduced to an optimal level. Sometimes, in careless or uninformed usage, people speak of eliminating externalities. This would seldom, if ever, be optimal since internal costs of control as well as external costs are involved in the solution.

While relating the externality phenomenon to property rights has helped to clarify it and its relationship to prevailing institutional arrangements, the possibilities of internalizing pollution-type externalities through private exchange seems to be extremely small. Typical pollution phenomena are ones in

---

* One frequently noted related point which seems to us of limited importance, but which we discuss briefly because of the prominent role it has played in the literature in recent years, is that when negotiation between the parties is possible, imposing a tax on the external cost generating activity will lead to non-optimal results. This can be illustrated by reference to Figure 8-1. If a tax equal to the marginal cost of off-site damages is levied upon the waste discharger, his marginal net gain for a given quantity of waste discharged is measured by curve CZ'' minus curve AY (that is, waste discharge reduction cost avoided minus damage cost imposed). This difference is indicated by curve CZ'. At the optimum point Z' (as discussed in the text), his marginal gains are cancelled by the marginal damages imposed, so that his net gain is zero. Acting by himself, if marginal off-site damage costs are imposed upon him, the waste discharger would tend to move to this point. But if the damaged party can negotiate with the waste discharger, he will have an incentive to induce the waste discharger to cut back even further than this optimal point. In fact, he will be willing to pay the waste discharger to reduce his discharge to the point where his marginal net gain equals the marginal damage imposed. This is indicated by point B' in Figure 8-1. Since we feel (as argued below) that the role of private negotiation in pollution-type externalities is likely to be minor, we do not think that this theoretically interesting point is of much practical significance. For further discussion, see Ralph Turvey, "On Divergencies Between Social Cost and Private Cost," *Economica*, Vol. 30, No. 1119 (August 1963).

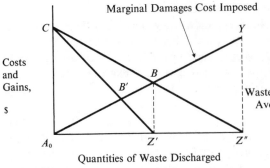

FIGURE 8-1

which numerous parties are affected (often in individually small amounts summing to a large total) by one or more, and often very many, sources of residuals discharge. The possibilities of organizing effectively for exchange in this situation, especially on the part of the damaged parties, would seem to be almost nil. This problem goes under the name "transactions costs" in the literature. There are major costs, to the damaged parties, of getting together to negotiate in their common interest. Moreover, since a particular party will tend to benefit from the improved environment (which usually has the characteristics of a public good) whether he participates in the exchange or not, it is in his particular interest not to participate. This phenomenon is known as the "free rider" problem.

Thus, we seem to be left with the possibility that some form of collective action through government is needed to effectively internalize pollution-type externalities. There is no necessity or even presumption that improvement is possible, of course. For example, evasion may be a problem and compliance and administrative costs may be excessive. Although these possibilities are given little attention in this book, they are important.

8.2 TAXING THE WASTE DISCHARGER

In our initial discussion of the use of publicly administered incentives for the control of external costs, we will assume that the total external cost, or damage, function is linear. This means that marginal damages are constant, and somewhat simplifies the exposition. Later, after we have discussed the effects of discharges on streams, we will examine the question of the actual character of damage functions.

We can depict the response of a waste discharger to a tax equal to the marginal damages his discharge imposes with the aid of Figure 8-2.

Notice that in this diagram, maximum waste discharge occurs at the origin and units of waste withheld are measured along the horizontal axis. This arrangement permits us to show the waste discharger's marginal cost curve for

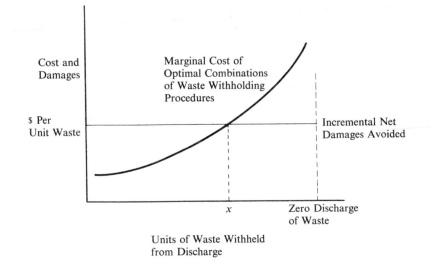

FIGURE 8-2

withholding waste in a manner similar to that in which marginal cost curves are normally displayed. If an effluent charge (or we may refer to it as a tax—these words are used interchangeably in this connection) is levied on each unit of waste discharge equivalent to the incremental damage it imposes, the waste discharger will have an economic incentive to reduce his discharge to the point where the marginal cost of a further unit of reduction is just equal to the marginal damage imposed. In other words, he will withhold the amount of waste x. At this point the difference between the external cost avoided and the internal cost incurred to avoid it is at a maximum. Moreover, the waste discharger will have an incentive to seek the least costly means for achieving the level of waste reduction he chooses. A manufacturing firm, for example, would have an incentive to choose the least costly combination of such alternatives as treatment of waste waters, process changes, and production adjustments. As we shall see in Chapter 10, our national policy on water pollution has tended to stress treatment of waste waters after generation to the exclusion of other alternatives even though empirical research has shown alternatives such as process change to be important.*

We will explore the use of effluent charges in water quality management further at various places in this and the next few chapters, but before doing so we must review another issue. There has been a significant interest, in both academic and policy circles, in the possible use of subsidies for the control of waste discharge. A question of interest therefore is whether a system of payments

---

* See, for example, George O. G. Löf and Allen V. Kneese, *The Economics of Water Utilization in the Beet Sugar Industry* (Washington, D.C.: Resources for the Future, Inc., 1968).

to waste dischargers could be worked out which would have the same allocative results as a system of effluent charges based on marginal damages. The answer is that *in principle* it could be, but in practice it is likely to be virtually impossible to do so, and it is probably undesirable to try. As we will see at the end of Chapter 10, the subsidy schemes which have actually become embodied in our national policy are far from being able to achieve an efficient allocative result. In the economics literature, payments to waste dischargers have come to be known as "bribes" and we will adopt that terminology here.

8.3   BRIBES

In this section we first demonstrate that a system of bribes is conceivable which would achieve the same result as an optimal charges scheme. We argue that this is true despite some recent statements to the contrary.* We conclude, however, that administrative and informational problems rule out payments for serious consideration as an effective and efficient water quality control measure. Our discussion of bribes also provides a useful opportunity to explore further how a rational waste discharger would respond to a system of charges.

Consider first the response of the firm emitting the pollutant, which is assumed to be proportionate to output. The firm has a total cost curve, $TC = f(x)$. If pollutant emitted is now taxed at a rate equivalent to c per unit output, TC is now $TC_T = f(x) + cx$.

If, on the other hand, a subsidy or "bribe" is paid for reducing pollution emission from a specified level, x^*, TC is still the same except for a constant:

$$TC_s = f(x) - c(x^* - x), \qquad x < x^*$$

Marginal cost is the same for both the tax and bribe situations, i.e., $f'(x) + c$ as compared with $f'(x)$ in the original situation. With a tax, one unit of additional output entails not only additional expenditure on labor, etc., but also c of tax. With a bribe, one more unit requires the same additional expenditure on labor, etc., along with giving up c of bribe.

If $f(x)$ is viewed as a long-run cost function, the same statement may be made from the point of view of a firm on the list of those which are eligible for bribe payments, but the precise final adjustment of the industry, which requires zero industry profits on *opportunity* costs, depends on whether new entrants are permitted and on who is eligible to receive bribes.

---

* See D. F. Bramhall and E. S. Mills, "A Note on the Asymmetry Between Fees and Payments," *Water Resources Research*, Third Quarter 1966, pp. 615–16; M. J. Kamien, N. L. Schwartz, and F. T. Dolbear, "Asymmetry Between Bribes and Charges," *Water Resources Research*, First Quarter 1966, pp. 147–57; and A. Myrick Freeman III, "Bribes and Charges: Some Comments," *Water Resources Research*, First Quarter 1967, pp. 287, 298. See also F. T. Dolbear, "On the Theory of Optimum Externality," *American Economic Review*, Vol. 57, No. 2 (March 1967) and Richard A. Tybout, "Pricing of Pollution and Other Negative Externalities," *The Bell Journal of Economics and Management Science*, Spring 1972, Vol. 3, No. 1, pp. 252–66.

If new entrants are not permitted and the industry was initially in equilibrium with each firm producing x^* (at minimum point on long-run average cost curve), introduction of a bribe system will result in the exit of some firms sufficient to increase price by c (assume constant cost industry). For firms still producing, price covers factor outlays *and* the bribes foregone because they are producing (instead of reducing pollutant by not producing). Firms leaving the industry continue to receive bribes of cx^* each.

In contrast, suppose only the original firms (making only "normal" profits) are eligible for bribes but that entry is free. The result now will be the exit of all of the original firms (who will continue to receive their bribes) and the entry of new firms not eligible for bribes. The pre-bribe situation will be restored and the regulatory authority will find that it has been spinning its wheels. If the bribe system is to be effective, potential entrants also must be bribed.

If the assumption of proportionality between waste load and output is abandoned, and one assumes that waste loads can be reduced by treatment or other methods, a payment per unit reduction of waste load still will produce the same balance between production cutback and treatment (or other methods) as a charge of equivalent amount. This can be shown conveniently by the method of Lagrange multipliers.

Let the output of waste reduction be a function of the level of use of a number of alternative inputs which might include treatment, recycle, reduction in output, etc. We can then write a production function for waste reduction.

$$Q = f(X_1, X_2, \ldots, X_n)$$

where the X_i are alternative means of reducing waste discharge.

Given any quantity of waste reduction, Q^*, the firm will try to produce it as cheaply as it can. This means it is trying to minimize its costs M (in the sense of foregone net revenue as well as outlays) on the inputs used to produce Q^*, where the cost is given by

$$M = P_1 X_1 + P_2 X_2 + \cdots + P_n X_n$$

where P_1 is the cost per unit of input 1, etc. The firm is constrained in minimizing M by the production function indicated above.

This contraint can be written in the form:

$$f(X_1, X_2, \ldots, X_n) - Q^* = 0$$

This expression is multiplied by the artificial variable λ and added to the expression M (which is to be minimized) to obtain the Lagrangian expression:

$$M_\lambda = P_1 X_1 + P_2 X_2 + \cdots + P_n X_n + \lambda[f(X_1, X_2, \ldots, X_n) - Q^*]$$

This expression is minimized in the standard way by setting each of its partial derivatives to zero:

$$\frac{\partial M_\lambda}{\partial X_1} = P_1 + \lambda \frac{\partial f}{\partial X_1} = 0$$

$$\frac{\partial M_\lambda}{\partial X_2} = P_2 + \lambda \frac{\partial f}{\partial X_2} = 0$$

$$\cdots\cdots\cdots\cdots\cdots\cdots$$

$$\frac{\partial M_\lambda}{\partial X_n} = P_n + \lambda \frac{\partial f}{\partial X_n} = 0$$

$$\frac{\partial M_\lambda}{\lambda} = f(X_1, X_2, \ldots, X_n) - Q^* = 0$$

This set of $n + 1$ simultaneous equations can in principle be solved for the optimal values of the n inputs $X_1, X_2, \ldots, X_n$ and the Lagrangian multiplier λ.

If we write the first two equations as

$$P_1 = -\lambda \frac{\partial f}{\partial X_1} \qquad \text{and} \qquad P_2 = -\lambda \frac{\partial f}{\partial X_2}$$

and divide one equation by the other, we get

$$\frac{P_1}{P_2} = \frac{\partial f / \partial X_1}{\partial f / \partial X_2}$$

Since $\partial f / \partial X_1$ is equal to the marginal (physical) product of X_1 and likewise $\partial f / \partial X_2$ is the marginal product of X_2, we can write

$$\frac{P_1}{P_2} = \frac{MP_1}{MP_2}$$

which is, as we saw in Chapter 2, the optimizing rule for minimizing costs. When this rule holds for all input combinations, the cost of increasing output of waste reduction by a small increment by means of one input is equal to the marginal cost of increasing it by the same increment by using more of any other input. Thus, when the MC of waste reduction is equated to the unit effluent charge or bribe, the MC of reducing waste by all alternative means is equated and no further cost reductions can be achieved by trading off the alternative means.

Since the costs associated with waste disposal are generally low relative to other costs of production and since the firm has the option of treating or otherwise modifying final waste output, the effects of waste disposal costs on prices, location, and decisions to enter or leave an industry usually will be small.

However, where decisions on location and/or industry entry or exit are involved, the administration of a system of payments becomes, as has already been implied above, particularly troublesome. Payment must be continued after shutdown of a plant, if the procedure is to have the desired results. While this might be manageable, serious problems would occur if a shift in demand for the product should increase the potential profitability of the plant, or if other dynamic adjustments should take place. Moreover, plants might introduce processes that produce a greater quantity of waste in order to obtain payment for reducing waste.

Even more perplexing would be the handling of proposals for new industrial locations. The administrative authority would have to stand ready to make payments to industrial plants which never do locate in the area but which would do so if a payment reflecting the costs their effluents would impose were available to them.* Payments on this basis would of course be an open invitation to extortion. If charges were levied, however, the authority only would have to provide the prospective firm with an estimate of the per-unit charge to be placed on its effluent.

This section has permitted us to show that under idealized conditions payments and charges serve equally well to achieve optimal amounts of waste discharge reduction. Moreover, we have seen that this is true whether we are speaking about the short run or the long run and for multiple alternatives to reduce waste as well as for output reduction. We have found also, however, that the informational and administrative requirements of the payments scheme are so extensive as to rule it out for serious consideration.

Also important in this connection is the fact that, at least in the eastern states, watercourses are often legally regarded as the property of the public at large. From this perspective, effluent charges can be regarded as payments for the privilege of using a scarce public asset—the waste assimilative capacity of waterways. For these various reasons, our further discussion focuses on charges rather than subsidies. However, before we can fruitfully pursue this discussion, we must review some aspects of the effects which waste discharges actually have on watercourses.

8.4   EFFECTS OF WASTE DISCHARGES ON WATERCOURSES

While a deep understanding of the details of a water quality management problem requires considerable knowledge of its natural science and engineering aspects, we will not try to review these in detail here. A suitable review for those interested can be found elsewhere.† We will just introduce a few relationships

---

* This is to avoid making the payment contingent on actually engaging in the activity.

† See Part I of Allen V. Kneese and Blair T. Bower, *Managing Water Quality: Economics, Technology, Institutions* (Baltimore: The Johns Hopkins Press, 1968).

which are necessary for the understanding of the subsequent development.

We may, for our purposes, think of waste discharges as containing *degradable* and *non-degradable* substances. This distinction carries implications for forecasting waste concentrations and other characteristics of interest in receiving waters, for types of controls possible, and also for economic policies designed to deal with externalities. Household sewage is the most widespread and well-known source of degradable waterborne residuals. But industrial waste is greater in terms of total volume of organics discharged. These organic substances draw upon the dissolved oxygen in water during a process of biological degradation which eventually converts them to stable inorganic materials.* Meanwhile, a heavily loaded stream may experience oxygen reduction sufficient to kill fish or even, with extremely large loadings which exhaust dissolved oxygen, to cause unpleasant odors and completely disrupt the ecology of the stream.

A measure of organic waste load is biochemical oxygen demand (BOD), which indicates the amount of oxygen drawn up (demanded) in the process of decomposition of the waste. The rate at which a given quantity and type of organic waste exerts oxygen demand is a function of a variety of factors, among which the most important are the chemical characteristics and the temperature of the receiving water, as well as the type of waste.

The rate at which BOD is exerted combined with the rate at which oxygen is restored determine the level of dissolved oxygen (DO). Water bodies have a certain ability to dissolve oxygen which gets into the water through the water-atmosphere interface by a process known as reaeration. The amount of oxygen which can be dissolved in water is primarily a function of temperature, and under summer temperature conditions the saturation level is 7–10 parts per million (ppm) of oxygen in the water. In flowing water the combined effect of a BOD load continuously discharged at a specific location and recreation in the stream results first in a decrease and then in an increase in DO as the waste is carried downstream. This phenomenon is described by a characteristic curve known as the "oxygen sag."

The variables in the oxygen sag are described by standard equations known as the Streeter equations.† The Streeter equations can be viewed intuitively in one of two ways. First, one might envision a given absolute quantity of oxygen-demanding waste being put into a container of water that has specified reaeration characteristics. The initial biochemical oxygen demand is measured in ppm and thus depends on the density of the waste material in relation to the volume of water in the container. As the biological reactions proceed, the

---

* This is not the end of the story since these inorganic materials are plant nutrients which often cause problems of excessive enrichment of water bodies. We will not treat this important problem explicitly here.

† The oxygen sag was first formulated in H. W. Streeter, "A Study of the Pollution and Natural Purification of The Ohio River, III, Factors Concerned in the Phenomena of Oxidation and Reaeration," Public Health Bulletin No. 146, 1925, reprinted 1958. Subsequently modifications have been made; for example, H. A. Thomas, Jr., "The Dissolved Oxygen Balance in Streams," Lecture No. 4, Seminar on Waste Water Treatment and Disposal, Boston Society of Civil Engineers, 1957.

unsatisfied BOD is reduced as time passes at a constant rate per unit time. As time progresses, the oxygen-demanding waste is gradually consumed (that is, converted into inorganic substances) and the reaeration process continues, with the level of dissolved oxygen again reaching the saturation level for water of those particular characteristics when the oxygen-demanding waste is completely consumed.

Alternatively, one can think of a flowing stream with uniform characteristics over a certain reach in which there is a constant input of oxygen-demanding waste at a certain point. We now can think of distances downstream as being exactly equivalent to time in the former way of looking at this situation. Thus, as we proceed downstream, we will find first a decrease in the dissolved oxygen content as oxygen is consumed in the biochemical reactions on the oxygen-demanding waste, and finally a rise in the dissolved oxygen content to the saturation level still further on downstream. While the subsequent formulas have been written in terms of time, they could just as well be written in terms of distance provided the equivalencies stipulated above are met.

Biochemical oxidation is indicated as a first order differential equation of the form

$$\frac{dL}{dt} = -k_1 L_t$$

where L_t is the unsatisfied BOD (ppm), t is time (days), and k_1 is a rate constant which is a function of the characteristics of the waste and the water temperature. If L_a is the initial first stage BOD and is interpreted as the constant of integration, the result of integrating the above equation is

$$L_t = L_a e^{-k_1 t}$$

Reaeration is also indicated as a first-order process. It is a function of the difference between actual DO concentration and saturation concentration, as follows:

$$\frac{dC}{dt} = k_2(C_s - C_t)$$

where C_t is the concentration (ppm) of DO at time t and C_s is the saturation concentration; k_2 is once again a rate constant which is primarily a function of temperature.

When the two reactions are combined and the resulting equation written in terms of the DO deficit ($D_t = C_s - C_t$):

$$\frac{dD}{dt} = k_1 L_t - k_2 D_t{}^*$$

---

* See G. M. Fair, J. C. Geyer, and D. A. Okun, *Water and Wastewater Engineering*, Vol. 2 (New York: John Wiley & Sons, Inc., 1968), for a good explanation of the derivation.

After substituting $L_a e^{-k_1 t}$ for L_t, we have

$$\frac{dD}{dt} = k_1 L_a e^{-k_1 t} - k_2 D_t$$

This is a first order differential equation of the general form

$$\frac{dy}{dx} + Py = Q$$

with
$$Q = k_1 L_a e^{-k_1 t}$$

Following standard procedures which may be found in any text on differential equations, the solution of this equation is

$$D_t = \frac{k_1 L_a}{k_2 - k_1} (e^{-k_1 t} - e^{-k_2 t}) + D_a e^{-k_2 t}$$

where D_a is the deficit and L_a is the BOD concentration, both at time $t = 0$. The time at which the maximum deficit occurs, say (t_c), can be found by taking the derivative of the above equation with respect to time, setting the result to zero, and solving for t_c. The resulting expression is:

$$t_c = \frac{1}{k_2 - k_1} \ln \left[\frac{k_2}{k_1} \left(1 - \frac{(k_2 - k_1) D_a}{k_1 L_a} \right) \right]$$

At the location corresponding to this time the deficit is:

$$D_c = \frac{k_1 L_a}{k_2} e^{-k_1 t_c}$$

While the above equations were first devised to describe the behavior of DO in a single reach of a stream subject to a single waste discharge, they can be applied to multiple reaches, since the deficit at the downstream end of one reach is also the initial deficit (D_2) at the upstream end of the next reach. Such straightforward use of the equations is possible only under highly simplified conditions. The basic equations describing DO behavior have been elaborated in a number of ways to handle more complex situations which we will discuss in Chapter 10.

Nondegradable substances discharged to watercourses exhibit great variety in constituents and effects. Their quantity at various points in a stream is comparatively easy to predict when the amount discharged is known, since they are merely diluted, not degraded. On the other hand, a complex variety of damaging effects on the utility of the receiving water stems from these substances; prominent among them are corrosiveness, toxicity, and hardness.

Control of waterborne waste discharges can be accomplished in basically two ways. The first is by internal controls which are primarily applicable to industry and the second is via treatment. As we have already mentioned, empirical studies have shown that industry often has great scope for reducing waste discharge through such means as more tightly managed production processes, recycling, and by-product recovery. Both municipal and industrial waste streams can be treated via processes whose technologies need not detain us here. We should note, however, that treating the waste water stream does not destroy the physical substance contained in it. Thus, minimizing the costs of protecting one environmental medium may well cause unwarranted degradation in the quality of others. We will explore this point in some detail in Chapter 11.

In addition to internal controls and treatment, the quality of a receiving stream can usually be improved by measures to enhance its assimilative capacity. One device is to augment the low flows of a river through releases of water from reservoir storage. This may have two types of positive effect. One is to increase dilution of the wastes discharged into the stream. The second is that under some conditions greater streamflow can increase the reaeration coefficient k_2 by inducing turbulence. Another means for improving the assimilative capacity of the stream is to introduce air into it mechanically, as with a compressor and hoses. Finally, it is frequently possible, especially in compact urban-industrial regions, to achieve cost economics by collecting industrial and municipal wastes together in large collective treatment plants. We will explore these more complicated but very important aspects of water quality management further in subsequent chapters.

8.5 PROBLEMS IN DETERMINING CHARGES: THE NATURE OF DAMAGE FUNCTIONS

Basic to an optimum system of effluent charges, or for that matter any procedure seeking to achieve an economically optimal level of water quality, is delineation of the "damage cost function," which is the functional relationship between the amount of a waste discharged and total damages. The simplest situation occurs when this function is linear, i.e., each additional unit of waste discharge results in an equal increment of cost. Such a situation is illustrated in Table 8-2 where it is assumed that five plants are arrayed along a stream, that streamflow increases along the course of the stream (say, because a tributary enters), and that the waste it contains is non-degradable (say, chloride). The non-degradability assumption simplifies the example because only dilution is involved.

Damages at each plant, indicated in the sixth column of the table, are arbitrarily chosen for illustrative purposes, but damage at a given plant is directly proportional to the chloride concentration. Thus, at Plant 5, a chloride concentration of 2.0 produces damages of $1,000 per day, but a concentration of 4.0 produces damages of $2,000 per day.

Since damage per day is assumed to be in direct proportion to concentration, a level of charges equal to incremental damage costs can be worked out for each

TABLE 8-2

SIMPLE ILLUSTRATION OF COST DISTRIBUTION

Plant no. (serially located along stream)	Chloride load discharged (1000 lb per day)	Chloride load at plant intake (1000 lb per day)	Flow Condition I				Flow Condition II			
			Streamflow (mill. gpd)	Chloride concentration (1000 lb. per mill. gal.) [gpd]	Damage per day $1000	Cumulative total damage per day $1000	Streamflow (mill. gpd)	Chloride concentration (1000 lb. per mill. gal.) [gpd]	Damage per day $1000	Cumulative total damage per day $1000
1	1.0	.0	1.0	.0	.00	.00	.5	.0	.00	.00
2	.5	1.0	1.0	1.0	1.00	1.00	.5	2.0	2.00	2.00
3	1.5	1.5	1.0	1.5	3.00	4.00	.5	3.0	6.00	8.00
4	1.0	3.0	2.0	1.5	3.00	7.00	1.0	3.0	6.00	14.00
5	.5	4.0	2.0	2.0	1.00	8.00	1.0	4.0	2.00	16.00

Flow Condition I

Damages caused at:	Damage caused by:				Sum of damages caused to $1000
	Plant 1	Plant 2	Plant 3	Plant 4	
	All values in $1000				
Plant 1	.00	.00	.00	.00	.00
Plant 2	1.00	.00	.00	.00	1.00
Plant 3	2.00	1.00	.00	.00	3.00
Plant 4	1.00	.50	1.50	.00	3.00
Plant 5	.25	.125	.375	.25	1.00
Sum of damages caused by:	$4.25	$1.625	$1.875	$ .25	$8.00

Flow Condition II

Damages caused at:	Damage caused by:				Sum of damages caused to $1000
	Plant 1	Plant 2	Plant 3	Plant 4	
	All values in $1000				
Plant 1	.00	.00	.00	.00	.00
Plant 2	2.00	.00	.00	.00	2.00
Plant 3	4.00	2.00	.00	.00	6.00
Plant 4	2.00	1.00	3.00	.00	6.00
Plant 5	.50	.25	.75	.50	2.00
Sum of damages caused by:	$8.50	$3.25	$3.75	$ .50	$16.00

Source: Kneese and Bower, *Managing Water Quality* (Baltimore: Johns Hopkins Press, 1968).

level of flow and for each plant. For example, at flow level I the charge for Plant 1 is \$4.25 per unit of waste discharged which is the sum of the damages caused by Plant 1 to Plants 2, 3, 4, and 5. The total assessment would be \$4,250,000. This charge is the same regardless of the level of discharge of the other plants. If Plant 1 reduced its discharge by half in response to the charge levied on it, its total assessment would drop by half to \$2,125,000—the amount by which downstream damages are reduced.* This "separability" characteristic of linear damage functions is important since it greatly reduces the amount of information which a regulatory authority must have to implement an efficient effluent charge system.

The relative simplicity of a system of effluent charges based upon linear damage functions arises from the fact that each waste discharger's marginal damage costs can be determined separately from every other's. In contrast, non-linearities produce interaction between waste discharges in the sense that the incremental external cost associated with one cannot be determined unless the level of discharge of the other is known.

Let us look at these two cases a bit more formally. The first case is where damage functions are *linear* and therefore *separable*. Assume there are two waste dischargers located along a stream and that they both discharge a degradable waste, i.e., BOD.† Assume further that the damages which result from the BOD which they discharge can be expressed as a simple multiple of the area under the DO deficit curve from the first plant to a distance T days downstream; that is:

$$C = K \int_0^T D \, dt\ddagger.$$

---

* That is, in given flow conditions Plant j suffers damages of $_oD_j$ from upstream discharges, c_i, as of situation o. Plant 1's share of Plant j's damage is

$$^1D = \frac{c_1}{c_1 + \sum_{i=2}^{J-1} c_i} \, _oD_j$$

If Plant 1 reduces its discharge to kc_1 ($K < 1$), then the chloride concentration at Plant j is reduced and the new damage at Plant j is

$$\frac{kc_1 + \sum_{i=2}^{J-1} c_i}{c_1 + \sum_{i=2}^{J-1} c_i} \, _oD_j$$

Plant 1's proportionate share of this new damage is also reduced to

$$\frac{kc_1}{kc_1 + \sum_{i=2}^{J-1} c_i}$$

Thus, Plant 1's share of the new damage, caused by the change in its discharge, is:

$$^1_1D = \frac{kc_1}{kc_j + \sum_{i=2}^{J-1} c_i} \cdot \frac{kc_1 + \sum_{i=2}^{J-1} c_i}{c_1 + \sum_{i=2}^{J-1} c_i} \, _oD_j = k^1_o D$$

† This example is developed in Jon C. Liebman, "The Optimal Allocation of Stream Dissolved Oxygen Resources," Cornell University Water Resources Center (Ithaca, New York, 1965), p. 41ff.

‡ Notation relating to the oxygen sag is explained in the previous section of this chapter.

where C is the damage, K is a constant, and D is the DO deficit at any point. Writing D as a function of $L_1 + L_2$ (the amount of BOD discharged at Plant 1 and Plant 2 respectively) and D_a (the initial deficit), and performing the integration gives an expression of the form

$$C = K(K_1L_1 + K_2L_2 + K_3D_a)$$

where K_1, K_2, and K_3 are functions of the parameters of the Streeter equations. It follows that the damage due to the first discharge is KK_1L_1 which is independent of the level of the second discharge or the initial deficit; and the damage due to the second discharge is KK_2L_2, which is independent of the level of the first discharge and the initial deficit.

The second case consists of damage functions in which this type of independence does not exist. If the damage cost of an additional part per million of deficit is greater when the deficit is large than it would be if the deficit were smaller, damages attributable to individual waste discharges are no longer independent.

Assume, for example, that damage is a multiple of the integral of the squared deficit:

$$C = K \int_0^T D^2 \, dt$$

Then, integration yields an expression of the form

$$C = K(K_1L_1^2 + K_2L_2^2 + K_3L_1L_2 + K_4L_1D_a + K_5L_2D_a + K_6D_a^2)$$

In this equation, the damages attributable to the first discharge are made up of the first, third, and fourth terms. The third term depends upon the level of the second discharge, and therefore the first firm's marginal damage is a function of the second firm's discharge as well as of its own. Instead of merely needing to know damage functions and being able to achieve an optimal solution by imposing damage costs on the waste dischargers and letting them respond, the agency must now know the cost functions for waste reduction at each interdependent point of waste discharge. It must determine the optimum level of waste reduction for each point *before* charges are assessed on effluents in order to obtain an optimal solution. This means that the effluent charges system loses one major advantage over other systems of control such as payments of effluent standards. This point is explored further in the next chapter.

Its comparative lack of complication may well commend an assumption of linearity even when it is known that the discharge-damage relation is actually somewhat more complex. The fact that taking account of greater complexity may rapidly increase costs and yield strongly diminishing returns must be kept in mind in designing an actual system of charges. In other words, among the incremental costs that should not be neglected are the costs of refinements of the system of charges.*

Also, in practice, a public agency may set standards for water quality in a stream. This may follow a greater or lesser degree of economic analysis but is at the end a political decision. These standards can then be treated as a perfectly inelastic damage function, and charges can be effective and efficient means for achieving the standards. This type of situation, which is of great practical importance, is explored in considerable detail in Chapter 10. We now turn to a somewhat more elaborate and rigorous economic model of water quality management in a river basin.

---

* The use of linear separable functions may not be a good approximation of the actual conditions should any of the following situations hold to a significant degree: (1) damage costs definitely do not increase in direct proportion to the increase in waste concentration; (2) the relationship between different types of wastes is either synergistic or cancelling rather than additive; (3) a downstream treatment process removes two or more types of wastes coming from different sources. In the third case, an inevitable element of arbitrariness is introduced into allocating the costs to individual waste-discharging firms which emit different wastes or the same wastes in different proportions. When the costs of removing residual materials from intake water are strictly "joint," there is literally no non-arbitrary way of determining who is responsible for what. In some or many cases, however, the costs are probably not truly joint. In these cases, for any given level of concentration the cost of dealing with an increment of the waste can be estimated. In the first two cases, the complexity occurs because the cost for which Plant 2's discharge can be held responsible becomes in part a function of how much Plant 1 discharges. Currently much uncertainty exists concerning the character of damage functions, but there is evidence that some of them are to one or another extent non-linear.

CHAPTER 9

A Less Restrictive Model of Water Quality Management

The next step is to develop a more powerful and realistic economic model for analysis of water quality management. We wish, for example, to be able to abandon the assumption that damage costs are linear. Also we have previously assumed that there are no efficient water quality control measures that cannot be realized at the individual waste outfall or water supply intake. The assumption that such facilities could not reduce the overall costs associated with water quality management in a basin was useful for our initial discussion of technological external diseconomies, and probably descriptive of some real cases as well. But engineering-economic research has shown that there are many important instances where economies can be realized by collective measures such as low-flow augmentation, stream reaeration, groundwater recharge for quality improvement, effluent diversion or redistribution to make better use of natural assimilative capacity, the specialized use of streams or stretches of streams, and combinations of these. Where facilities involve scale economies which cannot be efficiently realized at individual outfalls or intakes and/or public good characteristics, it may be appropriate to have a regional authority with powers more extensive than those assumed in the previous chapter. It may be desirable that these extend to planning, financing, constructing, and operating of water quality improvement facilities. In this chapter we analyze certain aspects of these questions by means of a simple mathematical model.* Then we

---

* A more elaborate version of this model can be found in Allen V. Kneese and Blair T. Bower, *Managing Water Quality: Economics, Technology, Institutions* (Johns Hopkins Press, 1968); see especially the Appendix to Chapter 10 by Hayden Boyd. The present version is adapted from "Analyzing 'Externalities': 'Direct Interaction' vs. 'Asset Utilization' Models," by Herbert Mohring and J. Hayden Boyd, *Economica*, November 1971, pp. 347–61.

present a more intuitive discussion using the heuristic device of a basin-wide firm.

9.1   AN ASSET UTILIZATION MODEL

In more deeply examining criteria for optimum management of a "common property" resource like a water body, we find it desirable to use an "asset utilization" approach rather than the "direct interaction" approach which has characterized most of the theorizing about externality problems and which we used in the last chapter. This direct interaction approach has the merit of permitting ready use of simple graphic techniques. But the asset utilization approach seems to us to go more directly to the heart of the problem of optimizing the use of common property resources and is also more readily adaptable to the analysis of many different users. Of course, its results do not contradict anything that has been said in the last chapter. Let us start with the following model, devised to analyze certain aspects of transportation problems.

Define total highway cost of providing N trips per unit time as

(a)
$$TC = N \cdot C(N,K) + f(K)$$

The first term on the right-hand side represents the variable cost borne directly by drivers, C being the cost of one trip to a driver; the second term is the cost per time period of providing K units of highway capacity. The short-run marginal cost of a trip is:

(b)
$$\frac{\partial(TC)}{\partial N} = C(N,K) + N \cdot \frac{\partial C}{\partial N}$$

This type of model was first developed in connection with problems of highway tolls and highway investment, and it may be helpful to start with a brief exposition of a simple version of this analysis. Assume that each driver values travel time equally and incurs the same operating costs for his vehicle. Then, when the Nth adds his vehicle to $N - 1$ vehicles already on a given highway, he incurs a cost and, in addition, causes the remaining drivers to incur additional costs. In the continuous case, $C(N,K)$ is the variable cost borne by the Nth driver and $N \cdot (\partial C/\partial N)$ is the marginal congestion cost imposed on the remaining drivers. The fixed "common property" resource is the man-made, augmentable highway in this case, and it is common property because of its conditions of access.

Proper management would require that each driver pay a marginal cost price made up of two components: $C(N,K)$, the costs he bears directly, plus a toll equal to the costs he imposes on other drivers by adding to congestion equal to $[N \cdot (\partial C/\partial N)]$. Under certain conditions these external costs also represent the value of the marginal product of the common property resource service. The revenue from this toll can be interpreted as a reward to the authority for providing the services of the (temporarily) fixed factor.

As we noted in Chapter 7, toll collections in a congestive case would exactly equal the capital costs of an optimum capacity expansion if services of the common property asset can be produced at constant long-run cost. We now derive this result.

To find the cost-minimizing level of highway capacity, (a) must be differentiated with respect to K and then the resulting expression set equal to zero.

(c) $$\frac{\partial(TC)}{\partial K} = N \cdot \frac{\partial C}{\partial K} + f'(K) = 0$$

But if constant returns to scale prevail in the provision of trips (i.e., if a λ percent increase in K and N results in a λ percent increase in TC), C will be a function of N/K and equation (a) can be rewritten as:

(d) $$TC = N \cdot C \frac{N}{K} + P_K \cdot K$$

where P_K is the constant unit price per time period of capacity. Differentiating this expression with respect to K then yields:

(e) $$\frac{\partial(TC)}{\partial K} = -N^2 \cdot \frac{C'}{K^2} + P_K = 0 \qquad \text{where} \quad C' \equiv \frac{dC(N/K)}{d(N/K)}$$

or $$P_K K = N^2 \cdot \frac{C'}{K}$$

the amount to be spent on highway capacity. This is equal to the toll (derived earlier) required to achieve a welfare maximum when collected from all trips:

$$\underset{\substack{\text{(toll from} \\ \text{each trip)}}}{N} = N\left(N \cdot \frac{\partial C}{\partial N}\right) = \left(N^2 \cdot \frac{C'}{K}\right)^*$$

This development of the economics of highway tolls and highway capacity can now be adapted to the case of waste discharge to a water body.

First, let us assume N business firms are located around a lake which provides both water supply and residual absorption services. This common property resource yields no other services. The discharge of wastes reduces the utility of the lake for water supply.

---

* The estimation of $C(N,K)$ presents some difficult and subtle problems that are not discussed here. An especially challenging one is to place a value on the extra time required for a trip by reason of congestion.

Industrial firm i $(i = 1, \ldots, n)$ manufactures Y^i units of a product sold in a competitive market at a price P_i. The firm also uses X_i units of an input (labor) purchased competitively at rate W. Output of Y^i is also a function of the amount of waste material (Z_i) which the firm puts in the lake and the quality of water obtained from the lake (q). Each firm produces the same type of waste. Here we neglect adaptations other than output effects to simplify the exposition. Other adaptations might include process changes, waste water treatment, and water supply treatment.

Quality of the lake water depends on the amount of waste discharge of each of the n firms and certain natural attributes of the lake (L) which may be altered by the application of resources (say, by inducing mixing). These natural attributes are not affected by waste discharges.

The objective is taken to be maximizing the difference between the value of output $\sum P_i Y^i$ and the sum of the cost of X inputs $\sum W X_i$ and the cost of securing the desired lake characteristics, L, for the n firms subject to constraints resulting from the interrelationships among water supply and waste disposal.

(f) Max $U = \sum P_i Y^i (X_i, Z_i, q) - \sum W X_i - C(L) - \lambda [q - Q(Z_1, \ldots, Z_n, L)]$

The constraint says the quality of water available for input depends on waste discharges to the lake and lake assimilative capacity.

When this expression is differentiated with respect to X_i, Z_i, q, and L [q being determined by $q = Q(Z_1, \ldots, Z_n, L)$], the following first order conditions are obtained for the maximization problem:

(g)
$$\frac{\partial U}{\partial X_i} = P_i Y^i_{X_i} - W = 0 \qquad (i = 1, \ldots, n)$$

This equation says the value of the marginal product of inputs (labor) should equal the price of these inputs.

(h)
$$\frac{\partial U}{\partial Z_i} = P_i Y^i_{Z_i} + \lambda Q_{Z_i} = 0 \qquad (i = 1, \ldots, n)$$

(i)
$$\frac{\partial U}{\partial q} = \sum P_j Y^j_q - \lambda = 0 \qquad (j = 1, \ldots, n)$$

(j)
$$\frac{\partial U}{\partial L} = \lambda Q_L - C' = 0$$

λ is the implicit value of a unit of water quality (measured at the optimum position for the system), and is equal to the value of the sum of the marginal products of a unit change in quality, (q).

Equation **(j)** says the marginal value of a unit change in lake characteristics (L) is to be equated to the marginal cost of L.

If **(i)** is substituted into **(h)**, the result is:

(k) $P_i Y_{Z_i}^i + Q_{Z_i} \sum P_j Y_q^j = 0 \qquad (i, j = 1, \ldots, n)$

The ith private firm acting in its own interest will ignore the effect on the productivity of all firms via water quality, q, resulting from an increase in its Z_i. Even the effect on Y_q^i of an increase in Z_i is negligible in comparison with $Y_{Z_i}^i$ if there are enough dischargers. Thus to attain the socially optimum Z_i's, a tax should be imposed on each unit of Z_i emitted equal to the second term of **(k)**. The Z_i's and the X_i's will be reduced. That is, the partial derivatives of the Y^i differ according to whether these taxes are imposed or not.

Some possible uses of the lake however, might themselves be subject to congestion, say, recreational uses, and therefore would have to be priced by the authority.

The effluent charge collected by the lake authority would by analogy with the highway toll case in certain instances exceed, equal, or fall short of the long-run cost of improving lake characteristics. If the lake is naturally present and investments only augment its capacity, part of the effluent charge will represent an inframarginal rent (or net yield) on the existing asset. The revenue from the charge can only fall short of long-run cost under conditions of decreasing cost above a certain degree.*

The analysis presented above can now be extended to a situation in which the firms are located along a stream rather than a lake. Of the n firms located along a stream, Firm 1 is furthest upstream (i.e., no waste discharge above it), Firm 2 is next, and Firm n is furthest downstream (i.e., an infinite sink is downstream from it). The quality of water available to a particular firm i is then a function of a river characteristic (R) and waste discharge by only the firms $1, \ldots, i-1$ above it on the river. The maximization problem for the entire river basin now becomes:

(j) $\text{Max } V = \sum P_i Y^i(X_i, Z_i, q_i) - \sum WX_i - C(R)$
$$+ \sum \lambda_i [q_i - Q^i(Z_1, \ldots, Z_{i-1}, R)]$$

The first order conditions are:

(k) $P_i Y_{X_i}^i - W = 0$

(l) $P_i Y_{Z_i}^i + \sum_{j=i+1}^{n} P_j Y_{Q_j}^i Q_{Z_i}^j = 0$

(m) $\left(\sum_{j=1}^{n} P_j Y_{Q_j}^j \right) Q_R^j - C' = 0$

Equation **(k)** will again be obtained by profit maximization and **(l)** by levying a charge on Firm i equal to the value of the second term if sites of all activities are given and fixed.

---

* For a development of this point, see Boyd in Kneese and Bower, *op. cit.*

But suppose an entrepreneur (or a river authority) wishes to place a new activity in the existing array of sites. Take as an example a bathing beach which generates no wastes but has a high marginal product for high water quality. Say the choice is between site O (upstream) and site $n + 1$ (between n and the infinite sink).

At the upstream location, the beach would involve adding $P_0 Y_Q^0 Q_R^0$ to the right-hand side of (m) which might justify some additional investment in R but would leave previous optimal waste discharges unaltered. If, however, site $n + 1$ were chosen, a term such as $P_{n+1} Y_{Q_{n+1}}^{n+1} Q_{Z_i}^{n+1}$ would have to be added to each of the equations (l) in addition to adding $P_{n+1} Y_{Q_{n+1}}^{n+1} Q_R^{n+1}$ to (m).

As a result, maximizing the objective function would require each firm i for which $Q_{Z_i}^{n+1}$ is negative to reduce its level of waste discharge. This would require diverting inputs from production of Y's so that

(n)
$$\sum_{i=1}^{n} (P_i Y^i - W X_i)$$

will decline from its previous level. One way of reflecting this would be to levy a tax equal to the difference on the new activity.

The model developed in this section suggests the need for a basin-wide authority which will:

(1) Levy a charge on waste discharge.
(2) Explore the production function and implement resource improving (augmenting) investments where efficient.
(3) Control land use.

9.2 A MORE INTUITIVE PRESENTATION— THE BASIN-WIDE FIRM

The model in the previous section has yielded certain insights and criteria but understanding of the subject may benefit from a more general discussion. Accordingly we proceed to a verbal presentation. In it we restate the main results of the model and extend them. Also, a new heuristic device is introduced— the "basin-wide firm." Experience has shown that many readers find this device illuminating.

The point of the example of such a firm is to illustrate some of the principles involved in taking account of the technical interdependencies in a river basin when economies of scale in water quality management measures are available.

Assume that a single firm conducts all water-using industrial enterprises, all water and waste treatment facilities (no privately owned septic tanks, water softeners, etc.), and all water transportation and related facilities. Assume further that the firm operates all hydroelectric facilities, owns all land and structures in the flood plain, and is the sole provider of flow regulation. The firm must also control all recreational use of the watercourse. Finally, assume that the firm operates in markets that are either competitive or in which public regulatory authorities set prices equal to marginal costs at levels of output which just clear the market.

The decision criteria which the firm would use in regard to disposal of wastes in order to maximize its profits are those generally appropriate to other aspects of optimum resource use confronted by the firm. The firm would select the combination of water quality control measures (water supply treatment, waste generation and treatment, flow augmentation, waste water releases coordinated with stream flow, etc.) and downstream damages that would minimize its over-all costs (including those associated with disposal of its wastes) at its most profitable level of activity. This would be accomplished by equating the relevant incremental costs associated with waste disposal for all alternatives. As pre-viously indicated, these costs would include any foregone valuable outputs which are sacrificed to improve the efficiency of the waste disposal system.

The firm would transport effluent to a collective treatment plant where scale economies can be realized, if this is less costly than treatment at the individual discharge points. In fact, the firm would continue to transport effluent to lower-cost plants until the marginal costs of transportation and the marginal treatment costs saved are equal.

The firm, we have assumed, would in its selfish interests "internalize" all pertinent costs. A water resources agency in a basin cannot internalize all of them, and *consequently it must attempt to have the opportunity costs of water resources use, including waste disposal, reflected in the decisions of entities which are simultaneously considering* other resources costs. This must be done by levying an appropriate charge for the use of the common property asset.

To return to our illustrative basin-wide firm, the firm's general objective is to maximize profits, which implies that the component of costs associated with waste disposal (as well as all other costs) will be minimized at the profit-max-imizing level of output. If, for example, the firm could lower its costs by doing a little less effluent treatment and permitting a little more damage, or by doing a little more water treatment and a little less waste reduction, or a little more augmentation of low flows and a little less temporary storage of wastes, or a bit more process adjustment and a little less direct reaeration of the stream, etc., its overall profit position could not be at a maximum. As part of its general profit-maximizing activities, the firm would integrate its waste control activities with other aspects of its water-related operations. One major linkage is via the effects of flow regulation.

Thus, in computing the costs of alternative water quality control devices, the firm would need to consider complementary and competitive relationships among different water uses and alteration of the stream's flow regimen. Accordingly, flow-augmentation costs would have to be determined in light of the fact that this alternative is often complementary with navigation (for example) but at least partly competitive with irrigation, flood damage reduction, power, and recreation. Any net benefits associated with other uses foregone in using flow augmentation to improve water quality in the optimum system are counted among the costs associated with quality improvement through flow augmentation. Moreover, the firm would consider the full marginal costs of producing particular products including those costs which are imposed on other activities by waste disposal.

If markets adequately registered the population's evaluation of all goods and services bought and sold by the hypothetical firm, its solution to the waste disposal problem would be "efficient," as we have come to understand that term.

Note that all consumer demands for the services of water in the basin must be reflected in the firm's decision on how the water should be used, including direct demands for water services, as for recreation, sewage removal, household consumption, and the direct demands that come to be expressed through the demand for the products whose manufacture or transport may make use of the water services of the basin in some way.

While we have made many extreme assumptions in developing this example and certainly do not propose establishing basin-wide firms, some important points have been illustrated.

First, the example makes it clear that public policies which explicitly recognize water quality management as a problem of optimizing an interdependent system in a region will result in consideration of many alternative control measures. Accordingly, implementation of such policies is more likely to approach a least-cost system than if narrowly circumscribed conventional approaches are adopted. Our discussion in the next chapter will show that taking the more comprehensive and flexible approach can result in large cost savings.

Second, the example reveals that implementing the regional approach requires the planning, design, and integrated operation of many interdependent elements in the system. Our illustrative firm found it in its selfish interest to "internalize" all these elements and under our assumptions found their optimum planning and operation in its interest as a matter of seeking maximum profit.

No water management agency will or should internalize all the relevant elements of the system. The degree to which they are internalized may vary. The agency may itself plan, design, and operate only clearly collective measures, for example, reservoirs and reaeration devices, and use direct controls or incentives (charges) to articulate these with the rest of the relevant economic system. In other instances, a regional agency may find it serves efficiency to go much further. For example, a regional agency might plan, design, and operate virtually all water-related facilities in a region including water and waste water treatment plants. Even in this case it would still have to devise means to appropriately influence industrial process design and plant location.

9.3 EFFLUENT CHARGES AND COLLECTIVE MEASURES FOR WATER QUALITY MANAGEMENT

Fortunately, devising an appropriate effluent charges policy for an agency which incorporates economically desirable collective measures in its system requires no new principles whatsoever. The ideal charge still will be equal to the marginal external cost imposed. The residual external marginal cost imposed by waste discharge, when control at relevant points of waste discharge is induced to an optimal level by effluent charges, is the measure of the marginal benefit of the collective quality improvement facility—say, a flow-regulating reservoir. In other words, it measures the reduction in overall system cost (and therefore the benefit produced) when collective measures are introduced which improve water quality marginally.

Let us assume (unrealistically) that the agency creates the entire assimilative capacity of the river by producing a flow of water. Assume further that this flow can be produced at a constant average and marginal cost. Finally, assume that increases in assimilative capacity can be produced efficiently in small increments. If it acted efficiently, the agency would increase assimilative capacity in such a way that the marginal cost of the last increment in capacity to control the effect of a waste would be equal to the effluent charge on that waste, which in turn is equal to the marginal cost of waste control at outfalls. In this instance the proceeds from the effluent charge reflecting the marginal external cost would be exactly sufficient to cover the total cost of producing the assimilative capacity.

Given the same situation except that we now assume that the marginal cost of further increments of capacity is rising, the relationship between the yield from charges and total cost of the investment is different. In this case the effluent charge payments will exceed the amount necessary to pay the total cost of the investment when optimum capacity is attained. Conversely, if the marginal cost of expanded assimilative capacity declines over the relevant range, the proceeds from the charge would be insufficient to cover the cost of the capacity expansion. This is true even though it reduced the overall costs associated with the regional waste disposal system.* If the regional agency implements measures which do not augment assimilative capacity but rather reduce waste loads (like collective treatment) it should follow the equal marginal cost rule in making its decisions and charge the waste disposers whom it is serving the marginal treatment cost (which equals the marginal external cost) of handling the particular kind of waste involved.

We assumed above that the regional authority created all of the assimilative capacity of the stream. This assumption makes for a theoretically neat outcome but is unrealistic. There is always some natural waste assimilative capacity available in a stream. This in no way affects the appropriate criterion for the agency's investment decisions, i.e., the equal marginal cost rule, but it does affect the financial results. When the agency levies a charge reflecting marginal external costs in the presence of natural assimilative capacity, part of the payment made is a "pure rent" on the scarcity value of the natural capacity. As we have indicated earlier, this is analogous to a charge levied on the use of public lands (a grazing fee, for example). Accordingly, when natural assimilative capacity exists, the proceeds from the charge will be more than sufficient to pay for an

---

* See the Appendix by Boyd in Kneese and Bower, *op. cit.*

economically justified augmentation of assimilative capacity produced under constant cost conditions.

Depending on how much naturally occurring assimilative capacity was initially available, it might take rather sharply decreasing costs in the provision of collective facilities for the agency to incur a deficit if it implemented only economically justifiable facilities and levied charges equal to the marginal external cost.

The above discussion has assumed that collective facilities can be expanded more or less continuously. Since some of them, such as reservoirs, involve substantial indivisibilities, this is not very realistic for small systems. But the principles are the same even when durable and lumpy investments are made. Of course it will be necessary to make long-run projections with their attendant uncertainties. Other measures such as mechanical reaeration can be expanded more or less continuously. Ground water recharge operations represent an intermediate situation. Moreover, as a system becomes larger and more diverse, even absolutely large additions become small relative to the total system and can be implemented on the basis of comparatively short-run considerations.

9.4   UNMEASURED VALUES: CONSTRAINTS ON THE OBJECTIVE

The policies so far described would in essence produce the system of water quality management facilities achieved by a competitive firm* so situated and integrated as to "internalize" the pollution-caused "externalities." If there were no problems in the manner in which the market registers water quality values, this solution would be quite consistent with the general rationale of a market system.

However, public bodies can and should take account of those aspects of water quality for which market evaluations do not presently exist, cannot be imputed, or cannot be accepted. These may include matters such as general aesthetic effects, public health, and perhaps others. So long as acceptable methodologies for measurement are not available, we may term these "unmeasured values." In general, we mean by this term values related to water quality which are widely thought to exist but for which we have no quantitative monetary estimates. Although, as we have previously seen, much encouraging progress has been made in the measurement of values formerly thought of as unmeasurable, we still face a situation in which we cannot rely on having estimates of all relevant values as a routine matter.

Two ways of handling unmeasured values come to mind. One way would be to label them "intangible" and disregard them in planning and designing water quality management systems. We have already seen in Chapter 6 that for a

---

* Or one regulated by a public authority on the basis of criteria which would produce competitive market results.

long time the federal water resource agencies handled them this way. Then, when the proposed system designs are actually to be considered for authorization by representatives of the public, side information could be provided on aesthetic effects, public health, and other matters considered relevant to arriving at a decision in the public interest.

The second approach is to include hypotheses about such values in the process of system planning by expressing them in physical terms and treating them as constraints upon the objective.* For example, if social choice should dictate that the oxygen level in a stream must at all times be high enough to support fish life, the system must be planned to minimize the real cost associated with waste disposal subject to the constraint, or "minimum standard," that DO is to be kept at a specified level. This may require a different combination of units with different operating procedures than a system planned without the standard or constraint. Presuming the constraint is effective and not automatically achieved if measurable costs (including damage costs) are minimized, it will increase the cost of the system, with the extra cost representing the limitation which the constraint places upon the objective.

To be consistent with efforts to achieve maximum welfare, the planning process should consider constraints "provisional" and view them as matters for research and study in order to discover how well they represent the preferences of society. One way of studying them from this point of view is to test their cost sensitivity. By varying a constraint by small amounts, redetermining the optimum system, and relating the change in costs to the associated physical changes (i.e., effects on oxygen levels, appearance, aquatic life, etc,. in specific stretches of stream), information can be provided which will permit considered choices to be made by political representatives.

One useful way of stating the results of experiments with the constraints that are not valued directly by, or imputable from, the market is in terms of what they must "at least be worth." For example, a social judgment may be made that DO is to be maintained beyond the point indicated by the cost-minimizing solution in order to preserve or enhance a recreational fishery. A comparison of the otherwise optimized system with and without the constraint will not establish precisely what the avoided destruction of fishing pleasure is worth, but it will indicate the *least* value that must be attached to it if the level of control procedures is to be worthwhile. Or the additional cost of a higher level of certainty of achieving the desired DO level can be estimated. If constraints are imposed representing goals not directly commensurable with the values stated in monetary terms in the objective function, marginal conditions analogous to those indicated earlier must still hold if the cost-minimization objective is to be fulfilled. The optimum system is not attained until a situation is reached in which it is impossible to make incremental "tradeoffs" between alternatives that will lower costs without violating the constraint.

---

* Recall our discussion in Chapter 6 of the two ways in which constraints on the objective function can be regarded. Here we do not regard them as representing *in principle* incommensurable values.

The planning of efficient systems and experimentation with the constraints require large amounts of data and extensive knowledge of physical and economic relationships. Rapid and flexible computational techniques for estimating the physical characteristics and patterns of water quality and for carrying out the actual minimization (maximization) procedure are essential. In the following chapter we will comment on some of these and discuss some results.

Once a combination of system elements has been decided upon, it will be needed to induce optimum waste reduction at individual outfalls. The charge used to do this must be just high enough to achieve the standard, and it must not be possible to expand the large-scale measures at an incremental cost less than the increment alcost which can be avoided at the individual outfalls. If several wastes are involved, the expected value of all incremental costs avoided by an expansion in the large-scale measures must be added together and compared with the cost of expanding the measure.

We may generalize by saying that once a constraint is established by a duly constituted, well-informed political decision-making process, it may be viewed as representing a damage function which has a perfectly inelastic segment at the specified quality level and degree of certainty. When this view is taken, the analysis with respect to appropriate levels of effluent charges and investment criteria presented in earlier sections holds exactly.

Once more we must return to the question of the information needed to implement the procedure we have outlined. As already indicated the need is extensive. The specific character of the information required to make reasonably dependable analyses of systems, including cost sensitivity analysis of constraints, in complex river basins will become clearer when we consider a few applications in the next chapter.

CHAPTER 10

Applications

Regional water quality management systems that incorporate something like the full range of efficient alternatives are still in the planning stage in the United States, although collective regional-scale measures for water quality improvement have been instituted in a few cases by local, state, private, and/or federal agencies. More systematic planning for regional water quality management is evolving, however, and progressively more comprehensive and sophisticated planning approaches are being taken.

The study of the Delaware Estuary, which is the main one we review in this chapter, illustrates the progress which has been made in analytical techniques and in the incorporation of economic reasoning into the planning process. As always the application of operational analytical models requires some drastic simplifications often including working with relationships assumed to be linear and treating stochastic elements as though they were deterministic. In the final part of the chapter we will report briefly on a study which explicitly incorporated some stochastic elements. The reader should relate this material to the "production function revisited" discussion in Chapter 7.

10.1 THE DELAWARE ESTUARY STUDY

The Delaware River Basin, though small by American standards and draining an area of only 12,765 square miles, has a population of over six million persons. Portions of the basin, especially the Lehigh sub-basin and the Delaware estuary

334

area, are among the most highly industrialized and densely populated regions in the world, and it is in these areas that the main water quality problems are encountered. The Delaware estuary, an 86-mile reach of the Delaware River from Trenton, New Jersey, to Liston Point, Delaware (see the map in Figure 10-1), is most important in terms of the quantity of water affected, the area involved, the extent of industrial activity, and the number of people affected.

Despite early industrial and municipal development in the basin, very little was done to deal with water quality problems until the last few decades. The Interstate Commission on the Delaware River Basin (INCODEL) was formed in 1936, and under its auspices the states in the basin signed a reciprocal agreement on water quality control. This provided the legal basis for construction of treatment plants by municipalities after World War II. The standards of treatment achieved were not particularly high (on the average not much more than removal of the grosser solids), and the residual waste load from the plants, together with industrial discharges, continued to place heavy oxygen demands on the estuary. Especially during the warm summer months DO falls to low levels or becomes exhausted in a few portions of the reach of the estuary from Philadelphia to the Pennsylvania-Delaware state line.

Features of the Study

In 1957–58, at the request of the Corps of Engineers, the U.S. Public Health Service made a preliminary study of water quality in the Delaware estuary. The data it produced regarding the quality of the estuary led state and interstate agencies concerned with water quality to request a comprehensive study of the estuary under the provisions of the Federal Water Pollution Control Act. The study was begun in 1961 by the Water Supply and Pollution Control Division of the Public Health Service, and in the summer of 1966 a report was issued by the Federal Water Pollution Control Administration (*Delaware Estuary Comprehensive Study: Preliminary Report and Findings*).

The study provides an excellent opportunity to illustrate points developed theoretically earlier.

a. It is of considerable theoretical and methodological interest because an economic optimization model was an inherent part of it.

b. It provides some insights into the possibilities for large-scale collective measures in a regional system for water quality management. However, the limited consideration given to alternatives to conventional treatment at individual points of waste discharge is a weak part in an otherwise strong report. Several possibilities were noted, but they were not analyzed in the detail that study of treatment possibilities was.

c. It is a good illustration of how cost-sensitivity analysis can be applied to alternative physical goals.

d. The study provided the basic data for an analysis of effluent charges as a means to induce an efficient pattern of waste reduction.

Among the notable contributions of the estuary study was the development and application of a rigorous mathematical representation of the causal relationships defining the waste assimilative and transport characteristics of the estuary. The model permits estimating the effects of increases or decreases in the waste load discharged in a particular section on all other sections throughout the estuary area. A model of this character is an essential element in a systematic analysis for regional water quality management, whether or not an estuary is involved. This model, which characterizes physical, biological, and chemical relationships in the estuary, was tied to an economic optimization (linear programming) model. This permitted the identification of cost-minimizing solutions which could then be compared with other solutions more consistent with conventional administrative modes of water quality control.

It is not consistent with the objectives of this book to present a full discussion of the water quality model of the estuary area but we will try to give a feel for it and show how it was linked to a linear programming cost-minimization model.*

The Model

The Delaware Estuary was divided into 30 reaches and the Streeter oxygen balance equations† were adapted and applied to these interconnected segments. This led to a system of linear first-order differential equations. The transfer functions which depict the change in DO in segment i due to an input of waste in segment j fortunately simplify to a set of ordinary linear relationships if steady state conditions are assumed, i.e., the discharge rate is constant and temperature and river flow are taken as parameters. In fact, the transfer relationships can be represented by an ordinary matrix of a_{ij} coefficients such as we have encountered several times before.‡

This result is fortunate because it means these coefficients can be incorporated readily into a linear set of constraints which fit the linear programming format.

Assume that the watercourse consists of m homogeneous segments and c_i is the DO target in segment i. The target vector $\mathbf{c}$ of m elements can be obtained by changes of inputs to the water resource from combinations of the m segments. Define a program vector $\mathbf{x} = (x_j, x_1, \ldots, x_n)$ which generates DO improvements

---

* The discussion of the next several pages is based on Matthew J. Sobel, "Water Quality Improvement Programming Problems," *Water Resources Research*, Vol. 1, No. 4 (Fourth Quarter, 1965).

† Recall Chapter 8, "The Concept of External Costs."

‡ This result is explained by Sobel, *Ibid.*, as follows: "The transfer function for DO response in segment i due to an input of frequency ω in segment j is

$$\phi_{ij}(\omega) = a_{ij}(\omega) \exp z\theta_{ij}(\omega)$$

where $\theta_{ij}(\omega)$ is the phase shift, $a_{ij}(\omega)$ is the amplitude attenuation, and $z = \sqrt{-1}$. It can be shown that $\theta_{ij}(\omega)$ is an arctangent function whose value $\to 0$ as $\omega \to 0$; as $\omega \to 0$, $\phi_{ij} \to a_{ij}(0)$; $a_{ij} \equiv a_{ij}(0)$ is the DO response in segment i per unit of steady-state input in segment j." Sobel attributes the development of this result to V. V. Solodovnikov, *Introduction to the Statistical Dynamics of Automatic Control Systems* (New York: Dover Publications, 1960).

through the mechanism of the constant coefficients of the linear system already described—a_{ij} = DO improvement in segment i per unit of x_j; $i = 1, \ldots, m$; $j = 1, \ldots, n$; and, of course, $x_j > 0$.

If we let A be the (m by n) matrix of a_{ij} coefficients then $A\mathbf{x}$ is the vector of DO changes corresponding to $\mathbf{x}$.

Now recalling that $\mathbf{c}$ is the vector of target improvements we have two restrictions on $\mathbf{x}$, namely, $A\mathbf{x} \geq \mathbf{c}$ and $x \geq 0$. The reader will have noticed that mathematically these are sets of linear constraints such as those found in a standard linear program. All we need is an objective function to complete the problem.* Let $\mathbf{d}$ be a row vector where d_j = unit cost of x_j, $j = 1, \ldots, n$. Notice that this assumes linear cost functions. We have already seen that programs with linear constraints and non-linear objective functions can usually be solved if the non-linear function is not too complicated. So this condition would not necessarily have to hold. Anyway, now we can write the problem as a standard linear program,

$$\min \mathbf{dx}$$
$$\text{s.t.} \quad A\mathbf{x} \geq 0$$
$$\mathbf{x} \geq 0$$

The actual programs needed to solve the problem encountered in the Delaware estuary were somewhat more complicated. The reader interested in the details should consult the paper by Sobel.† Here we merely wanted to give a feeling for how the problem was set up as a linear program.

Of course, the transfer coefficients (a_{ij}) relate to a steady-state condition (specified conditions of stream flow and temperature). Thus the model turns out to be totally deterministic and the variability of conditions is handled by assuming extreme conditions usually associated with substantial declines in water quality. As we will see later, these assumptions can obscure economic problems of great significance.

Analysis of Objectives

The strategy of the Delaware study was to use the model to analyze the total and incremental costs of achieving five "objective sets," each representing a different package and spatial distribution of water quality characteristics, with the level of quality increasing from set 5 (representing 1964 water quality) to set 1. The water quality characteristics and associated levels and the areas to which they apply are shown for objective set 2 in Table 10-1. The 30 sections referred to in the table are shown on the map in Figure 10-1. An effort was then made to measure benefits associated with the improvement in water quality indicated by the successive objective sets. At the same time, limited analysis was made of collective measures which might substitute efficiently for waste treatment

---

* The linear programming technique is reviewed in Chapter 2.
† *Ibid.*

TABLE 10-1

WATER QUALITY GOALS FOR OBJECTIVE SET 2

Sections (column ranges): Trenton (1), Bristol, Torresdale, Philadelphia, Camden, Chester, Wilmington, New Castle, Liston Point (30)

Water quality parameter[a,b]	1	2	3	4	5	6	7	8	9	10	11	12	13	14	15	16	17	18	19	20	21	22	23	24	25	26	27	28	29	30
Dissolved oxygen[c]	5.5					5.5		4.0											4.8	5.0							5.0			6.5
DO 4/1–6/15 and 9/16–12/31	6.5																													6.5
Chlorides[d]													50		250															
Coliforms (no./100 ml.)	5,000[e]					5,000[e]			5,000[f]																					5,000[f]
Coliforms 5/30–9/15	4,000[e]			4,000[e]	5,000[e]	5,000[e]			5,000[f]																5,000[f]					4,000[e]
Turbidity (Tu)	N.L. + 30																										N.L. + 30			
Turbidity 5/30–9/15	N.L.		N.L.		N.L. + 30																			N.L. + 30			N.L.			
pH[g] (pH units)	6.5–8.5																												6.5–8.5	
pH[g] 5/30–9/15	7.0–8.5				6.5–8.5																			6.5–8.5					7.0–8.5	
Alkalinity[g]	20–50					20–50		20–120																						20–120

TABLE 10-1 (Cont.)

Parameter	1	2	3	4	5	6	7	8	9	10	11	12	13	14	15	16	17	18	19	20	21	22	23	24	25	26	27	28	29	30
Hardness[h]	95					95		150							150															
Temperature[g] (°F)	Present levels																										Present levels			
Phenols[h]	.001						.001	.005								.005	.01													.01
Syndets[h]	.5						.5	1.0																						1.0
Oil and grease, floating debris	Negligible																										Negligible			
Toxic substances	Negligible																										Negligible			
Section:	1	2	3	4	5	6	7	8	9	10	11	12	13	14	15	16	17	18	19	20	21	22	23	24	25	26	27	28	29	30

[a] mg/l unless specified.
[e] Maximum level.
[i] Average during period stated.

[b] Not less stringent than present levels.
[f] Monthly geometric mean
N.L. = Natural levels.

[c] Summer average.
[g] Desirable range.

[d] Maximum 15-day mean.
[h] Monthly mean.

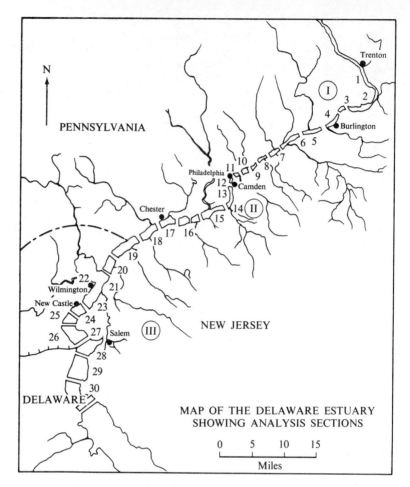

Source: FWPCA, Delaware Estuary Comprehensive Study.

FIGURE 10-1

over certain ranges. These included the dredging of bottom deposits that exert
an oxygen demand, reoxygenation of the estuary, and diversion of wastes from
the estuary.

Water Quality Objectives

Table 10-2 shows several water quality parameters with the associated levels for
the five objective sets. A few further comments about the objective sets may be
useful.

Objective Set 1. This is the highest objective set. It makes provision for large
increases in water-contact recreation in the estuary. It also makes special

TABLE 10-2

COMPARISON OF WATER QUALITY GOALS FOR OBJECTIVE SETS 1–5 (SET 5 REPRESENTS CONDITIONS IN 1964)

Water quality parameter	Set	1	2	3	4	5	6	7	8	9	10	11	12	13	14	15	16	17	18	19	20	21	22	23	24	25	26	27	28	29	30
Section:		Trenton		Bristol		Torresdale		Philadelphia		Camden								Chester			Wilmington			New Castle				Liston Point			
Dissolved oxygen mg/l summer average	1	6.5						6.5		5.5		4.5						4.5	5.5		5.5	6.5						6.5	7.5		7.5
	2	5.5						5.5	4.0										4.0		5.0							5.0		6.5	
	3	5.5						5.5	3.0												3.0	4.5							4.5		6.5
	4	4.0						4.0	2.5														2.5		3.5					5.5	
	5	7.0			5.1		5.8							1.0					1.0					4.2							7.1
Chlorides, mg/l max. 15-day mean	1																	50	250												
	2													50				250													
	3													50		250															
	4											50		250																	
	5							50			100	250		400				1,340				2,400									

TABLE 10-2 (Cont.)

Parameter	Set	1	2	3	4	5	6	7	8	9	10	11	12	13	14	15	16	17	18	19	20	21	22	23	24	25	26	27	28	29	30
Coliforms no./100 ml 5/30–9/15	1	4,000[a]							5,000[a]									5,000[a]						4,000[a]					4,000[a]		
	2		4,000[a]		4,000[a]		5,000[a]		5,000[b]											5,000[b]					5,000[b]						
	3			4,000[a]		5,000[b]																						5,000[b]			
	4	5,000[b]								5,000[b]	Present levels																				
m.g.m.[b] →	5		2,600		2,700		6,800		25,000					63,000			66,000		51,000		22,000		7,000				1,900			700	
Turbidity turbidity units 5/30–9/15	1	N.L.							N.L. + 30											N.L.					N.L.						
	2		N.L.			N.L. + 30														N.L. + 30						N.L.				N.L.	
	3			N.L.			N.L. + 30																		N.L. + 30			N.L.			
	4	N.L. + 30																		N.L. + 30								N.L.			
Maximum level →	5		23		28		29		24					22			24		27		27		37				43			43	
pH, pH units desirable range 5/30–9/15	1	7.0–8.5					6.5–8.5													6.5–8.5											
	2		7.0–8.5			6.5–8.5																			6.5–8.5						
	3			7.0–8.5			6.5–8.5																					6.5–8.5			
	4	6.5–8.5									Present levels									Present levels					6.5–8.5						
Present range →	5	7.0–8.7					6.9–7.6							6.6–7.3					6.4–7.0						5.6–7.6					6.1–7.8	

TABLE 10-2 (Cont.)

Parameter	Set	1	2	3	4	5	6	7	8	9	10	11	12	13	14	15	16	17	18	19	20	21	22	23	24	25	26	27	28	29	30
Alkalinity, mg/l desirable range	1					20–50			20–120																				20–120		
	2					20–50			20–120																	20–120					
	3					20–50			20–120																				20–120		
	4					20–50			Present levels																		Present levels				
Present range→	5	25–51					33–46								34–50				13–41						4–25				10–49		
Hardness, mg/l monthly mean	1	95					95		150									150													
	2	95					95		150								150														
	3	95					95		150								150														
	4	95					95		150					150																	
	5	83									122									467											
Phenols, mg/l monthly mean	1	.001																	.001	.01											.01
	2	.001					.001		.005							.005	.01														.01
	3	.001					.001		.005							.005	.01														.01
	4	.005												.005	.01																
	5	.01		.02		.03			.04					.03		.05		.05			.06										

a Maximum level. b Monthly geometric mean. N.L. = Natural levels.

provision for 6.5 ppm levels of dissolved oxygen to provide safe passage for anadromous migratory fish during the spring and fall migration periods. Thus this objective set should produce conditions in which water quality is basically no obstacle to the migration of shad and other anadromous fishes.

Objective Set 2. Under this objective set the area available for water-contact recreation is constricted. Some reduction in sport and commerical fishing would also be expected because of the lower dissolved oxygen objective. This set, like objective set 1, makes special provision for high dissolved oxygen during periods of anadromous fish passage.

Objective Set 3. This set is similar to set 2. Although there is no specific provision for raising dissolved oxygen during periods of anadromous fish migrations, there is comparatively little difference in the survival probability under objective sets 2 and 3. Under the waste-loading conditions envisioned for objective set 3, the estimated survival twenty-four out of twenty-five years would be at least 80 percent—compared with 90 percent for set 2.

Objective Set 4. This provides for a slight increase over 1964 levels in water-contact recreation and fishing in the lower sections of the portion of the estuary studies. Generally, water quality is improved slightly over 1964 conditions and the probability of anaerobic conditions occurring is greatly reduced.

Objective Set 5. This would maintain 1964 conditions in the estuary. It would provide for no more than a prevention of further water quality deterioration.

Costs of Alternative Programs

The costs of achieving objective sets 1 through 4 by various combinations of treatment and other measures for the waste-load conditions expected to prevail in 1975–80 are shown in Table 10-3.

Benefits from Improved Water Quality

The Delaware Estuary Comprehensive Study pioneered by broadening the range of benefits considered in the water quality planning process and by introducing quantitative estimates of recreation benefits into the process. While the benefit figures were necessarily rather rough, they appear to be sufficiently accurate to comprise a general guide to the decision-making process.

Three general categories of recreation benefits were considered: (1) swimming, (2) boating, (3) sport fishing. Analyses conducted at the University of Pennsylvania, and based on a highly simplified model of recreation participation, indicated a large latent recreation demand in the estuary region. Another study, separately sponsored, tended to confirm the order of magnitude of the estimates.*

---

* Paul Davidson, F. Gerard Adams, and Joseph Seneca, "The Social Value of Water Recreational Facilities Resulting from an Improvement in Water Quality: The Delaware Estuary," in Allen V. Kneese and Stephen C. Smith (ed.), *Water Research* (The Johns Hopkins Press for RFF, 1966).

TABLE 10-3

SUMMARY OF TOTAL COSTS OF ACHIEVING OBJECTIVE SETS 1, 2, 3, AND 4
(COSTS INCLUDE COST OF MAINTAINING PRESENT (1964) CONDITIONS AND
REFLECT WASTE-LOAD CONDITIONS PROJECTED FOR 1975–80.)
FLOW AT TRENTON = 3,000 CFS

(million 1968 dollars)

Objec-tive set	Uniform treatment			Zoned treatment			Cost minimization		
	Capital costs	O&M costs[a]	Total costs	Capital costs	O&M costs[a]	Total costs	Capital costs	O&M costs[a]	Total costs
1	180	280 (19.0)	460[b]	180	280 (19.0)	460[b]	180	280 (19.0)	460[b]
2	135	180 (12.0)	315[c]	105	145 (10.0)	250[c]	115	100 (7.0)	215[c]
3	75	80 (5.5)	155[c]	50	70 (4.5)	120[c]	50	35 (2.5)	85[c]
4	55	75 (5.0)	130	40	40 (2.5)	80	40	25 (1.5)	65

[a] Operation and maintenance costs, discounted at 3 percent, twenty-year-time horizon; figures in parentheses are equivalent annual operation and maintenance costs in millions of dollars/year.

[b] High-rate secondary to tertiary (92–98 percent removal) for all waste sources for all programs. Includes in-stream aeration cost of $20 million.

[c] Includes $1–$2 million for either sludge removal or aeration to meet goals in river sections nos. 3 and 4.

In computing the monetary values associated with recreation demand under each objective set, a number of factors were considered, including recreation-bearing capacity of the estuary as influenced by improved quality. A range of benefits was calculated by the application of alternative monetary unit values to the total use projected for the estuary. The analyses indicated that the increase in direct quantifiable recreation benefits for set 1 would range between $160 million and $350 million, for set 2 between $140 million and $320 million, for set 3 between $130 million and $310 million, and for set 4 between $120 million and $280 million. Since municipal and industrial benefits were deemed to be small and to some extent cancelled by negative features in regard to industrial water use, these ranges were taken to be rough estimates of the total benefits from improved water quality in the estuary.

A comparison of the recreation benefits with the cost estimates (Table 10-4) shows that objective set 4 appears to be justified, even when the lowest estimate of benefit is compared with the highest estimate of cost. The incremental costs of going from set 4 to set 3 suggests that set 3 is marginally justifiable. On the assumption that some of the more widely distributed benefits of water quality

TABLE 10-4

COSTS AND BENEFITS OF WATER QUALITY IMPROVEMENT
IN THE DELAWARE ESTUARY AREA[a]

(million dollars)

Objective set	Estimated total cost	Estimated recreation benefits	Estimated incremental cost		Estimated incremental benefits	
			minimum[b]	maximum[c]	minimum[b]	maximum[c]
1	460	160–350				
			245	145	20	30
2	215–315	140–320				
			130	160	10	10
3	85–155	130–310				
			20	25	10	30
4	65–130	120–280				

[a] All costs and benefits are present values calculated with 3 percent discount rate and twenty-year time horizon.
[b] Difference between adjacent minima.
[c] Difference between adjacent maxima.

improvement may not have been appropriately taken into account, it can probably be justified. Clearly, however, the incremental benefits of going to sets 2 or 1 are vastly outweighed by the incremental costs.

Collective Measures for Water Quality Improvement

Some attention was given to the possibility of achieving improved water quality by means of collective measures such as dredging the estuary to reduce benthal oxygen demand, collecting wastes for treatment in regional treatment plants, diverting wastes from critical reaches of the estuary to Delaware Bay or to the Atlantic Ocean, and providing mechanical reoxygenation of the estuary. Some of these measures looked promising on the basis of preliminary reconnaissance, but they received little emphasis in the study. For example, it appeared that even the great cost of collecting certain industrial wastes and piping them from the estuary to the Atlantic Ocean would reduce the overall costs of achieving at least the higher objective sets, but this result is not stated in the report proper.

Rough estimates of the total cost of reaching various DO objectives by mechanical reoxygenation produced perhaps the most spectacular results. These are shown below, the costs being present values calculated with 3 percent discount rate and twenty-year time horizon:

Objective Set	Cost (millions)
1	$70
2	$40
3	$12
4	$10

The DO conditions of objective set 2—namely, 4 ppm of dissolved oxygen in the critical reaches during the summer and 6.5 ppm during anadromous fish passage—could be reached through reoxygenation at not much greater cost than simply maintaining present conditions with even the least-cost waste treatment alternative. However, as reoxygenation would meet only the DO objective, and the additional costs of meeting other water quality objectives were not presented, it is impossible to tell how reoxygenation might enter into the efficient achievement of the various objective sets.

It is unfortunate that these collective measures were not adequately explored. Enough was done, however, to suggest that such measures should enter into a strategy for dealing with the water quality problems of the estuary. The study of the Potomac, part of which is discussed below, was much more adequate in its consideration of the range of technological alternatives.

Effluent Charges on the Delaware Estuary

Following the planning study described in the previous sections, another study of particular interest to economists was done using the same models and data. This was a study of the possible use of effluent taxes or charges as an economic incentive for controlling waste discharge. It is of particular interest because of the economists' traditional view that external diseconomies should be taxed. The study was done in connection with the work of a special interdepartmental committee on water quality control headed by Gardner Ackley, at the time Chairman of the President's Council of Economic Advisers. The written reports were prepared by the Federal Water Pollution Control Administration headquarters staff, primarily by Edwin Johnson.*

Assuming that direct controls would be effective and that waste dischargers would respond rationally to economic incentives, the study analyzed four programs for achieving alternative dissolved oxygen objectives in the estuary.

The first, and in a sense a standard of comparison for the others, is the least-cost linear programming solution (LC). This solution uses the mathematical programming technique described earlier to obtain the minimum cost distribution of waste removals. To implement this program as a control policy would

---

* See *Report on the Effluent Charge Study*, Mimeo 1966, Federal Water Pollution Control Administration and Edwin Johnson, "A Study in the Economics of Water Quality Management," *Water Resources Research*, Vol. 3, No. 2 (Second Quarter, 1967). An excellent discussion of the effluent charges study is also found in Grant W. Schaumberg, Jr., *Water Pollution Control in the Delaware Estuary*, Harvard Water Program, May 1967, mimeo.

require precise information on waste treatment costs at all outfalls and direct controls on all waste discharges. It would result in radically different levels of treatment and treatment costs at different outfalls. The reason is simply that it would concentrate treatment at those points where the critical oxygen sag can be reduced most inexpensively.

The second is the Uniform Treatment Solution (UT). In this solution each waste discharger is required to remove a given percentage of the wastes previously discharged before discharging the remainder to the stream. The percentage is the minimum needed to achieve the DO standard in the stream and is the same at each point of discharge. This solution may be considered typical of the conventional administrative effluent standards approach to the problem of achieving a stream quality standard.

The third is the Single Effluent Charge Solution (SECH). This solution involves charging each waste discharger in the estuary the same price per unit of waste discharge. The solution examines responses of individual waste discharger and identifies the minimum single charge which will induce sufficient reduction in waste discharge to achieve the standard.

The fourth is the Zone Effluent Charge Solution (ZECH), which uses a uniform effluent charge in each zone instead of a uniform charge over all reaches of the estuary. In Figure 10-1 the zones are designated by Roman numerals.

In none of these cases is there an explicit measurement of damages resulting from water quality degradation. Rather, the stream standard is used as a surrogate which may be viewed as a perfectly inelastic damage function. The problem then becomes one of meeting efficiency (least-cost) and equity (cost-distribution) criteria.

Before turning to a discussion of specific results in relation to the first criterion, we will state the general conclusions which the FWPCA staff drew from this study.

a. Effluent charges should be seriously considered as a method for attaining water quality improvement;

b. Costs of waste treatment induced by a charge level will approach the least costly treatment;

c. A charge level of 8 to 10 cents per pound of oxygen demand material discharged appears to produce relatively large increases in critical dissolved oxygen levels;

d. Major regional economic readjustments from a charge of that level are not anticipated to occur in the study area;*

---

* In all but a few cases the total cost (cost of treatment plus effluent charge) was less than 1 percent of the value of output. In most cases it was a small fraction of 1 percent. See Johnson, *op. cit.*, Table 8. Another study shows roughly similar results with costs of waste treatment averaging approximately 1 percent of *value added* in several industries. David F. Bramhall and Edwin S. Mills, *Future Water Supply and Demand* (Maryland State Planning Dept., April 1965).

e. Administrative costs and difficulties of managing an effluent charge method are greater than conventional methods of water quality improvement. However, the problems are not insurmountable and are not sufficiently great to negate the advantages of the charge method;

f. Compared to a conventional method of improving water quality, the charge method attains the same goal at lower costs of treatment, with a more equitable impact on waste dischargers. Also, the charge provides a continuing incentive on the discharger to reduce his wastes discharge and provides a guide to public investment decisions.

Efficiency Considerations

Table 10-5 indicates the economic costs associated with the program for two levels of water quality. The 3–4 ppm standard was considered the practical maximum attainable in the estuary by the FWPCA staff.

TABLE 10-5

COST OF TREATMENT UNDER ALTERNATIVE PROGRAMS

DO Objective (*ppm*)	Program			
	LC	UT	SECH	ZECH
	(*million dollars per year*)			
2	1.6	5.0	2.4	2.4
3–4	7.0	20.0	12.0	8.6

The analysis indicates that the effluent charges system would produce the specified quality levels at about one-half the cost of the uniform treatment method. Especially at the higher quality level, the cost-saving is of a highly significant magnitude. The present value of the cost stream saved is on the order of $150,000,000.

The least-cost system is capable of reducing costs somewhat further since it programs waste discharges at each point specifically in relation to the cost of improving quality in the critical reach, but this comes at the cost of detailed information on treatment costs at each point and a cost distribution such that very high costs would be incurred at some points of discharge and little or no cost at others. Many people would presumably regard this as inequitable. The least-cost system is closely approached by ZECH at the higher quality level. In effect, this procedure "credits" waste dischargers at locations remote from the critical point with degradation of their wastes in the intervening reach of a stream before they arrive at the critical reach.

This is a necessary condition for full efficiency when effluent charges are used to achieve a standard at a critical reach in a stream. The reason that the ZECH does not achieve quite the same efficiency as LC is that the "credit" is not specific to the individual waste discharger but is awarded the blocks—three in this case.

At an effluent charge of 8–10 cents per pound of BOD which the staff estimated would be needed for the zoned effluent charge program,* the funds (rent on the assimilative capacity of the stream) collected by the administrative agency would amount to about $7 million per year. Nevertheless, for the 3–4 ppm DO objective, the total cost to industry and municipalities as a whole—effluent charge plus cost of treatment—is about the same as the cost of treatment only under the uniform treatment program. About half of this outlay does not represent an actual resources cost but if deemed desirable could be redistributed back to waste dischargers on the basis of equity criteria, used for general government purposes, or devoted to collective measures for improving water quality.

An important efficiency advantage of the effluent charges programs as contrasted with the LC program is their relatively lesser demand for information and analytical refinement. A study of the type already performed for the Delaware Estuary could serve as the basis for an effluent charge scheme. An order of magnitude estimate of the required charge is provided and adjustments and refinements could be made if necessary as responses to the charge reveal themselves. Actually, since the costs do not take account of the possibility of process change, the proposed charge is probably too high and could be adjusted downward at a later point. Also, the charge provides a continuing incentive for the discharger to reduce his waste load by placing him under the continuing pressure of monetary penalties. He is induced to develop new technology and as it develops to implement it. As new technology develops, the effluent charge could be gradually reduced while the stream standard is maintained or the standard could be allowed to rise if this is deemed desirable. The direct control measures implicit in the LC program, on the other hand, as well as the effluent standard of the uniform treatment program, provide only a limited incentive to improved technology. Moreover, the minimum cost program would require not only detailed information about current cost levels at each individual outfall but also about changes in cost with changing technology in regard to industrial processes, product mix, treatment cost, etc.

A more subtle point with respect to comparing effluent charges and effluent standards (even efficient ones, from the limited cost minimization point of view) is that unless a price is charged for any residual damage imposing use of the common property resource, the relative prices of final and intermediate goods will not reflect full social costs and resource misallocation will occur. So while it could be possible to achieve the same quality of water with standards as with charges it would not usually be possible to obtain the same overall allocation of resources. An exception would occur when the optimal waste discharge is one that imposes no external costs at all. In that case whatever residual waste

---

* See Federal Water Pollution Control Administration mimeo, Table 6.

discharge would occur under an optimal standards system would impose no external costs and therefore no charge should be made for it.

10.2   STOCHASTIC ASPECTS—THE POTOMAC STUDY AGAIN

Our discussion of water quality management has been in purely deterministic terms. We could have modified this somewhat by couching it in terms of expected values. However, we have already seen in earlier chapters that the expected value is not necessarily the only moment of the distribution of costs and returns of interest to decision makers. Moreover, the concept of a standard is a more complex one than first meets the eye, once probability elements are admitted.

As we have seen, too, operational analytical models are incapable of handling stochastic elements in a sophisticated way. Thus, about the only way the time dependent and random elements can be explored at the present time is via simulation. The kinds of inputs demanded by simulation models have already been discussed in Chapter 7 and we will not repeat them here since they carry over straightforwardly to the economic analysis of water quality systems.

Application of simulation to water quality problems so far has been limited. But one aspect of Davis' study of the Potomac estuary* (portions of which have already been discussed in Chapter 6) is sufficient to show the possible importance of more systematic investigation of stochastic elements in water quality management. As we noted in our earlier discussion of the Potomac, where the primary emphasis was on the alternative cost technique of benefit evaluation, the design of the system proposed by the Corps of Engineers was based on a conventional water quality objective. It was that DO concentrations in the estuary would not fall below 4 ppm based on the 24-hour monthly mean for the minimum month. A standard kind of mass curve analysis was used to check that the yield of the proposed reservoirs system would be sufficient to meet the objective. As we saw before, this analysis makes the untenable assumption that future streamflow will be a replication of the past.†

To help illuminate the probability aspect of the standard, a stochastic hydrology was applied to the reservoir simulation program.‡

Table 10-6 presents some results on the implication of different probabilities of violating 2 and 4 ppm DO levels when different systems of reservoirs are operated to achieve DO targets. In this presentation the Corps assumption that low-flow regulation is the only means used to counteract the residual deficit, after about 90 percent treatment, is used. This is done to spell out clearly the implication for reservoir storage, even though in an optimized or least cost

---

* Davis, *op. cit.*
† See Chapter 7.
‡ See Chapter 7.

TABLE 10-6

PERCENT OF TIME MONTHLY MEAN DO IS LESS THAN 2.0 PPM FOR
500-YEAR TRIALS AT DIFFERENT DO TARGET AND SYSTEM CAPACITIES

Storage Capacity (acre feet)	DO Target	Pct. time < 2 ppm	Pct. time < target
82,000	2 ppm	.25	.25
140,000	2 ppm	.03	.03
600,000	4 ppm	.35	3.30
770,000	4 ppm	.22	1.03
970,000	4 ppm	.0	.33

system the incremental costs of achieving lower probabilities of violation would be less. It is interesting to note two main points emerging from this analysis.

(1) Reducing the probability of violating the 4 ppm objective from 3.30 percent to .33 percent costs about 370,000 acre-feet in storage and around 50 million in dollars. The .33 percent level is about equivalent to objective used in the Corps study.

(2) If a system is operated to avoid violation of a 2 ppm target, about the same low-level of violation of the 2 ppm level can be achieved with 82,000 A.F. of capacity as with 770,000 A.F. of capacity in a system operated to achieve a 4 ppm target. Thus what the level of the standard is meant to accomplish becomes a profoundly important question when reservoirs are used in a water quality management system. Put in another way, how much security concerning oxygen not falling to very low levels are we willing to sacrifice to keep it at higher levels more of the time? It is not necessarily true that a system operated to achieve high levels as much of the time as possible will provide greater security against extreme failure than a smaller system operated to achieve lower levels as much of the time as possible. In fact in the Potomac instance quite the opposite was true. Water was released for the higher objective and when it was exhausted the target was missed by large margins.

10.3   CONCLUSIONS

In the last half-decade or so, much has been done to apply economic concepts based on partial equilibrium analysis to problems of water quality management. These studies have been illuminating, but the time has come when we must try to reach out beyond these approaches into the much more difficult area of general equilibrium analysis. This effort will occupy us in the next chapter.

CHAPTER 11

Residuals and General Equilibrium:
Toward a "Spaceship" Economics

So far we have followed the traditional economics approach to questions of pollution. We have treated a particular environmental problem—like water pollution—in isolation, assuming that the rest of the economy is functioning ideally, or at least approximately so. A similar tendency is also evident in government institutions devised to control these problems and in professional work on them. Thus we have at the federal, state, and often at the municipal level independent units of government to deal with waterborne wastes, wastes discharged to the atmosphere, and solid wastes. Similarly, professional and research skills in the natural sciences and engineering tend to break down into the same categories. Although many reasons can be named for this balkanization, in some measure, at least, it results from failure to recognize the strong interdependencies which exist between the various waste streams and the control measures appropriate to them.*

Instead of using the usual air-water-solids characterization of environmental pollution, we will discuss it in this chapter in terms of the main sectors of the economy which present a residuals disposal or reuse problem. An attempt will be made to develop an economic theoretical structure for organizing thought about this problem.

---

* As this book was being written the federal government agencies and some state and local agencies were being reorganized to consolidate authority over the range of types of pollution problems. But the process was far from complete and how successful it would be remained to be seen.

Three main members belong to this theoretical structure. The first is the concept of mass conservation or materials balance drawn from physics and chemical engineering. The second is a general equilibrium model of the Walras–Cassel–Leontief type, and the third is what we have dubbed a partial-general model which retains many of the insights of the other two but is more detailed and realistic.

11.1   A MATERIALS BALANCE APPROACH

Environmental pollution and its control can from one perspective be viewed as a materials balance problem for the entire economy.* A highly simplified schematic diagram of how the goods and residuals production process works is indicated in Figure 11-1.

Finished goods in the schematic diagram can be either consumer goods, like food and automobiles, or intermediates in the productive process. The inputs to the system are fuels, foods, and raw materials; they are partly converted into finished goods and partly become non-marketable residuals. Except for increases in inventory and recycling, finished goods also ultimately enter the residuals stream. For the sake of simplicity, we begin our consideration of the materials flow after the basic fuel, food, and raw materials have been produced by mines, farms, forests, and wildlife areas, but before they enter into processing. This approach, however, does neglect some significant discharges of residual materials into the environment—for example, mine tailings, acid mine drainage, and salt water pumped up with crude oil.

In an economy which is closed (no imports or exports) and in which there is no net accumulation of stocks (plant, equipment, inventories, consumer durables, or residential buildings), the amount of residuals which is inserted into the natural environment must be approximately equal to the weight of basic fuels, food, and raw materials entering the processing and production system, plus oxygen taken from the atmosphere.† This result leads to the corollary that residuals disposal is an even larger operation than basic materials production.

Figure 11-2 shows a materials flow in detail and relates it to the various sectors of the economy. In an open economy (such as any city, state, or nation engaged in trade across its boundaries), it would be necessary to add flows representing imports and exports. Similarly, in any economy undergoing stock

---

* As far as we know, the idea of applying materials balance concepts to waste disposal problems was first expressed by Frank A. Smith in *The Economic Theory of Industrial Waste Production and Disposal* (draft of a doctoral dissertation, Department of Economics, Northwestern University).

† To simplify our language, we will not repeat this essential qualification at each opportunity, but assume it applies throughout the following discussion. In addition, we must include residuals such as oxides of nitrogen (NO_x) arising from reactions between components of the air itself but occurring as combustion by-products.

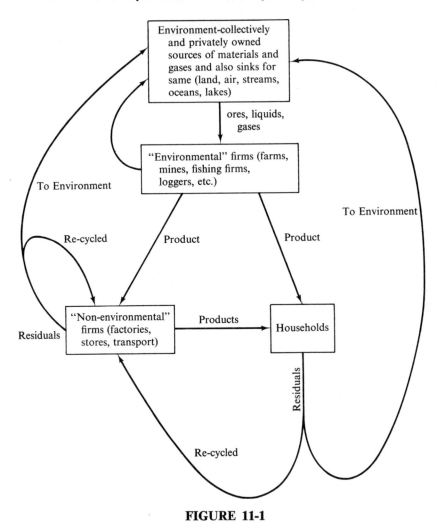

FIGURE 11-1

or capital accumulation, the production of residuals in any given year would be less by that amount than the basic inputs. In the United States, accumulation would account for about 10 to 15 percent of basic annual inputs, and there is some net importation of raw and partially processed materials—amounting to 4 or 5 percent of domestic production. Table 11-1 shows the weight of raw material produced in the United States in several recent years, plus net imports of raw and partially processed materials.

Of the "active" inputs,* perhaps three-quarters of the overall weight is

---

* Excluding stone, sand, gravel, and other minerals used for structural purposes, ballast, fillers, insulation, etc. We also disregard gangue and mine tailings in this tally.

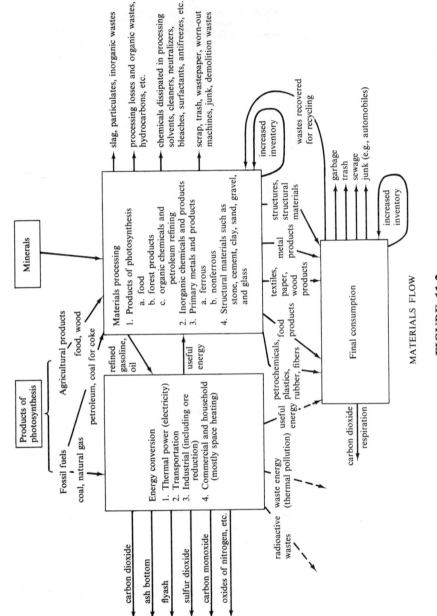

MATERIALS FLOW

FIGURE 11-2

TABLE 11-1

WEIGHT OF BASIC MATERIALS PRODUCTION IN THE UNITED STATES
PLUS NET IMPORTS, 1963–65

(10^6 tons)

Material	1963	1964	1965
Agricultural (incl. fishery and wildlife and forest) products:			
Food and fiber:			
Crops	350	358	364
Livestock and dairy	23	24	23.5
Fishery	2	2	2
Forestry products (85% dry weight basis):			
Sawlogs	107	116	120
Pulpwood	53	55	56
Other	41	41	42
Total	576	596	607.5
Mineral fuels	1,337	1,399	1,448
Other minerals:			
Iron ore	204	237	245
Other metal ores	161	171	191
Other nonmetals	125	133	149
Total	490	541	585
Grand total[a]	2,403	2,536	2,640.5

[a] Excluding construction materials, stone, sand, gravel, and other minerals used for structural purposes, ballast, fillers, insulation, etc. Gangue and mine tailings are also excluded from this total. These materials account for enormous tonnages but undergo essentially no chemical change. Hence, their use is more or less tantamount to physically moving them from one location to another. If this were to be included, there is no logical reason to exclude material shifted in highway cut and fill operations, harbor dredging, land-fill, plowing, and even silt moved by rivers. Since a line must be drawn somewhere, we chose to draw it as indicated above.

Source: A. V. Kneese, R. U. Ayres, and R. C. d'Arge, *Economics and the Environment: A Materials Balance Approach* (Resources for the Future, Inc., 1970; 2nd Printing, 1971), p. 10.

eventually discharged to the atmosphere as carbon [combined with atmospheric oxygen in the form of carbon monoxide (CO) or carbon dioxide (CO_2)] and hydrogen [combined with atmospheric oxygen as water (H_2O)] under current conditions. This results from combustion of fossil fuels and from animal respiration. Discharge of CO_2 can be considered harmless in the short run.

Large "sinks" (in the form of vegetation and large water bodies, mainly the oceans) re-absorb this gas, although there is some evidence of net accumulation of CO_2 in the atmosphere. Some experts believe that the latter is likely to increase greatly (as much as 50 percent) by the end of the twentieth century, possibly giving rise to significant—and probably adverse—weather changes.

The remaining residuals are either gases [like CO, nitrogen dioxide (NO_2), and sulfur dioxide (SO_2)—all potentially harmful even in the short run]; dry solids like rubbish and scrap; or wet solids like garbage, sewage, and industrial wastes suspended or dissolved in water. In a sense the solids are the irreducible limiting form of waste. By the application of appropriate equipment and energy, all undesirable substances can be removed from water and air streams*—but what is left must obviously be solid. From this viewpoint, a primary interdependence between the various residuals streams is clearly revealed. And it becomes clear that "treatment" does not reduce the amount of residuals the environment must absorb but only changes their form.

But solid residuals, or for that matter those that remain in a liquid or gaseous state, do not necessarily have to be discharged to the environment. In many instances, it is possible to recycle them economically back into the productive system. The materials balance view underlines the fact that the total materials throughput necessary to maintain a given level of production and consumption can decrease, up to a point, as the efficiency of utilization (e.g., recycling) increases. If recycling of a material is pushed too far, however, overall consumption of materials may increase. Similarly, the useful lifetime of goods is closely related to the net throughput of the system. The longer cars, buildings, machinery, and other durables last, the fewer new materials are required to compensate for depreciation or to sustain a given rate of capital accumulation.

Finally, the more efficient fuel combustion processes can be made (in the strict energy conversion sense), the fewer waste products will be left for the environment to receive for a given total energy production. Perfect utilization of carbonaceous fossil fuels would leave mainly water and carbon dioxide as residuals, while nuclear energy conversion leaves small but troublesome quantities of residuals.

11.2   SIGNIFICANCE FOR ECONOMICS

One may well ask what the significance of the materials flow and balance view is for the economics of natural resources use. Clearly, no economist would advocate conservation of materials or recycling for its own sake (although other professionals perhaps would).

To see the significance, we must step back and take a broad view of the resources production and allocation process. The function of allocating resources to alternative ends has traditionally been accomplished in our society

---

* Except CO_2 which, as noted above, may be harmful in the long run.

by private exchange. As we have already seen, modern welfare economics concludes that if (1) preference orderings of consumers and production functions of producers are independent and their shapes properly constrained, (2) consumers maximize utility subject to given income and price parameters, and (3) producers maximize profits subject to the price parameters, a set of prices exists such that no individual can be made better off without making some other individual worse off. For a given distribution of income, this is an efficient state. Given certain further assumptions concerning the structure of markets, this Pareto optimum can be achieved via a pricing mechanism and voluntary decentralized exchange.

However, as we first saw in Part III, this exchange process breaks down unless all (or reasonably all) desirable services yielded by material objects or people can be reduced to private ownership without monopolization. In the social economics of private production from natural resources, instances of such breakdown have been observed, analyzed, and policies devised to deal with them. In Chapter 4, for instance, the common property problems in fishing and petroleum were discussed.

Still, the situation in each instance was viewed as a "market failure" in a partial equilibrium sense. Again in our discussion of water quality we recognized the market failure resulting from the common property aspects of residuals discharge to watercourses (as well as from scale economies in control measures) and built our analysis around a partial equilibrium approach to managing the resulting externalities. But water pollution is one of a wider class of problems resulting from the disposal of residuals.

Air and water used to be the economist's favorite examples of "free goods" (goods so abundant that their marginal value to any user, or potential user, is zero). These media served the function of "infinite sinks" for most of the residuals which are, as the materials balance view so clearly shows, an inevitable accompaniment of production and consumption activities. Of course, for generations, isolated instances existed where local air or water masses became loaded with residuals. Thus we have many instances in the economics literature of references to "smoke nuisance from a factory chimney," etc. While economists have become much more sophisticated in their applied analysis of pollution problems, a tendency still exists to regard externalities as somewhat freakish anomalies.

Economic and population growth has shown that this characterization is stretching the bounds of credibility. Congestion phenomena abound (the common property of space) and environmental pollution has become painfully evident to most people.

What appears to be developing is a vast asymmetry in the adequacy of our property institutions (which, of course, underlie all private exchange) to handle resources allocation problems. On the one hand, in the production of basic natural resources commodities, property institutions serve well in most instances to lead production into highest productivity channels now and in the future. On the other hand, the flow of residuals back to the environment is heavily to media where property institutions can function only imperfectly if at all. Once these media become overloaded on a large scale, they are free goods no more but rather *natural resources* of ever-increasing value as economic development proceeds.*

To recapitulate the points of this and the previous sections briefly: (1) Technological external diseconomies resulting from discharge of residuals to the environment are not freakish anomalies in the processes of production and consumption but an inherent and normal part of them when the environmental media are no longer free goods. (2) These external diseconomies are quantitatively negligible in a low population or economically undeveloped setting, but they become progressively more important as the population rises and the level of output increases (i.e., as the natural reservoirs of dilution and assimilative capacity become exhausted). (3) At a certain stage they cannot be properly dealt with by considering environmental media, such as air and water, in isolation. (4) Isolated and ad hoc taxes and other restrictions are not sufficient for their optimum control, although they are essential elements in a more systematic and coherent program of environmental quality management.

In view of this it is important to develop not only improved measures of the external costs resulting from differing concentrations of residuals in the environment but also more systematic methods for projecting emissions of external cost producing residuals, technical and economic tradeoffs among them, and the effects of recycling on environmental quality. Economists are as yet poorly equipped with economic theory and analytical techniques appropriate to these matters. However, some first efforts in the direction of providing more general models for the analysis of environmental pollution problems have been made, and we will discuss them in the following sections.

11.3   THE NATIONAL I-O MODEL

Leontief has proposed an extension of the basic national open I-O model (see Chapter 2) which would permit forecasting of residuals emissions and of the effects of certain types of policy measures. The following exposition of his

---

* Frank Knight perhaps provides a key to why these elementary facts have played so small a role in economic theorizing and empirical research:

> The next heading to be mentioned ties up with the question of dimensions from another angle, and relates to the second main error mentioned earlier as connected with taking food and eating as the type of economic activity. The basic economic magnitude (value or utility) is service, not good. It is inherently a stream or flow in time. [F. H. Knight, *Risk, Uncertainty, and Profit* (Boston and New York, 1921)].

Almost all of standard economic theory is in reality concerned with services. Material objects are merely the vehicles which carry some of these services, and they are exchanged because of consumer preferences for the services associated with their use or because they can help to add value in the manufacturing process. Yet we persist in referring to the "final consumption" of goods as though material objects such as fuels, materials, and finished goods somehow disappeared into the void—a practice which was comparatively harmless so long as air and water were almost literally "free goods."

proposal is based on the mathematical appendix of Leontief's article in the *Review of Economics and Statistics*.* Although interpretation of the mathematics is straightforward, we shall describe the system in some detail because non-marketable residuals are handled somewhat differently from ordinary commodities.

The physical input-output balance with residuals included in the system is shown by the matrix equation in Table 11-2. We have m ordinary goods and $n - m$ residuals, making a total of n inputs and outputs.

Each of the A matrices is a matrix of input-output coefficients. For example:

a_{ij} is the amount of the ith ordinary input required per unit of the jth ordinary output (sub-matrix A_{11}).

a_{ik} is the amount of the ith ordinary input required to produce a unit of the kth pollutant reduction output (sub-matrix A_{12}).

a_{ki} is the amount of the kth residual resulting from producing a unit of the ith ordinary output (sub-matrix A_{21}).

a_{kl} is the amount of the kth residual produced as a result of a unit reduction in the lth pollutant (sub-matrix A_{22}).

To see what is involved in this system of equations, let us separate out one of them and write it in full. Assume we have three ordinary commodities and two residual reduction activities,† a total of five outputs, or "inputs," in all. Take, for example, the first equation (1), which is formed by multiplying each member of the first row of A* by the corresponding members of the X vector of industry outputs and adding these products together, thereby obtaining the first member, y_1, of the vector of final outputs, Y:

(1)
$$[1 - a_{12} \ -a_{13} \ -a_{14} \ -a_{15}] \begin{bmatrix} x_1 \\ x_2 \\ x_3 \\ x_4 \\ x_5 \end{bmatrix} = y_1$$

or, $x_1 - a_{12}x_2 - a_{13}x_3 - a_{14}x_4 - a_{15}x_5 = y_1$

Note that in the matrices of input-output coefficients we have regarded a_{ii} and a_{kk} as zero so that industry output is always net of its own output that *it* uses.

This equation simply says that the total output of the first commodity minus the amount used in the production of x_2, x_3, x_4, and x_5 is equal to the amount of the first commodity, y_1, going to final demanders. The last four terms account

---

* Wassily Leontief, "Environmental Repercussions of the Economic Structure: An Input-Output Approach," *Review of Economics and Statistics*, Vol. III (August 1970), pp. 262–71.

† We speak of pollution reduction activities rather than industries because in any application the pollutant reduction activities often will be a part of an ordinary industry. In some cases it may be desirable to account for these separately.

TABLE 11-2

PHYSICAL INPUT–OUTPUT BALANCE

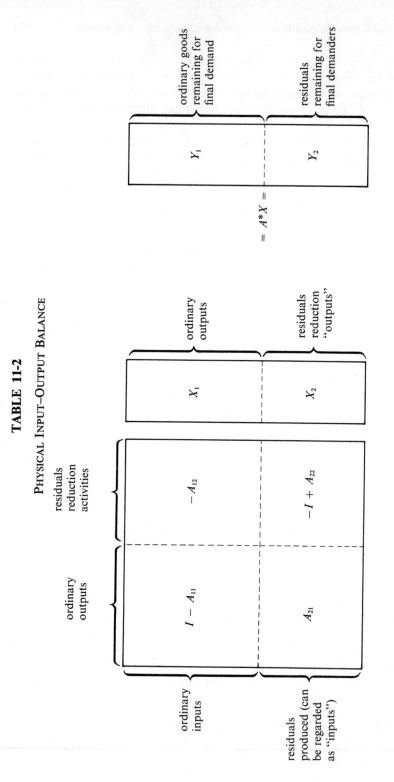

ordinary goods remaining for final demand

Y_1

residuals remaining for final demanders

Y_2

$= A^*X =$

residuals reduction activities

ordinary outputs

X_1

residuals reduction "outputs"

X_2

$-A_{12}$

$-I + A_{22}$

ordinary outputs

$I - A_{11}$

A_{21}

ordinary inputs

residuals produced (can be regarded as "inputs")

Commodities, or industries, are indexed as follows:

$$\underbrace{1, 2, \ldots, i, \ldots, j, \ldots, m}_{\text{ordinary goods}} \quad \underbrace{(m+1), \ldots, k, \ldots, l, \ldots, n}_{\text{residuals}}$$

for all of the x_1 used in production, whether for ordinary goods or residuals reduction.

Now consider an equation **(2)**, in the bottom part of the square matrix, **A***, say the last one for the nth commodity, which is a residual. Note that since the output of the residuals-processing industry is here measured as residuals reduction, the signs of the elements of the two lower quadrants are reversed from those of the two upper:

(2)
$$\begin{bmatrix} a_{51} a_{52} a_{53} a_{54} & -1 \end{bmatrix} \begin{bmatrix} x_1 \\ x_2 \\ x_3 \\ x_4 \\ x_5 \end{bmatrix} = y_5$$

or, $\qquad a_{51}x_1 + a_{52}x_2 + a_{53}x_3 + a_{54}x_4 - x_5 = y_5$

This says the residual which is commodity number five generated in the production of x_1, x_2, x_3, and x_4 *minus* the amount by which this residual is reduced equals the amount which goes to final demanders.

Thus in abbreviated matrix form, the physical input-output balance is $\mathbf{A^*X = Y}$, where $\mathbf{X}$ and $\mathbf{Y}$ are vectors of industry outputs and deliveries of final goods, respectively. Industry outputs include residuals reduction, and final goods include non-market residuals received.

The system of equations, $\mathbf{A^*X = Y}$, can be solved for the vector $\mathbf{X}$, industry outputs, by premultiplying each side by the inverse of the matrix, $\mathbf{A^{*-1}}$, obtaining $\mathbf{X = A^{*-1}Y}$. Thus if $\mathbf{A^{*-1}}$ has been calculated for a given industrial structure, the industry outputs, $\mathbf{X}$, that would be associated with any specified bill of final goods, $\mathbf{Y}$, can be calculated easily, given, of course, the peculiar assumptions of the input-output scheme as commonly formulated. The main one is that the input coefficients, the a's, are fixed no matter what the size of an industry's output. There is only one way to produce an output, a way which is completely described by one column of a coefficients. It is this assumption that facilitates calculation of economy-wide effects of certain policy changes or changes in final demands.

If the value added in the production of a unit of a commodity is known, this schema can be used to calculate the prices of the commodities that will rule under certain specified conditions. First we express the input-output balance between prices and values-added, as in equation **(3)** in Table 11-3. $\mathbf{P}$ is a vector of prices of outputs, partitioned into ordinary goods and residuals, as before, and $\mathbf{V}$ is a vector of values-added, partitioned in the same way. The square matrix is different, however, in that $\mathbf{A^*}$ has been transposed (its columns and rows have been interchanged so that, for example, element a_{ki} is now where element a_{ik} used to be).

In addition, the coefficients involving residuals generation [those in $\mathbf{A_{21}}$ and in $(-\mathbf{I} + \mathbf{A_{22}})$] have been modified. They have been reduced by a factor which reflects the proportion of residual generated by an industry the elimination of

TABLE 11-3

Input–Output Balance Between Prices and Values-Added

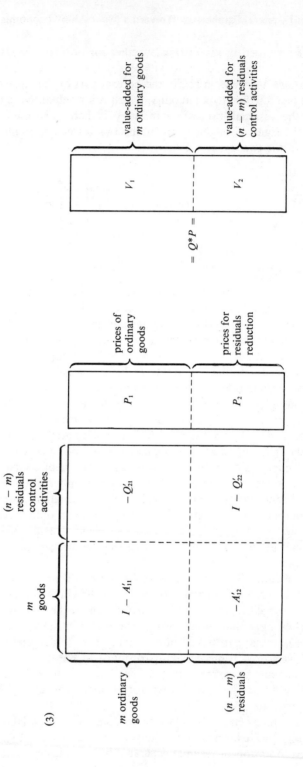

which is paid for by it. Thus if industry i generates a_{ki} residual per unit of output (a_{ki} is in A_{ki}) and pays for the elimination of 100 r_{ki} percent of it, we replace a_{ki} by $q_{ki} = r_{ki}a_{ki}$. A similar modification is made for residuals produced by the residual control industries—of the a_{kl} found in the quadrant $(-I + A_{22})$.

After these modifications, A_{21} becomes $-Q_{21}$ and $(-I + A_{22})$ becomes $(I - Q_{22})$. Note that signs are changed to have the price of the product minus the sum of required inputs times their prices be equal to value added for each industry.

In matrix form, the price-value added balance is expressed as $Q^*P = V$. As before, we can premultiply both sides by Q^{*-1} and in this way determine the prices that must rule for a given set of values-added *and* q's: $P = Q^{*-1}V$. Note that if each industry pays for the whole per unit cost of residuals eliminated that it has produced (i.e., if r_{ki} and r_{kl} equal one), then $Q_{21} = A_{21}$ and $Q_{22} = A_{22}$.

By using the relationships established in these equations, various interesting analyses can be performed. For example, calculations can now be made of changes in residuals resulting directly and indirectly from a change in final demand* or the net increase in production needed to achieve a specified reduction in residuals while holding final goods production constant. This analysis accounts not only for the resources needed by the residuals control sector but the resources used indirectly to control residuals from the supplying industries.

Equations (3) and those derived from it balance the system in value terms and admit the possibility of some residuals being controlled by the manufacturing industries themselves (but still in activities separable from their normal production process) rather than only by the residuals control sector.

The appeal of the *I–O* approach as extended to include residuals generation and control lies in the ease with which it can be implemented. The economy-wide *I–O* approach is best suited for residuals problems where location of discharge does not matter, or at least is not a dominant consideration, either for natural or policy reasons. For example, should the increase in atmospheric CO_2 become a problem of real concern, the *I–O* approach would permit testing the influence of different patterns of final demand on CO_2 discharge, given that the production technology of the economy did not change or changed in accordance with the projections of technical and residual coefficients. In this case the specific location of the discharge does not matter, because more or less uniform dilution occurs globally.

In those cases where concentration, exposure, and assimilative capacity do vary with location, an "ideal" policy would take account of these differences, but certain considerations, cost of implementation, for example, may point to the desirability of national emission standards even in these cases. In this curcumstance, the national *I–O* model will still be of some use. For example, the implications for residuals and industry outputs of alternative patterns of

---

* When the change in final demand is a unit increase in the ith good or service, ordinary inputs required and residuals generated are the elements of the ith column of A^{*-1}.

final demand and levels of residuals control can be played out, although the linkage with environmental effects must then be extremely loose.

Another calculation that can be made is one in which patterns of final demand are projected under the assumption of no residuals control and with present or projected production technologies, including residuals generation coefficients, going into the future. One can get an impression of alternative possible futures by means of these "projections."

The *I-O* approach as we have described it so far has some notable shortcomings, however:

(1) The system as discussed up to this point is on a national scale whereas pollution "problem sheds" tend to be on a regional scale, and sometimes the region is quite small.

(2) It has not accounted in a logically complete manner for the residuals generated in production and consumption in the initial attempts at application. In principle, however, the pollutant categories could be expanded to include *all* residuals. If the classification were detailed, there would be many pollution "control" industries with zero output.

(3) It is usually not correct to think of residuals control as taking place in a separate residual control sector or even in separate residual control activities, especially in the case of industrial activities. In most industries, process changes resulting in residual control and greater production of marketable products are important alternatives to separate residual control activities either outside or within the industry. The only way such changes resulting either from new application of existing technology or development of new technology can be inserted into the *I-O* approach is by changing coefficients relating residuals generation to output. No internal optimizing method is available for selecting industrial processes in view of their residual generation characteristics and other economic attributes.

(4) The model focuses on residuals generation and discharge. It does not analyze what happens to residuals once they enter into the environment nor does it incorporate any consideration of damages. The processes of transportation and transformation in the environment, as affected by hydrological, meteorological, biological, and other natural system conditions, have a significant bearing on the damaging effects of a given amount of residuals discharge.

(5) The model focuses on residuals control costs but gives no attention to the value of the loss in function of common property resources

when their quality deteriorates due to the effects of residuals discharge.

Some of the deficiencies of the *I–O* approach as just described can be remedied within its framework, but only at the cost of considerable complication. For example, the limitation of national scale of the model immediately suggests regional *I–O* models.

11.4 REGIONAL AND INTERREGIONAL I-O MODELS

National boundaries seldom describe a satisfactory area for the analysis of pollution problems. These problems tend to conform more nearly to natural regions ranging from the entire globe (as with CO_2 and DDT) to small stretches of river or highly localized airsheds. In principle this fact could be accommodated in the *I–O* approach by developing a set of linked interregional models for the nation. Little logical or mathematical difficulty is involved in converting the national to an interregional model. The extensions are straightforward, and consist primarily of adding rows and columns specifying imports and exports to and from the various regions. The problem lies in data requirements.

A set of coherent *I–O* models for subnational regions is needed. Many tables have been constructed for individual states and regions, and recently at least a crude set of linked interregional tables has been made available for the United States (this was done at Harvard University under the sponsorship of the Economic Development Administration). The Harvard tables have not been adapted for work on residuals problems.*

11.5 ACCOUNTING FOR RESIDUALS IN A LOGICALLY COMPLETE MANNER

The residuals generation aspect of the present *I–O* models does not completely account for all materials flows, including residuals, which are generated by the various parts of the real world system. No environmental sector is included, and all residuals not processed are viewed as ending up in the final demand sector. Moreover, interdependencies among solid, liquid, and gaseous residuals in production, consumption, and transformation (treatment) processes are not identified or accounted for.

---

* A substantial amount of work has been done on specific regional environmental problems involving the *I–O* approach. See John H. Cumberland, "A Regional Interindustry Model for Analysis of Development Objectives," *Regional Science Association Papers*, Vol. 16, 1966, pp. 65–94; Cumberland, "Application of Input-Output Technique to the Analysis of Environmental Problems," prepared for The Fifth International Conference on Input-Output Techniques, Geneva, January 11–19, 1971; and Walter Isard *et al.*, "On the Linkage of Socio-Economic and Ecologic Systems," in *Regional Science Association Papers*, Vol. 21, 1968, pp. 79–100.

In a recent monograph by Ayres, d'Arge, and Kneese,* models have been explored which provide for a logically complete accounting of materials flowing into production and consumption processes in the economy and thence to the environment. The approach proceeds by specifying a set of equations representing materials balances in conjunction with equations representing an interdependent economic system. We will treat it only briefly because so far it has had little empirical application. The approach has called attention to the importance of the conservation of mass in considering residuals processes. Essentially all raw materials (in terms of mass) which enter the extractive and materials processing activities of the economy must be returned to the environment as residuals. This fact is not controverted by the application of treatment processes, since they only transform materials and do not destroy them. Some estimates of residuals generated in the U.S. economy have been made based on materials balance concepts, and other applications in analysis and forecasting are being explored.

11.6   SCHEMATIC ILLUSTRATION OF A MATERIALS BALANCE MODEL

Perhaps the simplest and most direct way in which a comprehensive materials balance might be illustrated would be an adaptation of the activity analysis format, as shown on Table 11-4. Row headings indicate particular goods or services. Activities (which could be industries but don't have to be) are indicated by column headings. Final consumption activities (here combined into one column) are also included in the format.

A negative entry in a cell indicates the quantity of the good (measured by weight except for services, which must be measured in conventional units) on that row which is used as an input by the corresponding activity. A positive entry in a cell indicates the amount of the good on that row which is produced by the corresponding activity. For example, suppose that on row 3 a -22 appears in column 6 and $+37$ in column 9. This would mean 22 units of good No. 3 are used as an input to activity No. 6 and 37 units of good No. 3 are produced by activity No. 9.

Resources coming from the environment are always inputs; hence the negative signs are as indicated. Purely intermediate goods and services are used only within the industrial sector. Hence all rows sum to zero for this sector.

Final goods and services have net positive balances for the industrial sector,

---

* Allen V. Kneese, Robert U. Ayres, and Ralph C. d'Arge, *Economics and the Environment: A Materials Balance Approach* (Washington: Resources for the Future, Inc., 1971). For later comments on this approach, see Roger G. Noll and John Trijonis, "Mass Balance, General Equilibrium, and Environmental Externalities," *American Economic Review*, Vol. LXI (September 1971), pp. 730–35 and A. O. Converse, "On the Extension of Input-Output Analysis to Account for Environmental Externalities," *American Economic Review*, Vol. LXI (March 1971), pp. 197–98.

TABLE 11-4

Format for Materials Balance

Outputs and/or inputs	Industrial activities				Final consumption activities (e.g. households)	Total for all economic units	Total to environment from:		Total from environment to:	
	1	2	...	Total			industry	final consumption	industry	final consumption
Resources 1. 2. ...	—		—	—	—	—	0	0	—	—
Intermediate goods and services 1. 2. ...	—	+		0	0	0	0	0	0	0
Final goods and services 1. 2. ...	—	+		+	—	0	0	0	0	0
Residuals (including pollutants) 1. 2. ...	-5 0	0 -2	$+3_I$ $+2_I + 4_A$	0 or $\pm$ -2 $+4$	0 or $+$ $+2_I + 3_W$ $+3_A$	0 if all is processed; + if not (some goes to environment) 7	4	$_3H$		
Column total (excl. services)	0	0	0	0	0	0	$\Big\}\,B$		$\Big\}\,C$	

369

but the totals for all economic units are zero since goods and services going to the final consumption sector are regarded as inputs into the consumption activity.

Residuals may go into an activity which transforms them, perhaps producing some salable product along with other residuals, or they may go to the environment. The destination might be indicated by a subscript, say A for atmosphere or W for water. In the case of residual No. 1, for example, five units are "processed" by activity No. 1, of which three come from industry and two from households. These units contribute to the production of the outputs of activity No. 1, which may include other residuals. Households also discharge three units of residual No. 1 to water bodies.

In the case of residual No. 2, two units are used as input by activity No. 2, all of them coming from industry activities. Industry activities also discharge four units to the atmosphere along with three discharged by households.

Residual row totals for all activities will be zero if all of a given residual produced is processed. If not, the row total will be positive with some of the residual going to the environment.

Neglecting inventory changes, column totals of tangibles should be zero for each activity, as should also the totals coming from and going to the environment $(B = C)$.

Needless to say, the practical implementation of a materials balance accounting system would encounter a host of difficulties that have not been touched on here. This format is useful for thinking about pollution problems, however, since it provides the basis for viewing the choice of production and consumption activities and their levels as a programming problem that treats the production and processing of residuals as an integral part of the whole.

11.7   AN OPERATIONAL PARTIAL-GENERAL MODEL

In this section we outline a more partial model which retains many of the essentials of the insights gained from the general equilibrium models, but which is much more sophisticated in its handling of residuals and the environment. It can be made operational in analyzing residuals management problems in a regional context. The model is partial in that it does not incorporate a full materials balance, and it takes certain cost and demand information as externally given rather than determined internally in the model. On the other hand, it does incorporate the possibility of alternative production processes in industry as well as treatment of residuals streams and provides an economic analysis of tradeoffs among discharges to different environmental media. It also traces residuals in the environment and associates them with damages at receptor locations. This "model" is more accurately viewed as a set of models operated by an executive program rather than a single model in a strict sense. Nevertheless, for the sake of brevity we shall usually refer to it as a model. Unfortunately, we can give the reader no more than a feeling of how the model works since a detailed discussion would become too extensive. Considering this model also gives us an opportunity to extend our previous discussions of the application of mathematical programming to natural resources problems to include some non-linearities—specifically a non-linear objective function.

The *regional* residuals management approach developed by Russell and Spofford* consists of a set of three interlinked models which are depicted schematically in Figure 11-3 and described briefly below. We discuss here only the simplest version of the overall set of models. It is assumed that residuals discharge is continuous and unchanging once set at a particular level and that conditions (e.g., wind speed and direction, water flow) in the atmosphere and watercourses are fixed. The reader will recall from Chapter 10 that the Streeter equations have a simple solution under these conditions. The same is true of the equations characterizing the atmospheric diffusion system. Also we assume there is no direct interaction among residuals once they are discharged. These assumptions can be relaxed in the actual model but they greatly simplify our exposition.

The essential components of the overall model follow:

A linear programming model relates inputs and outputs of the various production processes and consumption activities at specified locations within a region—including the unit amounts and types of residuals generated by the production and consumption of each product, the costs of transforming these residuals from one form to another (i.e., solid to gas, liquid to gas, liquid to solid), and the costs of disposing of residuals in the natural environment (i.e., transportation costs, the cost of landfill operations, etc.).

The programming model permits choices among *production processes, raw material input mixes, by-product production, recycle of residuals,* and *in-plant adjustments and improvement,* all of which could reduce the total quantity and/or the type of residuals to be transformed by *treatment processes* and/or *disposed of* in the natural environment. The residuals generated are not assumed fixed (or given) either in form or in quantity. The residuals-environmental quality management system optimizes production of goods and residuals. Allowance is made in the model for the reduction of the residuals originally generated. Also, provision is made for choices among transformation processes and hence among the possible forms of the residual to be disposed of in the natural environment (i.e., solid, liquid, or gas). Damages and costs to receptors are reflected through environmental diffusion models and residuals-receptor damage functions as "shadow prices"—i.e., marginal costs—to be applied to the variables in the LP model representing residuals discharged to the natural environment. Emissions standards and ambient standards can also be examined by means of this model.

---

* A relatively full discussion of this approach is found in Clifford S. Russell and Walter O. Spofford, Jr., "A Quantitative Framework for Residuals Management Decisions," in Allen V. Kneese and Blair T. Bower, eds., *Environmental Quality Analysis: Research Studies in the Social Sciences* (Baltimore: The Johns Hopkins Press, forthcoming).

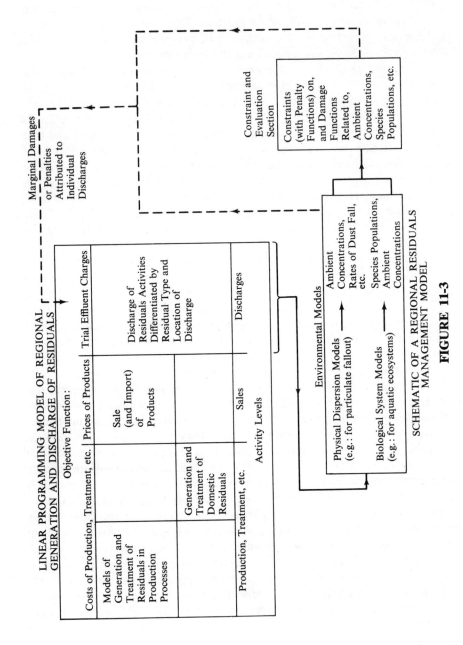

LINEAR PROGRAMMING MODEL OF REGIONAL
GENERATION AND DISCHARGE OF RESIDUALS

Objective Function:

Costs of Production, Treatment, etc.	Prices of Products	Trial Effluent Charges
Models of Generation and Treatment of Residuals in Production Processes	Sale (and Import) of Products	Discharge of Residuals Activities Differentiated by Residual Type and Location of Discharge
Generation and Treatment of Domestic Residuals		
Production, Treatment, etc.	Sales	Discharges

Activity Levels

Marginal Damages or Penalties Attributed to Individual Discharges

Environmental Models

Physical Dispersion Models (e.g.: for particulate fallout) ⟶ Ambient Concentrations, Rates of Dust Fall, etc.

Biological System Models (e.g.: for aquatic ecosystems) ⟶ Species Populations, Ambient Concentrations

Constraint and Evaluation Section

Constraints (with Penalty Functions) on, and Damage Functions Related to, Ambient Concentrations, Species Populations, etc.

SCHEMATIC OF A REGIONAL RESIDUALS
MANAGEMENT MODEL

FIGURE 11-3

Environmental Diffusion Models

Atmospheric diffusion, stream diffusion, and noise diffusion models are used to relate the amounts and types of residuals discharged into the natural environment—both to the atmosphere and to watercourses—to the amounts (i.e., ambient concentrations) and types of residuals that are present at various receptors (man, animals, plants, and inanimate objects).

In the case of non-interacting residuals, the total quantity (i.e., concentration) of a given residual at any point in time and space may be evaluated independently of the discharges of other types of residuals. In addition, if the rate of change of concentration of a given residual (that is, decay) may be expressed either independently of, or as a linear function of, the concentration, the total quantity of the given residual at any point in time and space may be expressed as a linear sum of the contributions from all sources. For a discussion of this result with respect to water, see Chapter 10. Environmental diffusion models are used to compute the effect, i.e., concentration, at any point, i, due to a specified discharge from any source, j. Whereas the residuals are non-interacting and rates of change are linear functions of concentration, the separate effects may be added to one another, yielding the total effect from all sources within a specified region. If modification of the environment (e.g., low flow augmentation) is not considered explicitly as a management alternative, this may be depicted mathematically for the kth residual and for steady-state conditions with the following set of linear relationships:*

Source, j

$$\begin{array}{l} R_1^{(k)} = a_{11}x_1^{(k)} + a_{12}x_2^{(k)} + \cdots + a_{1n}x_n^{(k)} \\ R_2^{(k)} = a_{21}x_1^{(k)} + a_{22}x_2^{(k)} + \cdots + a_{2n}x_n^{(k)} \\ \quad\vdots \qquad\quad \vdots \qquad\quad \vdots \qquad\qquad \vdots \\ R_m^{(k)} = a_{m1}x_1^{(k)} + a_{m2}x_2^{(k)} + \cdots + a_{mn}x_n^{(k)} \end{array} \qquad (*)$$

(Receptor, i)

or in matrix notation as, $R^{(k)} = A \cdot X^{(k)}$ where

$x_j^{(k)}, \ j = 1,\ldots,n;$ $k = 1,\ldots,p;$	= quantity of the kth residual discharged from the jth source during the time interval, Δt.
$a_{ij}, \ i = 1,\ldots,m;$ $j = 1,\ldots,n;$	= unit transfer coefficient indicating the quantity (i.e., concentration) at receptor location, i, due to a unit discharge of a given residual at source, j.
$R_i^{(k)}, \ i = 1,\ldots,m;$	= the total quantity (i.e., concentration) of the kth residual at receptor location, i.
n	= number of sources of the kth residual.
m	= number of receptor locations.
p	= number of residuals in the analysis.

---

* This set of equations is for the kth residual only. Similar equation sets would be required for other residuals. The superscript k will be omitted in the discussion of a later section with no intended loss of generality.

The quantities of a specified residual discharged to the environment, x_j, $j = 1, \ldots, n$, are given as output of the LP model and the transfer coefficients, a_{ij}, $i = 1, \ldots, m$; $j = 1, \ldots, n$, are computed from environmental diffusion models (for deterministic, steady-state conditions)*. The vector of ambient concentrations of a given residual at all receptor locations, R_i, $i = 1, \ldots, m$, due to that residual discharged from all sources is the output of the system of equations (*). This vector, **R**, in turn, is used as input to the receptor-damage models (functions). If modification of the environment is considered as an alternative, the transfer coefficients must be recalculated appropriately.

Ambient Standards

Where damage functions are not available, ambient standards may be used. In this situation, marginal damages (and costs) will not be defined except for the "binding" constraints, in which case the marginal damages are implicitly assumed to be infinite (or at least greater than the shadow prices of the corresponding binding constraints). For this situation, equation set (*) may be modified to include ambient standards as follows:

$$
\begin{aligned}
a_{11}x_1 + a_{12}x_2 + \cdots + a_{1n}x_n &\leq S_1 \\
a_{21}x_1 + a_{22}x_2 + \cdots + a_{2n}x_n &\leq S_2 \\
\vdots \qquad\qquad \vdots \quad\ \ \vdots& \\
a_{m1}x_1 + a_{m2}x_2 + \cdots + a_{mn}x_n &\leq S_m
\end{aligned}
$$

or in matrix notation, $\mathbf{AX} \leq \mathbf{S}$, where **S** is a vector of ambient standards. Since this is a linear constraint set, it can be transferred in its entirety directly into the LP model.

Damage Functions

When damage functions are available, it will be possible to compute marginal damages for all sources at the locations of residual discharge. It is assumed that the functions are continuous and have continuous first derivatives. For this case, the damages at each location, due to the kth residual $D_i^{(k)}$, $i = 1, \ldots, m$, are assumed to be functions only of the corresponding ambient residual concentrations, $R_i^{(k)}$, $i = 1, \ldots, m$, or expressed mathematically,†

$$
D_i^{(k)} = f(R_i^{(k)}) \qquad i = 1, \ldots, m \qquad\qquad (**)
$$

The form of the assumed damage function is depicted in Figure 11-4 below.

---

* The reader may wish to refer back to page 337 where a discussion is presented of how such a matrix is formed for a water quality situation.

† Damages which are a function of several residuals can also be handled conveniently using this scheme. As we shall see, partial derivatives rather than total derivatives could be used in the evaluation of marginal damages.

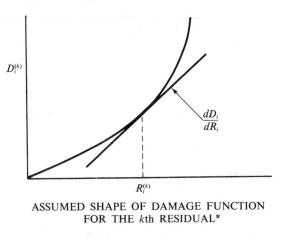

ASSUMED SHAPE OF DAMAGE FUNCTION
FOR THE kth RESIDUAL*

FIGURE 11-4

* The shape of this function is assumed to be monotonically increasing. The actual path of
the curve would depend upon the specific residual, and the types and numbers of receptors
present.

The purpose of this exercise is to compute the total marginal damages
corresponding to each residual source. For the kth residual, the total damages
to all receptors and/or uses in the region is given by:

$$D_T^{(k)} = D_1^{(k)} + D_2^{(k)} + \cdots + D_m^{(k)} = \sum_{i=1}^{m} D_i^{(k)}$$

As shown by equation (**), the actual damage, D_i, is a function of the ambient
concentration, R_i. Therefore, the following expressions for marginal damages
associated with the kth residual obtain*

$$\frac{\partial D_T}{\partial x_1} = \frac{dD_1}{dR_1} \cdot \frac{\partial R_1}{\partial x_1} + \frac{dD_2}{dR_2} \cdot \frac{\partial R_2}{\partial x_1} + \cdots + \frac{dD_m}{dR_m} \cdot \frac{\partial R_m}{\partial x_1}$$

$$\frac{\partial D_T}{\partial x_2} = \frac{dD_1}{dR_1} \cdot \frac{\partial R_1}{\partial x_2} + \frac{dD_2}{dR_2} \cdot \frac{\partial R_2}{\partial x_2} + \cdots + \frac{dD_m}{dR_m} \cdot \frac{\partial R_m}{\partial x_2}$$

$$\vdots \qquad \vdots \qquad\qquad\qquad\qquad \vdots$$

$$\frac{\partial D_T}{\partial x_n} = \frac{dD_1}{dR_1} \cdot \frac{\partial R_1}{\partial x_n} + \frac{dD_2}{dR_2} \cdot \frac{\partial R_2}{\partial x_n} + \cdots + \frac{dD_m}{dR_m} \cdot \frac{\partial R_m}{\partial x_n}$$

* Here again, the superscript k has been omitted for purposes of exposition.

However, from equation set (*), $\partial R_1/\partial x_1 = a_{11}$, $\partial R_2/\partial x_1 = a_{21}$, $\partial R_m/\partial x_1 = a_{m1}$, and so on, the above equation set reduces to:

$$\frac{\partial D_T}{\partial x_1} = a_{11}\frac{dD_1}{dR_1} + a_{21}\frac{dD_2}{dR_2} + \cdots + a_{m1}\frac{dD_m}{dR_m}$$

$$\frac{\partial D_T}{\partial x_2} = a_{12}\frac{dD_1}{dR_1} + a_{22}\frac{dD_2}{dR_2} + \cdots + a_{m2}\frac{dD_m}{dR_m}$$

$$\vdots \qquad\qquad \vdots \qquad\qquad\qquad \vdots$$

$$\frac{\partial D_T}{\partial x_n} = a_{1n}\frac{dD_1}{dR_1} + a_{2n}\frac{dD_2}{dR_2} + \cdots + a_{mn}\frac{dD_m}{dR_m}$$

or in matrix notation as, $\partial \mathbf{D}_T/\partial \mathbf{x} = \mathbf{A}^T \cdot (d\mathbf{D}/d\mathbf{R})$. The marginal damages are evaluated using this equation set, and the resulting vector $\partial D_T/\partial x_j, j = 1, \ldots, n$, is returned to the interindustry LP model as prices on the residuals discharged to the environment.

The procedure outlined in the last few pages is summarized below:

a. Given a residual discharge set, $x_j, j = 1, \ldots, n$, and a matrix of transfer coefficients, $a_{ij}, i = 1, \ldots, m; j = 1, \ldots, n$, solve equation set (*) for $R_i, i = 1, \ldots, m$.

b. Evaluate the slopes of the various damage functions, dD_i/dR_i, $i = 1, \ldots, m$, at the points, $R_i, i = 1, \ldots, m$, computed in step (a) above.

c. Using this result, evaluate the marginal damages caused by residuals being discharged to the natural environment.

d. Use the marginal damages, computed in step (c), as prices on residuals discharged in the LP model and resolve the LP model for a new set of residuals discharges, $x_j, j = 1, \ldots, n$.

The Response Surface and Marching up It

We further explain this iterative process for determining the optimum value of of the objective functions by invoking the concept of the gradient which we introduced briefly in Chapter 2. The objective function used in this problem may be thought of as comprised of four parts: (a) gross consumption benefits (i.e., total willingness to pay),* (b) opportunity costs of traditional production inputs, (c) residuals treatment costs, and (d) subsequent damages to man due to

---

* In the actual problem, piecewise linear demand functions are used.

ambient concentrations of residuals in the environment. Stated more formally:

F = Benefits $(q_i, i = 1, \ldots, k_1)$ − Production costs $(q_i, i = 1, \ldots, k_1)$

     − Treatment costs $(w_i, i = 1, \ldots, k_2)$ − Damages $(x_i, i = 1, \ldots, k_3)$

where q_i = activity levels of k_1 production processes,

            w_i = activity levels of k_2 treatment processes,

            x_i = activity levels of k_3 residual discharge activities.

The gradient (grad $\mathbf{F}$) is a vector of first order partial derivatives of the function $F(x_1, x_2, \ldots, x_n)$ computed at a point, $X^{(k)}$, i.e.,

$$\nabla \mathbf{F} \equiv \text{grad } \mathbf{F} \equiv \hat{e}_1 \frac{\partial F}{\partial x_1} + \hat{e}_2 \frac{\partial F}{\partial x_2} + \cdots + \hat{e}_n \frac{\partial F}{\partial x_n}$$

where $\hat{e}_1, \hat{e}_2, \ldots, \hat{e}_n$ are unit vectors in the 1st, 2nd, $\ldots$, nth directions respectively. For our purposes the most important theorems on gradients are given in the following statement:

> Thus the direction of the gradient is the direction in which the function increases most rapidly, while the direction opposite to that of the gradient is that in which the function decreases most rapidly; the magnitude of the gradient gives the rate of increase or decrease.*

The objective function describes a surface in multi-dimensional space which is constrained in a linear programming problem by the constraint set $\mathbf{AX} \leq \mathbf{b}$. In OR jargon the former is known as the response surface.

At any point on the response surface, the coefficients of the linear plane tangent to it are described mathematically by grad $\mathbf{F}$. For a linear objective function, the gradient is, simply, a vector of linear coefficients. Consequently, in the linear case the gradient is everywhere the same. For a non-linear objective function, however, the gradient varies from point to point along the response surface and, thus, is restricted to having local properties.

The iterative technique of using marginal damages from one iteration as shadow prices on the amounts of residuals discharged to the environment on the following iteration is identical to computing the local gradient of the objective function at a point and using the vector of first order partial derivatives as linear coefficients to approximate the shape of the response surface in the vicinity of that point. Naturally, this linear approximation to the more complex non-linear surface is mot accurate near the point of computation and the error between the linearized surface and the actual surface increases as one travels away from the initial point.

---

* R. Courant, *Differential and Integral Calculus*, Vol II (New York: Interscience Publishers, Inc., 1961).

The gradient of the objective function ($F =$ Benefits $-$ Production costs $-$ Treatment costs $-$ Damages) may be expressed as:

$$
\text{grad } \mathbf{F} = \hat{q}_1 \frac{\partial B}{\partial q_1} + \hat{q}_2 \frac{\partial B}{\partial q_2} + \cdots + \hat{q}_{k_1} \frac{\partial B}{\partial q_{k_1}}
$$

$$
- \hat{q}_1 \frac{\partial C}{\partial q_1} - \hat{q}_2 \frac{\partial C}{\partial q_2} - \cdots - \hat{q}_{k_1} \frac{\partial C}{\partial q_{k_1}}
$$

$$
- \hat{w}_1 \frac{\partial C}{\partial w_1} - \hat{w}_2 \frac{\partial C}{\partial w_2} - \cdots - \hat{w}_{k_2} \frac{\partial C}{\partial w_{k_2}}
$$

$$
- \hat{x}_1 \frac{\partial D}{\partial x_1} - \hat{x}_2 \frac{\partial D}{\partial x_2} - \cdots - \hat{x}_{k_3} \frac{\partial D}{\partial x_{k_3}}
$$

where $\hat{q}_i, i = 1, \ldots, k_1;$ $\hat{w}_i, i = 1, \ldots, k_2;$ and $\hat{x}_i, i = 1, \ldots, k_3,$

are unit vectors, and where $\mathbf{Q}$, $\mathbf{W}$, and $\mathbf{X}$ are vectors of activity levels previously defined. The partial derivatives, $\partial B/\partial q_i$, $i = 1, \ldots, k_1$, are nothing more than the prices, P, of final products and in the present model are constants; $\partial C/\partial q_i$, $i = 1, \ldots, k_1$, are the marginal opportunity costs of traditional production inputs considered in this model to be constant; $\partial C/\partial w_i$, $i = 1, \ldots, k_2$, are linear cost coefficients for residuals treatment activities; and $\partial D/\partial x_i$, $i = 1, \ldots, k_3$, are the marginal damages which for this model are not constants, i.e., they vary according to the specific location on the response surface and must be re-computed for each location.

Since the linear coefficients provided by the partial derivatives for the non-linear portion of the objective function vary along the response surface, a question of the location of the optimum and thus the step size for these variables arises. For the non-linear situation, if no step size is specified, the linear program will go immediately to a solution which will be on the boundary of the feasible region specified by the constraint set $\mathbf{AX} \leq \mathbf{B}$, and which will almost certainly be far from the actual (non-linear constraint) peak of the response surface. If the step size is too large, it may similarly be impossible to get close to the peak. The program may "step over" the peak so to speak, as in the case where no step size was specified. If the step sizes are small, a large number of iterations may be required to approach the peak, resulting in excessive costs of calculation. The following is a description of how this problem can be approached in simple circumstances and is illustrative of one technique which has actually been used. To explain the technique, we need to define the *magnitude* of the gradient.

For purposes of further discussion, the gradient of a function $F(X)$ was defined above as:

$$
\nabla \mathbf{F} \equiv \text{grad } \mathbf{F} = \hat{e}_1 \frac{\partial F}{\partial x_1} + \hat{e}_2 \frac{\partial F}{\partial x_2} + \cdots + \hat{e}_n \frac{\partial F}{\partial x_n}
$$

The *magnitude* of the gradient is simply the directional derivative of the function describing the response surface taken in the direction of the greatest rate of increase in the function, i.e., in the direction of steepest ascent. Mathematically, it is the maximum value of dF/ds, where s is a distance parameter measured in any direction from a point. When dF/ds is maximized, the direction of s is, by definition, the direction of the *gradient*.

The magnitude of the gradient is given by the following formula:

$$|\text{grad } \mathbf{F}| \equiv \left(\frac{dF}{ds}\right)_{\text{max}} = \sqrt{\left(\frac{\partial F}{\partial x_1}\right)^2 + \left(\frac{\partial F}{\partial x_2}\right)^2 + \cdots + \left(\frac{\partial F}{\partial x_n}\right)^2}$$

For the method described here, the linear constraint set contains a subset of constraints which limits the size of the steps or adjustments that can be made to the vector of decision variables, $\mathbf{X}$, in each of the successive iterations, k, $k + 1, k + 2$, etc. This constraint ensures that the selection of the next position along the response surface is restricted to that portion of the surface most closely approximated by the newly created linear surface. Selecting a step size which moves the process along rapidly but which does not step over the optimum (at least not too frequently or by too much) is the key to all gradient methods of non-linear programming. In general, it is a simple enough matter to find the local direction of steepest ascent for the unconstrained problem, i.e., the local gradient. But how far one should step once the direction has been found is another question entirely.

The $(k + 1)$th step size along the gradient, $\delta_g^{(k+1)}$, may be expressed as a multiple of the magnitude of the local gradient, $|\nabla \mathbf{F}^{(k)}|$.* That is,

$$\delta_g^{(k+1)} = \lambda^{(k+1)} |\nabla \mathbf{F}^{(k)}|$$

where

$|\nabla \mathbf{F}^{(k)}|$ = the magnitude of the local gradient computed at the kth point along the route of ascent, and

$\lambda^{(k+1)}$ = scalar multiple of the gradient.

The ith component of the step size is:

$$\delta_{g_i}^{(k+1)} = \lambda^{(k+1)} \left[\frac{\partial F(x)}{\partial x_i}\right]$$

Thus, not only is the step in the *direction* of the gradient, $\nabla \mathbf{F}$, but here we indicate that the step length is itself a function of the magnitude of the gradient. This is an essential feature for finding an interior optimum by the gradient

---

* This is one possibility for selecting a step size. Other schemes might also be used. See, for example, T. Saaty and J. Bram, *Nonlinear Mathematics* (New York: McGraw-Hill Book Co., 1964).

method for when one approaches the optimum, i.e., $\nabla F \rightarrow 0$, the step length gets shorter and shorter until finally at the optimum the step length is equal to zero.

Thus, the constraints relating to step length are adjusted in each iteration by applying the scalar multiple λ to the computed magnitude of the gradient at the preceding step. Accordingly, the restrictions representing step length are themselves variables which are adjusted at each step in the program. As the surface flattens out near its peak, step lengths become automatically shorter and "stepping over" is avoided (if, of course, the λ's are properly chosen). Of course, we have stepped over many problems ourselves in explaining the procedure. Selecting an appropriate λ is a significant problem, and adjustments need to be made to prevent the number of iterations from approaching infinity as the peak is approached and the response surface becomes very flat.*

11.8   CONCLUDING COMMENT

At the time this text was being written, a more sophisticated version of the set of models just described was being applied to an actual region. While not a complete general equilibrium approach, it is the first time that a residuals management problem is being attacked in a relatively complete and systematic manner and in full recognition of many tradeoffs which have been neglected or treated simplistically in partial approaches to air, water, or solid waste problems.

Considering the brief period (much less than a decade) during which economics work on residuals problems as such has been going on (and even then at a modest level), respectable progress can be reported at both the theoretical and applied levels. It would be pretentious to claim that anything more than a preliminary understanding of environmental economics has been achieved. Nevertheless, economics has been the only discipline which so far has been able to provide a reasonably orderly conceptual structure for the considerations of these difficult and urgent problems which could span the distance from basic science and technology to human values. The theory has not yet been completely unified—traditional conservation economics, economic growth, and the economics of residuals management and recycling, while clearly tightly interrelated, are still pursued within somewhat isolated conceptual departments. It is a worthy challenge to the new generation of economists (and professionals in related disciplines) to close these gaps and broaden and deepen our theoretical equipment for understanding and analyzing the rational use of our natural endowments in pursuit of the values of human beings.

---

* This is only one of a number of possible approaches to the non-linear programming problem. Considerable progress has been made in the last decade in the development of general, non-linear algorithms that can handle both non-linear objective functions and non-linear equality and inequality constraints. See, for example, F. A. Fiacco and G. P. McCormick, *Nonlinear Programming: Sequential Unconstrained Minimization Techniques* (New York: John Wiley & Sons, 1968).

PART V

Conclusions and Deep Problems

CHAPTER 12

Time for Stock-Taking

The Road We Have Travelled

In this last chapter we look back over the material we have covered in the context of a number of important general questions. What have we learned about economic theory that helps analyze problems in the management of natural resources? Where are the difficulties? Is economic theory of help in predicting what the future has in store for society? Can it help us to make decisions that will presumably affect future events or will we be swept along willy-nilly to unknown and perhaps terrible future states?

Our objective has been to provide an account of those parts of allocation theory that seem to be especially useful in the analysis of problems in the management of natural resources *and* which do not receive much attention in the usual courses in economic theory. The first step was a rapid review of the basic ideas of allocation theory, including the sources of market failure, this being central to the later concern with resource problems that are not wholly encompassed within private economic entities.

Substantial attention was given to the idea, and some of the basic techniques, of maximization subject to side conditions or restrictions. One of these techniques, linear programming, was given considerable attention along with the closely related tool of input-output analysis, since these tools have and will play an important role in the empirical analysis of resource management systems. Although basic ideas are important, the reader will want to consult specialized sources to develop a certain amount of technical expertise in manipulating these tools.

Since some important natural resource problems are part of the more general problem of capital accumulation, far more space has been devoted to capital theory and related matters than in a conventional text. A simple model of capital accumulation was presented. Some of the implications of steady growth of various types were brought out. We have taken the liberty of giving considerable emphasis to our own comments on the problem of how rapidly capital should be accumulated and of how natural resources might be introduced into the problem. Two types of more specific problems involving management over time were discussed, each of them involving the economic system in interaction with a natural system. The first of these natural systems was the comparatively simple one of mineral depletion, the second was a simple example, cast in terms of a fishery, of the immensely more complicated problem of managing economic-biological systems.

In view of the tremendous importance of government investment related to natural resources, we gave detailed discussion to benefit-cost analysis, starting with basic ideas of discounting and optimizing the various features of an investment opportunity. Two basic problems were the selection of the rate of discount and the problem of multiple objectives. Here again we have not confined ourselves to a recounting of the views to be found in the literature but have discussed our own at length. In particular, we have been critical of the internal rate of return as a selection criterion, certain methods of cost allocation, and the routine inclusion of income redistributive effects as an element in project evaluation.

Various concepts in public investment theory were illustrated by applications, including "rescue" operations, flood damage control, recreation benefits, the analysis of options for managing water quality in a river basin, and inland waterways operation.

Problems of residuals management were discussed in terms of water quality management and from two points of view: one, the management of the external effects, and the other the management of the "asset" whose services are implicitly being utilized by the process of effluent discharge. The latter orientation led to the important conceptual device of the basin-wide firm. Concrete illustrations were provided by studies of water quality management in the Delaware and Potomac estuaries.

Some aspects of residuals management need to be approached comprehensively. A completely comprehensive residuals theoretical model was introduced in the form of a materials balance accounting. While the application of a complete materials balance scheme with attention to location would be extremely complex and beyond present capability, a more limited application is possible, involving only a partial materials balance and one region. A theoretical model of this type which will permit choices via linear programming was presented. A variant of this model is currently being applied to a concrete situation.

In summary, we have found that many problems which otherwise seem capable of causing great confusion can be resolved by application of some of the most elementary and basic concepts of economics. The confusion concerning benefit-cost ratios is an example of this. On the other hand, we found as we pursued our discussion that some realistic elements of the natural resources situation were putting greater and greater strain on our usual theoretical equipment—especially the simpler versions of static or comparative static partial equilibrium theory. Problems of technological change and stochastic processes, not to speak of uncertainty of outcomes, were omnipresent. In the later stages we found it necessary to depart from the simpler partial equilibrium formulations of problems entirely in an effort to deal with the pervasive externality problems associated with residuals disposal and congestion phenomena resulting from increasingly heavy use of common property resources. While we feel that the introduction of general equilibrium theory is useful to aid understanding of these phenomena, the models we used still suffer from grave deficiencies. To a substantial extent these result from the simplifying assumptions which we made about production processes and the static character of the models.

In particular, a great deal of work needs to be done before we are in a position to assess the worth of input-output and feasible applications of the various types of programming to problems of effluent management. For example, consider the problem faced by the policy maker who would like to control a family of residuals by means of taxes imposed on their discharge. How can he discover this optimum set of taxes, taxes which ideally may vary according to effluent, location of discharge (this may imply variation by concentration of dischargers), location of those affected, and so on? One method would be experiment, with an attempt being made to estimate the net change in benefits with each small alteration in the set of prices. Clearly this option is out of the question since large adjustments of real capital might be involved ultimately, and these might take so much time that progress would hardly be visible. The problem must therefore be analyzed in some way to permit a search on paper for a set of prices that will at least yield a substantial improvement if not the optimum. But application of such analysis—whether by simulation, programming, or other technique—may involve such drastic simplification either because of the sheer complexity of reality or because of ignorance of relevant functions (especially damage functions) that important opportunities for economization are missed.

We have not attempted to give an account of the economics of particular resources except as seemed useful in order to provide an introduction to the application of theoretical ideas from allocation theory. In consequence, there has been no attention given to industrial organization, something that would have been essential had this been a text on the economics of the various natural resources.

Preparation for the Long Term

By and large, the orientation of this book has been toward problems of the present and the immediate future. A number of problems, however, that involve action now will have important effects extending far into the future. How useful is our theory in the analysis of these problems?

In the most general terms, the problems of the future will involve the pressure of population on natural resources. This is also a way of characterizing the problems of the past, but the complexion of the problem has changed considerably. We shall still be faced with the possibility of increases in the cost of particular natural resource products or services—food, materials, energy—but in the future something new will have been added and is already here in some measure. Never before have problems of congestion confronted us in so ubiquitous a manner as now, and it is as certain as anything in human affairs can be that these will become far more severe in most countries within the coming decades. The other new element is effluents in such quantities and of such a nature as to impose increasing costs in deterioration of health and in destruction of natural beauty to the point of threatening changes in basic physical and biological processes on regional or global scales. The new element in the situation is not that man's activities are having region-wide effects. This has been happening everywhere human population has increased sufficiently, beginning with pastoral activities on so intensive a scale as to result in overgrazing and continuing with the clearing of forests and the extension of cultivation. In some regions, the resulting changes in the behavior of the ecosystems has been profound and costly to the people of the region. Much extension of cultivation has taken place without causing strongly adverse effects on humans—although cultivation obviously has changed the behavior of ecosystems in a fundamental way. What is new is an "unintended" flow of effluents resulting from new ways of conducting agriculture, of manufacturing, and of consuming that bring the possibility of *adverse* effects on a scale much larger than ever before. It behooves us to ask whether our intellectual constructs can contribute to understanding what may lie before us.

Economic theory has been formulated pretty much on the assumption of complete information or has incorporated certain stochastic elements only with considerable difficulty. Can it be applied to problems that involve not only stochastic elements, but that are shot through with basic uncertainties?

There is a six-way flow of substances and services between the various "environments," businesses, and households. Unfortunately, we are at this date very much in the dark as to the effects of each of these classes of flows. For example, cigarettes have been shown (obviously not with certainty) to be an agent of catastrophe for a large number of persons. How many more substances like this are we ingesting in water and food and breathing in the air? What kinds of physical and psychic difficulties will emerge in the future as the result of different types of congestion?

Alas, the unsuspected effects of our way of life are but one facet of our ignorance and uncertainty. Suppose that the *effects* were all measurable. We should like then to do something to reduce the more serious of them, but what should be done? What caused them? While there no doubt are many measures that could be taken with some considerable confidence of *their* effects, the unfortunate state of affairs is that many aspects of natural systems are so poorly understood that in many cases we should be at a loss to suggest remedial measures.

Here then is a different situation for which to devise economic theory. What constitutes economizing behavior in situations of this sort? What theoretical constructs seem to be especially useful in contexts characterized by massive uncertainties by way of directing our attention to strategic variables that we should attempt to estimate? Is the best we can do to suggest that we act in such a way as to insure against catastrophic effects? If this is the best, how do we decide that sufficient and appropriate action has been taken?

Perhaps the most serious difficulty in theorizing and trying to prescribe actions that affect the very long run is that of specifying the social welfare function. The difficulty, however, would seem to be less for the formulation of positive theory than for prescription, for any attempt to prescribe for the long pull ought to call attention to and deal with possible inconsistencies in the ruling social welfare function. These are more likely to be present in considering right action for the increasingly uncertain picture we see as our vision is directed forward in time. One of the difficulties may be viewed as revolving around two aspects of the population in the society—the identity of the persons included and the number of persons.

The reader will recall that for contemporaneous problems we urged a view that ascribed great importance to efficiency calculations based on market prices. This was done on the ground that it was possible to adjust public policy to take reasonably good account of other aspects of the social welfare function other than the benefits associated with efficient production. An individual experiences over a lifetime the results of a whole series of public decisions on many matters, made, we might imagine, in the name of efficiency, and with certain distributional consequences. These consequences will be largely offsetting, thus enabling him to find his place in the socially agreed distribution of income. Where large effects on personal income flow from a particular public decision, special attention is possible.

Unfortunately, the ideas of offsetting effects and consensus on distribution are not available in the case of members of the same society who are separated by a substantial interval of time. Offsets of effects of public decisions on particular individuals over a long period of time are not possible. What is more, the decisions in question do not constitute a set, each member of which is not very important, but rather they color and determine major features of the society at various points in time. They are of a class with the contemporaneous decisions on the income distribution aspect of the social welfare function.

What can the economic theorist do? On the one hand, he can accept the decisions made by the present society with respect to capital accumulation, present consumption and destruction of natural resources, and with respect to production and consumption activities carrying with them the possibility of future damage to natural resources as an expression of the social welfare function. In this case, his task will be to formulate theory that will facilitate the prediction of the successive states of the economy that will unfold as this social welfare function governs the society's responses to the changing stock of natural and man-made capital and to changes in the stock of knowledge.

On the other hand, if the theorist feels that there are defects in the process by which society determines courses of action having important effects on the distant future, perhaps even leading to actions that are seriously inconsistent, he may want to abandon his role as observer, point out the inconsistencies, and perhaps try to specify those aspects of the social welfare function that would be or ought to be adopted by society if the process of determination were "satisfactory."

Any attempt to summate utilities over time can be and probably should be viewed as following the latter course, since it implies a very special view of the social welfare function. The question must then be asked whether the particular manner of viewing the social welfare function is adequate from an ethical point of view or whether some other type of language might facilitate discussion.

The question of the number of people for which "we" are trying to maximize welfare is a question that involves the passage of time since numbers can be changed only slowly. We have already discussed the conundrum of per capita utility versus total utility for the society. But suppose that problem is resolved. The proper economizing acts will depend on the size and growth of the population. Indeed, the growth of population may be one of the variables on which we can act. Here we encounter the unfortunate fact that there is no theory of population worthy of the name. All of the speculation on future population seems to be essentially an exercise in arithmetic calculation based on the inertia that is present in the rate of population growth stemming from the fact that it takes a fair number of years for people to grow to childbearing age and pass on through it. As we pass through and beyond the influence of this inertia, the estimates become more and more speculative.

Most of the speculation about population problems has focused on the developing countries, with dispute over the role of population in economic growth. No real agreement has developed on this issue nor has the clarity of the discussion been enhanced by a persistent intermixing of issues concerning population *growth* and population *size*. Some have argued that population is a positive force in economic development because it permits specialization and scale economies (an issue of size). On the other hand, it is argued that rapid population growth is adverse because of the undesirable effect it has on age structure (an issue of rates of change). Large families have been considered conducive to economic development because dependency creates high motivation. One could continue to spell out issues that have been raised, but a firm conclusion one can draw from the discussion is that there is no *simple* relationship between population growth, rates of economic development, levels of per capita income, and other variables of interest to society.

To say that past attempts to add up the utilities of groups living at different times have not been very attractive certainly does not mean we do not have obligations to those who will succeed us. It may be possible to clear the way for theorizing about such obligations by specifying a few limiting characteristics of the inter-generational social welfare function. Unfortunately, the attainment of even this modest goal is fraught with difficulty in a pluralistic society since even limited characteristics cannot be related to *agreed* fundamental philosophic positions. Indeed, one of the main difficulties here, we suspect, is that a far from negligible number of people entertain philosophical-religious positions that carry no implications whatsoever for our behavior as it might affect future generations.

Not very many are thoroughgoing individualists (in the worst sense of the word), however, and the number who are thoroughgoing "my-generationists," although not individualists, is probably similarly small. Still, there are surely many who would not dismiss as nonsensical the query: "Should we worry at all about the survival of future generations?" At the other end of the spectrum, there may even be a few whose position is implicitly rather similar to maximizing the undiscounted sum of utility of all persons existing from now on on the assumption that all have the same utility function of a specified form.

Our own entry for consideration as a modification of the social welfare function is a modest one that would be compatible with a variety of philosophic-religious positions: Our actions should not be such as to foreclose the attainment of a position with respect to nonexhausting resources by future populations that is attainable by us. How limited this suggestion is can be indicated very briefly by noting that it says nothing about preserving exhausting resources nor does it say anything about the cost of attaining the position wanted. Perhaps this is merely a roundabout way of saying that doing things that foreclose return to the prior situation are to be avoided. Obviously, this notion would require considerable clarification, but we think exploration of its implications might yield something of interest.*

Perhaps some of the implications of this idea can be brought out by imagining ourselves to be in the shoes of those living in the future. We can then ask certain questions that they almost certainly will be asking. For example, "Do I regret that the goods and services I consume do not and cannot contain as high a material and energy content as those of the late twentieth century?" While the offhand answer of most people probably would be "yes," further reflection might well lead to a reply of "no" or "not very much." Technological progress between now and then certainly will have served to mitigate the effects of higher prices for energy and materials (if these had occurred, as seems likely). Just as important is the enormous flexibility with which consumers can reform their budgets so as to provide satisfying lives even with radical changes in the composition and/or level of consumption as measured in constant prices. With "adequate" food, clothing, shelter, and medical care, are high levels of materials and energy consumption necessary for a full life?

---

* Irreversibility has an important role in the work on conservation of S. V. Ciriacy-Wantrup. He advocates what he terms a "safe minimum standard of conservation." See his *Resource Conservation—Economics and Policies* (Berkeley: University of California Press, 1952), especially pp. 251ff.

A second question might be: "Are the material 'essentials' of life limited by a population that is too large? Do I suffer from congestion because those living in the twentieth century and later failed to start limiting population?" The likely answer to this question is not nearly so clear as for the first. Even if those of the twentieth century failed to start limiting population by deliberately adopted measures, population in this country, at least, might have stopped growing because of endogenous forces. More disturbing, does the person born into a society of high congestion regret that his ancestors were so prolific or does he find himself unable to conceive that a less congested society would be more desirable?

A third question might be: "Are we poorer in services flowing from the 'environment' because of actions by the people of the twentieth century that could have been avoided, perhaps at very little cost to them? How many sources of natural beauty are gone that we might have enjoyed? Is the productivity of the land or water bodies greatly diminished?"

Note the difference between material flows and environmental flows. Maintenance of material and energy flows at high levels for a long period of time might present obstacles because of rising costs associated with the exploitation of lower grade deposits or because of difficulties associated with the disposal of residual products such as tailings and radioactive wastes. This would be likely to occur even with population held down far enough to avoid excessive congestion. In contrast, the alternative cost of maintaining environmental flows not only can be held down by a combination of population control and technological progress but may be quite small. It would seem that any theoretical approach to the problem of economizing in this situation which gave substantial weight to the well-being of those living later would end with very high valuations for actions that would avoid sacrificing environmental service flows. Let us try to put the point in another way. If we contemplate man in the future living in what in certain respects is a wasteland, it is hard to imagine that the possibility for "converting" environment into capital goods (which could be reproduced in part by recycling) could make up for the loss.

A number of specifications of at least some of the aspects of the social welfare function have been suggested. One that is enjoying considerable current attention is the "ecology ethic," a term that must have been used first by a person unacquainted with either ecology or ethics. Perhaps this point of view has something in common with Schweitzer's view of the sacredness of living things or with the concept of the Pueblo Indians and others of living in harmony with nature. The issue is posed perhaps most sharply in connection with the question of preserving endangered species. The California brown pelican is endangered by DDT, the whooping crane has been hunted almost to extinction, and the blue whale may not make it. Scientists often discuss the importance of the genetic material which might be lost for scientific research, ecological imbalances, etc. All of which may be important. But one can't help but suspect that underlying all of this is the feeling that there is something ethically wrong about man destroying a species of living things, especially among the higher life forms, whose destruction he should avoid or prevent *even if* the cost outweighs any foreseeable benefit in terms of direct human utility from the creature. While we must confess an emotional sympathy with this viewpoint, it does still leave us with an unanswered question. Presumably even the most dedicated ecologist would be unwilling to incur a great cost in human suffering to preserve an animal species with little direct utility to humans. On the other hand, if the cost of preservation were very small, presumably even the most devoted utilitarian would not wish to destroy the species for such a small gain. But the difficult questions lie in the middle ground and the ecology ethic, however attractive, seems to leave us without a criterion of choice, although it provides a partial guide.

The ecology ethic involves the idea of avoiding transition to states that can't be reversed (often termed irreversibilities), and this was true also of the suggestion we made. An important distinction can be made between the two, however. Many, if not all, supporters of the ecology ethic wish to avoid crossing these thresholds because they believe that Nature ought to survive, whether its survival is good or bad for humans. This probably would be the position held by a pantheist, for example, although no doubt many supporters of the ecology ethic are not pantheists and perhaps not theists of any sort.

Our suggestion, in contrast, viewed preservation of options as being desirable (to us) because of our concern for future humans. The question of why we should be concerned at all about humans of the future opens up even more fundamental questions which will not be discussed here.*

Changing Preferences and Man's Adaptation

One of the basic assumptions which we as economists make in developing welfare economics models is that tastes and preferences are exogenously given. This effectively forecloses us from inquiring into the normative basis for the utility functions which we assume all consumers to have. Of course, economists realize that tastes are not immutable or God-given, but trying to introduce taste-formation into the corpus of economic theory would present us with complexities as yet unmeasured.

---

* The reader interested in pursuing these matters further will wish to consult an article by Lynn White, Jr., "The Historical Roots of Our Ecologic Crisis," appearing in *Science*, Vol. 155, No. 3767, March 10, 1967, p. 1203. White asserts that the historical roots of the ecologic crisis are to be found in the anthropocentrism of Christianity, which resulted historically in man's indifference to the fate of things nonhuman and his unthinking exploitation of nature. He says that there can be no hope of solving the crisis without the diffusion of something like the spirit of St. Francis, who talked with the birds and animals. While his view of the role of Christian doctrine in the formation of attitudes toward nature no doubt has some historical validity, he does seem to neglect a major aspect of Christian (and Judaic) doctrine present from the earliest times, to wit, love thy neighbor. If love motivates us—and it surely does motivate many Christians and non-Christians alike—the perception that one's action toward nature in harming other people surely leads to the conclusion that something had better be done about the action. It appears to us that the strength and clarity of this perception are far greater now than at any time in the past, and for a very good reason. We rather clearly have it within our power to produce environmental changes on scales that did not appear to be possible before.

The idea behind the exogenously given tastes assumption is that fully informed consumers (the usual assumption of consumer welfare theory) will weigh off all alternative options available to them in a rational and intelligent manner. Perhaps a weaker but still possibly satisfactory version of this concept would be to assume that, even though the consumer is not fully informed, the gaps in his information are random and that he has an equal probability of becoming informed or educated about all things bearing on his welfare. Whether this assumption could be supported in fact is doubtful in view of the likelihood that there is a bias against acquiring information about and tastes for unowned and unpriced collective goods. Let us consider a specific instance. The automobile is a private good. It is in the interest of the automobile and fuel industries to cultivate a taste for new, elaborate, powerful, and expensive automobiles. These are large and economically potent industries whose advertising touches virtually every person in the country every day. It is, of course, possible that rather than more or larger cars being sold as a result of competitive advertising, the separate companies cancel each other's efforts. But it is hard to believe that all glamour, sex symbolism, and other blandishments do not have some effect on the number and types of automobiles sold.

The other side of the coin is that the automobile is a notorious user of common property resources. It is by far the largest single source of air pollution in the United States and its rusting hulks render the landscape hideous over large areas of the country. It requires urban space to an extreme degree. Yet since everyone, and therefore no one, owns these common property resources, no one has much incentive to try to educate and propagandize the public about their value. Thus when we view taste and preference formation in a dynamic context, we find it hard to argue that there are no biases.

Another more physiological and deeply psychological way of viewing this phenomenon of taste change is the "man adapting" concept widely propounded by René Dubos. Dubos writes:

> The human saga has been the endless search for new environments; and each new move has required adaptive changes to the painful and danger-ous . . . . The most a man can do its to make sure that the environmental changes he brings about do not outstrip his adaptive potentialities . . . .
>
> Some of [the] delayed and indirect consequences will naturally affect physical health and will therefore be measurable objectively. But others will be concerned with more subtle qualities of human life and will require qualitative value judgments. Because man is so adaptable, he can learn to tolerate murky skies, chemically treated waters, and lifeless land . . . .
>
> The most important values, unfortunately, are not definable in terms of specific qualities or characteristics of nature—they involve man's relation to his total environment.*

---

* René Dubos, "Air, Water, and Earth," *Looking Ahead*, Vol. 16, No. 6 (Washington: National Planning Association, September 1968.)

The essence of this thought is that while man may not on the surface be aware of any destructive effects of environmental deterioration, because his tastes adjust themselves, chronic physical and mental health problems are often the end result. If true, the implication of this for economic theory is that a consumer's choices at any moment of time cannot be taken as an expression of his best interest *as he would see it* if he knew what was happening to him. The difficulties this presents for economic welfare theory are serious.

Perhaps an even deeper question than that raised by Dubos is as follows: What if man adapts to what we would, from our present perspective, view as a badly deteriorated environment but with no manifestly harmful mental or physical effects—indeed let us say he is very happy? This is what we might term the 1984 question.* We might visualize man living at very high densities, sealed off from any natural environment (because it is toxic), benignly stoned on much improved psychedelic drugs, resting on his effortless exerciser. Is there anything in a relativistic view of preferences which would provide grounds for judging such a state to be unwholesome? The answer appears to be no—but we shiver at the thought.

If good theory is to be formulated, it must be conceived with some image of the situation to which it applies. This is the main difficulty for the theorist thinking about the long run—our image of it is very hazy even with respect to its general outlines. Nevertheless, it may be worthwhile speculating a bit about the general characteristics that future development may have.

By now it should be clear to everyone that steady growth theorizing cannot possibly have more than a very partial relevance to the concrete problem of the future development of the economy and society. We have already seen how growth could conceivably come to a halt even if nature imposed no limitations whose impact would increase. The halt could result from either a consumer glut or the accumulation of a quantity of capital so great that there were no further opportunities for investment. Nor does it seem impossible that net savings might be zero before either of those limiting conditions was reached. If this did not happen, development of new opportunities for investment might be limited (not simultaneously) by a cessation of growth in the stock of technological knowledge. If the system as a whole should exhibit large diseconomies of scale, this too presumably would be reflected in the exhaustion of investment opportunities.

To many, however, it is becoming increasingly clear that limitations stemming from "nature's niggardliness" must have an important place in our thinking and probably will have a controlling influence on development long before any of the above conditions is realized. It is not so much that the cost of food may rise because of the comparatively fixed supply of agricultural land or that the cost of materials may rise because of exhaustion of good deposits. These may

---

* Some may already have adapted. Consider the following statement, said to have been made in a smoggy state: "When you've seen one redwood tree, you've seen them all."

still turn out to be important elements in the picture, especially in some countries. In many countries, however, and even for all of them taken together, the limiting aspects of nature may first turn out to be limitations on her capacity to receive and absorb the many types of debris from human activities without serious deterioration.

One way to perceive some of the major adaptations which would have to be made is to imagine the evolution of a self-contained society. Let us assume away the problem of the intergenerational social welfare function by assuming that population is stable and that its members do not age or die. That is, "I" as I am now will continue. Let us suppose also that we understand the functioning of natural systems and how this is altered by various human activities.

Economizing considerations would require the gradual alteration of consumption patterns and production processes in response to pressures on natural systems as capital and output, and therefore returns to the environment, rose. The cost of newly-mined mineral products very likely could be expected to rise as lower and lower grades were mined.* At the same time, the supply of material reclaimed from scrap would be increasing, since with a higher price it would pay to undertake the expensive collection activities required as scrap is assembled from more dispersed and scattered sources. In those cases where new production could take place from an "inexhaustible" source, such as sea water, without undue damage to the environment, there would be an upper limit to the increase in price, as noted earlier.

It might be noted that complete recycling of materials in the sense of recovering all of the materials input for reprocessing and use is impossible. Many materials are dispersed so widely in the course of use (e.g., paints, thinners, solvents, fuels and other materials converted to gases, cleaners, etc.) that collection is impossible. Even for those which appear to be of a more fixed nature, such as metals in formed shapes, the ubiquitous processes of oxidation and friction insure a partial dispersal that cannot be avoided. Also, recycling requires the input of other materials and energy, and may in fact produce its own pollutants. Thus, the optimum extent of recycling depends on the circumstances of the moment and requires a calculation of all of the relevant costs. It is likely, of course, that at the present time recycling of certain materials is below optimum because of deficiencies in the cost calculations. Some social costs are not properly reflected in decisions.

In the case of energy, the costs of the "inexhaustible" sources (breeder fission reactors and fusion) and the costs of energy from mineral sources (petroleum, coal, etc.) would be expected gradually to converge and then diverge, with energy from fossil fuel sources becoming less and less important and perhaps eventually disappearing altogether. Given our assumption of a constant population, food production certainly would pose no problem, since we should be able to do at least as well as we are now.

---

* Recall that the mining of one-half percent copper ore requires the mining and grinding, and disposal of a little more than twice as much barren rock as for one percent ore.

With increasing output, we would be putting greater and greater strains on the environment. As these strains developed, the idealized society we are considering would take steps to reduce the demands on the services of the environment. If the inventory of radioactive substances escaping to the atmosphere as the result of energy from fission rose to the danger point, effective steps would be taken to economize on this form of energy and perhaps to reduce the escape of radioactive material to the atmosphere. If pesticides finding their way to soil and water bodies threatened permanent damage, their use would be reduced. In sum, as the pressures mounted, the ideal adjustment would involve a combination of a number of measures, including adjustment of the consumer budget away from products whose production entailed dangerous or damaging effluents, and the redesign of products and processes to reduce the activities producing damaging effluents and to reduce the flow of certain effluents to places where they can produce damage. A similar readjustment would take place to reduce the impact of congestion effects.

These alterations of the consumer budget and production processes would take place in such a way as to maximize product, taking into consideration all service flows from the environment, including those not now appropriated, whether those flows go directly to enterprises or to individuals. We would have made a rational sacrifice in the "quality of the environment" up to the point where this sacrifice was balanced by satisfactions from the extra flow of *particular* types of goods made possible by this sacrifice.

It is likely that it would take a very long time before this society would approach a "steady state" very closely, but it would be highly likely that the primary production of *certain* substances would be greatly curtailed or even eliminated. These curtailments could easily be so important or so pervasive as to require large changes in consumption patterns and production methods, but even with these the general style of life might be similar to that of the present. Perhaps the factors most likely to result in great change would be the possible need to restrict the production of atomic electric power (presumably from breeder reactors) in order to control the stock of dispersed radioactive material in the atmosphere and on the surface of the earth, and in water bodies or local and regional heat disposal problems arising from the large consumption of energy.

If the assumption of a constant population is abandoned, even the most general outlines of the future are greatly obscured. The inertia inherent in the present age distribution of this country's population would insure continued growth for several decades to come even if the net reproduction rate were to drop to maintenance level tomorrow (an average of a little more than two babies during a lifetime for each female born). While it appears to us that our institutions function well enough to cope with our growing difficulties even if population continues to grow for some time, failure to curb this growth rather soon would subject our system to increasing strains since the need for radical readjustments in certain directions would be more likely. The age distribution of a stable population would be quite different from the present and past distributions in this and many other countries, however, and these also would require important changes in many aspects of economic and social life.

In the United States, the natural increase in population from 1968–69 was about .8 percent per year. Net civilian immigration added another .2 percent, giving a total increase of about 1.0 percent. If the decline in the net reproduction rate from about 1.7 in 1960 to about 1.1 a decade later should continue (where 1.0 would indicate age-specific fertility rates which, if continued, would eventually stabilize the population), U.S. population would stabilize in several decades or perhaps even decline, not because of any act of positive control but simply because of the unfolding of the determining forces.

The picture is entirely different for the world as a whole, and especially so for the less developed countries. After making estimates of future birth and death rates, the United Nations concludes that world population will almost double between 1969 and 2000, with the rate of growth being about 2.2 percent per year in the less developed countries as against 1.0 percent for the developed countries. The ratio of the populations in the less developed countries to those of the developed is estimated to be 10:3 in 2000. And if governments do not attain positive control over population growth by that time and growth still continues, the disparities and the pressures on available resources will continue to mount until finally growth is brought to a grinding halt by increases in death rates.

In the face of the uncertainty surrounding population growth, economic theory could proceed to analyze problems of capital accumulation and resource degradation on the basis of various assumed patterns of population growth. This of course is what has been done in the past, with population growth usually assumed to be a constant, including zero growth, a popular assumption. We should like to be able to put the theory to work, however, But how does a catalogue of paths and outcomes help if there is no way to make an effective choice of any particular one? It would be very useful, of course, to have a theory of population growth that would in fact enable prediction, a theory that indicated the important variables involved, and thereby would permit the elaboration of various possibilities for control.

Control of population may be possible, however, without having a complete theory of population growth at hand. Although it may be impossible to predict what would happen to population in the absence of deliberate societal control measures, control measures are available which may be sufficient to limit growth. Whether positive control in the sense of being able to move population up or down as wished is achievable is far from certain.

Here we encounter the need to inquire into the formation of societal consensus. If this is strong enough, methods adequate to the task probably could be put into effect. But will society do so? Does today's society really care if it and the immediately following generations build up a population inertia that in turn will result in a path for society that will be very painful for later generations? Certainly the economist is under an obligation to try to make sure that present society is aware of the likely future results of its present actions bearing on population growth. Thus the catalogue of possible paths is of some use after all!

In elaborating these possibilities, it probably would be useful to experiment with more specific forms of the social welfare function, partly to make ethical implications more explicit. One possible modification, already hinted at in earlier pages, would be to abandon the monotonic relation between welfare and goods, perhaps thinking of the same level of welfare as attainable with widely different quantities of goods and services, provided certain specific minimum requirements are met. Another modification involves the "environment." At the conceptual level, service flows from the environment to households are an element of welfare and of course the service flows from the environment to businesses also affect welfare indirectly. Finally, it would seem that the conundrum of whether to maximize per capita utility or total societal utility might be resolved by including population itself or its derivative effects in the welfare function.

An even more difficult puzzle is how to incorporate the people of other societies, present and future, into the analysis. While a social welfare function can be conceived that incorporates them, the possibility of specifying a function on which there might be agreement among the different societies seems even more remote than for a single society.

Another possible route for analysis in the face of this difficulty would be that of international trade theory. The new element in the analysis would be real external diseconomies among the traders (nations). This factor would extend the range of outcomes considerably. Differences among the social welfare functions of the various societies, especially with respect to their views on future generations, would be an important element in determining the range of outcomes. For example, certain types of national behavior could bring all systems to a halt rather than merely altering the terms of trade, as in the usual analysis.

Envoi

Economic theory is unique among social science theories. Its strength arises from its strong devotion to the concept of an interdependent system and from the effort to be reasonably precise in formulation. As a result of these features the theory has a built-in tendency to consider alternatives and tradeoffs and has yielded useful theorems and hypotheses. Finally, the relatively rigorous formulation of the theory has made it comparatively easy for economists to explain it to other scientists and to work in interdisciplinary relationships with them.

Thus our criticisms and reservations are far from a call to abandon the inherited body of theory or to try to make discontinuous jumps to other formulations. Rather, it is to be hoped that economists and other scientists will be moved to build on the theory, to extend it, to improve it, and to make it an even more useful tool than it now is for decision making in the interest of society.

Index